M000247401

# Mastering Data Visualization with Microsoft Visio Professional 2016

Master the art of presenting information visually using Microsoft Visio Professional 2016 and Visio Pro for Office365

**David J Parker**

[PACKT] PUBLISHING
enterprise
professional expertise distilled

BIRMINGHAM - MUMBAI

# Mastering Data Visualization with Microsoft Visio Professional 2016



First published: May 2016

Production reference: 1240516

Published by Packt Publishing Ltd.
Livery Place
35 Livery Street
Birmingham B3 2PB, UK.

ISBN 978-1-78588-266-1

www.packtpub.com

# Credits

**Author**
David J Parker

**Commissioning Editor**
Veena Pagare

**Acquisition Editor**
Tushar Gupta

**Content Development Editor**
Viranchi Shetty

**Technical Editor**
Vivek Arora

**Copy Editor**
Angad Singh

**Project Coordinator**
Izzat Contractor

**Proofreader**
Safis Editing

**Indexer**
Monica Ajmera Mehta

**Graphics**
Kirk D'Penha

**Production Coordinator**
Conidon Miranda

**Cover Work**
Conidon Miranda

# About the Author

**David J Parker's** background has been in data visualization ever since he struggled to produce lists of hospital equipment from Computer Aided Design models of buildings as a budding architect in the '80s. He moved into building and infrastructure asset management in the late '80s using a Unix system and gradually migrated to Windows-based systems throughout the '90s.

He became a European Business partner of Visio Corporation in 1996 and presented the database-linked Visio solutions that he was providing merchant banks in London and New York with at several international conferences. David started bVisual Ltd. in 1998, which provides Visio-based solutions to various industries, and became a Silver-level Microsoft partner.

He has been a Microsoft MVP (Visio) for the last 12 years and has helped Microsoft Corp, UK and Western Europe, by providing Visio solutions, training, website content, and presentations. David has had several books on Visio published and has been presenting Visio/SharePoint integration courses for many years for Microsoft Western Europe, from Oslo in the North down to Lisbon in the South. He has presented at SQL and SharePoint Saturday conferences and writes a regular blog for people interested in Microsoft Visio.

# Table of Contents

# Preface

It is difficult to look at a technology website or publication without some mention of data visualization. There is so much data available now, and there will be even more in the future. Data is not useful information unless it can be understood, so tools that can aid comprehension are essential. Microsoft has recently been making large strides in the business intelligence space with tools such as the Power BI stack, but Microsoft Visio has been an operational intelligence tool for businesses since the mid-nineties. Over the years, Visio has matured even more and added many features to provide links to data and special data graphics to visualize this data easily. Technologies advance, expectations increase, and Visio continues to evolve to provide greater capabilities and flexibility. For many, BI (Business Intelligence) is concerned with the slicing and dicing of data, usually using charts and graphs to provide greater insight, but there are many times when information is best presented with less constrained visual forms. This is where Visio excels with thousands of pre-drawn shapes available and its ability to be customized easily. This makes Visio the OI (Operational Intelligence) of choice for many.

Microsoft Visio is a multipurpose graphical application that comes with a large variety of templates that cover a wide spectrum of business uses. A Template is a preconfigured Visio document with a selection of Stencils (or libraries) of Masters (or shapes). There are also a vast number of custom stencils available from the web (of varying quality and capabilities). Traditionally, Visio has been used mostly for organization charts, process flows, and network diagrams, but it can do much more than that. Many of the built-in templates come with add-ons that enhance the core application to provide specific actions for a specialized user. This can turn a multipurpose interface into a vertical solution centered one.

There are millions of Visio users around the globe, and over a billion Microsoft Office users who are using a similar and familiar interface. However, every time I show how simple it is to link Visio shapes to data, and how the data can be easily visualized, I get the same reaction, "I didn't know Visio could do that!" Visio is considered part of the extended Microsoft Office family, but at the time of writing this book, Visio does not have the web-based add-ons that the main applications have. Nor is there a lightweight web Visio version, unlike the other Office applications. However, it is easy to see that there is a progression in this direction, and a large part of the latency is down to the complexity of maintaining the integrity of such a complex application that combines vector graphics and data.

The closest similarity to another Office product is not to PowerPoint, but to Excel. Every shape, and that includes text, in Visio has a programmable ShapeSheet behind it, just like a worksheet in Excel, complete with cells that contain customizable formulas. Also, Visio comes with VBA built in, which makes it easy for power users to write macros, and for developers to prototype. The mature type library can be programmed by standard .NET developers, and there is even a JavaScript object model for the Visio Viewer and Visio Web Access control.

Personally, I discovered the power of Visio in the mid-nineties, several years before Microsoft acquired the product/company. I was an early beta-tester of the ODBC data links that were introduced then, and of the newer data-linking feature that was added in 2007. I have been providing custom templates, stencils, and solutions ever since because Visio has the depth to solve a lot of business data visualization scenarios.

I cannot deny that I get some pleasure from creating Visio shapes that respond to data value changes. It feels like life is breathed into them, and they continue to live independently, turning a canvas into a constantly updated information dashboard.

I believe the skills and the principles outlined in this book will be relevant for many years to come, and they will enable businesses to intelligently comprehend operational data.

# What this book covers

*Chapter 1, Data within Visio Essentials*, reviews the evolution of data within Visio from the early nineties to the present day. The chapter also introduces the key features and add-ons in Visio that make data visual.

*Chapter 2, Understanding How Data Is Stored within Visio*, presents the different ways in which data is stored within Visio documents, pages, and shapes. It explains the relationship between the Visio API and the unique ShapeSheet and introduces the concept of structured diagrams.

*Chapter 3, Linking Data to Shapes*, explains how data can be imported into Visio documents and linked to shapes, both manually and automatically. It also shows how multiple hyperlinks can be automatically created by data,

*Chapter 4, Using the Built-In Data Graphics*, demonstrates how the built-in Data Graphics ( Icons Sets, Data Bars, Text Callouts, and Color by Value) can easily display data values.

*Chapter 5, Using the Pivot Diagram Add-On*, explains how this useful add-on can breakdown and aggregate data and be overlaid with refreshable data.

*Chapter 6, Creating Custom Master Shapes*, reveals how built-in Masters can be enhanced to provide better data visualization, and how custom Masters can be created from scratch.

*Chapter 7, Creating Custom Data Graphics*, shows how built-in Data Graphics and Graphic Items can be modified and new ones created.

*Chapter 8, Validating and Extracting Information*, explains how diagrams can be checked for conformance and integrity, and how data can be exported from Visio diagrams.

*Chapter 9, Automating Structured Diagrams*, demonstrates how data can be used to create Structured Diagrams automatically by connecting shapes together, by adding them to containers and lists, and by associating callout shapes.

*Chapter 10, Sharing Data Diagrams*, explains the different options available for sharing Visio data and graphics with other viewers, especially if they do not have Visio available.

*Chapter 11, Choosing a Deployment Methodology*, discusses the different ways in which custom templates, stencils, and code can be distributed for others to create their own data diagrams.

# What you need for this book

Either Microsoft Visio Professional 2013+, Microsoft Visio 2010 Premium, or Microsoft Visio Pro for Office 365 are required for all of the examples in this book.

Most of the code examples in this book are written using Visual Basic for Applications because it is included within Microsoft Visio.

Microsoft Excel, Microsoft Access, and the Microsoft SQL Server are used as data source examples.

# Who this book is for

This book is aimed at the departmental-level operational intelligence professional or Microsoft Office power-user. It is also intended for SharePoint/Office365 developers who want to include visual data in corporate websites.

# Conventions

In this book, you will find a number of text styles that distinguish between different kinds of information. Here are some examples of these styles and an explanation of their meaning.

Code words in text, database table names, folder names, filenames, file extensions, pathnames, dummy URLs, user input, and Twitter handles are shown as follows: "However, the supporting files are all present and include a file called `data.xml` that contains all of the data for each shape."

A block of code is set as follows:

```
<!DOCTYPE html>
<html>
  <head>
    <h1>Visio Viewer Example</h1>
  </head>
  <body>
        <object id="DrawingControl1" height="500" width="700"
          classid="clsid:F8CF7A98-2C45-4c8d-9151-2D716989DDAB" >
             <param name="ToolbarVisible" value="1">
             <param name="Src" value="http://www.bvisual.net
             //examples/BaUNetworkDiagram.vsd">
          </object>
  </body>
</html>
```

**New terms** and **important words** are shown in bold. Words that you see on the screen, for example, in menus or dialog boxes, appear in the text like this: "It is listed as **Microsoft Visio Document** when the **Developer** | **Insert** | **ActiveX controls** | **More Controls** button is pressed."

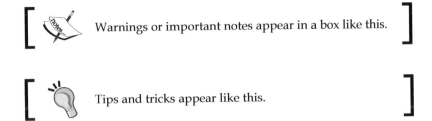

[ Warnings or important notes appear in a box like this. ]

[ Tips and tricks appear like this. ]

# Reader feedback

Feedback from our readers is always welcome. Let us know what you think about this book—what you liked or disliked. Reader feedback is important for us as it helps us develop titles that you will really get the most out of.

To send us general feedback, simply e-mail `feedback@packtpub.com`, and mention the book's title in the subject of your message.

If there is a topic that you have expertise in and you are interested in either writing or contributing to a book, see our author guide at `www.packtpub.com/authors`.

# Customer support

Now that you are the proud owner of a Packt book, we have a number of things to help you to get the most from your purchase.

## Downloading the example code

You can download the example code files for this book from your account at `http://www.packtpub.com`. If you purchased this book elsewhere, you can visit `http://www.packtpub.com/support` and register to have the files e-mailed directly to you.

You can download the code files by following these steps:

1. Log in or register to our website using your e-mail address and password.
2. Hover the mouse pointer on the **SUPPORT** tab at the top.
3. Click on **Code Downloads & Errata**.
4. Enter the name of the book in the **Search** box.
5. Select the book for which you're looking to download the code files.
6. Choose from the drop-down menu where you purchased this book from.
7. Click on **Code Download**.

You can also download the code files by clicking on the **Code Files** button on the book's webpage at the Packt Publishing website. This page can be accessed by entering the book's name in the **Search** box. Please note that you need to be logged in to your Packt account.

Once the file is downloaded, please make sure that you unzip or extract the folder using the latest version of:

- WinRAR / 7-Zip for Windows
- Zipeg / iZip / UnRarX for Mac
- 7-Zip / PeaZip for Linux

The code bundle for the book is also hosted on GitHub at `https://github.com/PacktPublishing/repository-name`. We also have other code bundles from our rich catalog of books and videos available at `https://github.com/PacktPublishing/`. Check them out!

# Downloading the color images of this book

We also provide you with a PDF file that has color images of the screenshots/diagrams used in this book. The color images will help you better understand the changes in the output. You can download this file from `http://www.packtpub.com/sites/default/files/downloads/12340T_ColorImages.pdf`.

# Errata

Although we have taken every care to ensure the accuracy of our content, mistakes do happen. If you find a mistake in one of our books—maybe a mistake in the text or the code—we would be grateful if you could report this to us. By doing so, you can save other readers from frustration and help us improve subsequent versions of this book. If you find any errata, please report them by visiting `http://www.packtpub.com/submit-errata`, selecting your book, clicking on the **Errata Submission Form** link, and entering the details of your errata. Once your errata are verified, your submission will be accepted and the errata will be uploaded to our website or added to any list of existing errata under the Errata section of that title.

To view the previously submitted errata, go to `https://www.packtpub.com/books/content/support` and enter the name of the book in the search field. The required information will appear under the **Errata** section.

# Piracy

Piracy of copyrighted material on the Internet is an ongoing problem across all media. At Packt, we take the protection of our copyright and licenses very seriously. If you come across any illegal copies of our works in any form on the Internet, please provide us with the location address or website name immediately so that we can pursue a remedy.

Please contact us at `copyright@packtpub.com` with a link to the suspected pirated material.

We appreciate your help in protecting our authors and our ability to bring you valuable content.

# Questions

If you have a problem with any aspect of this book, you can contact us at `questions@packtpub.com`, and we will do our best to address the problem.

# 1

# Data within Visio Essentials

From the very beginning, Visio was responsible for introducing the visual data paradigm for business information reporting. A key concept of Visio from the outset was smart shapes that could respond to information changes. This chapter reviews the evolution of data within Visio, from the introduction of a modifiable *ShapeSheet* in the very first version (v1.0) in 1992, through to the *Quick Import* feature in Visio 2016. It is important to understand the important enhancements in Visio's evolution. It will empower the prospective power user and developer with the knowledge of why some code is written a certain way, how it can be more efficient, and which solutions are potential dead-ends. It is always more productive to create any solution on top of a core product because the object model provides documented properties, methods, and events.

Visio has a number of add-ons that utilize the core Visio application object model, and that are presented as different templates or diagram types. Although some of these are very popular, such as the Organization Chart add-on, extending either the code or the associated master shapes can be problematic. However, some are still useful, so I will describe these in more detail.

When looking at extracts of code from other books, Internet pages, or even colleagues, it can be important to understand that the code may have been efficient for its time but could be better now. I have been guilty of this myself because I have offered code that worked well for many years, while a student has seen the potential of newer enhancements to the object model and proposed a better, more efficient solution.

All of the screenshots in this book come from Microsoft Visio Professional 2016, which was run in developer mode. The fact that screenshots of the latest version can still be used to describe core parts of the engine that have been enhanced since the first version demonstrates how the product has been built on firm foundations.

> **Running Visio in Developer Mode**
> Either tick the **Developer** tab in **Customize Ribbon** or **Run in developer mode** in **File** | **Options** | **Advanced** | **General**.

In this chapter, we shall cover the following topics:

- Why choose Visio for data diagramming?
- The evolution of data in Visio prior to the Microsoft acquisition
- The evolution of data in Microsoft Visio
- Reviewing the significant current OOTB add-ons
- Shedding a tear for the sadly missed OOTB add-ons

# Why use Visio for data diagramming?

Microsoft Visio first appeared as Visio from a company called **ShapeWare** in 1992. From the very beginning, it was designed as a smart diagramming system. Before long, the company changed its name to Visio Corporation and a new information graphics paradigm was born.

At that time, I was working as an implementation consultant for a Unix **CAD (Computer Aided Design)** system that had a link to a Unify database. I was using this system to provide personnel desk locations, space chargeback, and cable management to merchant banks in the city of London. In those days, you could not buy just the software and install it on your own PC or Mac; instead, you had to buy the hardware too. So, each workstation would cost about £20k ($30k). This is quite an investment, and the skills required were quite specialized, thus spending extra for a consultant to actually use it did not seem so expensive. The work for the merchant banks took me over to New York, and the cable management application even took me to NASA in Alabama.

However, the merchant banks that I worked for began to demand that any reports were formatted to an exacting standard. They had become used to the WYSIWYG interface in new Windows applications such as Word. "Unfortunately, this was not available directly in UNIX, so, I invested in Microsoft Access for reporting, via FTP. They soon also demanded better printed graphics than was possible in CAD, so I had to seriously reconsider my toolset. The consulting company that I worked for also sold a Windows CAD system that could not produce acceptable graphics either. It was also very difficult to automate, so I surveyed the available alternatives.

In the days before easy downloads from the Web were available, every computer magazine had a cover disk (a 3.5" stiffy, not a CD) with a few trial versions of programs on it, and I had previously tried one called Visio 2. I had been impressed with its parametric behavior and the provided ability to automate it using **Object Linking and Embedding** (**OLE**), so I decided to find out more about the current version at that time, which was version 4. I was excited to find that the technical edition had now brought the ability to import some types of CAD files, which meant that I would be able to utilize some of the drawings that I had been using for years. It also introduced the ability to link to databases via OLE.

I began to provide solutions using Visio Technical Edition linking to data in Sybase, Oracle, SQL Server, Access, and Excel using the database connectivity support that was introduced in Visio 4.

For example, I was linking 600 trader desks per floor on a single Visio page to the corporate Sybase database, and with a single macro I was able to refresh the text and color fill for each desk with the up-to-date occupant details. These floor plans were used by the help desk on these large open-plan floors to find traders who reported something amiss in their workstation. At first, I had to automate Visio from an external application, which I did with Microsoft Access or Excel as they already had **Visual Basic for Applications** (**VBA**) built in. I also wrote some code in **Visual Basic** (**VB**) as executables, but all these methods ran code across application boundaries, which slowed them down. I did manage to wrap VB DLLs with C++ to get them running within Visio as add-ons, but the coding time was increased by too much. Then, Visio itself introduced built-in VBA, so the code could execute far quicker within the Visio environment, and the time taken to write tactical solutions was reduced.

The parametric capability of Visio shapes enabled me to construct a single monitor SmartShape that changed size and appearance depending on one of the 33 different combinations of manufacturer and screen size that I entered into the Custom Properties of the shape.

> A case study is available at `http://bvisual.net/Case_Studies/ChaseManhattanBank.aspx`.

I was totally sold on the Visio paradigm and started a business based on providing Visio-based solutions shortly before Microsoft acquired Visio Corporation at the start of the year 2000.

Microsoft took over an extremely large amount of code and began the process of assimilating the application into the extended Microsoft Office family. This has had many challenges since the original Visio developers had no access to Windows or Microsoft Office code and practices. The "Big Three" Office applications (Word, Excel, and PowerPoint) have always blazed the trail as far as user interface design and file format are concerned, and Visio has followed behind at a respectful distance.

So, after the acquisition, Microsoft reviewed the breadth of features available within the many different editions of Visio (Standard, Technical, Professional, and Enterprise) that they had inherited and began to consolidate them. Over time, a large number of add-ons were added to the base product, and the Visio Corporation voraciously acquired many products that were using the Visio system (for example, IntelliCAD for CAD, InfoModeler for database modelling, and Kaspia for network discovery). Some of the products and code were incompatible with Microsoft's vision for Visio, so they were deprecated.

> For a more complete history of Visio, take a look at `http://visio.mvps.org/History`, which is maintained by the longest-serving Microsoft MVP for Visio, John Marshall.

However, the core engine of Visio has matured and expanded over many years of production use, with very little of it being removed. Therefore, skills learned around Visio shape development or automation have not been a waste of time, and most of the old documentation about these subjects is still relevant.

> An oldie, but a goody, Developing Microsoft Visio Solutions can be found at `https://msdn.microsoft.com/en-us/library/aa245244(v=office.10).aspx`.

There are three available editions of Visio 2013 and 2016: Standard, Professional, and Pro for Office365. In fact, the last two are exactly the same apart from the licensing method. This book is not about the Standard edition because it does not contain all of the data capabilities.

# The evolution of data in Visio before the Microsoft acquisition

The period between the years 1992 and 2000 saw Visio burst onto the scene and rapidly grow in size, acquiring almost every other product that used its drawing system. The first sales target was to out-sell the best-selling flowcharting tool of the time, ABC Flowcharter. This was done within 18 months, and Visio was on its way.

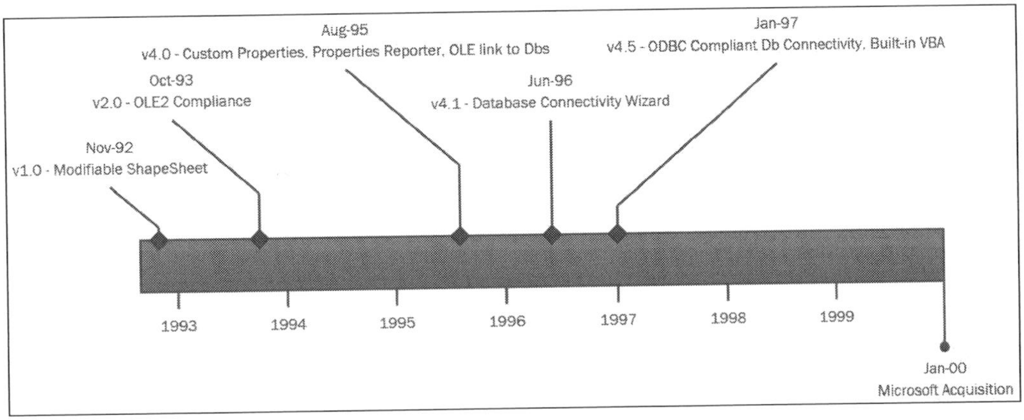


Beyond the Standard Edition was the Technical Edition, which contained CAD and engineering add-ons, and the Professional Edition, which contained database modelling and network diagramming. Eventually, there was also the Enterprise Edition with network discovery.

> Visit `http://www.visiocorp.info/boxes.aspx` for more information on the Visio Corporation.

The timeline displays the most relevant milestones of data diagramming, and a short explanation of each follows. They are relevant because these features still exist, and there are still code examples out there that use them.

# v1.0 – modifiable ShapeSheets

The intelligence in Visio comes from its unique modifiable ShapeSheet, which is reputedly modeled on an Excel worksheet. Every single shape in Visio has one, as does each page and even the document itself. So, it is important to understand it. It can be opened from the **Developer** ribbon by the **Shape Design | Show ShapeSheet** button. The following screenshot shows an example of a current ShapeSheet, and it also shows the **Shape Name** dialog:

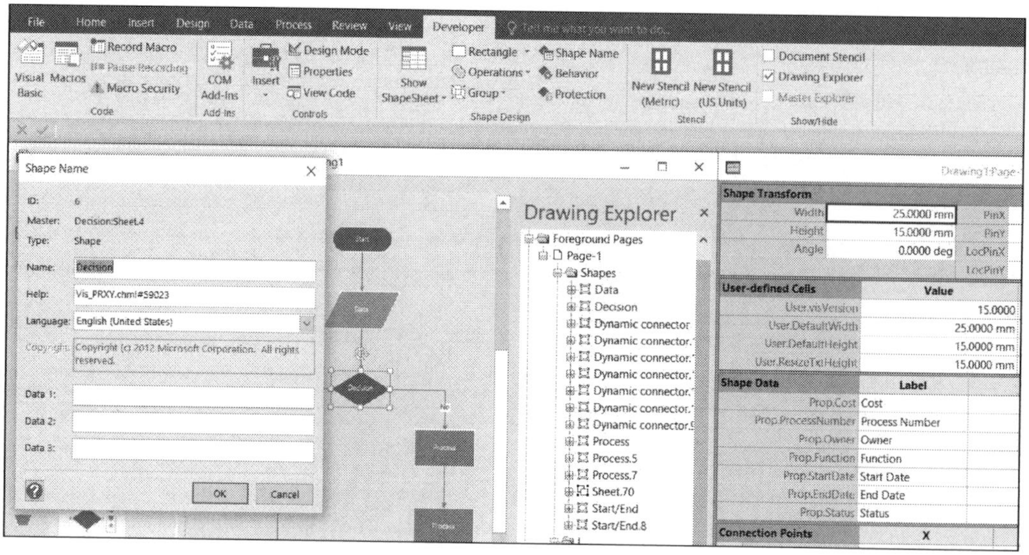


Note the **Data 1**, **2**, and **3** boxes on the **Shape Name** dialog can actually hold 64,000 characters, but only use it with caution because there are some old add-ons out there that use them. Initially, they were the only way to persist data in the shape. The ShapeSheet on the right of the screenshot shows how it is broken down into sections, rows, and cells. We will learn more about this in the next chapter. In the first version of Visio, there was no **User-defined Cells** or **Shape Data** section because it was introduced in version 4. The pre-cursor to **User-Defined Cells** was the **Scratch** section. Both of these sections are optional because they can be created, and have new rows inserted, as required. This is in contrast to the fixed, mandatory sections such as **Shape Transform** because every shape needs to have a location and rotation in the page that it is on.

In the center of the screenshot is the **Drawing Explorer** window, which displays the document, pages, shapes, and so on. We will learn more about that too in the next chapter.

# v2.0 – OLE2 compliance

OLE2 and the published object model allowed Visio to be controlled by programming languages such as Visual Basic 3. In fact, Visio was the first non-Microsoft product to have OLE2 compliance.

# v4.0 – Custom Properties, Properties Reporter, and the OLE link to DBs

**Custom Properties**, later renamed as **Shape Data** in 2007, not only provides a method of storing typed data for each shape, but also provides a dialog to view and edit them. The following screenshot shows that there is now a **Shape Data** popup dialog and a **Shape Data** window that was added years later:

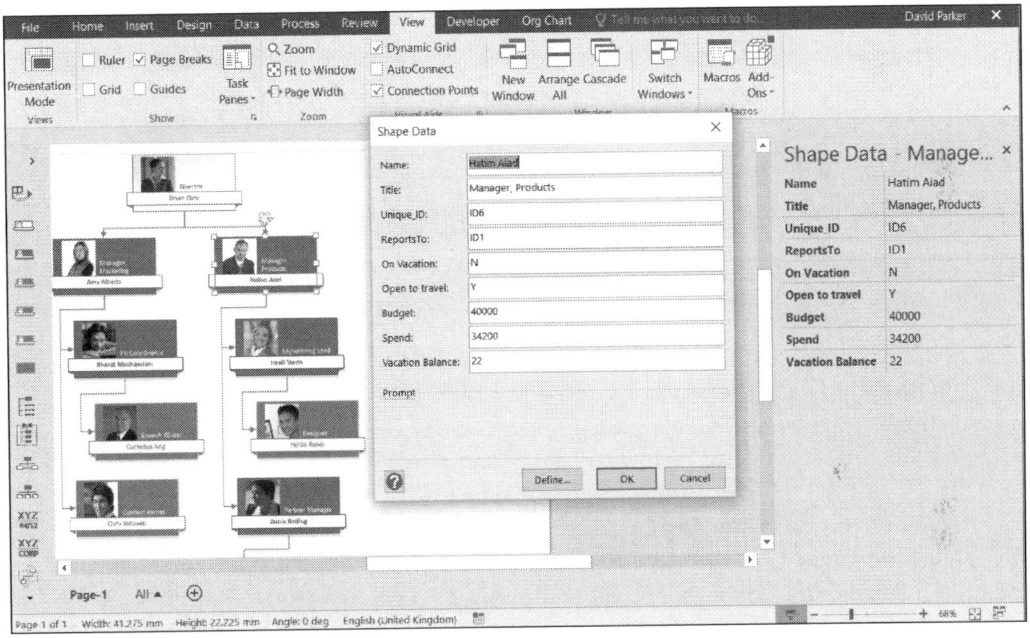


There will be much more about Shape Data in *Chapter 2, Understanding How Data Is Stored within Visio.*

**Properties Reports**, now called **Shape Reports**, provide a method to create simple tabular reports from data in Visio shapes. The following screenshot shows the **Reports** dialog, and there will be more about this feature in *Chapter 8, Validating and Extracting Information*:

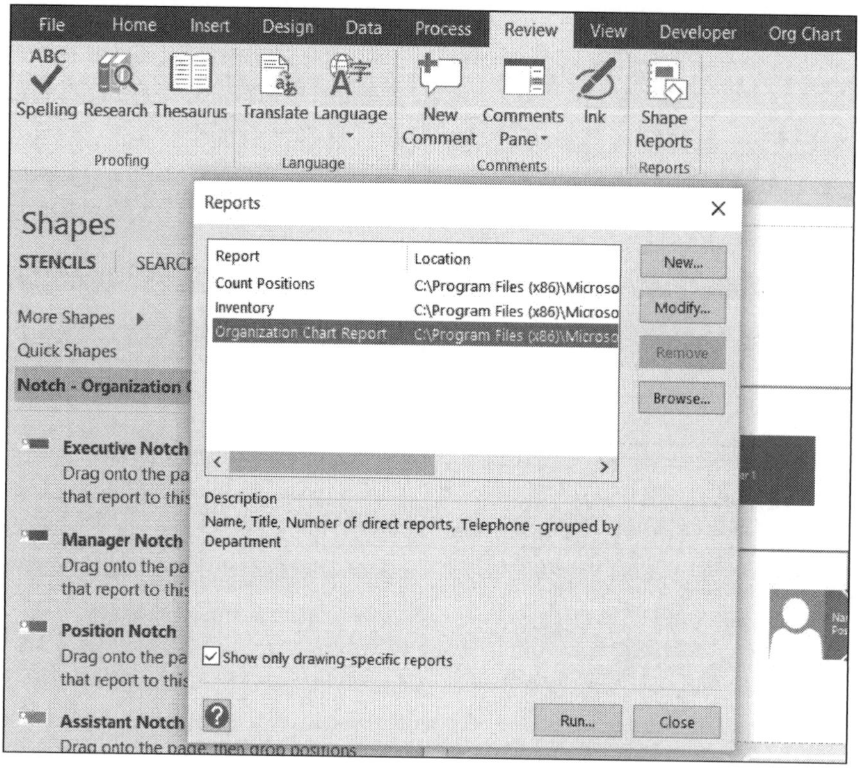


The OLE link to databases provides a method to read and write data to/from not only **Custom Properties/Shape Data**, but also from the newly provided **User-defined Cells**, and in fact, almost all the ShapeSheet cells and even the position of the shape in the page. The following screenshot shows the **Link to Database** dialog that can be opened from the **View | Macros | Add-Ons | Visio Extras** ribbon menu:

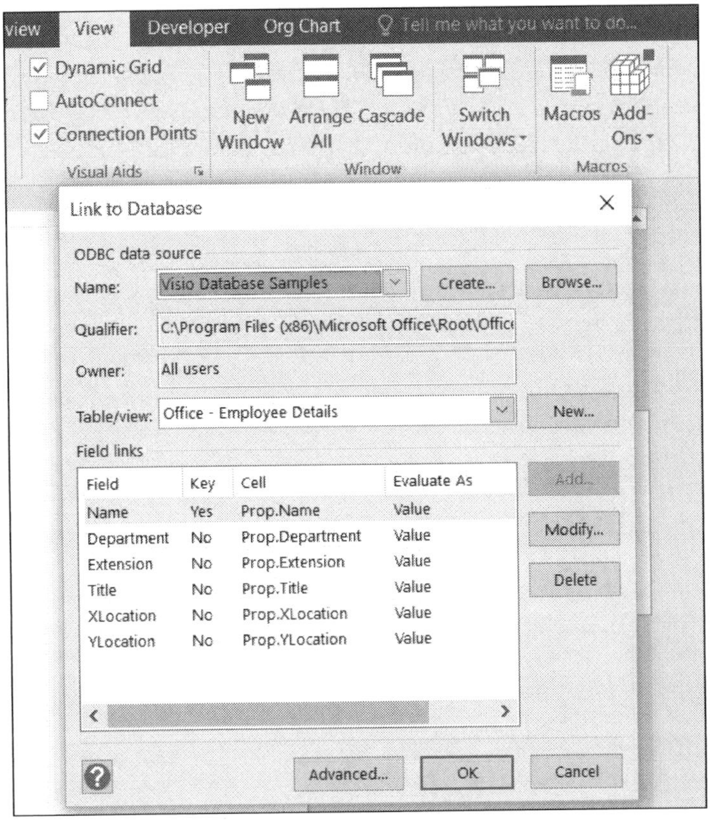


**User-Defined Cells** were an important addition in the ShapeSheet. They have just two columns: **Value** and **Prompt**. This means that formulae can be entered in the **Value** column with a description of what they are there for in the **Prompt** column. Before that, developers would use the **Scratch** section for formulae and descriptions of their purpose. This can make it difficult to understand the ShapeSheet code; however, the **Scratch** section does remain important for geometric calculations because of the capabilities of the X, Y, and A to D columns.

# v4.1 – the Database Connectivity wizard

This wizard provides an easy-to-use interface for data connectivity, and the following screenshot shows how it can be started from the **View** | **Macros** | **Add-Ons** | **Visio Extras** ribbon menu:

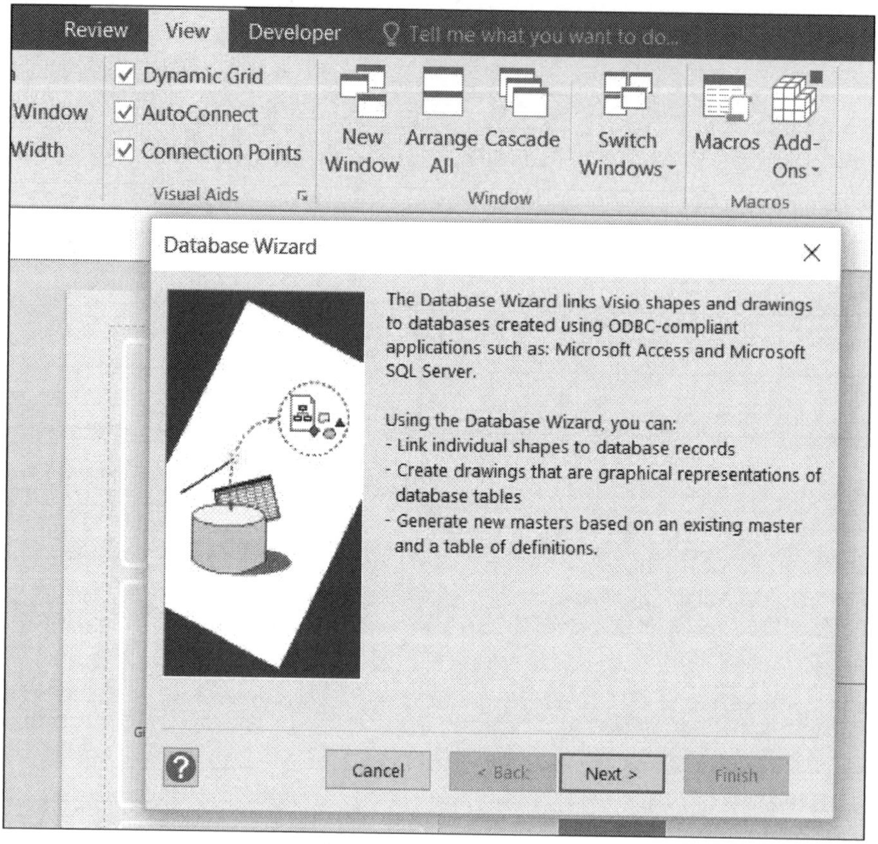


All of the data related add-ons under the **View** | **Macros** | **Add-Ons** | **Visio Extras** ribbon menu are part of one large add-on, and they are therefore not part of the core engine and object model in Visio. I have covered their functionality in an earlier book of mine (take a look at `http://www.visualizinginformation.com`), so it is not covered in this book.

# v4.5 – ODBC-compliant DB connectivity, built-in VBA

This version saw improvements in the database connectivity and ODBC compliance, and the inclusion of built-in VBA vastly increased the speed of scripts.

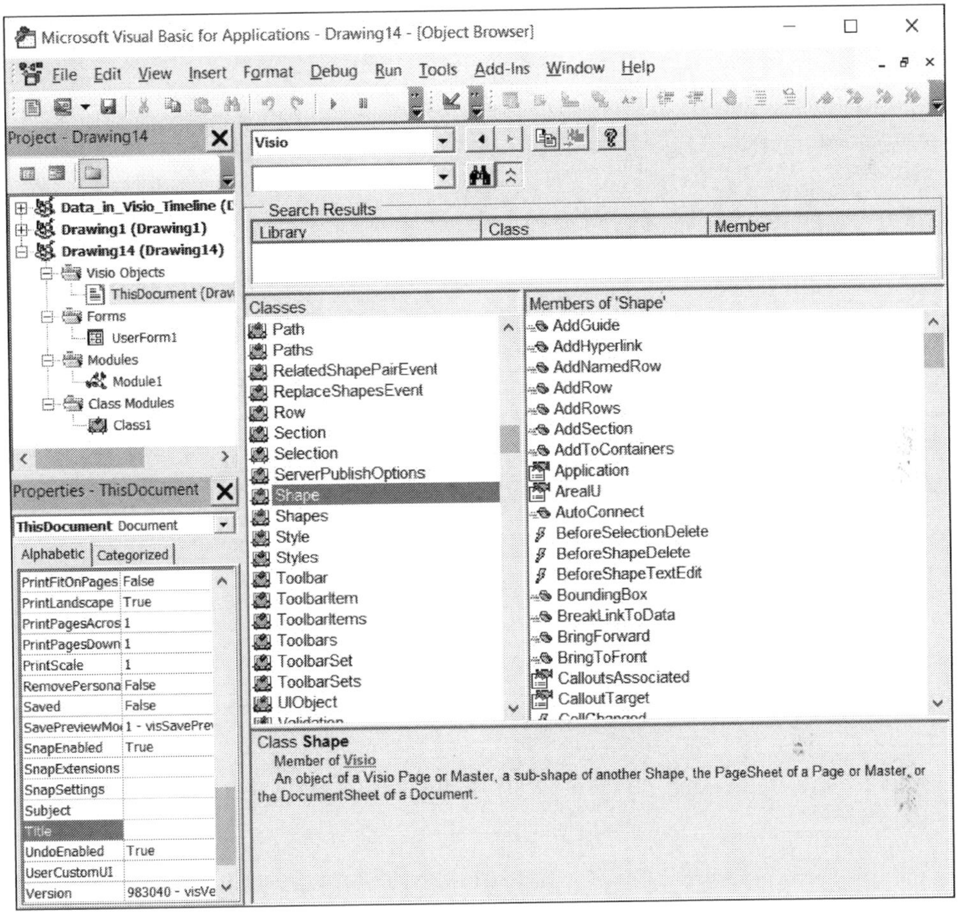


The speed improvements that I could make on automating updates utilizing the database connectivity add-on with VBA were really good. The time taken to update nearly 600 data-linked desks was reduced from 6 minutes to less than 60 seconds. This was a great improvement, but it was still relying on an add-on using ODBC. Although the add-on is capable of two-way connectivity (it can update the data source as well as refresh from the data source), it still has issues. For example, only one link is possible to a single shape. This is restricting in the corporate world, where for example the facilities, IT, and HR departments loathe merging their databases at source.

# The evolution of data in Microsoft Visio

Post-acquisition, Visio has seen its challenges, not only for the new custodians of the code base, but also for the Visio community. Microsoft has had to undertake some rationalization and integration with the extended Microsoft Office family. This has meant, for example, that developers have had to change the whole Visio user interface to use common Office elements. More latterly, this has meant changing the file structure of Visio documents to use the **Open Packaging Convention** (**OPC**) file format. The Visio community saw little improvement as far as data was concerned until Visio 2007, when the core engine was expanded at last. These features have been further enhanced since then, but they remain the cornerstone of data solutions in Visio 2016.

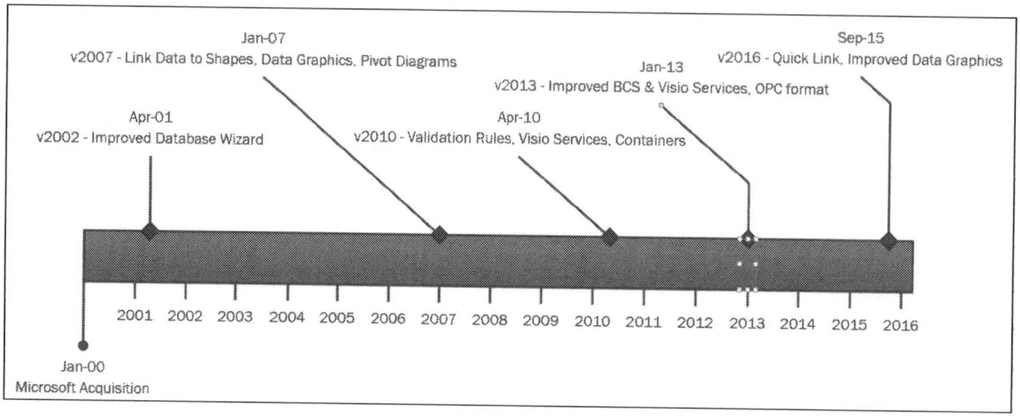


# v2002 – the improved database wizard

Some improvements to the database add-on kept us going for a while, but it uses older connectivity methodology and, as an add-on, it is difficult to extend, as explained earlier.

This add-on does have the ability to read and write data though, which can be useful for power-users and developers. For example, the position of a shape in a page, called its `PinX` and `PinY`, or its fill and line patterns and colors, could be captured from Visio and sent back directly to a table in the data source.

It is old, though, and other important information is unavailable, such as the containers that a shape is within, which call-out shapes are associated, or even which other shapes it is connected to. *Chapter 8, Validating and Extracting Information*, will cover extracting all types of information from a Visio diagram.

Most Visio users do not realize that there is a sample MS Access database called `DBSample.mdb` installed in the **Program Files** | **Office** | **lcid** folder. It is named **Visio Sample Database** in the **View** | **Add-Ons** | **Visio Extras** | **Link to Database** | **Name** drop-down list, and it contains a few tables to play with. The **Qualifier** box displays the installed location. However, I would recommend copying it to a writable folder on your local or network drive before updating it.

# v2007 – linking data to shapes, data graphics, and pivot diagrams

In Visio 2007, there was a plethora of new data features added to the core engine. This means that the Visio object model was extended for Professional edition users at the very least. A new property called `DataFeaturesEnabled` appeared on the `Application` object, and a `DataRecordsets` collection appeared on the `Document` object. Each normal `DataRecordset` appears in the new **External Data** window so that rows of data can be linked to shapes. Importantly, this data can be refreshed, either manually or after a set time period, while the document is open, or by code opening and refreshing each document. This provides extensibility for developers who can now create data automation code on firm foundations.

The new pivot diagram add-on also creates `DataRecordsets`, but these are not displayed in the **External Data** window.

> Detailed steps to download the code bundle are mentioned in the Preface of this book. Have a look.
>
> The code bundle for the book is also hosted on GitHub at `https://github.com/PacktPublishing/repository-name`. We also have other code bundles from our rich catalog of books and videos available at `https://github.com/PacktPublishing/`. Check them out!

The following screenshot from Visio 2016 shows two buttons (**Custom Import** and **Linked Data**) that replace the one called **Link Data to Shapes**, present in the earlier versions. There is no change to the foundation though:

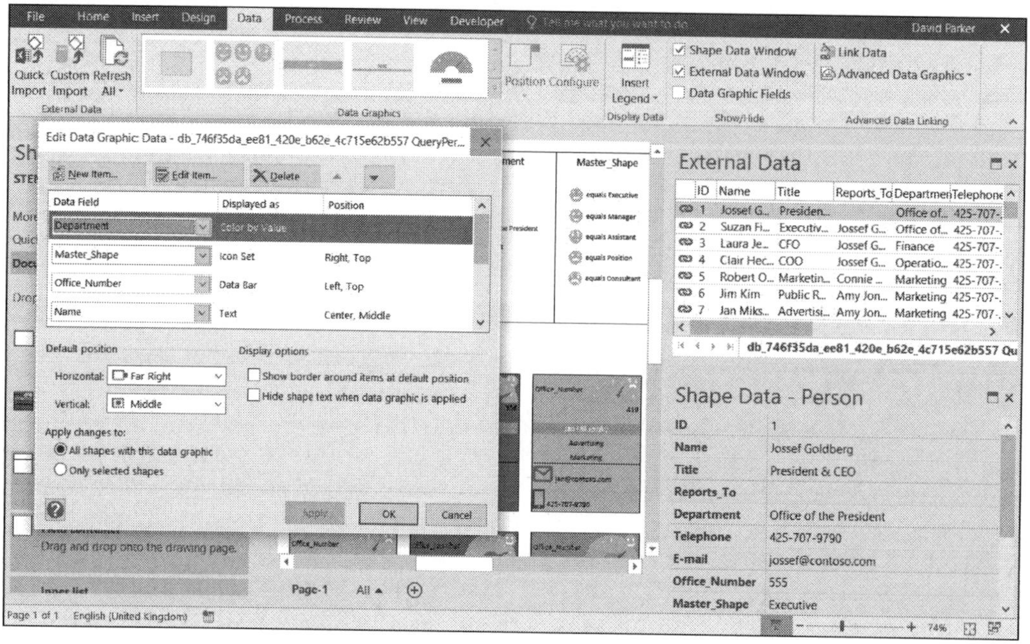


The **Quick Import** button, **Data Graphics** group, and **Data Graphic Fields** checkbox were introduced in Visio 2016, and they will be explained in the next chapter.

The **Display Data** | **Insert Legend** button was not introduced until Visio 2010.

# v2010 – validation rules, Visio services, and containers

Further integration with SharePoint was introduced in two ways.

- First, Visio could be used to create simple SharePoint Workflows, which could then be exported to SharePoint Designer for enhancement. Since it would be dangerous to export badly formed data to SharePoint, Visio 2010 was given a validation rules engine so that the structure of diagrams could be validated.
- Second, a Visio web part was provided in SharePoint that could not only display Visio documents faithfully, but also be partly refreshed from a suitable linked data source.

Validation and Visio services were originally only available in the Visio 2010 Premium edition, but Microsoft decided to offer all of the Premium content in the Professional edition from Visio 2013.

> My previous book, *Microsoft Visio 2013 Business Process Diagramming and Validation*, covers this topic in great detail. Take a look at `http://www.visiorules.com` for more information.

Container and callout shapes were introduced as part of a structured diagram concept, thus making it easier to construct and navigate diagrams.

Validation and structured diagrams are part of the object model and are discussed in more depth in *Chapter 8, Validating and Extracting Information*.

# v2013 – improved BCS, Visio services, and the OPC file format

The Visio file format has remained unchanged since Visio 2003, but it was time for Visio to join the rest of the Office applications and embrace the OPC file format. This is a zipped up document with many XML parts inside it; because it follows the OPC standard, it becomes accessible to some standard coding techniques.

In addition, this version saw the addition of Business Connectivity Services in SharePoint as a refreshable data source for Visio diagrams, and the need to publish documents to SharePoint was removed with native support of the new Visio file format by the Visio web part. Visio files can now be utilized in SharePoint web pages on any modern device, in any modern browser.

# v2016 – Quick Link and improved data graphics

The **Quick Link** button provides some automatic analysis of data in Excel worksheets, and some improvements were made to data graphics, such as the inclusion of icons in text callout items. These features are discussed in more detail in *Chapter 3, Linking Data to Shapes*.

# Other significant current add-ons that use data

There are a few add-ons that use data to generate diagrams, and they even provide the ability to export data. A couple of these utilize more specialist data such as **Schedule | Gantt Chart** and **Schedule | Timeline** for Microsoft Project. However, these three add-ons use data to create the layout of a diagram, which can then be enhanced with linked, refreshable data.

## The Organization Chart

First introduced in Visio 4.0, this popular wizard and its supporting add-on provide the ability to create hierarchical organization charts, and as the following screenshot shows, it can use Microsoft Exchange, Excel, text files, or an ODBC compliant data source:

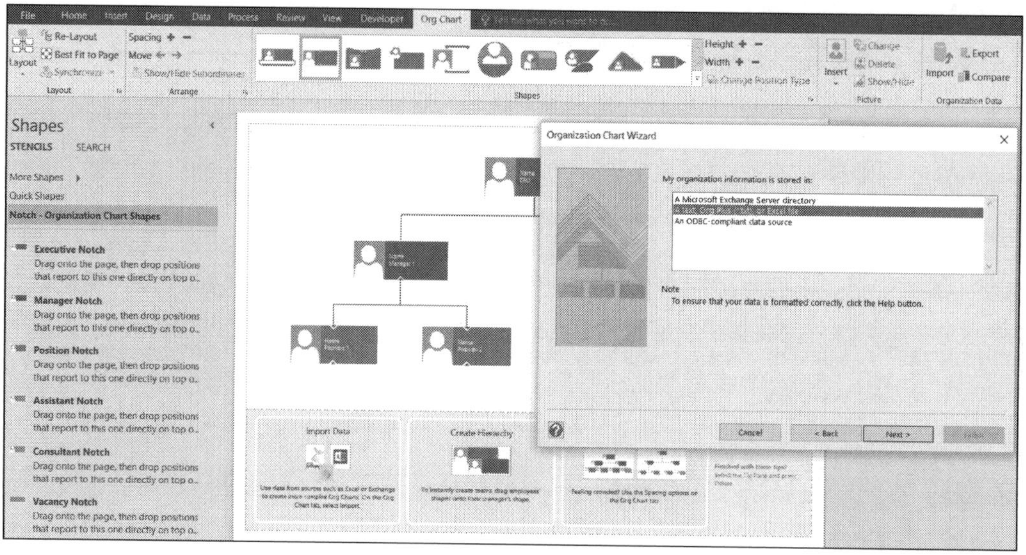


The imported data is used to create a hierarchical structure, but there is currently no refresh functionality. However, it can be overlaid with refreshable data using the **Data | Custom Import** feature that is covered in *Chapter 3, Linking Data to Shapes*. There is also the ability to compare two Visio documents in order to check what the differences are. It also has an export feature that outputs the shape data and hierarchical relationship to an Excel workbook, text, or CSV file.

This add-on has some other good features that some Visio users love. For example, it has the ability to insert images into the shape easily. This is all done using a non-extendable add-on, which makes it difficult to develop with.

# The Space Plan

First introduced in Visio 2003, this add-on provides the ability to import and, as the following screenshot shows, use **Microsoft Exchange**, **Excel**, **Active Directory**, or an **ODBC**-compliant data source.

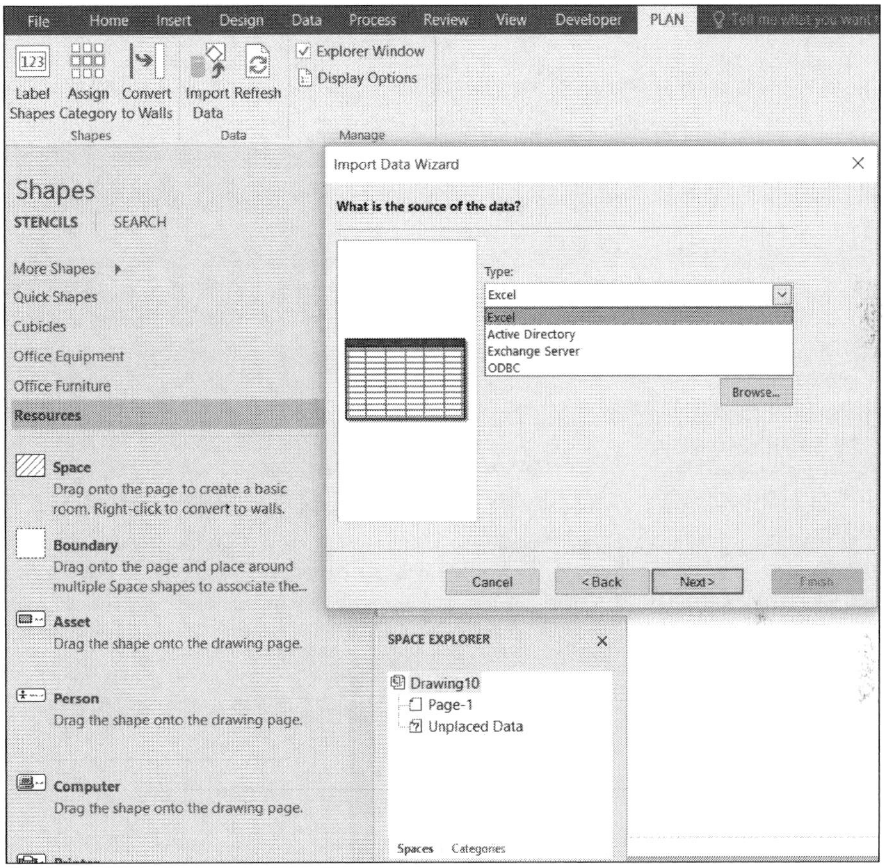


The imported data is displayed in the **Space Explorer** window, and it can be refreshed from the ribbon. Unless you need to directly import data from **Active Directory** or **Exchange Server**, or particularly like the **Space Explorer** tree view display or the ability to automatically add shapes onto other shapes (such as **Person** or **Asset** shapes onto **Space** shapes), then I recommend using the **Data** | **Custom Import** feature that is covered in *Chapter 3, Linking Data to Shapes*.

# The Pivot Diagram

This add-on uses the same **Data Selector** as the **Data | Custom Import** feature but with the extra capability of using **SQL Server Analysis Services** as a data source, as the following screenshot shows:

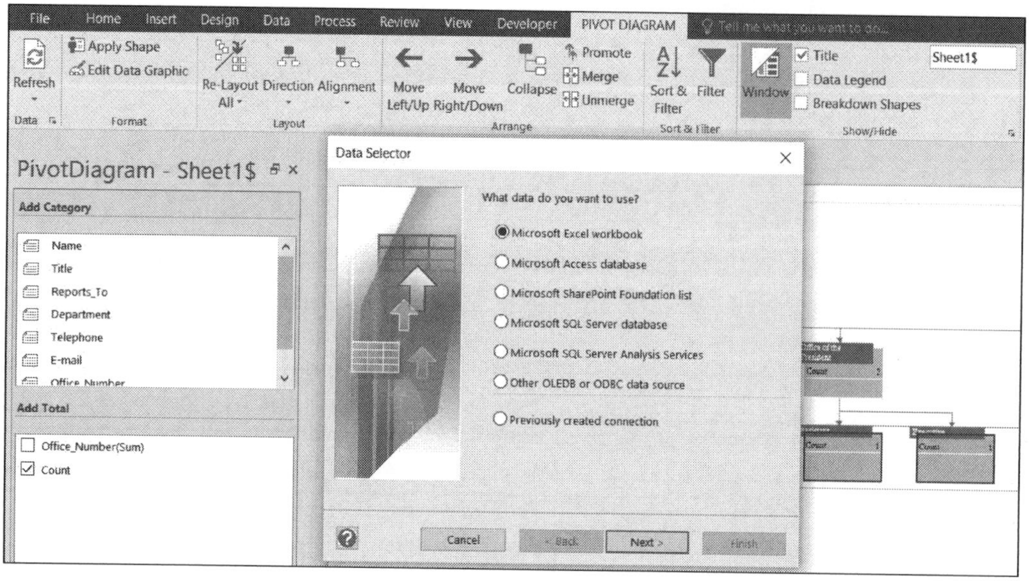


This add-on also utilizes the DataRecordsets collection that is covered in the next chapter, but DataRecordsets are hidden and numerous. This add-on, though, is worthy of more explanation and is covered in *Chapter 5, Using the Pivot Diagram Add-On,* since you can overlay with refreshable data by using the **Data | Custom Import** feature that is covered in *Chapter 3, Linking Data to Shapes.*

# Sadly missed add-ons that used data

There are a number of add-ons that have disappeared from Visio over the years. This could be for very good reasons, but we oldies still miss some of their capabilities. So, I mention them not only to warn you that some documentation you may find on the web is out-of-date, but also possibly to encourage reincarnations.

For example, the **Flowchart-TQM Wizard** and the **Network Diagram Wizard** were deprecated in Visio 2003, but they provided a method to not only add shapes with data, but also to connect them together. The data linking and structured diagram concepts have been added to Visio since then, so a reincarnation would need to account for these.

The network discovery tool was last seen back in the Visio 2000 Enterprise Edition, and it had many devoted users for many years after that. This add-on would discover the connectivity of items in a network, create a database, and then diagram parts of it on demand in a Visio diagram. There are several third-party applications that are now available that can generate Visio diagrams of your network.

What all of the afore mentioned deprecated add-ons have in common is that they were not part of the core engine, and therefore, were more difficult to maintain and almost impossible to extend with third-party code.

# A returning add-on...

There is also one deprecated add-on that is due to make a return by popular demand. This was and is the database modelling engine that originated in the code from the Infomodeler acquisition. It could be used to not only reverse-engineer databases, but also to forward-engineer and create reports. This eventually disappeared completely in Visio 2013, after first losing its forward engineering and reporting capability in earlier versions. It did have its limitations, but it was still very useful and is missed by quite a few users who need to understand, or explain to others, the complexity of a relational database structure. It will be returning in a limited form some time in 2016.

# Summary

You have learned about the evolution of data within Visio over the years, and how the core engine has been extended since Visio 2007 to include linking to refreshable data sources with enhanced graphics to represent these values.

The quest is to become proficient in creating refreshable data-linked graphics that accurately represent business intelligence. However, first we must look underneath the hood to see what makes Visio tick, which we will do in the next chapter.

# 2

# Understanding How Data Is Stored within Visio

A Visio user may choose to create a drawing from one of the many Microsoft templates, or even from a custom one. In each case, the user sees that a Visio document can have many pages. Each page can contain many shapes. The Visio user interface normally presents many shapes on stencils that the user can drag and drop onto a page. A user may also use the drawing tools to draw rectangles, ellipses, lines, or just add text. The user may use the ribbon buttons to add containers, callouts or connectors.

Data can be stored in Visio in many ways, and the developer chooses the way according to the needs of the usage scenario. This chapter will describe the important parts of the rich Visio object model so that a power user who writes macros, or a developer who writes add-ins, will know how to navigate around the various elements. It will also describe the important sections of the programmable ShapeSheet that is behind every shape. Lastly, it will show how the structured diagram concept can be understood using both the object model and the ShapeSheet.

A little knowledge of VBA will be useful, or just hit *Alt* + *F11* in Visio and explore....

In this chapter, we shall cover the following topics:

- An overview of data in Visio
- Introducing the Visio object model
- The ShapeSheet
- Structured diagrams

# A very quick introduction to data in Visio

There are many templates and tools within Visio that either import or export data.

The following diagram shows the various data sources or targets listed vertically in the center. The Visio features that can import data are on the left-hand side, and the features that export are on the right. There are many features that use data, but the most relevant features and data sources are enhanced with a thicker outline:

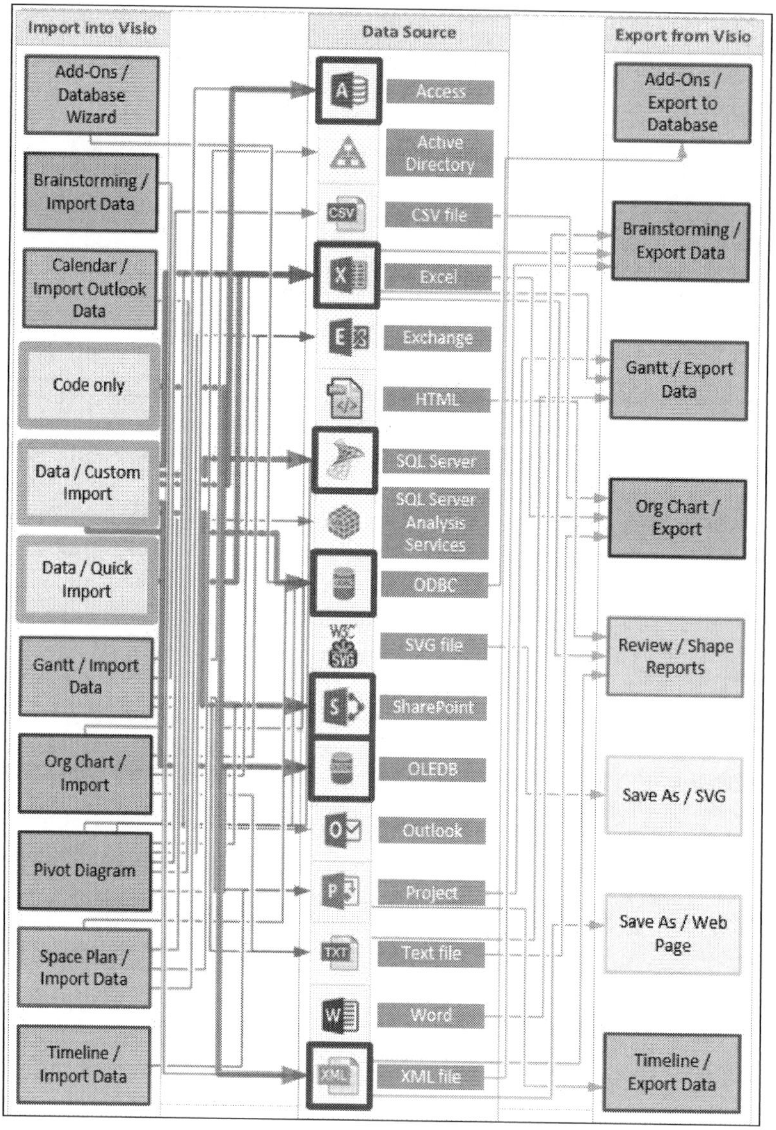

I have omitted SharePoint workflows from this diagram because it is so specialized.

> Visit http://blog.bvisual.net/2015/11/16/data-import-and-export-features-in-visio-2016-and-2013/ for more information about this diagram.

Most of these features utilize the Shape Data capability of Visio shapes, pages, and documents. The following table lists the Visio features that import values into Shape Data rows:

| Visio Features that Import Data into Shape Data / Source data | Access | Active Directory | Excel | Exchange | ODBC | OLEDB | SharePoint | SQL Server | SQL Server Analysis Services | Text file | XML file | Grand Total |
|---|---|---|---|---|---|---|---|---|---|---|---|---|
| **Business** | **1** | | **2** | **1** | **2** | **1** | **1** | **1** | **1** | **1** | | **11** |
| Org Chart / Import | | | 1 | 1 | 1 | | | | | 1 | | 4 |
| Pivot Diagram | 1 | | 1 | | 1 | 1 | 1 | 1 | 1 | | | 7 |
| **Data** | **1** | | **2** | | **1** | **1** | **1** | **1** | | | **1** | **8** |
| Code only | | | | | | | | | | | 1 | 1 |
| Data / Custom Import | 1 | | 1 | | 1 | 1 | 1 | 1 | | | | 6 |
| Data / Quick Import | | | 1 | | | | | | | | | 1 |
| **Maps and Floor Plans** | | **1** | **1** | **1** | **1** | | | | | | | **4** |
| Space Plan / Import Data | | 1 | 1 | 1 | 1 | | | | | | | 4 |
| **View / Add-Ons / Visio Extras** | | | | | **1** | | | | | | | **1** |
| Add-Ons / Database Wizard | | | | | 1 | | | | | | | 1 |
| **Grand Total** | **2** | **1** | **5** | **2** | **5** | **2** | **2** | **2** | **1** | **1** | **1** | **24** |

> SQL Server stored procedures can also be used as a data source in code in addition to the tables and views that are accessible from the user interface.

There are also Visio features that export values from Shape Data rows, as can be seen in the following table:

| Visio Features that Export Data from Shape Data / Target data | CSV file | Excel | HTML | ODBC | SVG file | Text file | XML file | Grand Total |
|---|---|---|---|---|---|---|---|---|
| **⊟ Business** | **1** | **1** | | | | **1** | | **3** |
| Org Chart / Export | 1 | 1 | | | | 1 | | 3 |
| **⊟ File / Save As** | | | | | **1** | | **1** | **2** |
| Save As / SVG | | | | | 1 | | | 1 |
| Save As / Web Page | | | | | | | 1 | 1 |
| **⊟ Review** | | **1** | **1** | | | | **1** | **3** |
| Review / Shape Reports | | 1 | 1 | | | | 1 | 3 |
| **⊟ View / Add-Ons / Visio Extras** | | | | **1** | | | | **1** |
| Add-Ons / Export to Database | | | | 1 | | | | 1 |
| **Grand Total** | **1** | **2** | **1** | **1** | **1** | **1** | **2** | **9** |

Many of the built-in shapes from stencils in Visio contain a pre-defined set of data rows. For example, the following screenshot of a cross-functional flowchart has the **Shape Data** window open for the selected **Start/End** shape. The **Data** ribbon tab contains more elements in the 2016 version because it now contains a gallery for **Data Graphics**:

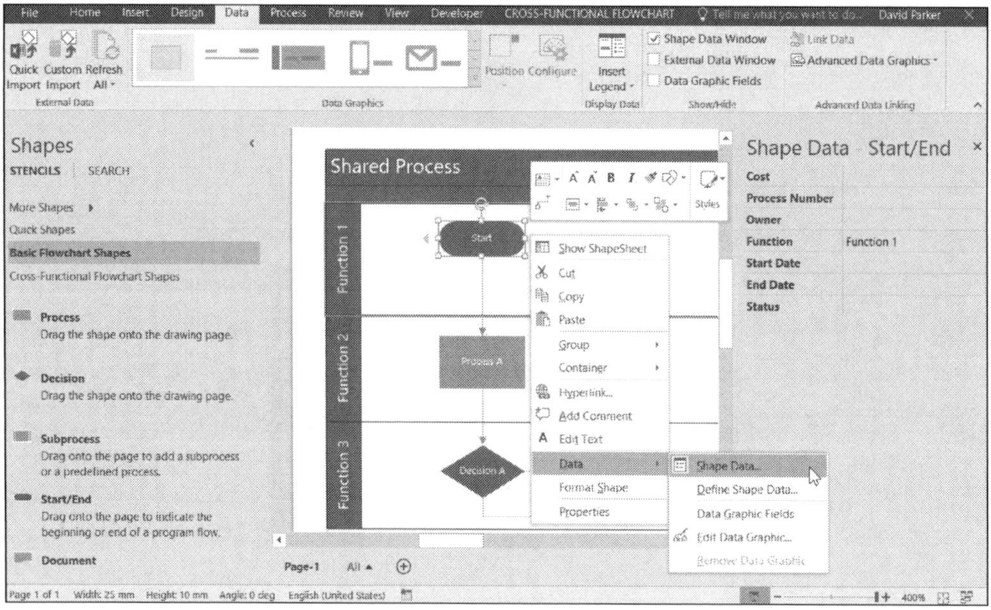

The **Shape Data Window** can be opened from the right-click menu of a shape (from **Data | Show/Hide | Shape Data Window**, or from **View | Show | Task Panes | Shape Data**). Many Visio users will just enter some text into each shape and may not even bother opening the **Shape Data Window**, and therefore they miss out on some of the best features of Visio!

There is an older **Shape Data** dialog too, which could also be used to view or edit data. The organization chart shapes, for example, have an extra right-click menu option labeled **Properties**, which opens up the **Shape Data** dialog, as shown in the following screenshot:

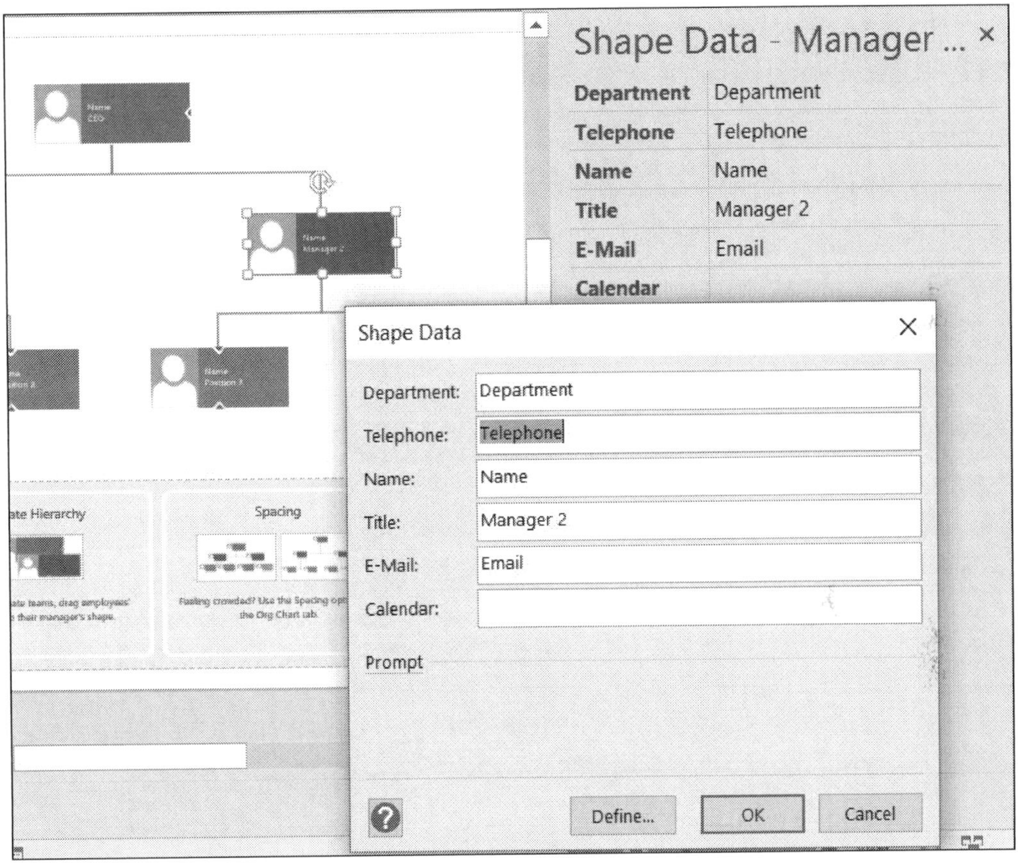


The dialog can only display a maximum of twenty rows, but the window has a vertical scroll bar that appears if there are too many to display.

# Defining Shape Data

Not every shape has these rows of data, but every shape could have them. There is a **Define Shape Data ...** option in the right-click menu on each shape and the **Shape Data** window header. There is also a **Define...** button on the **Shape Data** dialog. The following screenshot shows the **Define Shape Data** dialog for a flowchart shape:

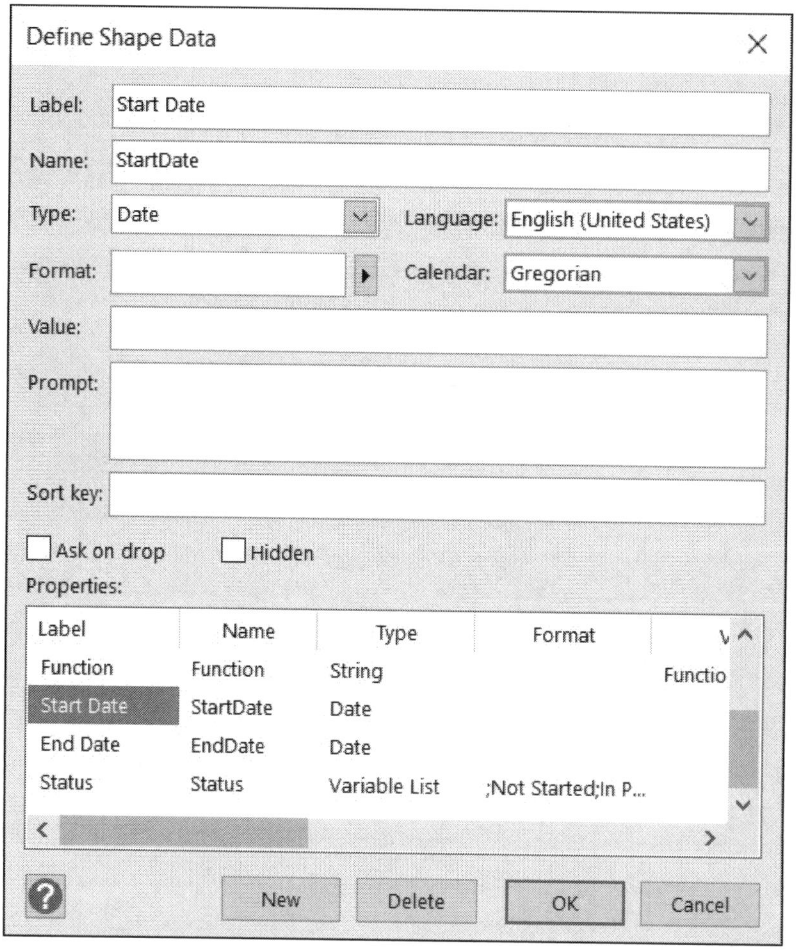


Defining shape data in this way can be quite time consuming, and there are limitations imposed by the dialog, such as the inability to enter formulas.

There is a way to create sets of data rows by using the **Shape Data Sets ...** option from the right-mouse menu of the **Shape Data** window header. This allows the definition to be copied from one shape to another, as seen in the following screenshot:

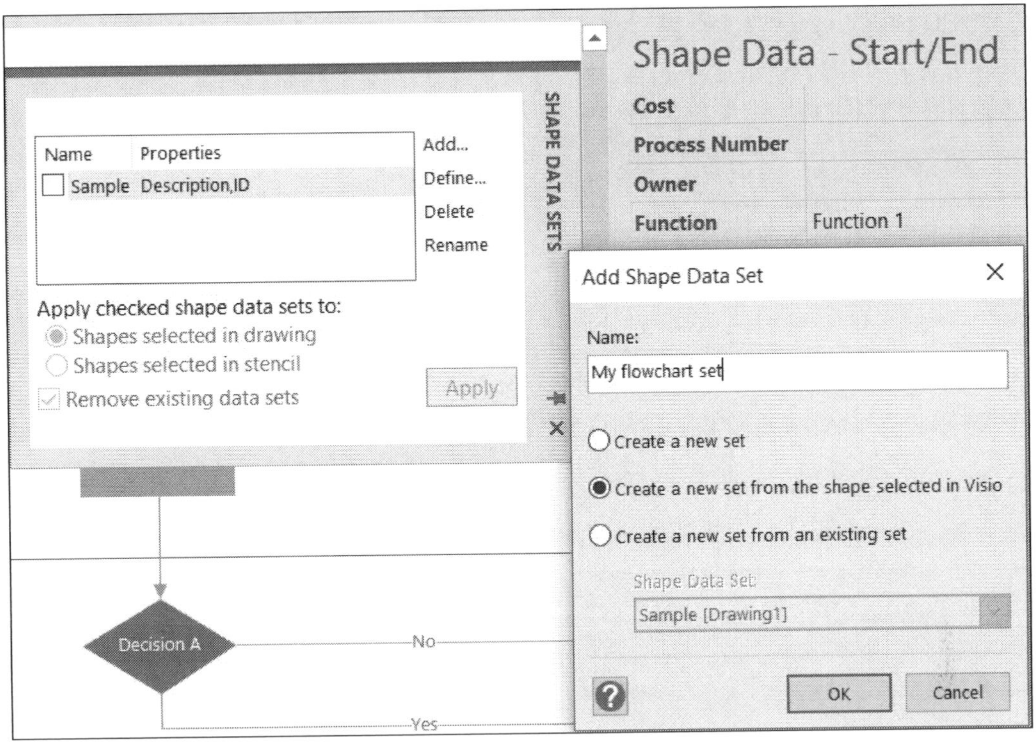


The data linking feature can also create shape data rows if they do not already exist in a shape. This can take some of the effort out of the task, but it also lacks refinement.

Also, this visible interface being changed into data on a Visio shape is not the only way that data can be stored. Therefore, it is important to get a grasp of what goes on under the covers so that the capabilities of Visio can be exploited to create more efficient solutions.

# Understanding the Visio object model

An object model defines how the various objects and collections relate to each other, and their properties, methods, and events. Knowing how to navigate around it is essential for writing quick code in VBA, or more capable code for an add-in or add-on.

# Starting with the Application object

The top-level object is the Visio `Application` object itself. This object contains a collection of documents that are currently open.

> Actually, there is also the `InvisibleApp` object, which a developer can use to interact with a diagram without the Visio application interface appearing on the screen.

Templates, drawings, and stencils are all types of Visio documents, although the user only sees stencils on the panels of shapes on the left of the drawing page. A drawing is usually created from a template document. However, a drawing can also be created from any existing drawing.

A **drawing document** consists of a collection of **pages**, each of which can contain a collection of **shapes**, and each **shape** can contain another collection of **shapes**, and so on. Although a shape can contain many levels of shapes collections, it does add more stress on the Visio engine if there are too many levels. A rule of thumb for shape developers is not to have it more than three levels deep.

A document has a Masters collection, and a Master contains a collection of shapes, and each shape can also contain a collection of shapes. A user sees a collection of icons displayed within a stencil.

In the following diagram of a partial object model, some objects are only available in the Visio Professional editions, as indicated by the container on the right:

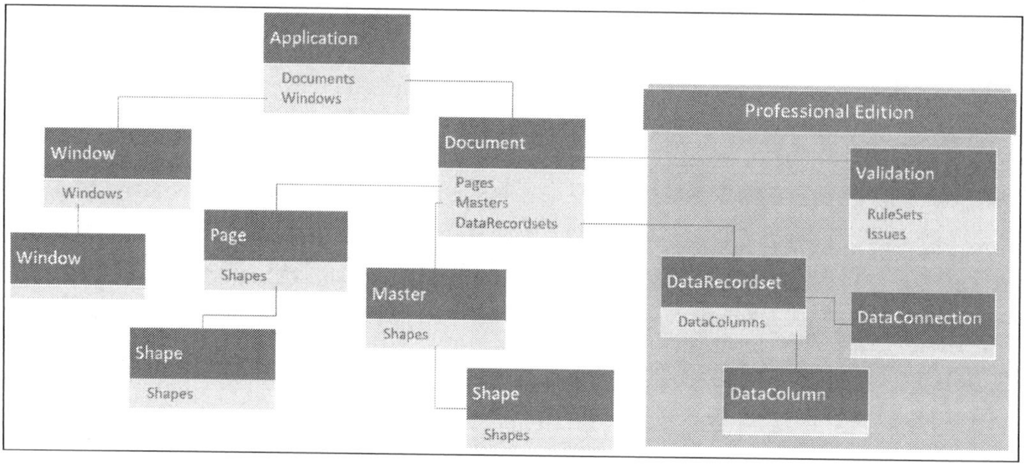

## Understanding the relationship of the Master shape and its shape instances

If a `Master` shape contains more than one shape on its page, then Visio will automatically group them together when the Master is dropped on to a page. Therefore, it is not good practice to have more than one shape in the `Master.Shapes` collection. Of course, this one shape can be a group shape itself, which can contain sub-shapes.

In fact, the application of data graphics to a shape will automatically turn it into a group shape if it is not one already. Therefore, it is good practice for all master shapes to be groups if there is any intention of using Data Graphics with them.

The action of dragging and dropping a `Master` shape from a stencil will create a `Shape` instance. If the `Master` shape does not exist in the document already, then it is first added to the Masters collection of the document. The Visio user can see the Masters collection of a drawing document by ticking **More Shapes | Show Document Stencil** in the **Shapes** window. Alternatively, the drawing's `Masters` node can be expanded in the **Drawing Explorer** window.

## Knowing how a shape can be identified

Every shape is automatically assigned a unique ID within its page, and a unique name within the shapes collection that it belongs to. A shape can be renamed in the UI with **Developer | Shape Design | Shape Name** by pressing *F2*, with a shape selected in the **Drawing Explorer** window or programmatically. There is no error created if you programmatically change the name of the Shape to one that exists already. Instead, the intended name is appended with the `Shape.ID`, separated by a dot. This is similar to the automatic name given to a shape when it is first dropped from a stencil. In this case, the shape is named the same as its Master, but of course, only the first one can be exactly the same, so subsequent ones are appended with the ID automatically.

There is an alternative to using the numeric `ID` property, which is the `NameID` property. The `NameID` property is in the form of `Sheet.nn`, where `nn` is the ID of the shape.

The following screenshot shows the partially expanded **Drawing Explorer** window and the **Developer | Shape Design | Shape Name** dialog opened for the selected `Class` shape that has been labeled **Application**. This shape has an **ID** of **1** because it was the first shape that was dropped onto the page:

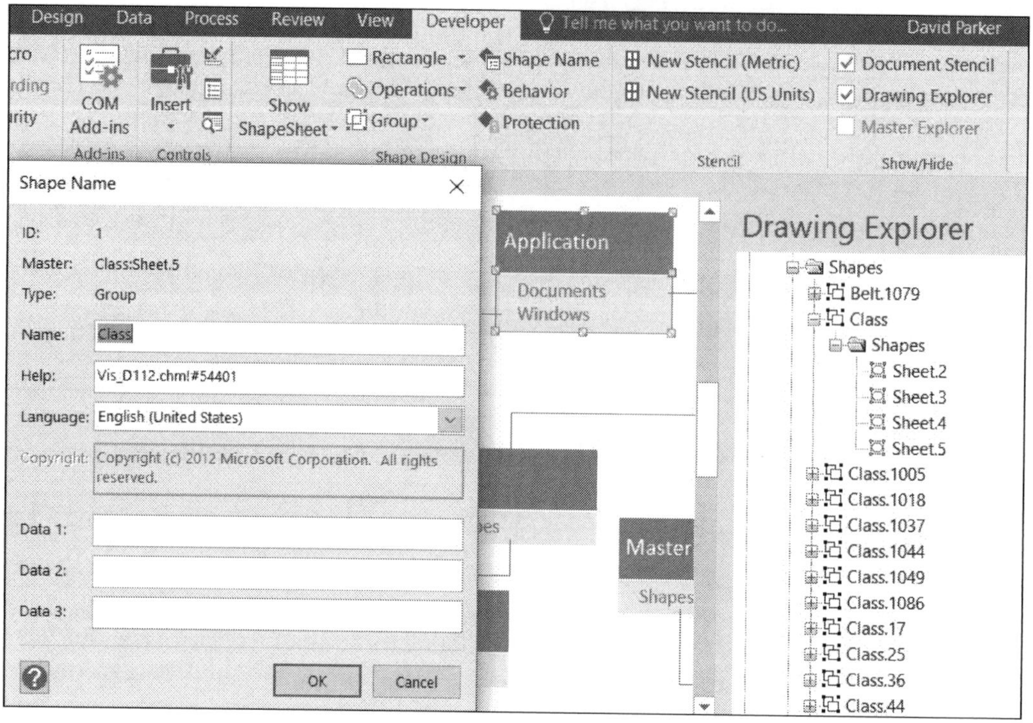


This shape is an instance of the Master named `Class`. The dialog displays **Class:Sheet.5** because **Sheet.5** is the name of the main shape in the `Class` Master. Notice that the **Name** property can be edited manually here. It can also be renamed in the **Drawing Explorer** tree view by selecting the name and then pressing *F2*.

Also, notice that the **Shapes** collection of this shape in the **Drawing Explorer** window shows four sub-shapes: `Sheet.2`, `Sheet.3`, `Sheet.4`, and `Sheet.5`. These were the next four shapes to be dropped on the page because they were already part of the `Class Master.Shapes(1).Shapes` collection. None of these four sub-shapes are among the ones labeled **Documents** and **Windows**. These two shapes are actually instances of the Master named `Member`, and they appear further down the tree view as the shapes named `Member` and `Member.35`, as shown in the following screenshot:

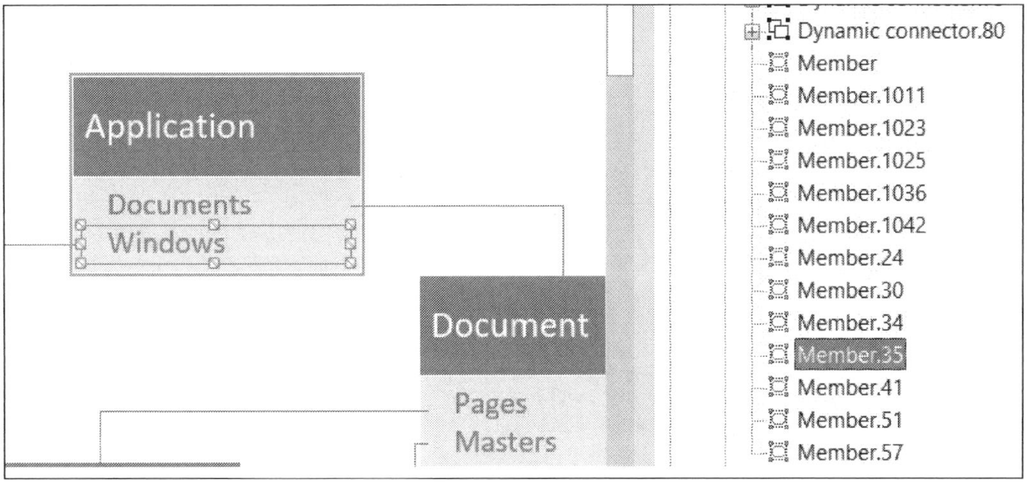


Even though these two shapes move and resize with the `Class` shape, they are not part of it. They are list item shapes, and the `Class` shape is a list shape that contains them. Their properties will be explained later in this chapter.

Notice the different icon in the tree view for shapes that are group type, and those, such as `Member.35`, which are not.

## How to use a globally unique identifier

A programmer also has the option of creating a **GUID** (**globally unique identifier**) for a shape by setting its `UniqueID` property. This GUID is unique for the whole application, while the numeric `ID` property is only unique within its page.

## The danger of using the Index property

The `Index` property of a shape is unique within its collection only, and it is assigned at the time of creation and is reflected in the z-order of the graphics. However, it can be changed by using methods such as `SendToBack` or `BringToFront`. In addition, the `DisplayLevel` cell can also change the apparent z-order of the graphics. Therefore, the `Index` property is rarely used to identify a shape.

## Reviewing shape text

It may seem sensible to refer to a shape by the text that appears on it, but of course, more than one shape can have the same text, and many shapes have no text. Every shape in Visio can contain text, which can contain multiple rows, formats, and references to other cell values.

In fact, there is no `Page.InsertText(...)` method, or similar, at all! If you use the macro recorder while using the **Home** | **Tools** | **Text** tool without a shape selected, then the `Page.DrawRectangle(...)` method is actually used, but the outline and fill of the rectangle are invisible. Of course, a power-user or developer can make them visible again.

Since the displayed text can be rich in content and contain references to values elsewhere, it is better to use the `Shape.Characters` property rather than the `Shape.Text` property in most cases.

> If a shape is using Data Graphics to display text with a Text callout graphic item, then the visible text will be part of a sub-shape.

Shape developers will sometimes prevent the text from being edited and only allow the Shape Data values to be edited and displayed in the text. Sometimes, the editable text is part of a sub-shape, and the top-level group shape does not allow edits. For example, the `Swimlane` shape in the **Cross-Functional Flowchart** template contains two sub-shapes. One of these is the header text, so the **Edit text** of group behavior has been unticked on the **Developer** | **Shape Design** | **Behavior** dialog, as shown in the following screenshot:

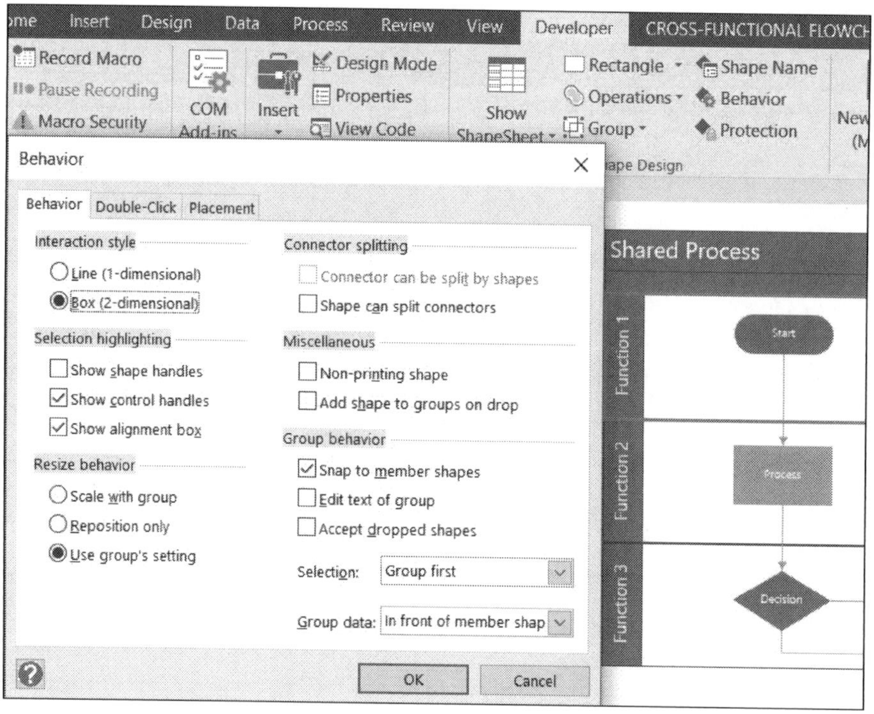

The `Shape.Text` property for the `Swimlane.9` shape does return `Function 1`, but the `Shape.Characters.Text` property returns an empty string.

With all this ambiguity around text, it is obviously not a good idea to use it to identify a shape.

# Understanding the DataRecordsets collection

The next chapter will go into detail about creating `DataRecordsets`, but it is important for the developer to understand the object model that is available in the Professional editions of Visio.

The following VBA code, `ListRecordsets()`, prints out all of the `DataRecordset` objects in the active document and then prints out some details of each column:

```
Public Sub ListDataRecordsets()
Dim drs As DataRecordset
Dim dcn As DataConnection
Dim dcl As DataColumn
Dim i As Integer
    For Each drs In ActiveDocument.DataRecordsets
        Set dcn = drs.DataConnection
        i = 0
        Debug.Print drs.ID, drs.Name, drs.CommandString
        Debug.Print , dcn.ConnectionString
        Debug.Print
        For Each dcl In drs.DataColumns
            i = i + 1
            Debug.Print i, dcl.Visible, _
                dcl.GetProperty(visDataColumnPropertyType), _
                dcl.Name, dcl.DisplayName
        Next
    Next
End Sub
```

mmediate

```
9            Process Steps$A1:F16        select * from `Process St
             Provider=Microsoft.ACE.OLEDB.12.0;User ID=Admin;Data

1            True          0             Steps           Steps
2            True          0             Assigned        Assigned
3            True          2             Complete %      Complete %
4            True          0             Responsibility
5            True          0             Email           Email
6            True          0             Call            Call
```

# Understanding the Validation objects

*Chapter 8, Validating and Extracting Information* will go into detail about using Validation, which is available in the Professional editions only.

The following VBA code, `ListRuleSets()`, prints out names of all of the rule sets and rules in the active document:

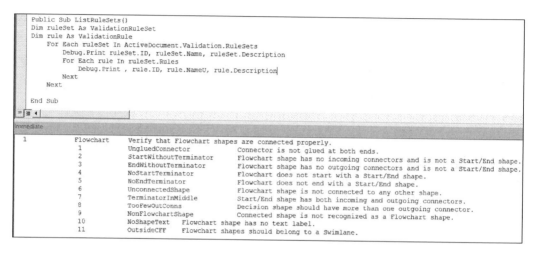

```
Public Sub ListRuleSets()
Dim ruleSet As ValidationRuleSet
Dim rule As ValidationRule
    For Each ruleSet In ActiveDocument.Validation.RuleSets
        Debug.Print ruleSet.ID, ruleSet.Name, ruleSet.Description
        For Each rule In ruleSet.Rules
            Debug.Print , rule.ID, rule.NameU, rule.Description
        Next
    Next

End Sub
```

Immediate

```
1             Flowchart     Verify that Flowchart shapes are connected properly.
               1            UngluedConnector             Connector is not glued at both ends.
               2            StartWithoutTerminator       Flowchart shape has no incoming connectors and is not a Start/End shape.
               3            EndWithoutTerminator         Flowchart shape has no outgoing connectors and is not a Start/End shape.
               4            NoStartTerminator            Flowchart does not start with a Start/End shape.
               5            NoEndTerminator              Flowchart does not end with a Start/End shape.
               6            UnconnectedShape             Flowchart shape is not connected to any other shape.
               7            TerminatorInMiddle           Start/End shape has both incoming and outgoing connectors.
               8            TooFewOutConns               Decision shape should have more than one outgoing connector.
               9            NonFlowchartShape            Connected shape is not recognized as a Flowchart shape.
               10           NoShapeText   Flowchart shape has no text label.
               11           OutsideCFF    Flowchart shapes should belong to a Swimlane.
```

Whether the rules check is written in code, as for the SharePoint Worklflow templates, or in XML, as in the flowchart templates, the rules need to be stored in the document in order to make for any issues to be tagged against them.

# Getting shapes selected in the UI

The Visio application has an `ActiveWindow` property, which has a `Selection` property that contains a collection of currently selected shapes in `ActiveWindow`, that is, if `ActiveWindow.Type` is equal to `Visio.VisWinTypes.visDrawing`. The first shape in this collection can also be referenced as the `PrimaryItem` of the `Selection` property in code, and it can be seen to have a thicker selection rectangle in the Visio UI.

## Understanding shape sections, rows, and cells

As previously stated, the power of Visio comes from the unique ShapeSheet that is part of every shape. However, some developers can find it a little strange at first. For example, there is no `Shape.X` or `Shape.Y` property to position a shape within a page. Instead, the developer must set the following property:

```
Shape.CellsSrc(VisSectionIndices.visSectionObject, VisRowIndices.
visRowXFormOut, VisCellIndices.visXFormPinX ).Formula
```

Alternatively:

```
Shape.Cells("PinX").Formula
```

The former verbose property uses enumeration constants to identify a cell. It will perform quicker than using the cell name, but it can be inconvenient at times.

There is no `Shape.Sections` collection that can be looped through. Instead, a developer should test whether a section exists before referencing it, that is, if that section is not one of the permanent ones. Indeed, this book is about data, and usually data is stored in an optional section such as `VisSectionIndices.visSectionProp (243)` and `VisSectionIndices.visSectionUser (242)`. These are the enumeration constants for the Shape Data (it used to be called **Custom Properties**) and User-Defined Cells sections.

# Getting to grips with the ShapeSheet

Every document, page, and shape has a ShapeSheet that contains a number of sections, rows, and cells. Cells contain formulas that produce a resultant value.

The document ShapeSheet is known as the `DocumentSheet` in the object model, but it can be referenced as `TheDoc` in a cell formula. Similarly, the page ShapeSheet is known as `PageSheet` in the object model, but it is referred to as `ThePage` in cell formulas.

There are a lot of mandatory sections in the ShapeSheet, and some of them do not even have their own enumerator in `visSectionIndices`. Instead, they come under `visSectionIndices.visSectionObject`. In fact, there are 38 shown on the **View Sections** dialog, but with only 24 section constants:

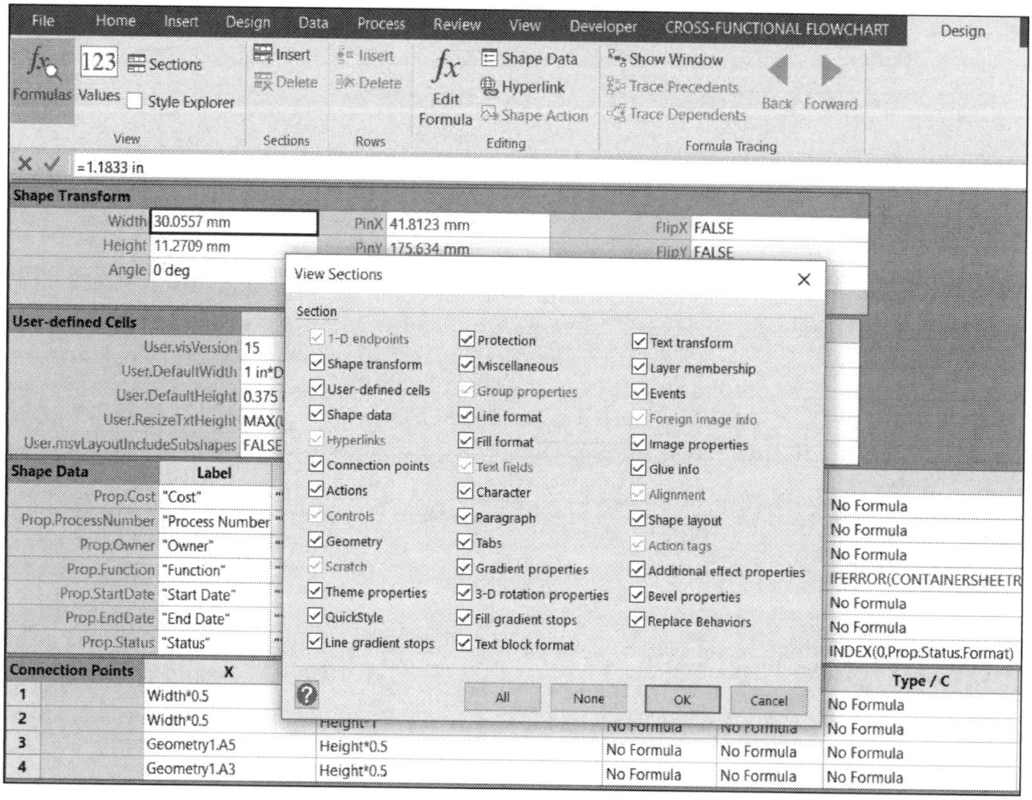


It is more efficient to reference a cell by its `SRC` (`Section`, `Row`, `Cell`) values than by its name. However, there are times when using the name is unavoidable.

If the ShapeSheet is open in the UI, then you can easily find the name of a cell by clicking in the cell, placing the cursor in the formula edit bar, and selecting the cell again. The name will appear in the formula edit bar. It can be removed again by pressing *Esc*.

The ShapeSheet has two display modes, **Formulas** and **Values**, which can be toggled using the **Design** | **View** | **Values** and **Formulas** button.

# Understanding the Shape Data section

The **Shape Data** section in the ShapeSheet is the most important for data in Visio because of the following points:

- It has a built-in user interface (the **Shape Data** window and the **Shape Data** dialog)
- It has some data typing
- It can be linked to data for automatic refreshes of values from the source
- Other ShapeSheet cells can reference these values and will then also be updated

In some solutions, point number 3 is the most important. For example, if the main consumption of a Visio diagram is through a SharePoint web page using the Visio Web Access control, then the whole diagram can be automatically refreshed from its data sources.

In earlier versions of Visio, Shape Data was called **Custom Properties**. In the following screenshot, the ShapeSheet displays the **Shape Data** section for the **Process** shape. The **Status** drop-down list in the **Shape Data** window presents the fixed list specified in the `Prop.Status.Format` cell:

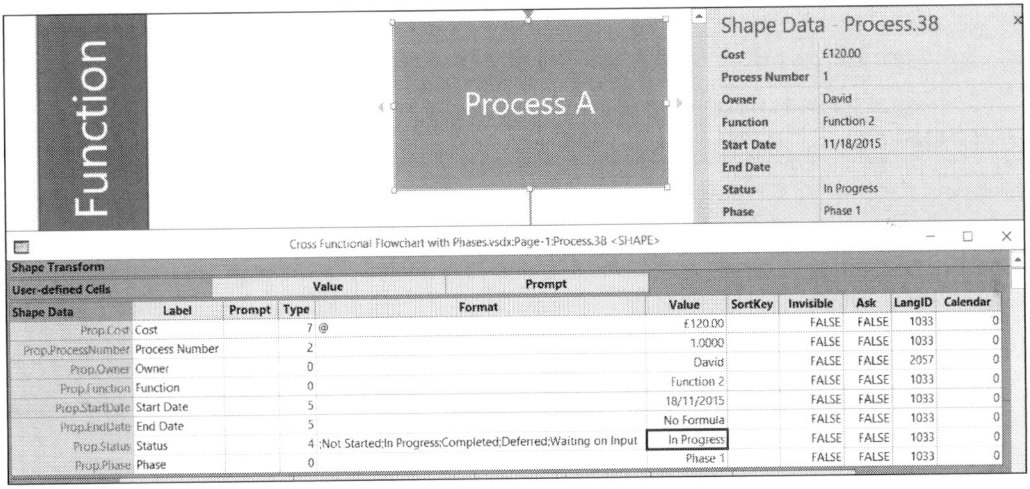


> Take a look at `http://blog.bvisual.net/2015/07/24/formatting-shape-data-in-visio/` for more information on formatting.

It is good practice to name each Shape Data row with something meaningful as it can be used for reference later. For example, in the previous screenshot, `Prop.ProcessNumber.Label` **will return the** `Process Number` **value.** `Prop.Function` **will return the same as** `Prop.Function.Value` **because** `Value` **is the default cell for** that section:

- The **Prompt** value will be displayed as a screen tip in the **Shape Data** window and dialog; it should be used more than it is.
- The **SortKey** cell can be used to provide automatic sorting of rows in the **Shape Data** window and dialog. Unfortunately, there is no way to re-order Shape Data rows (or any other rows) in the ShapeSheet, or even to copy more than one cell formula at a time.
- The **Invisible** cell is often used to control the visibility of a row dependent upon the value in another Shape Data row.
- If the **Ask** cell formula evaluates to **True** (non-zero), then the Visio user will be prompted for a value whenever the shape is dropped onto a page. This should not be used for shapes that will be automatically dropped. Strangely, this cell is known as `Verify` in the XML specification.
- The **LangID** cell contains a value representing the supported **Locale ID (LCID)** of the expected input language.
- The **Calendar** cell value is only relevant when the **Type** is **Date because it specifies the regional calendar type**.

There is another cell that is not visible in the ShapeSheet because it is read-only. This is called `DataLinked`, and it returns `True` if the row is linked to a row in a `DataRecordset`.

# Specifying the type of Shape Data

Visio Shape Data rows can specify the data type required in the **Type** cell, which will verify that only correct values are entered into the **Value** cell.

The **Define Shape Data** dialog allows the **Type** to be selected from a drop-down list, as shown in the following screenshot:

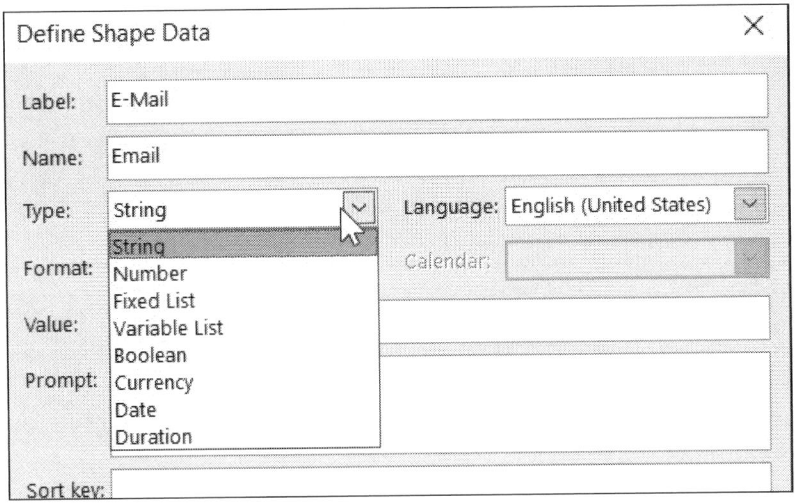


There is an enumerator for these types called `VisCellVals`, as can be seen in the following screenshot of the **Object Browser** in the VBA editor interface:

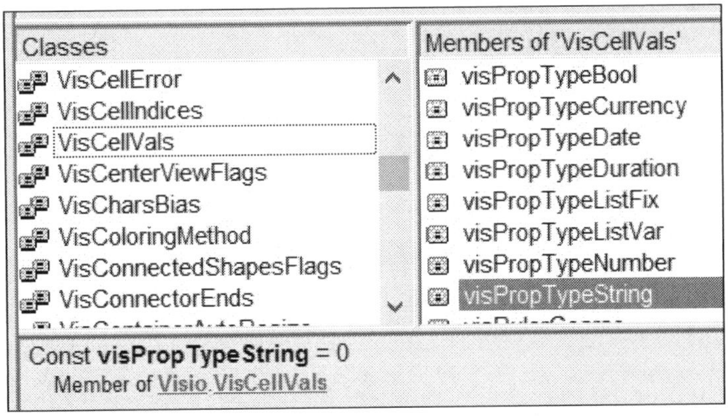


## Allowing text with the String type

This is the default if no type is defined, and can be defined with the `visPropTypeString (0)` constant. The text string can be 32,000 characters long, including multiple lines. It has been a constant embarrassment that the **Shape Data** window and dialog can only display a single line. A display format picture can be set in the **Format** cell.

## Offering choices with the Fixed List type

This provides the user with a choice from a fixed list of items, and it can be defined with the `visPropTypeListFix (1)` constant. The **Format** cell is used to define the items in the list with a separator. The default separator is a semi-colon, and no selection can be offered by including a zero-length item. For example, in the earlier screenshot of a **Process** shape, the formula in the `Prop.Status.Format` cell is as follows:

```
=";Not Started;In Progress;Completed;Deferred;Waiting on Input"
```

It is usual for the empty string to be at the beginning of the list so that it is index zero.

If the user selects an item from the drop-down list, then the `Value` formula is as follows:

```
=INDEX(n,Prop.Status.Format)
```

Here, `n` is the index number of the selected item in the semi-colon separated list.

This makes great sense because it does not rely on the text matching. It also serves as an example of the correct way to create the formula in code.

## Allowing only a numerical value with the Number type

Numbers are all stored as doubles and can be defined with the `visPropTypeNumber (2)` constant. A display format picture can be set in the **Format** cell.

## Simplifying True/False choices with the Boolean type

This has a default value of **False**, and it can be defined with the `visPropTypeBool (3)` constant.

An alternative would be to provide a Fixed List with **Yes/No** or **True/False**, as this would also provide the opportunity to have the **Yes/No/Maybe** choices or have an unset value.

## Offer some choices but allow others with the Variable List type

This provides a list that can be added to and defined with the `visPropTypeVarList (4)` constant.

The extended list is only in the shape instance that it is added to, and there is no checking for case. Consequently, a user that enters `complete` when there is already an item called `Complete`, he actually creates a new list item.

## Presenting a date picker with the Date type

This is actually a datetime type and can be defined with the `visPropTypeDate (5)` constant. A display format picture can be set in the **Format** cell.

This type is date and/or time, but the provided user interface only offers a date picker. The developer can create a different interface that provides date, date and time, or just time. The value is stored internally as a double.

## Measuring elapsed time with the Duration type

The elapsed time can be vary from weeks all the way down to seconds, and it can be defined with the `visPropTypeDuration (6)` constant. A display format picture can be set in the **Format** cell.

The default units for duration can be set in the **File** | **Options** | **Advanced** dialog, as shown in the following screenshot:

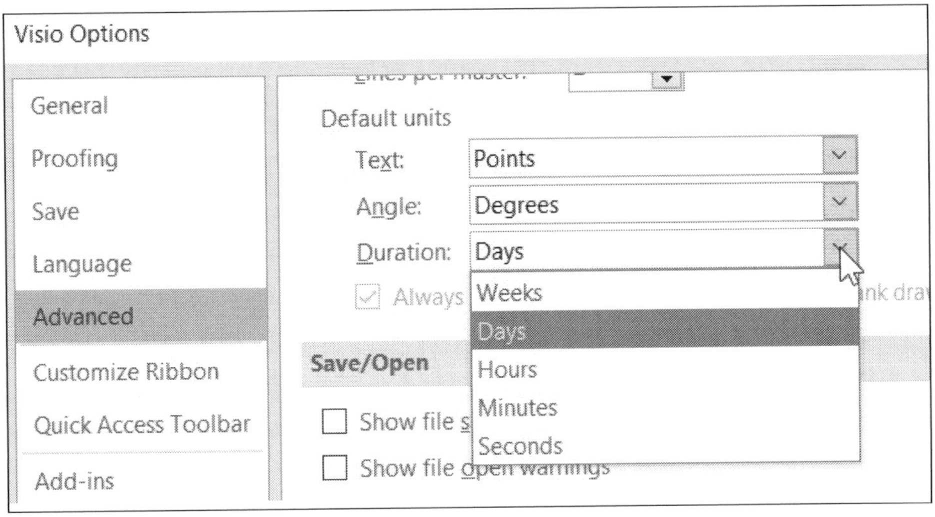


## Entering monetary values with the Currency type

It uses the system's regional settings and can be defined with the `visPropTypeCurrency (7)` constant. A display format picture can be set in the **Format** cell.

## Listing Shape Data rows in code

There are many times when it is necessary to retrieve the values of Shape Data rows in code. The following VBA sub-function, `ListShapeDataRows()`, loops through all of the rows in the **Shape Data** section of each shape in the active selection and prints out selected values:

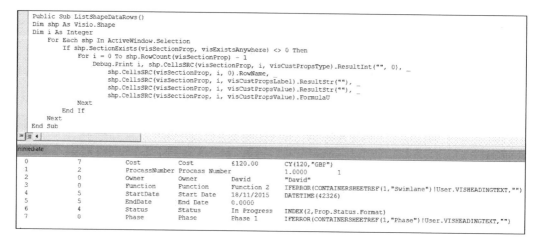

```
Public Sub ListShapeDataRows()
Dim shp As Visio.Shape
Dim i As Integer
    For Each shp In ActiveWindow.Selection
        If shp.SectionExists(visSectionProp, visExistsAnywhere) <> 0 Then
            For i = 0 To shp.RowCount(visSectionProp) - 1
                Debug.Print i, shp.CellsSRC(visSectionProp, i, visCustPropsType).ResultInt("", 0), _
                    shp.CellsSRC(visSectionProp, i, 0).RowName, _
                    shp.CellsSRC(visSectionProp, i, visCustPropsLabel).ResultStr(""), _
                    shp.CellsSRC(visSectionProp, i, visCustPropsValue).ResultStr(""), _
                    shp.CellsSRC(visSectionProp, i, visCustPropsValue).FormulaU
            Next
        End If
    Next
End Sub
```

Immediate

```
0    7    Cost           Cost            £120.00       CY(120,"GBP")
1    2    ProcessNumber  Process Number                1.0000        1
2    0    Owner          Owner           David         "David"
3    0    Function       Function        Function 2    IFERROR(CONTAINERSHEETREF(1,"Swimlane")!User.VISHEADINGTEXT,"")
4    5    StartDate      Start Date      18/11/2015    DATETIME(42326)
5    5    EndDate        End Date        0.0000
6    4    Status         Status          In Progress   INDEX(2,Prop.Status.Format)
7    0    Phase          Phase           Phase 1       IFERROR(CONTAINERSHEETREF(1,"Phase")!User.VISHEADINGTEXT,"")
```

The sample code refers to each row by the section, row, and cell values using the `Shape.CellsSRC(...)` property. However, they could be addressed directly using the `RowName` prefixed by `Prop.` with the `Shape.Cells(...)` property.

## Auto-generating hyperlinks from data

Hyperlinks are optional, and each row can be renamed for clarity. They are included as data because they can be automatically created using the **Data** | **External Data** | **Custom Import** feature. They appear on the right-click menu, above the **Edit Hyperlinks...** option.

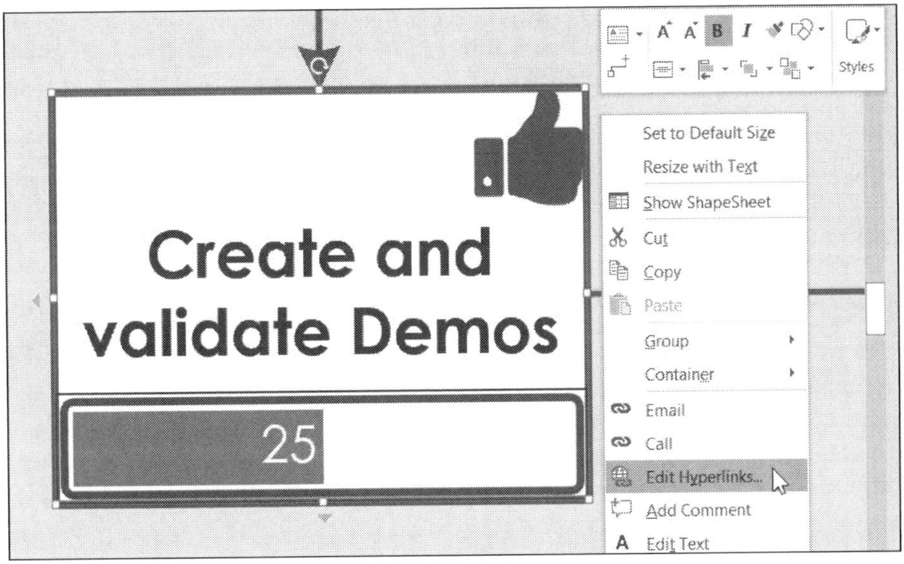


The **Hyperlinks** dialog can also be used to create or edit hyperlinks, as shown in the following screenshot. A shape can have zero, one, or multiple hyperlinks. They are all available for use in Visio, Visio Viewer, and Visio Web Access control in SharePoint web pages, but only the first visible one is available in the PDF export.

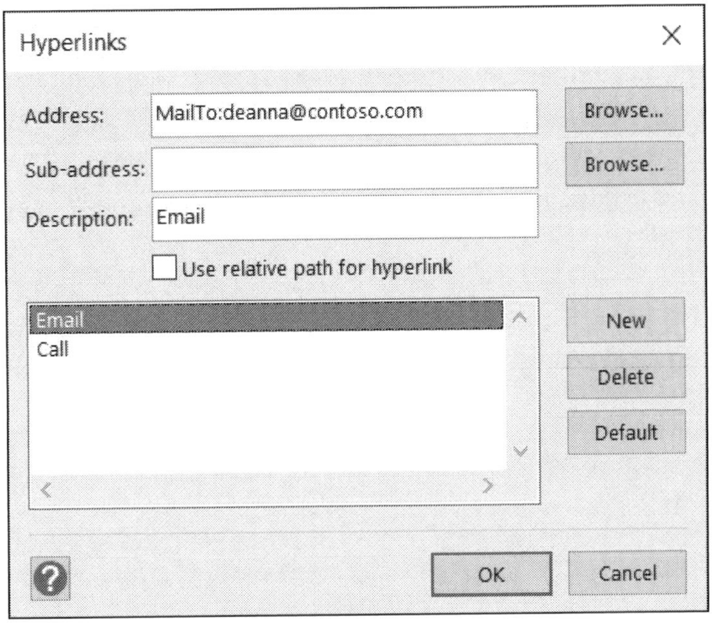

However, the ShapeSheet reveals some extra cells that you cannot get to with the dialog. The following screenshot shows the formula in the `Hyperlink._VisDM_Call.Address` cell, which has been created automatically by the **Link Data** feature:

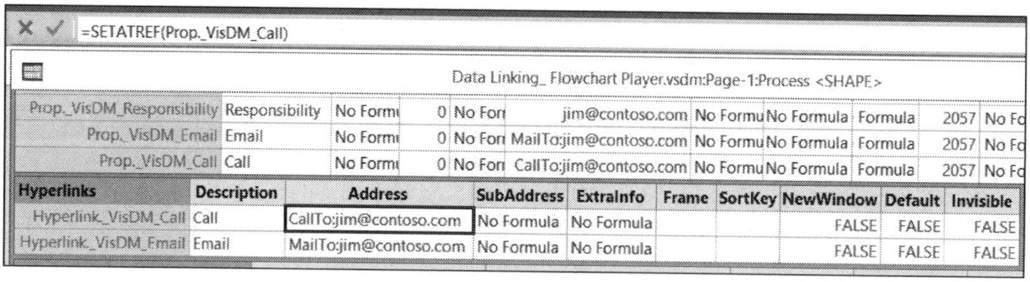
=SETATREF(Prop._VisDM_Call)
Data Linking_ Flowchart Player.vsdm:Page-1:Process <SHAPE>
Prop._VisDM_Responsibility Responsibility No Form 0 No For jim@contoso.com No Formu No Formula Formula 2057 No Fo
Prop._VisDM_Email Email No Form 0 No For MailTo:jim@contoso.com No Formu No Formula Formula 2057 No Fo
Prop._VisDM_Call Call No Form 0 No For CallTo:jim@contoso.com No Formu No Formula Formula 2057 No Fo
Hyperlinks Description Address SubAddress ExtraInfo Frame SortKey NewWindow Default Invisible
Hyperlink._VisDM_Call Call CallTo:jim@contoso.com No Formula No Formula FALSE FALSE FALSE
Hyperlink._VisDM_Email Email MailTo:jim@contoso.com No Formula No Formula FALSE FALSE FALSE

The `SETATREF(Prop.VisDM_Call)` function will redirect any updates to values entered in the **Hyperlinks** dialog's **Address** textbox to the `Prop._VisDM_Call.Value` cell.

> Each section has a default cell (if no cell is defined). So, `Prop._VisDM_Cell` is the same as `Prop._VisDM_Cell.Value`.

There are many different protocols that can be used with the hyperlinks in Visio, such as `file`, `http(s)`, `mailto`, `call`, and so on. They can be used to open relevant documents, either on the web or network, or to communicate with relevant individuals by e-mail, instant messenger, phone, or even to open up a mapping application at a specified location. There will be more examples of these in the next chapter.

Hyperlinks can also be used to go to a different page in the same Visio document and even to a particular shape.

The following VBA code loops through each shape in the active selection and prints out each hyperlink's details using two alternative methods. The first loops through the ShapeSheet **Hyperlink** section, and the second loops through the **Hyperlinks** collection:

```
Public Sub ListHyperlinkRows()
Dim shp As Visio.Shape
Dim i As Integer
Dim hyp As Hyperlink
Dim iSect As Integer
    iSect = visSectionHyperlink
    For Each shp In ActiveWindow.Selection
        If shp.SectionExists(visSectionHyperlink, visExistsAnywhere) <> 0 Then
            Debug.Print shp.ID, shp.Name, shp.Text
            Debug.Print
            For i = 0 To shp.RowCount(visSectionHyperlink) - 1
                Debug.Print i, shp.CellsSRC(visSectionHyperlink, i, 0).RowName, _
                    shp.CellsSRC(iSect, i, visHLinkDescription).ResultStr(""), _
                    shp.CellsSRC(iSect, i, visHLinkAddress).ResultStr(""), _
                    shp.CellsSRC(iSect, i, visHLinkSubAddress).ResultStr(""), _
                    shp.CellsSRC(iSect, i, visHLinkExtraInfo).ResultStr("")
            Next
        End If
        Debug.Print
        For Each hyp In shp.Hyperlinks
            Debug.Print hyp.Row, hyp.Name, hyp.Description, _
                hyp.Address, hyp.SubAddress, hyp.ExtraInfo
        Next
    Next

End Sub
```

mmediate

```
 27          Process       Provide internal download package

 0           _VisDM_Call   Call          CallTo:jim@contoso.com
 1           _VisDM_Email  Email         MailTo:jim@contoso.com

 0           _VisDM_Call   Call          CallTo:jim@contoso.com
 1           _VisDM_Email  Email         MailTo:jim@contoso.com
```

# Using the Off-page reference shape to jump around a document

The **Flowchart | Basic Flowchart Shapes** stencil contains a master called **Off-page reference** (OPC). This shape contains a formula that starts an add-on to create a twin shape elsewhere in the document, as shown in the following screenshot:

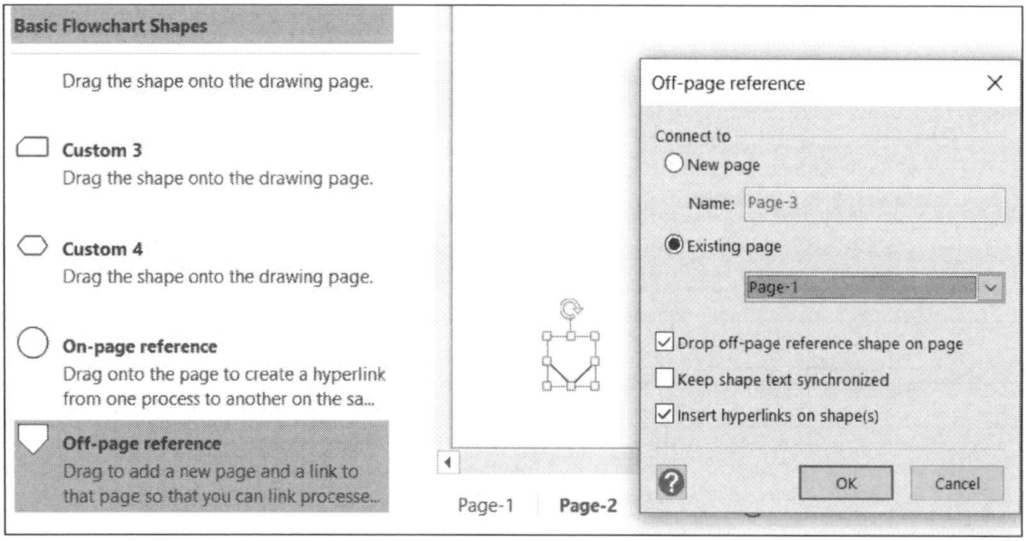


This shape can have both a hyperlink and a double-click event that jumps to the twin shape.

Each of the twin shapes contains some specific User-defined Cells that contain the unique identifiers of the other shape.

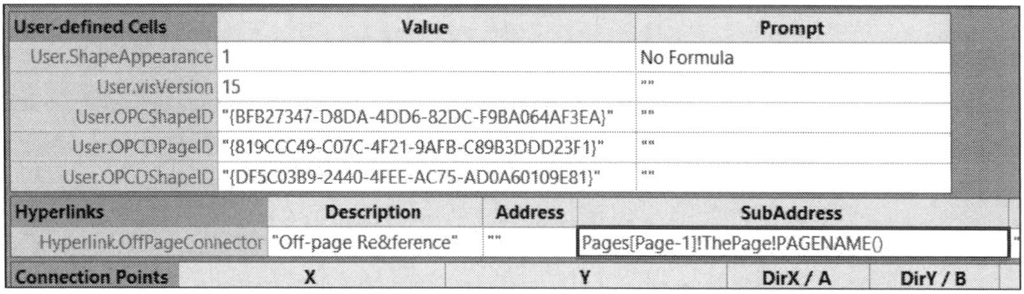
User-defined Cells
Value
Prompt
User.ShapeAppearance
1
No Formula
User.visVersion
15
""
User.OPCShapeID
"{BFB27347-D8DA-4DD6-82DC-F9BA064AF3EA}"
""
User.OPCDPageID
"{819CCC49-C07C-4F21-9AFB-C89B3DDD23F1}"
""
User.OPCDShapeID
"{DF5C03B9-2440-4FEE-AC75-AD0A60109E81}"
""
Hyperlinks
Description
Address
SubAddress
Hyperlink.OffPageConnector
"Off-page Re&ference"
""
Pages[Page-1]!ThePage!PAGENAME()
Connection Points
X
Y
DirX / A
DirY / B

The double-click event is possible because the `EventDblClick` cell has the formula `=RUNADDONWARGS("OPC","/CMD=2")`.

If the user decides to synchronize the text of each shape, then the `=RUNADDONWARGS("OPC","/CMD=3")` formula is entered into the `TheText` cell.

The add-on is initially fired whenever the shape is dropped onto the page because the `OnDrop` cell has the `=RUNADDONWARGS("OPC","/CMD=1")` formula. This will open the **Off-page reference** dialog and then add the correct values into the User-defined Cells as required.

The OPC add-on has been around for a very long time and can often be used in custom solutions.

> For more information, take a look at `http://blog.bvisual.net/2013/12/23/making-the-off-page-reference-hyperlink-url-safe`.

# User-defined Cells

This section is also optional and contains just two columns: **Value** and **Prompt**. Although formulas can be entered into either column, it is expected that **Prompt** will just be text that explains the purpose of the formula in the **Value** cell. Unfortunately, most developers do not bother to do this, which can make it more difficult to maintain code. Each row can also be renamed so that it can be referenced by formulas in other cells.

The following screenshot is from the **User-defined Cells** section of the Microsoft-supplied **Basic Flowchart Shapes | Process** shape, and it shows that some rows are used just to store data, while others are used to calculate values:

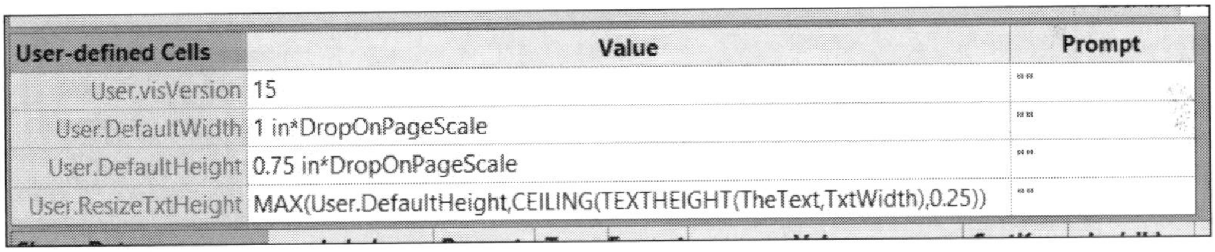

| User-defined Cells | Value | Prompt |
|---|---|---|
| User.visVersion | 15 | "" |
| User.DefaultWidth | 1 in*DropOnPageScale | "" |
| User.DefaultHeight | 0.75 in*DropOnPageScale | "" |
| User.ResizeTxtHeight | MAX(User.DefaultHeight,CEILING(TEXTHEIGHT(TheText,TxtWidth),0.25)) | "" |

The formulas in this section can be used to trigger value changes in other cells in the ShapeSheet.

Microsoft will use reserved row names in this section so that particular types of shapes can be recognized by the application. Unfortunately, there is no definitive list of these reserved names, and Microsoft can add to them at any time. Therefore, shape developers should try to ensure uniqueness and clarity as much as possible. The screenshot also shows one row named `User.visVersion`, which has been used for many years to denote the internal version number that the shape was produced for. There are quite a few row names that start with `vis` or `msv` that appear throughout the various templates and add-ons supplied by Microsoft. Some of these, pertaining to structured diagrams, are mentioned later in this chapter. A very useful one is `User.msvShapeCategories`, which contains a semicolon-separated list of categories that the shape belongs to. There is a `Shape.HasCategory(...)` method and a ShapeSheet's `HASCATEGORY(...)` function to test whether a shape belongs to a specified category. This function is often used in validation rules.

[ Take a look at `https://msdn.microsoft.com/EN-US/library/office/ff768297.aspx` for the Visio ShapeSheet reference. ]

# The Visio file format

Since the 2013 edition, Visio files are **Open Packaging Convention** compliant, which means that most of the contents are accessible for programmers using some standard techniques. This means that package parts can be more easily extracted, and even modified, without recourse to the Visio type library. Before the 2013 version, Visio files were either binary or monolithic XML files (which were approximately 10 times the size of the binary files). Now that Visio files are zipped-up XML packages, there is greater scope for extensibility. For example, the Visio Web Access control in SharePoint 2010 used XAML to render the graphics on a layer over the top of the Visio binary file. The files had to be published as Visio Web Drawings (`*.vdw`) to be used, and only the linked Data Graphics content was automatically refreshable. Since the 2013 version, native Visio files are rendered in the Visio Web Access control without needing Silverlight, and any shape cell that is referenced to a linked Shape Data row is automatically refreshable. This means that Visio documents can be viewed in any modern browser, on any modern device. This currently requires a suitable SharePoint client access license, but Microsoft is now committed to democratizing web access.

For security reasons though, any file that can contains VBA macros must have a different extension. The default file extensions for Visio files are as follows:

| Extension | File type |
|---|---|
| *.vsdx | Drawing |
| *.vsdm | Macro-enabled drawing |
| *.vstx | Template |
| *.vstm | Macro-enabled template |
| *.vssx | Stencil |
| *.vssm | Macro-enabled stencil |

The following diagram shows the internal package parts of a Visio document:

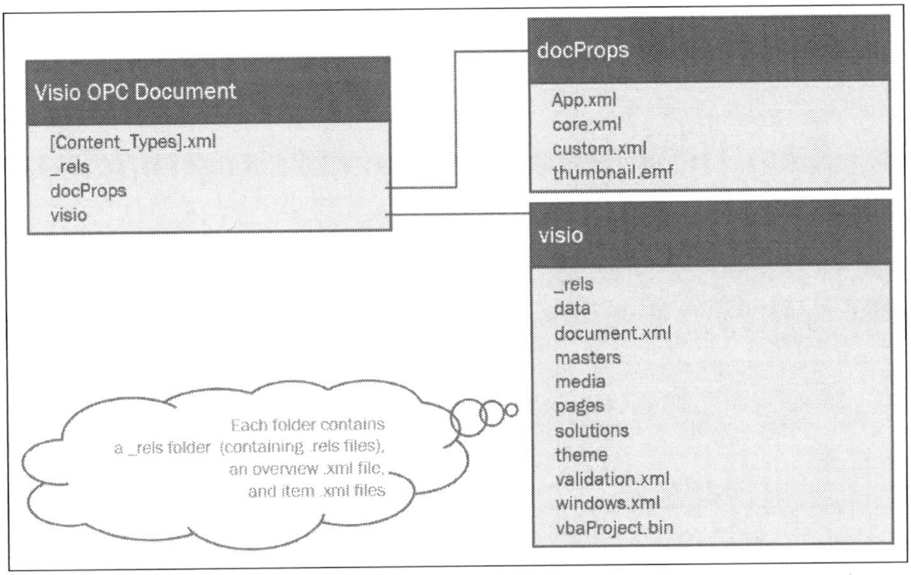


The data folder holds information about each of the `DataRecordsets` and not the data that is stored in each shape (although it might be the same).

> Take a look at `https://msdn.microsoft.com/en-us/library/system.io.packaging(v=vs.110).aspx` for more details on programming with the `System.IO.Packaging` namespace.
>
> Download the `[MS-VSDX].pdf` from `http://download.microsoft.com/download/8/5/8/858F2155-D48D-4C68-9205-29460FD7698F/[MS-VSDX].pdf` for a full specification of the Visio Graphics Service File Format.

# Storing data as hidden XML

A Visio document and certain cells can contain XML data as text enclosed within specific elements. This is called **SolutionXML**, and there are methods to test for their existence, add them, or remove them. This can be useful for storing data that does not need to be visible on the built-in interface. However, the information stored within XML is not easily accessible to ShapeSheet cell formulas. Therefore, its use is really for solution code. Indeed, several of the Microsoft supplied add-ons, such as the FM model, use SolutionXML for persisting data within a document.

This means that any solution data stored as SolutionXML can be more easily extracted without recourse to the Visio type library. As the page package part XML mixes shape graphics, structure, and data together, it can be useful for summarizing structure and relevant data in SolutionXML because it is kept in a separate package part.

# Knowing how shapes relate in structured diagrams

The **Insert | Diagram Parts** tab in the Visio interface provides the ability to add a **Container**, **Callout**, or **Connector** diagram part to a page, as shown in the following screenshot (these are the main parts of a structured diagram):

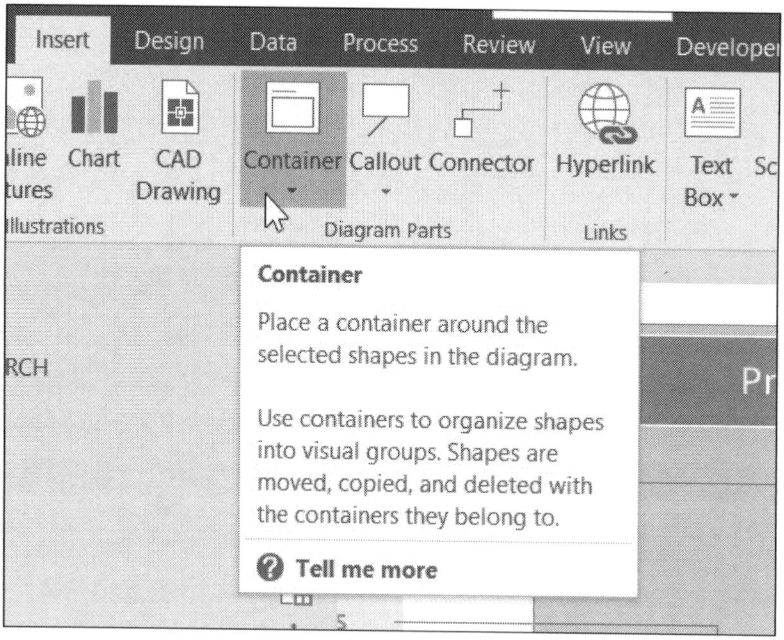

However, there are also other shapes available from various stencils that exhibit the same behavior. There is also a special type of container called **List** that can contain ordered items. There are several Microsoft-supplied shapes that are lists, including the **UML Class | Class** master shape, which is used in the following example. This List shape accepts other specific list item shapes.

This following screenshot contains all of the elements of a structured diagram, namely connections, containers, lists, and callouts:

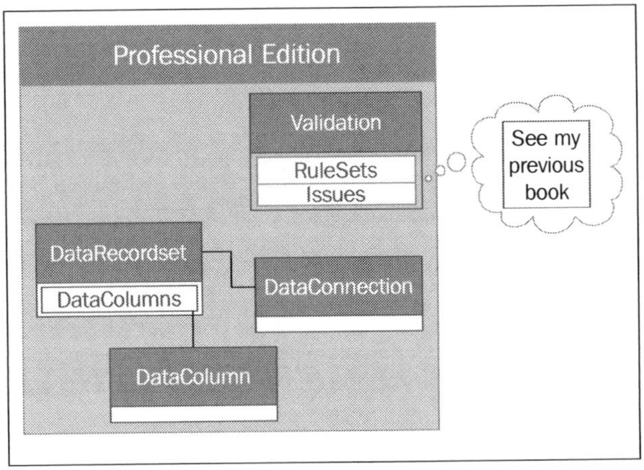


Everything but the two incoming connections at the top left of the screenshot are selected in order to limit the number of items under consideration in the following paragraphs.

Notice that the container shape has a thicker selection box because it is the first item selected, and it can be referenced as `Selection.PrimaryItem` in code.

> Take a look at `https://msdn.microsoft.com/en-us/library/office/ff959245(v=office.14).aspx#AddingDiagrams_UsingStructuredDiagrams` for more information.

# Connections

One of the most commonly used aspects of Visio diagrams is the ability of one shape being able to connect to another shape via a connector. The connector shape is a **one-dimensional** (**1D**) type (`Shape.OneD = 1`), and the glued shapes at either end are usually **two-dimensional** (**2D**) shapes (`Shape.OneD = 0`), as shown in the previous screenshot.

Attempting to retrieve the glued shapes from one of the connector shapes using the ShapeSheet can be a difficult task. The following screenshot shows that there are indeed references to the glued shapes at either end in the **BeginX**, **BeginY**, **EndX**, and **EndY** formulas:

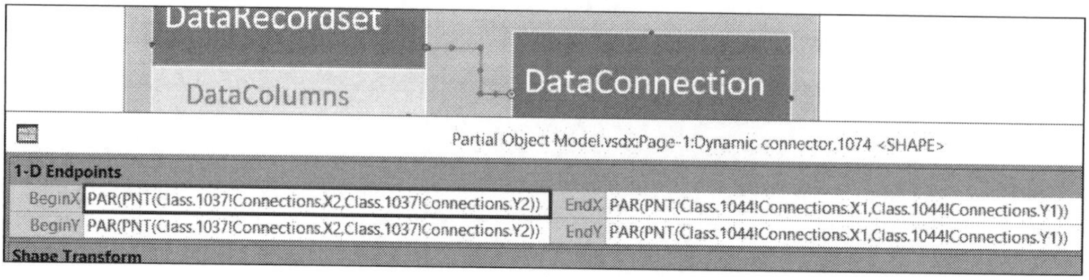


However, it is impossible to use these references in another ShapeSheet cell formula. In code, it would be possible to walk through the array returned by the `Cell.Precedents` property, and there are collections returned by the `Shape.Connects` and `Shape.FromConnects` properties. However, there is now an easier `Shape.GluedShapes(...)` method that can provide a filtered array of 1D and/or 2D glued shapes. The following screenshot shows a simple VBA `ListGluedConnections` sub-function, which produces an output from one 2D shape, through a 1D shape, to another 2D shape:

```
Public Sub ListGluedConnections()
Dim shp As Visio.Shape
Dim connectorShape As Visio.Shape
Dim sourceShape As Visio.Shape
Dim targetShape As Visio.Shape
Dim aryTargetIDs() As Long
Dim arySourceIDs() As Long
Dim targetID As Long
Dim sourceID As Long
Dim i As Integer

For Each shp In ActiveWindow.Selection
    arySourceIDs = shp.GluedShapes(visGluedShapesIncoming2D, "")
    For i = 0 To UBound(arySourceIDs)
        Set sourceShape = ActivePage.Shapes.ItemFromID(arySourceIDs(i))
        Debug.Print sourceShape.ID, sourceShape.Name, _
            sourceShape.Characters.Text
        Debug.Print , ">", shp.ID, shp.Name, shp.Characters.Text
    Next
    aryTargetIDs = shp.GluedShapes(visGluedShapesOutgoing2D, "")
    For i = 0 To UBound(aryTargetIDs)
        Set targetShape = ActivePage.Shapes.ItemFromID(aryTargetIDs(i))
        Debug.Print , , ">", targetShape.ID, targetShape.Name, _
            targetShape.Characters.Text
    Next
Next

End Sub
```

mmediate

```
1037          Class.1037    DataRecordset
              >              1074          Dynamic connector.1074
                            >              1044          Class.1044    DataConnection
1042          Member.1042   DataColumns
              >              1069          Dynamic connector.1069
                            >              1049          Class.1049    DataColumn
```

Not all diagram types need to consider the connector shape, but they do need to understand the hops from one 2D shape to another. Fortunately, there is a `Shape.ConnectedShapes(...)` method, as demonstrated in the following screenshot of a simple `ListConnections()` sub-function:

```
Public Sub ListConnections()
Dim shp As Visio.Shape
Dim targetShape As Visio.Shape
Dim aryTargetIDs() As Long
Dim targetID As Long
Dim i As Integer

For Each shp In ActiveWindow.Selection
    If Not shp.OneD Then
        aryTargetIDs = shp.ConnectedShapes(visConnectedShapesOutgoingNodes, "")
        For i = 0 To UBound(aryTargetIDs)
            Set targetShape = ActivePage.Shapes.ItemFromID(aryTargetIDs(i))
            Debug.Print shp.ID, shp.Name, shp.Characters.Text, ">>", _
                targetShape.ID, targetShape.Name, _
                    targetShape.Characters.Text
        Next
    End If
Next

End Sub
```

Immediate

```
1037          Class.1037    DataRecordset >>          1044          Class.1044    DataConnection
1042          Member.1042   DataColumns   >>          1049          Class.1049    DataColumn
```

In this case, the output can be simpler, as there are no connector shape details emitted.

> Take a look at `http://blog.bvisual.net/2013/05/21/getting-the-name-of-glued-connection-points` for information on getting the names of connection points.

## 1D to 1D connections

There are occasions when a 1D shape can connect to another 1D shape, but it needs to automatically generate a connection point on the target shape to do this.

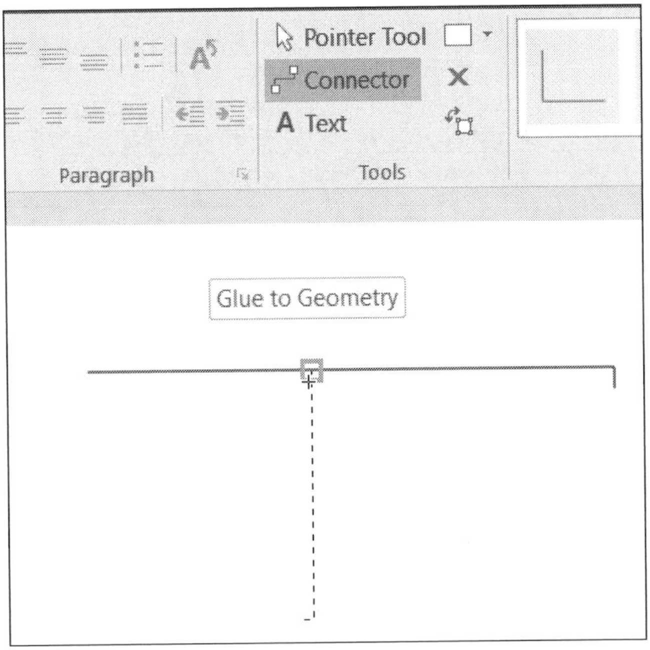


Once the lower connector shape is glued to the upper connector, then a glance at the **EndX** and **EndY** formulas (or **BeginX** and **BeginY** if it was connected at the other end) reveals the target shape. However, it shows that it is glued to a connections row, as shown in the following screenshot. This is possible because Visio automatically added a new connections row for this purpose, and it will remove it if the lower one is moved away:

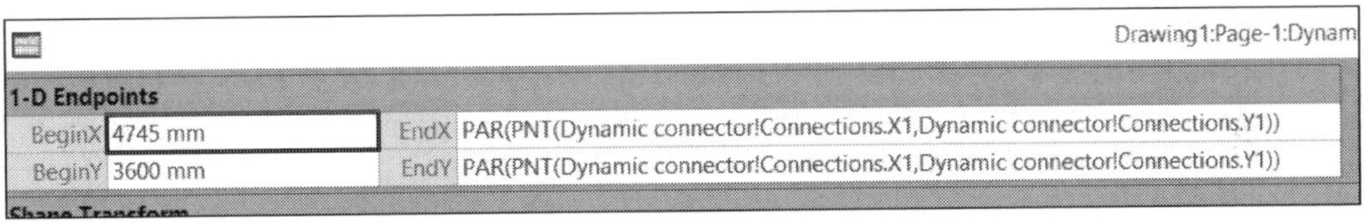


Using the glued-to-shape reference is impossible in another ShapeSheet cell formula, but in code, there is the `Shape.GluedShapes(...)` method.

## 2D to 2D connections

Also, the type of a connection point can be changed so that two non-1D shapes can be glued together, as shown in the following screenshot of a **Work peninsula** shape connecting to a **Corner surface** shape from the **Cubicles** stencil, which is in the **Maps and Floor Plans | Office Layout** template:

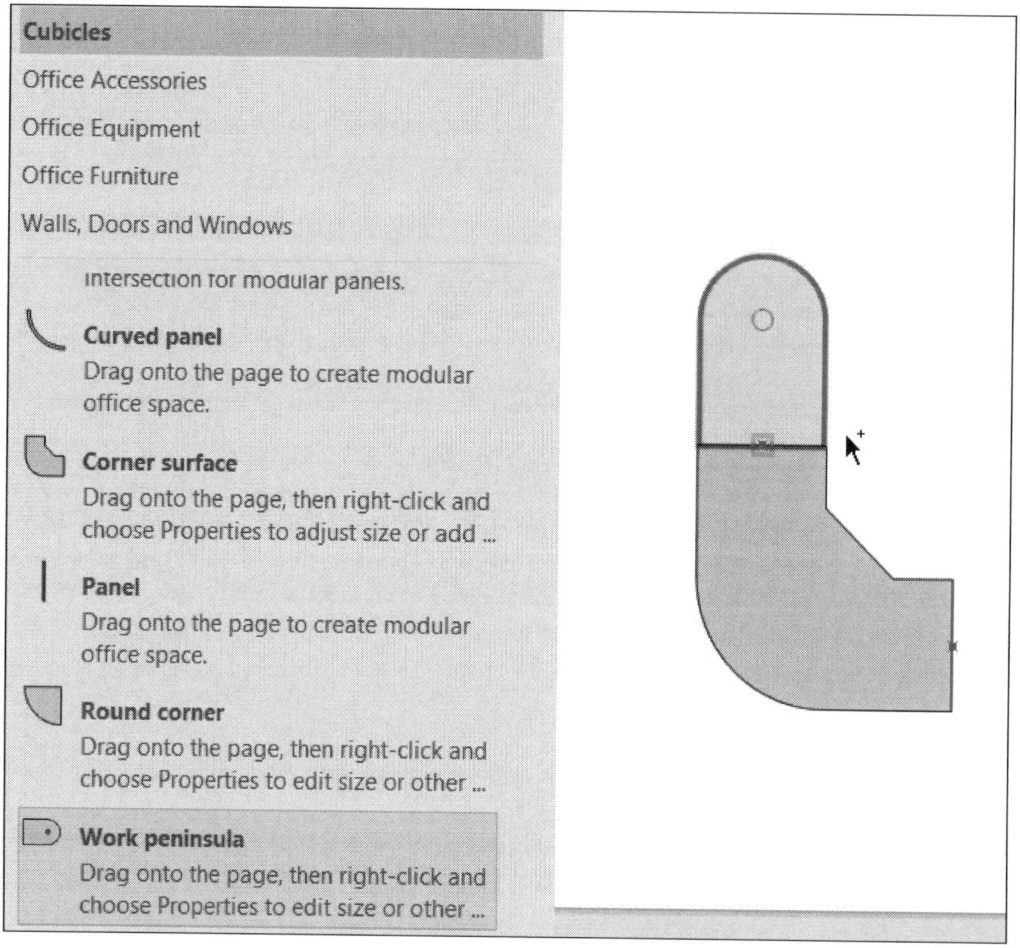


This type of connection can also dictate the angle at which one shape glues to the other. The following screenshot of the ShapeSheet of the **Work peninsula** shape shows that it has a **Connection Point** of `Type = 1` (`visCnnctTypeOutward`). The other shape has a connection point of `Type = 2` (`visCnnctTypeInwardOutward`), which enables one to glue to the other. The default is `Type = 0` (`visCnnctTypeInward`):

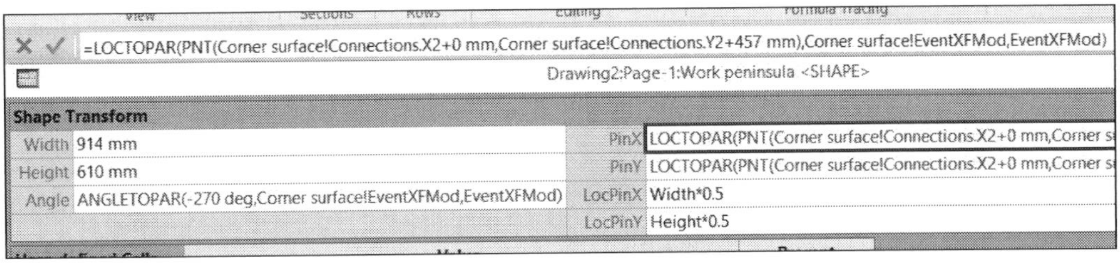


The **PinX** and **PinY** formulas do include references to the shape that they are glued to, but it is difficult to extract the other shape in another ShapeSheet formula. However, it is not so difficult in code because there is the `Shape.GluedShapes(...)` method.

## Why the Dynamic connector shape is special

The **Dynamic connector** shape is the default master that is used in Visio whenever a user uses the **Connector** tool without having a selected 1D master shape in the active stencil. This means that Visio will always create this master in the **Document Stencil** shape if it does not exist already. This fact is used by some of the Microsoft-supplied templates (as well as some third-party templates) because a custom version of Dynamic connector might already be present in the document. As usual, the **Match master by name** property should be ticked.

# Containers

The Visio interface also provides a context-sensitive **Format** ribbon tab when a **Container** shape is selected. This provides the user with the ability to change parameters such as **Margins**, **Container Style**, and **Heading Style**. It also enables the user to change the resize behavior, or lock the container, and so on. These actions can also be performed in code.

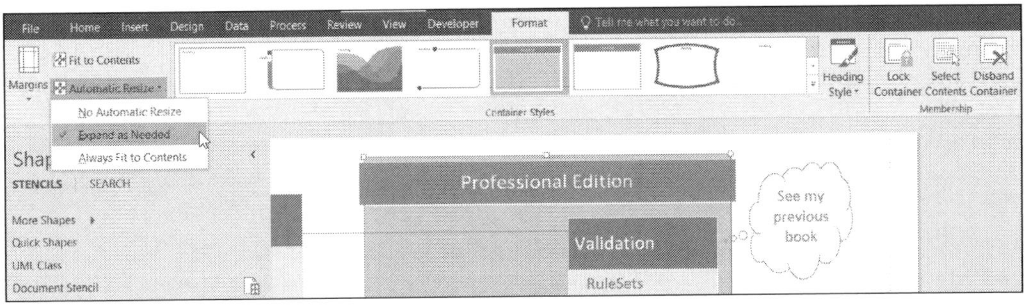

The following VBA code, `ListContainers()`, gets a list of all containers in the active selection that are not nested within another container. It then prints out each member within it that is not a member of a list and not a connector (a 1D shape):

```
Public Sub ListContainers()
Dim containerShape As Visio.Shape
Dim aryContainerIDs() As Long
Dim containerID As Long
Dim i As Integer
Dim memberID As Variant
Dim memberShape As Visio.Shape
Dim aryMemberIds() As Long

    aryContainerIDs = ActiveWindow.Selection.GetContainers(visContainerExcludeNested)
    For i = 0 To UBound(aryContainerIDs)
        Set containerShape = ActivePage.Shapes.ItemFromID(aryContainerIDs(i))
        Debug.Print containerShape.ID, containerShape.Name, containerShape.Text
        For Each memberID In containerShape.ContainerProperties.GetMemberShapes( _
                visContainerFlagsExcludeListMembers + visContainerFlagsExcludeConnectors)
            Set memberShape = ActivePage.Shapes.ItemFromID(memberID)
            Debug.Print , memberShape.ID, memberShape.Name, memberShape.Text
        Next
    Next

End Sub
```

Immediate

```
1079          Belt.1079     Professional Edition
               1018         Class.1018    Validation
               1037         Class.1037    DataRecordset
               1044         Class.1044    DataConnection
               1049         Class.1049    DataColumn
```

A shape is recognized in code as a normal container because it contains a specific User-defined Cell row named `msvStructureType`, which has a value of `Container`. There are a number of other User-defined Cells that control the graphical layout, but some specify what shapes are allowed or disallowed from being members.

The `User.msvSDContainerRequiredCategories` cell can contain an optional semicolon separated list of categories that any shape must have to become a member of the container.

The `User.msvSDContainerExcludedCategories` cell can contain an optional semicolon-separated list of categories that will prevent any shape that has one of these categories from becoming a member of the container. The Microsoft-supplied default value is `DoNotContain`. This means that any shape that has a `User.msvShapeCategories` value that contains `DoNotContain` will be unable to become a member.

# Lists

A **List** is a special type of container that includes `Shape.ContainerProperties.ContainerType = visContainerTypeList` (1). There are a number of examples of lists within the stencils provided by Microsoft, including the UML Class\Class shape in the previous example diagram. The following `ListLists()` VBA sub-function gets an array of all the container shape IDs in the active selection. Then, if the shape is a list, it prints it out with all of its members:

```
Public Sub ListLists()
Dim cntnrShp As Visio.Shape
Dim aryContainerIDs() As Long
Dim containerID As Long
Dim i As Integer
Dim memberID As Variant
Dim memberShape As Visio.Shape
Dim aryMemberIds() As Long

    aryContainerIDs = ActiveWindow.Selection.GetContainers(visContainerIncludeNested)
    For i = 0 To UBound(aryContainerIDs)
        Set cntnrShp = ActivePage.Shapes.ItemFromID(aryContainerIDs(i))
        If cntnrShp.ContainerProperties.ContainerType = visContainerTypeList Then
            Debug.Print cntnrShp.ID, cntnrShp.Name, cntnrShp.Text
            Debug.Print
            aryMemberIds = cntnrShp.ContainerProperties.GetListMembers
            If Not IsEmpty(aryMemberIds) Then
                For Each memberID In aryMemberIds
                    Set memberShape = ActivePage.Shapes.ItemFromID(memberID)
                    Debug.Print _
                        cntnrShp.ContainerProperties.GetListMemberPosition(memberShape), _
                        memberShape.ID, memberShape.Name, memberShape.Text
                Next
            End If
        End If
    Next

End Sub
```

Immediate

```
1018          Class.1018    Validation

1              1023         Member.1023   RuleSets
2              1025         Member.1025   Issues
1037          Class.1037    DataRecordset

1              1042         Member.1042   DataColumns
1044          Class.1044    DataConnection

1049          Class.1049    DataColumn
```

A shape is recognized in code as a normal container because it contains a specific User-defined Cell row named `msvStructureType` with a value of `List`. There are a number of other User-defined Cells that control the graphical layout, but as with a normal container, some specify what shapes are allowed or disallowed from being members.

> Take a look at `http://blog.bvisual.net/2014/12/24/a-visio-countdown-to-xmas` for more examples of lists.

The `Member` shapes contain a User-defined Cell named **MemberName** that contains the `=SHAPETEXT(TheText)` formula. This will simply present the text of the shape, as shown in the following screenshot:

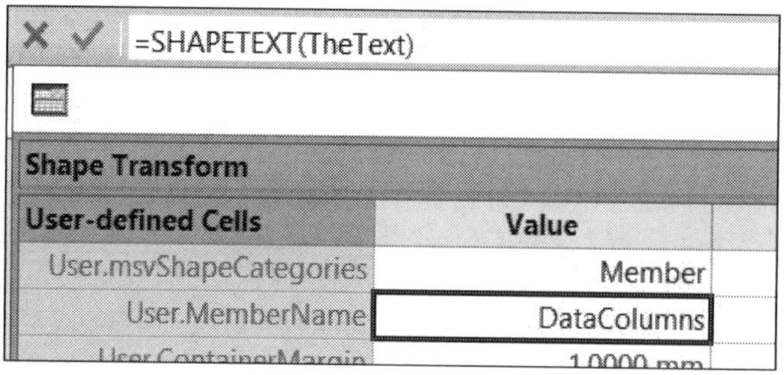


Microsoft could have easily gone further and included another User-defined Cell row (called, for example, `ParentClassName`) and used the `=IFERROR(SHAPETEXT(LISTSHEETREF()!TheText),"")` formula. This would then also present the text of the list that it belongs to. Alternatively, the `=IFERROR(SHAPETEXT(LISTSHEETREF()!User.EntityName),"")` formula would also provide the same result since the `Class` shapes contain a User-defined Cell named `EntityName`, which contains the `=SHAPETEXT(TheText)` formula.

On a similar theme, each `Member` shape could contain a cell with the `=ListOrder()` formula because it could then be surfaced in the graphics or reports more easily. The `Class` shape could also have a cell with the `=ListMemberCount()` formula, and this could also be surfaced in the user interface or reports.

# Callouts

Any shape (except a `Callout` shape) can have many associated `Callout` shapes. The following `ListCallouts()` VBA sub-function retrieves an array of callout shape IDs in the active selection, and then prints out the callout and target shape details:

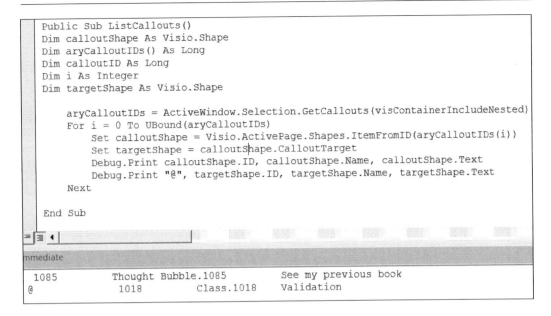

```
Public Sub ListCallouts()
Dim calloutShape As Visio.Shape
Dim aryCalloutIDs() As Long
Dim calloutID As Long
Dim i As Integer
Dim targetShape As Visio.Shape

    aryCalloutIDs = ActiveWindow.Selection.GetCallouts(visContainerIncludeNested)
    For i = 0 To UBound(aryCalloutIDs)
        Set calloutShape = Visio.ActivePage.Shapes.ItemFromID(aryCalloutIDs(i))
        Set targetShape = calloutShape.CalloutTarget
        Debug.Print calloutShape.ID, calloutShape.Name, calloutShape.Text
        Debug.Print "@", targetShape.ID, targetShape.Name, targetShape.Text
    Next

End Sub
```

mmediate

```
 1085          Thought Bubble.1085          See my previous book
@               1018          Class.1018    Validation
```

Alternatively, the `Shape.CalloutAssociated` property could have returned an array of any associated callouts for a shape.

A `Callout` shape is recognized by Visio because it has a `User.msvStructureType` row with the `Value = "Callout"`.

Again, Microsoft could have provided an extra cell in the `Callout` shapes with the `=IFERROR(SHAPETEXT(CALLOUTTARGETREF()),"")` formula. This could then be surfaced in the UI or reports more easily.

> Take a look at `http://blog.bvisual.net/2014/04/08/adding-configure-callout-functionality-to-visio-callouts/` for more information about adding extra functionality to the callout shapes.

# Summary

In this chapter, you learned about the rudiments of Visio, and how the ShapeSheet underpins a lot of its power in versatility. We also explored how to use the object model to retrieve information about the structure of the diagrams.

We have seen how much of the data is stored in the Shape Data section, and how other cells in the ShapeSheet can reference these values. To construct automatically refreshable diagrams from data, it is essential that a chain of inter-cell references ultimately end up with linked Shape Data values. So, the next chapter looks into the Link Data feature in Visio Professional.

# 3
# Linking Data to Shapes

Microsoft introduced the current data-linking feature in the Professional edition of Visio Professional 2007. This feature is better than the database add-on that has been around since Visio 4 because it is has greater importing capabilities and is part of the core product, and it has its own API. This provides the Visio user with a simple method of surfacing data from a variety of data sources, and it gives the power user or developer the ability to create productivity enhancements in code.

Once data is imported into Visio, the rows of data can be linked to shapes and then displayed visually, or they can automatically create hyperlinks. Moreover, if the data is edited outside of Visio, then the data in the Visio shapes can be refreshed so that the shapes reflect the updated data. This can be done in the Visio client, but some data sources can also refresh the data in Visio documents that are displayed in SharePoint web pages.

In this way, Visio documents truly become operational intelligence dashboards.

Some VBA knowledge will be useful, and the sample data sources are introduced in each section.

In this chapter, we shall cover the following topics:

- The new Quick Import feature
- How to import data from a variety of sources
- How to link shapes to rows of data
- Using code for more linking possibilities

# A very quick introduction to importing and linking data

Visio Professional 2016 added more buttons to the **Data** ribbon tab along with some new Data Graphics, but the functionality has basically been the same since Visio Professional 2007. The new additions, as seen in the following screenshot, can make this particular ribbon tab quite wide on the screen. Thank goodness that wide screens have become the norm!

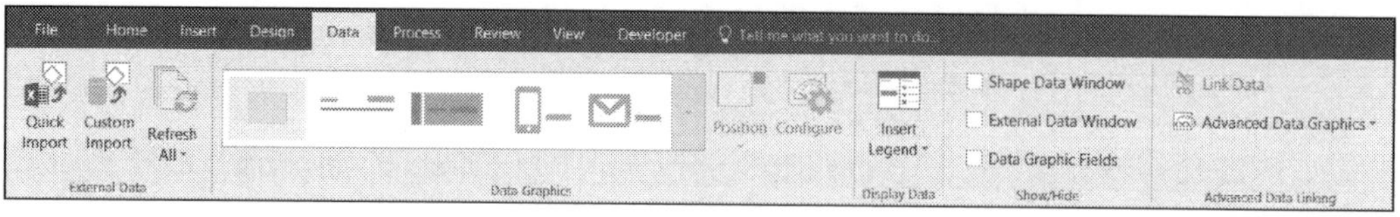


The process to create data-refreshable shapes in Visio consists of simply carrying out the following steps:

1. Import data as recordsets.
2. Link rows of data to shapes.
3. Make the shapes display the data.
4. Use any hyperlinks that have been created automatically.

The **Quick Import** tool introduced in Visio Professional 2016 attempts to merge the first three steps into one, but it rarely gets it perfectly, and it is meant only for simple Excel data sources. Therefore, it is necessary to learn how to use the **Custom Import** feature properly.

# Knowing when to use the Quick Import tool

The **Data** | **External Data** | **Quick Import** button is new in Visio 2016 Professional. It is part of the Visio API, so it cannot be called in code. This is not a great problem because it is only a wrapper for some of the actions that can be done in code anyway.

This feature can only use an Excel workbook, but fortunately, Visio installs a sample `OrgData.xls` file in the `Visio Content\<LCID>` folder. The **LCID (Location Code Identifier)** for US English is `1033`, as shown in the following screenshot:

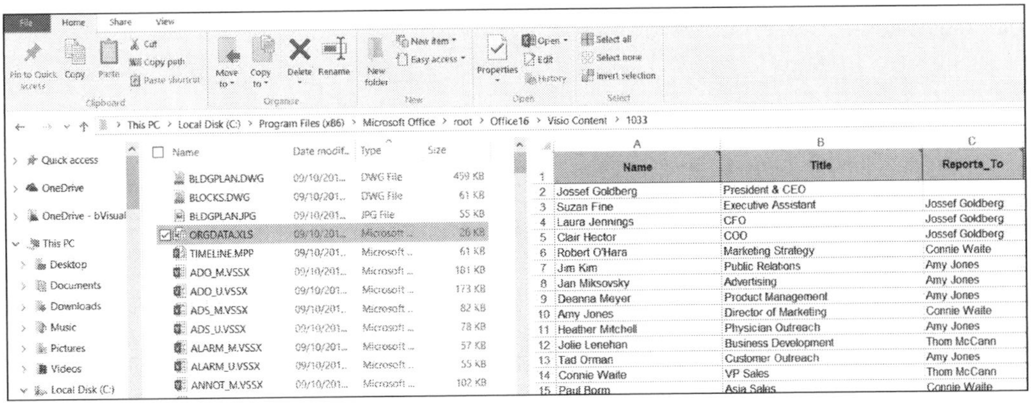


This Visio Professional 2016 32-bit installation is on a Windows 10 64-bit laptop. Therefore, the `Office16` applications are installed in the `Program Files (x86)\root` folder. It would just be `Program Files\root` if the 64-bit version of Office was installed. It is not possible to install a different bit version of Visio than the rest of the Office applications. There is no root folder in previous versions of Office, but the rest of the path is the same.

The full path on this system is `C:\Program Files (x86)\Microsoft Office\root\Office16\Visio Content\1033\ORGDATA.XLS`, but it is best to copy this file to a folder where it can be edited. It is surprising that the Excel workbook is in the old binary format, but it is a simple process to open it and save it in the new **Open Packaging Convention** file format with an `.xlsx` extension.

# Importing to shapes without existing Shape Data rows

The following example contains three **Person** shapes from the **Work Flow Objects** stencil, and each one contains the names of people, spelt exactly the same as in the key column in the Excel worksheet. It is not case sensitive, and it does not matter if there are leading or trailing spaces in the text.

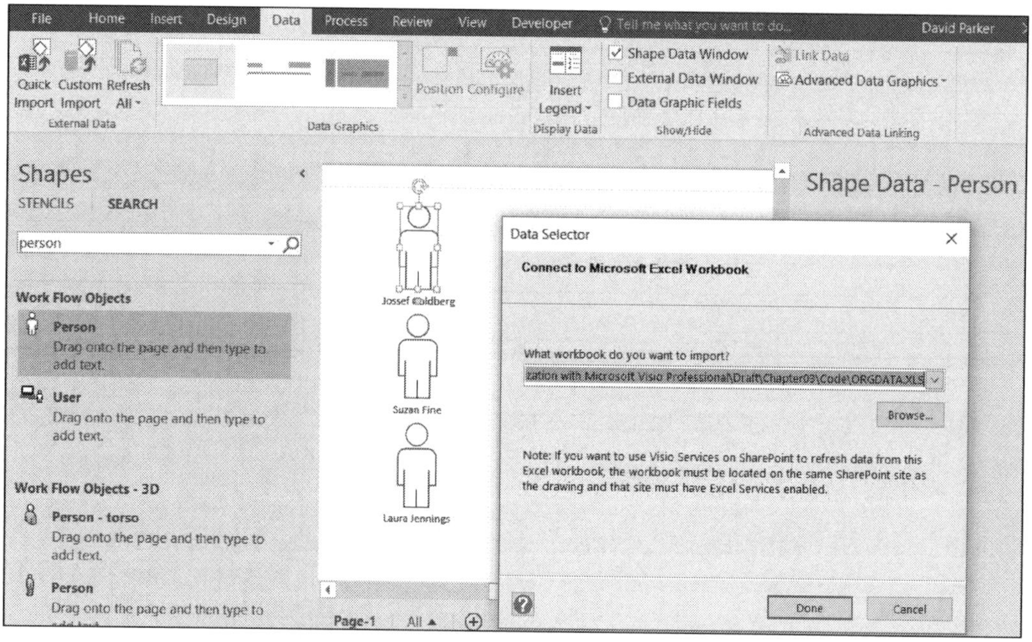


When the **Quick Import** button is pressed, a dialog opens up to show the progress of the stages that the wizard feature is going through, as shown in the following screenshot:

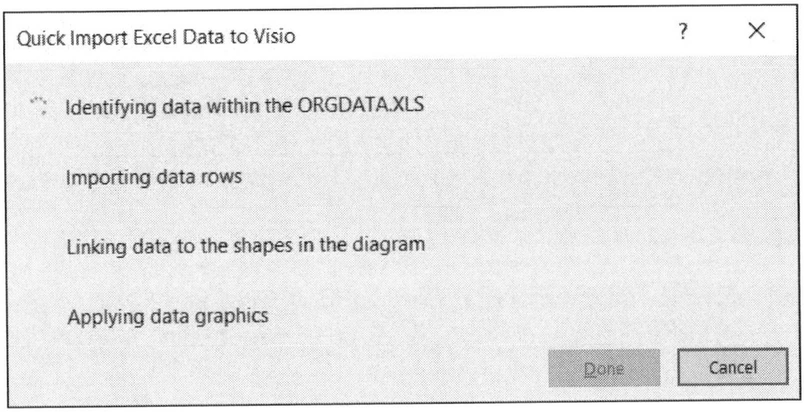


If the workbook contains more than one table of data, the user is prompted to select the range of cells within the workbook.

When the process is complete, then each of the `Person` shapes contains all of the data from the row in the **External Data** recordset where the text matches the **Name** column, as shown in the following screenshot:

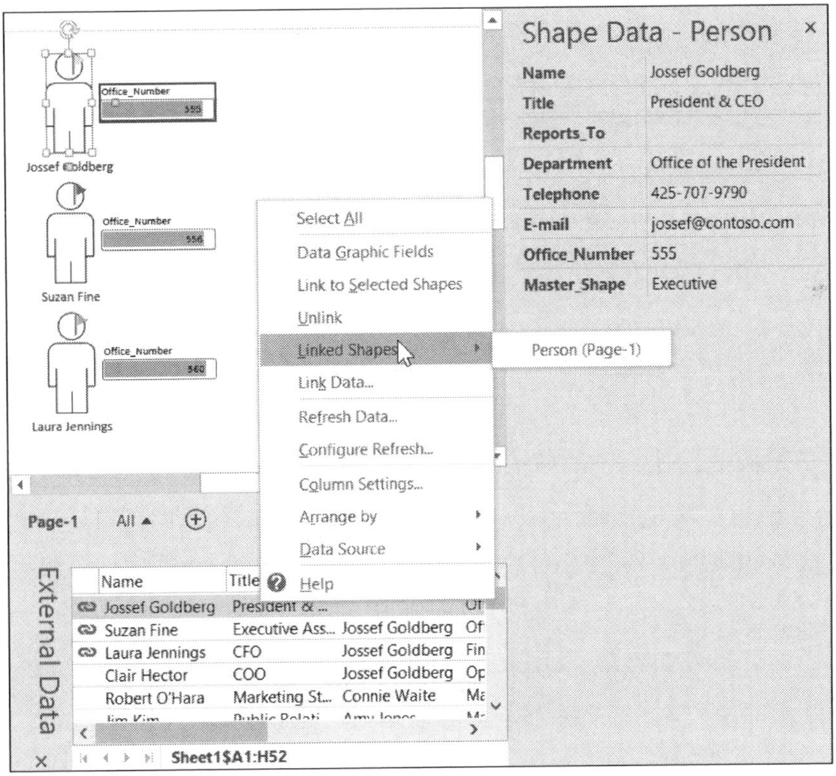

The linked rows in the **External Data** window also display a chain icon, and the right-click menu has many actions, such as selecting **Linked Shapes** for a row. Conversely, each shape now contains a right-click menu action to select the linked row in an **External Data** recordset.

The **Quick Import** feature has also added some default data graphics to each shape, which will be ignored in this chapter because it is explored in detail in *Chapter 4, Using the Built-In Data Graphics*.

Note that the recordset in the **External Data** window is named `Sheet1$A1:H52`. This is not perfect, but the user can rename it through the right-click menu actions of the tab. The **Properties** dialog, as seen in the following screenshot:

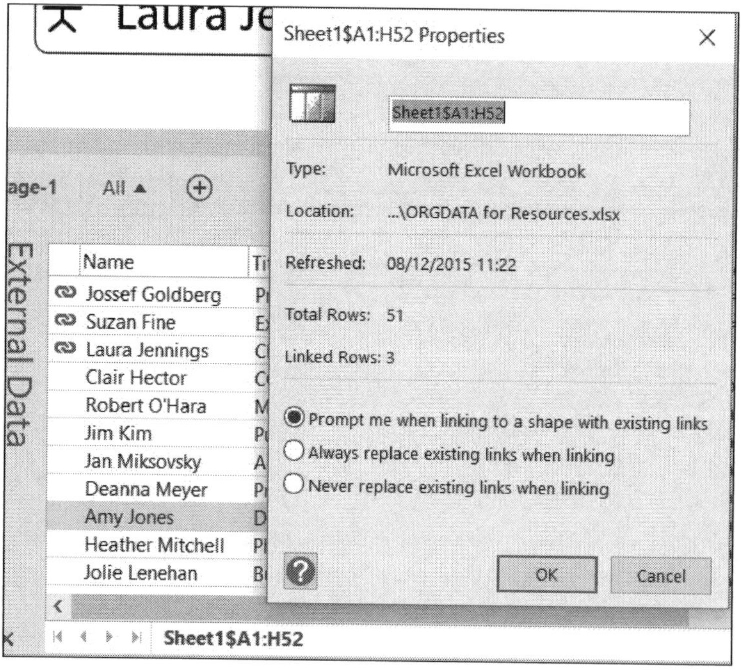


The user can also choose what to do if a data link is added to a shape that already has one.

[ A shape can be linked to a single row in multiple recordsets, and a single row can be linked to multiple shapes in a document or even on the same page. However, a shape cannot be linked to more than one row in the same recordset. ]

# Importing to shapes with existing Shape Data rows

The **Person** shape from the **Resources** stencil has been used in the following example, and as before, each shape has the name text. However, in this case, there are some existing **Shape Data** rows:

When the **Quick Import** feature is run, the data is linked to each shape where the text matches the **Name** column value:

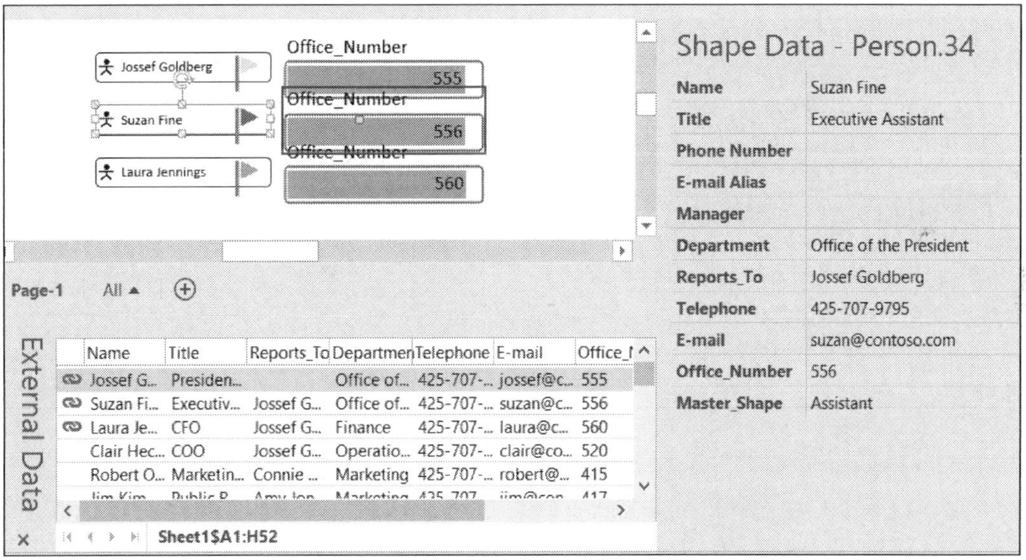


This feature has unfortunately created a problem this time because the **Phone Number**, **E-mail Alias**, and **Manager** Shape Data rows have remained empty, but the superfluous **Telephone**, **E-mail**, and **Reports_To** Shape Data rows have been added.

The solution is to edit the column headers in the worksheet to match the existing Shape Data row labels, as shown in the following screenshot:

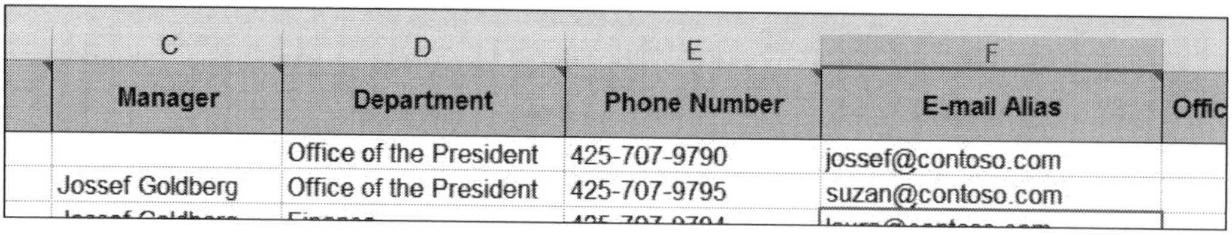

| | C | D | E | F | |
|---|---|---|---|---|---|
| | Manager | Department | Phone Number | E-mail Alias | Offic |
| | | Office of the President | 425-707-9790 | jossef@contoso.com | |
| | Jossef Goldberg | Office of the President | 425-707-9795 | suzan@contoso.com | |

Then, when the **Quick Import** feature is used again, the column headers will match the Shape Data row names, and the data will be automatically cached into the correct places, as shown in the following screenshot:

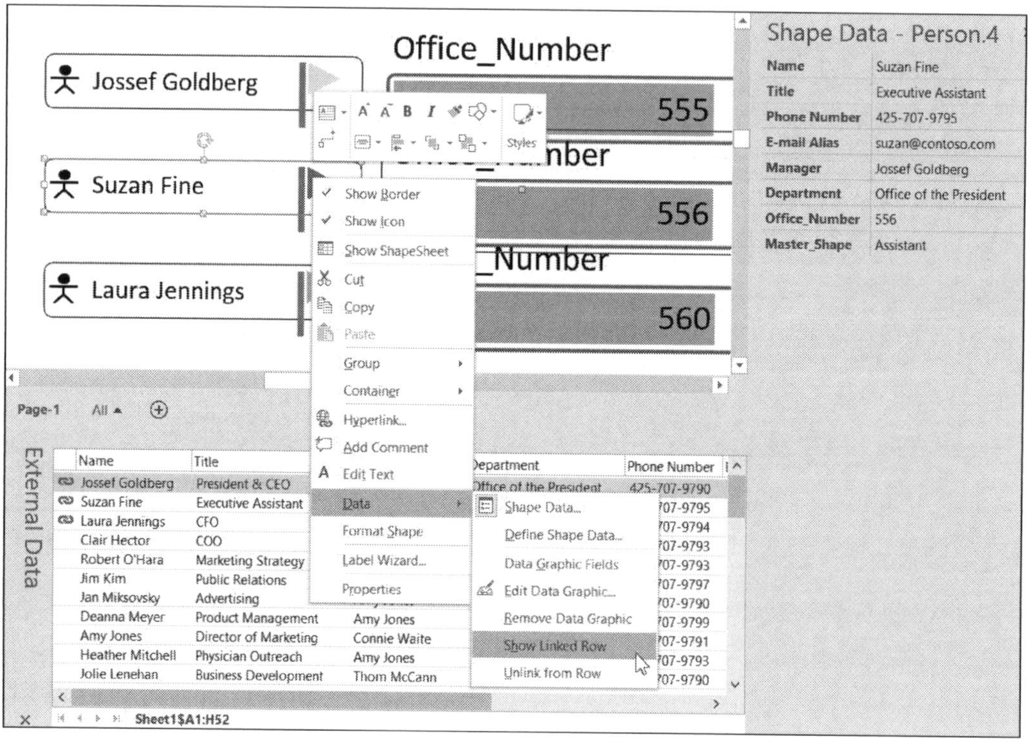


# Using the Custom Import feature

The user has more control using the **Custom Import** button on the **Data | External Data** ribbon tab. This button was called **Link Data to Shapes** in the previous versions of Visio. In either case, the action opens the **Data Selector** dialog, as shown in the following screenshot:

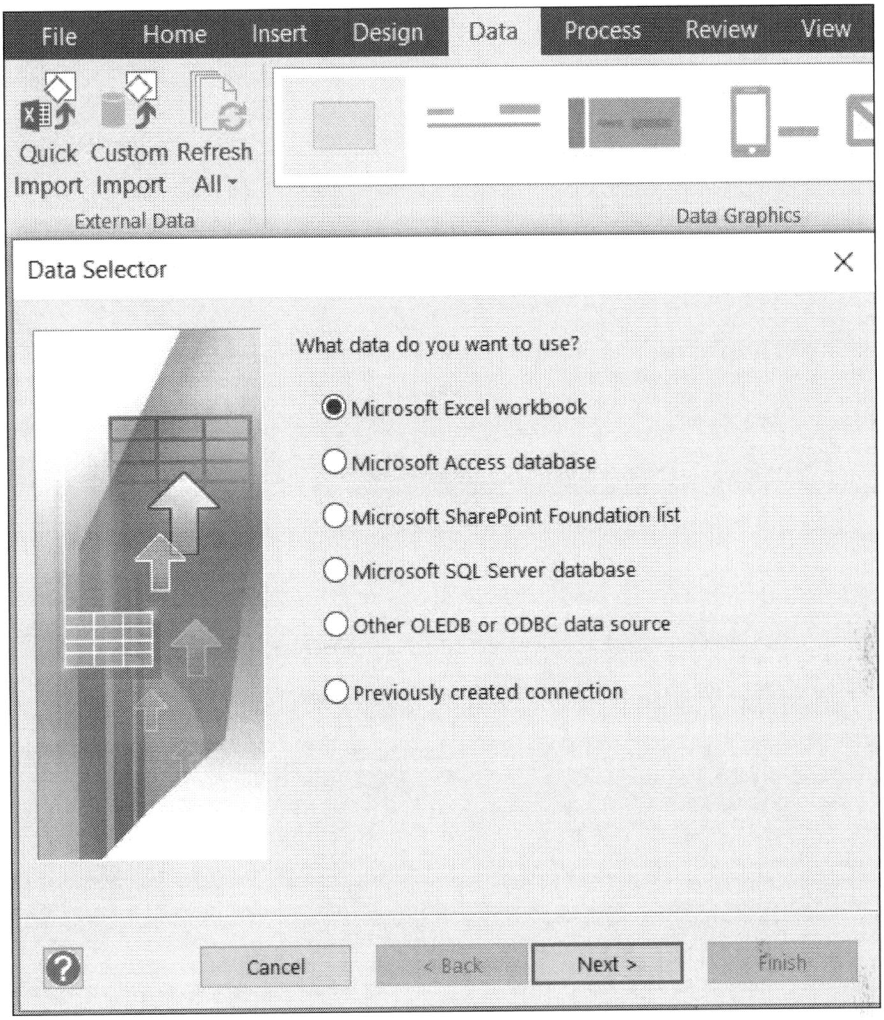


Each of these data sources will be explained in this chapter, along with the two data sources that are not available in the UI (namely XML files and SQL Server Stored Procedures).

## Importing from Excel workbooks

The `ORGDATA.xlsx` file has now been further enhanced in several ways so as to demonstrate some of the other possibilities.

The first sheet, which is the only one with any data in it, was renamed `Personnel`, and the table was formatted. The resultant table was renamed `PersonnelTbl`.

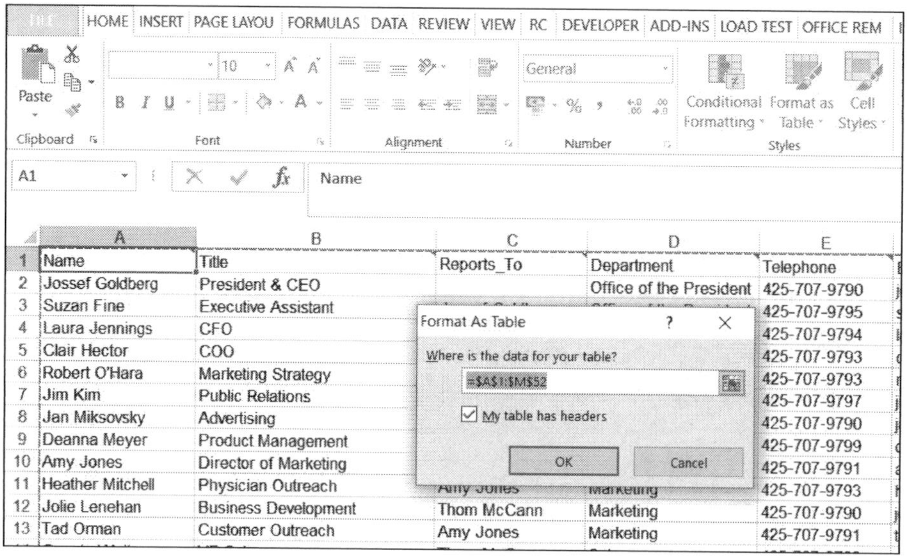


Extra columns were added to provide some hyperlinks:

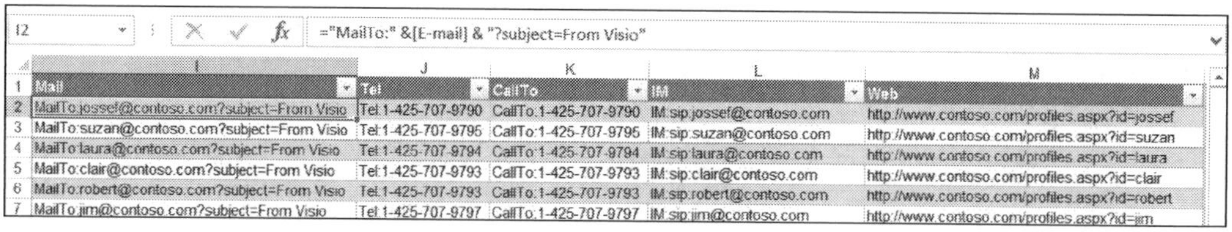


The following table lists the formulas used to create the example hyperlink columns:

| Column | Sample Value | Formula |
|---|---|---|
| **Mail** | `MailTo:jossef@contoso.com?subject=From Visio book sample` | `="MailTo:" &[E-mail] & "?subject=From Visio book sample"` |
| **Tel** | `Tel:425-707-9790` | `="Tel:"&[Telephone]` |
| **CallTo** | `CallTo:425-707-9795` | `="CallTo:"&[Telephone]` |
| **Call** | `Call:laura@contoso.com` | `="Call:"&[E-mail]` |
| **IM** | `IM:sip:clair@contoso.com` | `="IM:sip:"&[E-mail]` |
| **Web** | `http://www.contoso.com/profiles.aspx?id=robert` | `="http://www.contoso.com/profiles.aspx?id="&LEFT([E-mail], FIND("@", [E-mail])-1)` |

Each of these hyperlinks will be automatically created on each linked shape.

In the following example, the `OrgData.xlsx` file has been used with the **Organization Chart Wizard** to create a hierarchical layout. Only the **Name**, **Title**, and **Reports_To** data fields were used to do this.

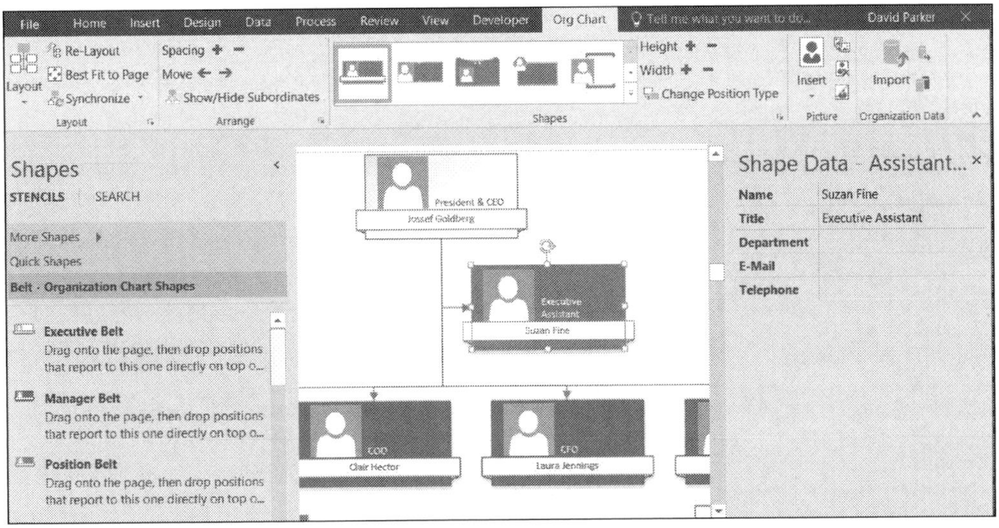


The data-linking features in Visio Professional 2016 do not currently automatically reorganize a diagram structure, but it can be used to update everything else. Therefore, the **Custom Import** button can be used to select the enhanced Excel workbook, as shown in the following screenshot:

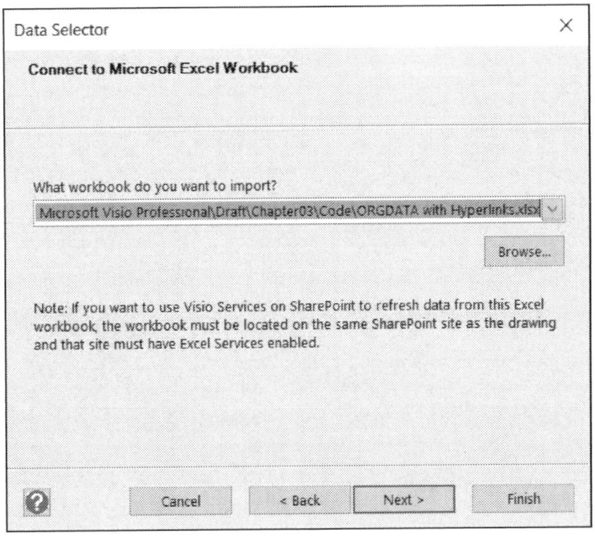

The **Data Selector** wizard then prompts for a worksheet table to be selected and ensures that the **First row of data contains column headings** checkbox is checked:

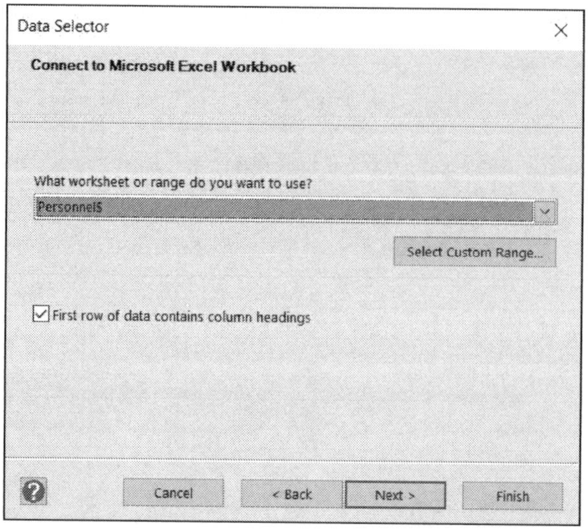


Alternatively, the user can opt to select a custom range of data from an Excel worksheet, but this is best avoided for repetitive tasks and should not be necessary in most cases.

The user then has the opportunity to make columns invisible by unchecking them in the **Select Columns** dialog, as seen in the following screenshot:

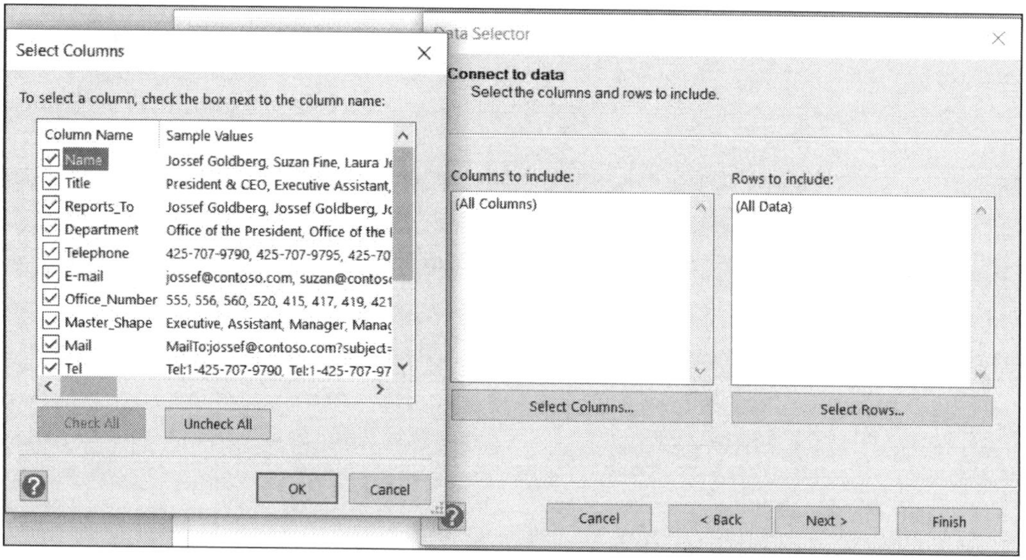

The invisible columns are not copied to Visio, and their data will not be transferred to linked shapes.

It is possible to filter the rows returned by some of the data linking sources, as shown in the following screenshot, in the menu available in the down arrow on a column header in the **Filter Rows** dialog:

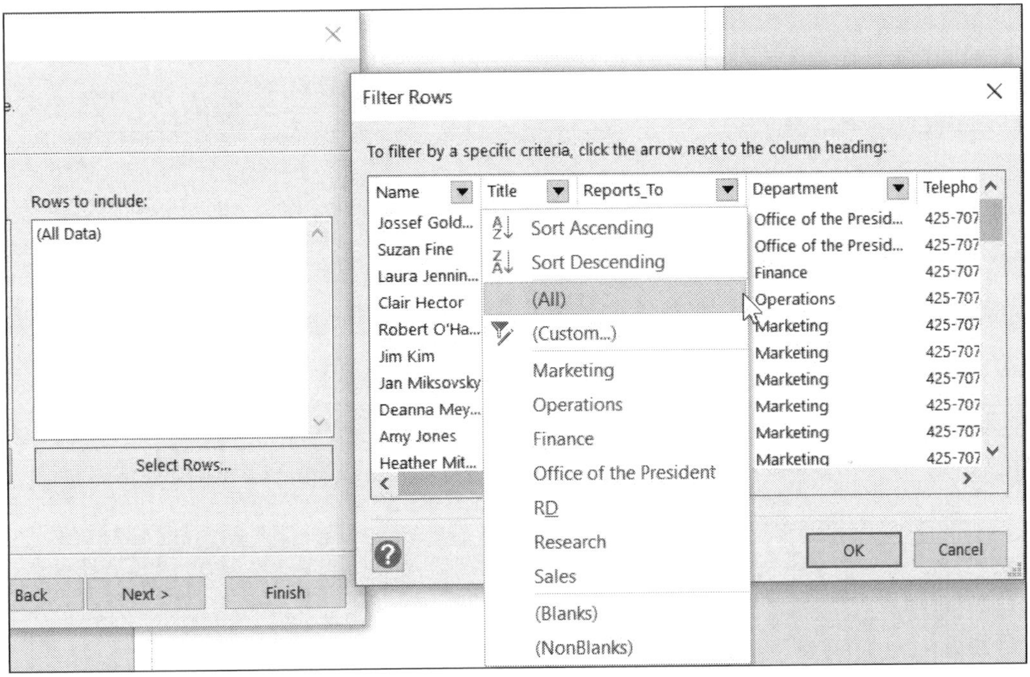

The next panel recommends the unique identifier for each row, which may be more than one column. It is important to do this if you want the data to be refreshable. The second option, at the bottom of the next screenshot, will not ensure that the right data is updated if a refresh is performed:

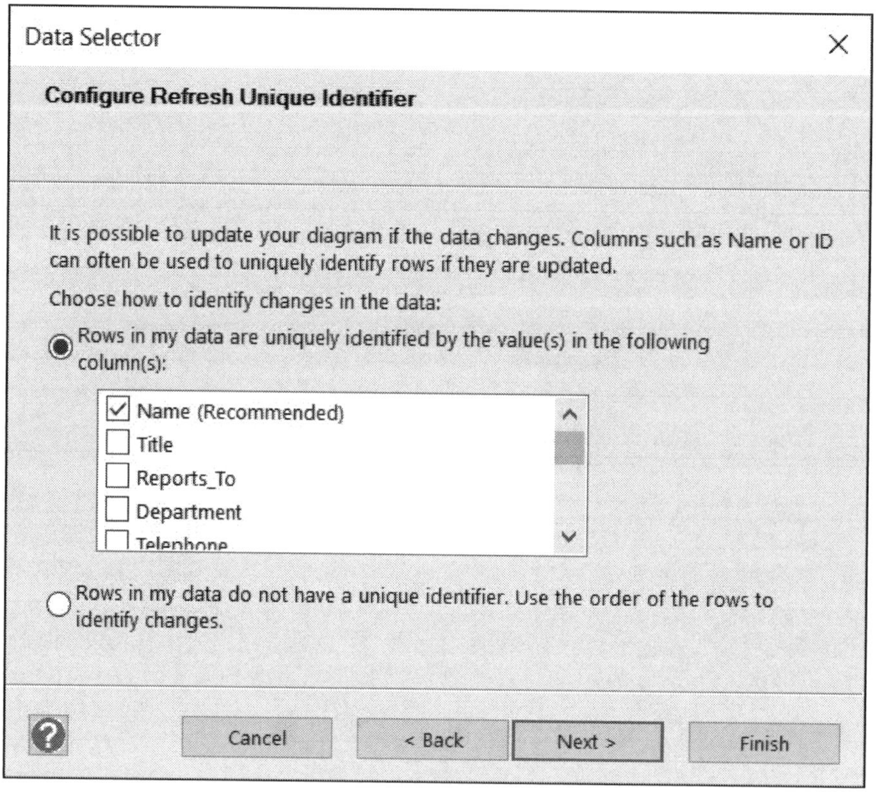


However, there are two actions to perform before importing the custom data. They are described next.

## Editing the column settings

The first action is to edit the **E-mail** column name in the **Personnel** recordset. The reason for this is that the matching of column name to Shape Data row name is case-sensitive, and these shapes already have a Shape Data row labeled **E-Mail** (with a capital **M**).

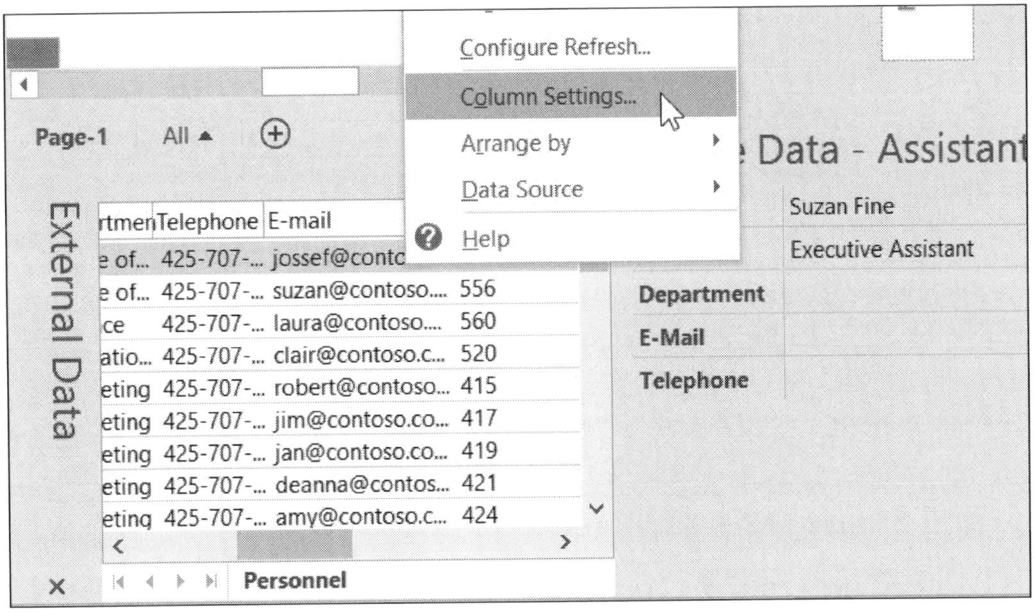


Unfortunately, and inconsistently, the **Column Settings** dialog is not case-sensitive, so just changing the case of `m` is not recognized. The solution is to rename it something else first, as shown (by adding an extra `x`) in the following screenshot:

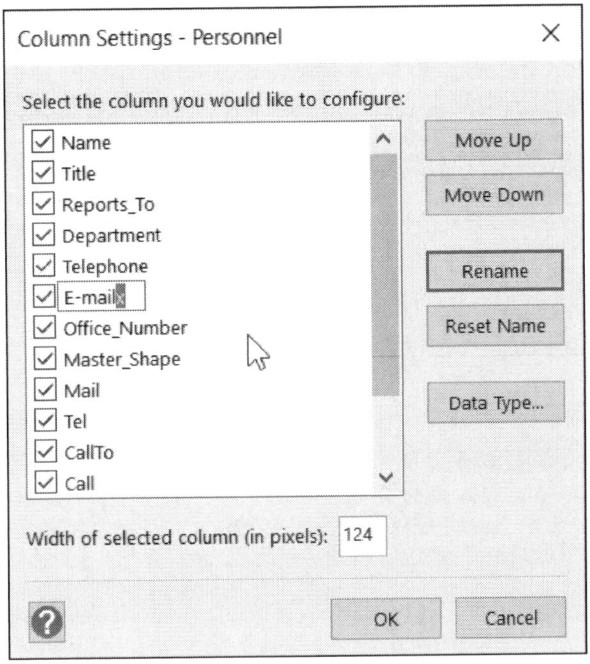

Annoyingly, it is necessary to close the **Column Settings** dialog and reopen it to make these two changes to the **E-Mail** column name.

> Renaming a column only changes the display name. The data source column name remains as it was so that data can be refreshed.

The **Data Type...** button provides the opportunity to view the assumed data type of each column. The following screenshot shows that the hyperlink columns, which are a special type of string, have been set correctly:

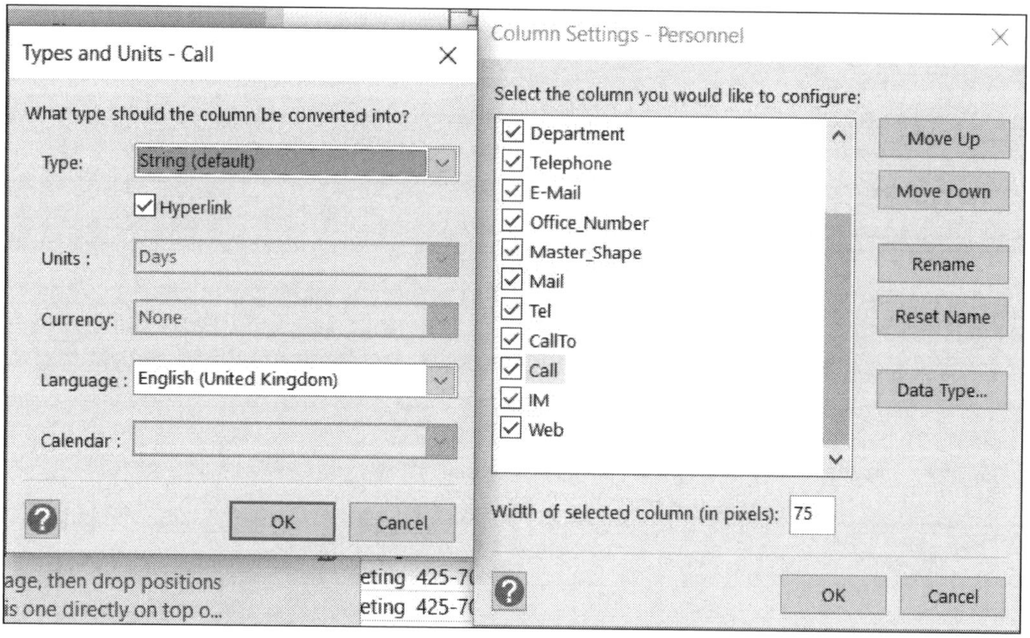


The columns are only made invisible in the UI, and their data will not be transferred to linked shapes. However, they still exist in the recordset that is cached into the Visio document.

## Preventing Data Graphics from appearing automatically

The second action is to uncheck the **Apply after linking data to shapes** option on the drop-down gallery of the **Advanced Data Linking\Advanced Data Graphics** button. This button was just called **Data Graphics** in earlier versions of Visio.

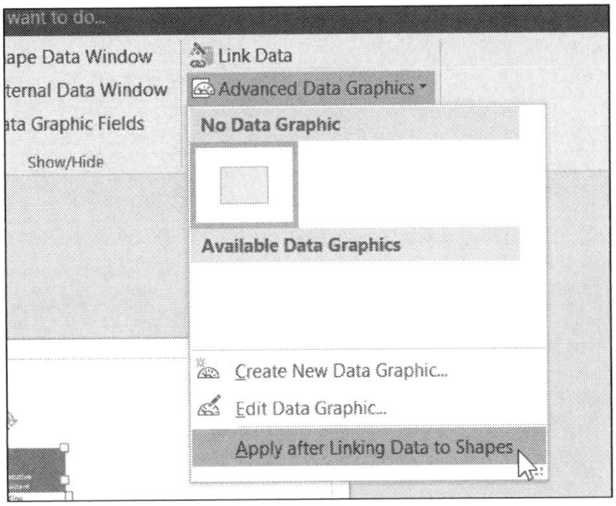


## Linking the data to the shapes

The **Automatic Link** dialog can be opened from the **Data | Advanced Data Linking | Link Data** button, or from the **Link Data...** option on the right-click menu of the **External Data** window:

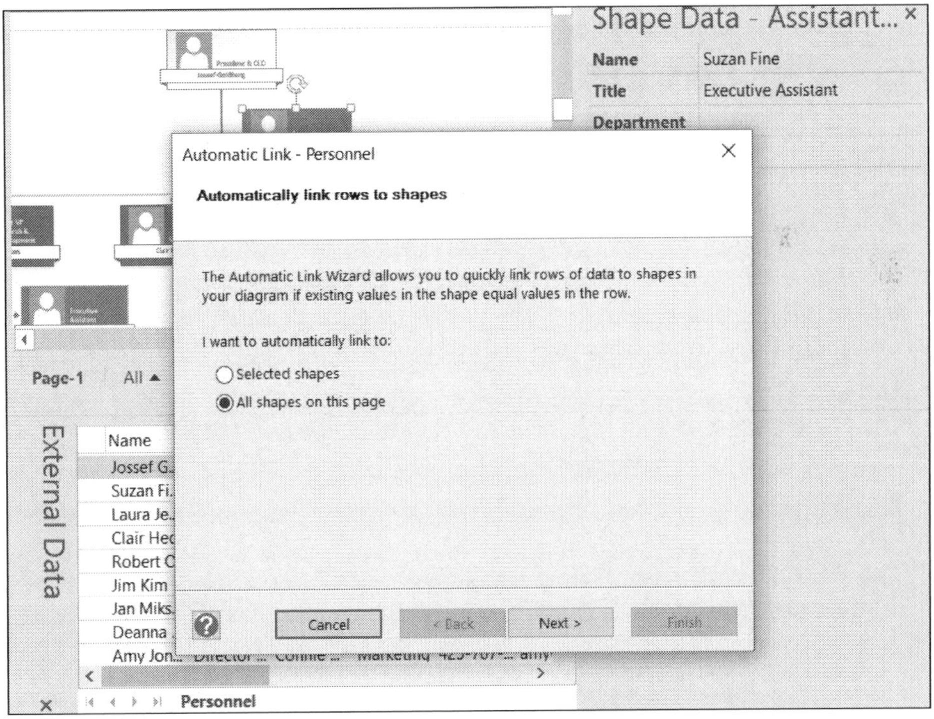

The wizard provides the opportunity to match one or more data column values with shape text or Shape Data row values:

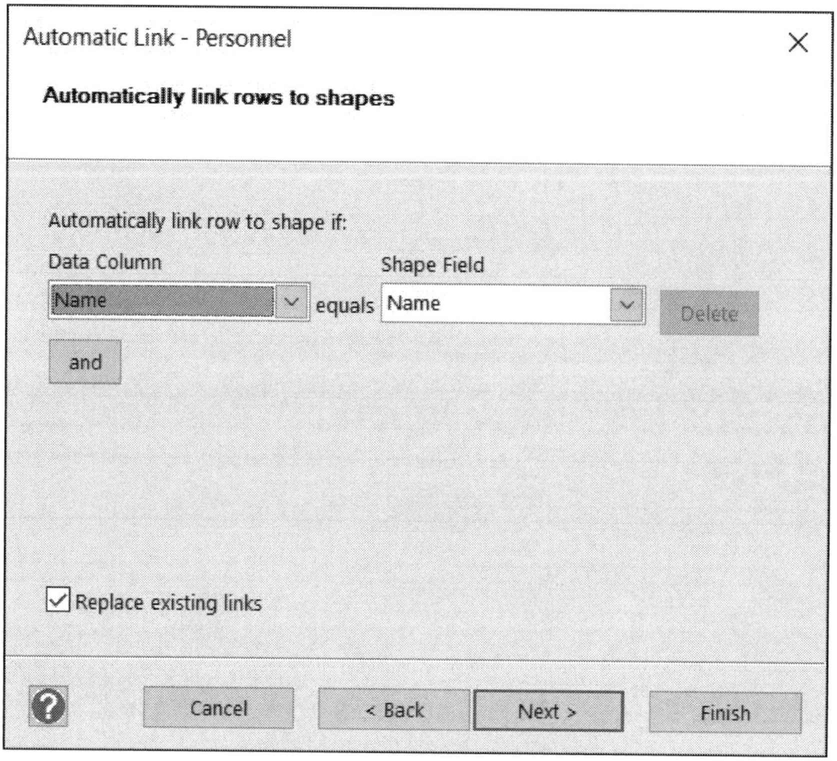


It does not matter if the **Replace existing links** checkbox is ticked in this case, but it should be unticked if multiple External Data recordsets are being linked to each shape.

The resultant shapes now have all of the data linked to the right Shape Data rows, and there are multiple hyperlinks created, providing access to e-mail, Skype, or just web pages.

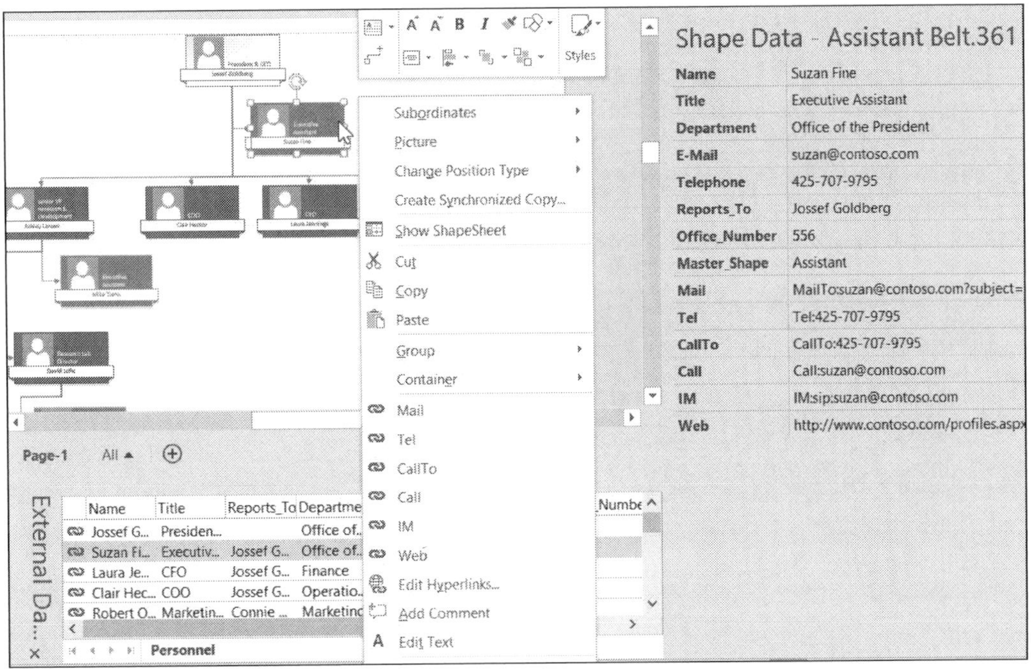


## Carrying out the same import from an Excel workbook with code

It can be laborious to repeat these types of import in many cases, so the following `ImportPersonnelFromExcel()` VBA sub-function will do it:

```
Const excelFileName  as string = "<excel file path>"

Public Sub ImportPersonnelFromExcel()

Dim doc As Visio.Document
Set doc = ActiveDocument

Dim cmd As String
Dim conString As String
Dim drs As Visio.DataRecordset

conString = "Provider=Microsoft.ACE.OLEDB.12.0;" & _
            "User ID=Admin;" & _
            "Data Source=" & excelFileName & ";" & _
            "Mode=Read;" & _
            "Extended Properties=""HDR=YES;IMEX=1;" & _
            "MaxScanRows=0;Excel 12.0;"";" & _
```

```
                "Jet OLEDB:Engine Type=34;"

    cmd = "select * from `Personnel$`"
    Set drs = doc.DataRecordsets.Add(conString, cmd, 0, "Personnel")

    Dim pKeys(1 To 1) As String
    pKeys(1) = "Name"
    drs.SetPrimaryKey VisPrimaryKeySettings.visKeySingle, pKeys

    Dim win As Visio.Window
    Set win = ActiveWindow
    win.Windows.ItemFromID(visWinIDExternalData).Visible = True
    'Change the display name the E-mail column
    Dim dataCol As Visio.DataColumn
    Set dataCol = drs.DataColumns.Item("E-mail")
    dataCol.DisplayName = "E-Mail"

    win.SelectAll
    Dim colNames(1) As String
    Dim fieldTypes(1) As Long
    Dim fieldNames(1) As String
    Dim idsofLinkedShapes() As Long
    colNames(0) = "Name"
    fieldTypes(0) = visAutoLinkCustPropsLabel
    fieldNames(0) = "Name"
    win.Selection.AutomaticLink drs.ID, colNames, _
        fieldTypes, fieldNames, _
        visAutoLinkDontReplaceExistingLinks + _
        visAutoLinkNoApplyDataGraphic, _
        idsofLinkedShapes

End Sub
```

The second argument for the `DataRecordsets.Add(...)` method does allow for various options apart from the default **0**, such as hiding the `DataRecordset` from being displayed in the **External Data** window:

| VisDataRecordsetAddOptions enum Constant | Value | Description |
|---|---|---|
| `visDataRecordsetNoExternalDataUI` | 1 | This prevents data in the new data recordset from being displayed in the External Data window. |
| `visDataRecordsetNoRefreshUI` | 2 | This prevents the data recordset from being included in the refresh operation and displayed in the Refresh Data dialog box. |
| `visDataRecordsetNoAdvConfig` | 4 | This prevents the data recordset from being displayed in the Configure Refresh dialog box. |
| `visDataRecordsetDelayQuery` | 8 | This adds a data recordset but does not execute the `CommandString` query until the next time you call the Refresh method. |
| `visDataRecordsetDontCopyLinks` | 16 | This adds a data recordset, but Shape Data links are not cut or copied. |

## Using Excel as a refreshable data source

Most of the data sources can be refreshed using the **Data** | **External Data** | **Refresh** button, which is also available in the right-click menu of the **External Data** window:

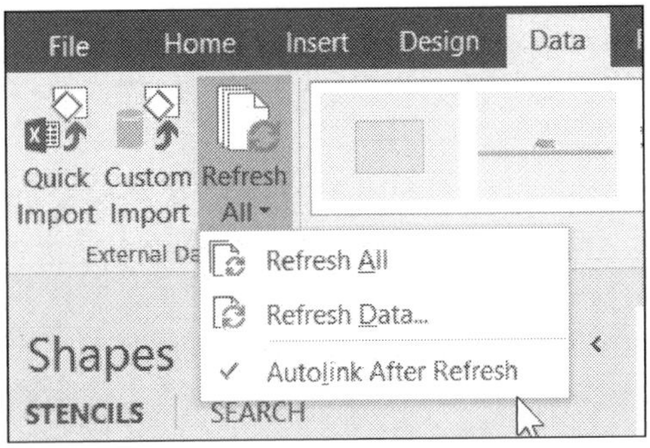

This will open the **Refresh Data** dialog, where all or individual recordsets can be refreshed, as shown in the following screenshot. It also has a **Configure...** button that displays the **Configure Refresh** dialog:

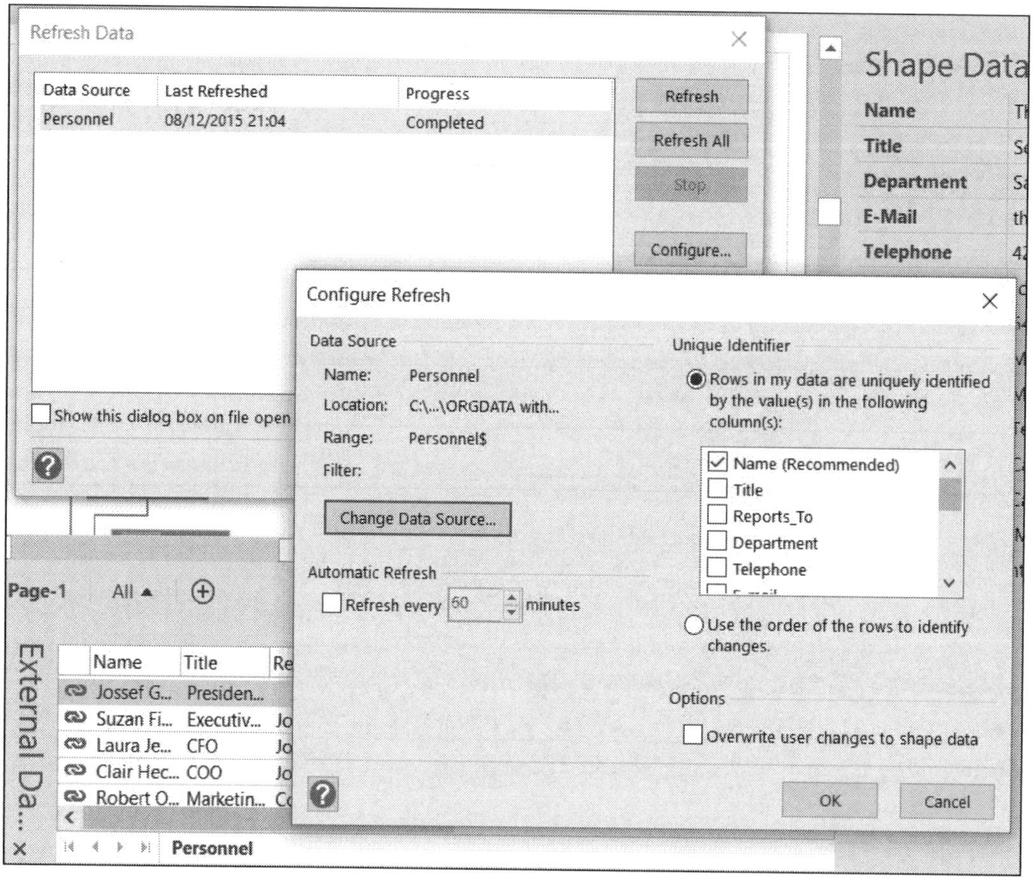

This dialog presents the opportunity to change data source using the **Change Data Source...** button; however, this should only be done to change to a matching data source, otherwise there will be a mismatch between columns and Shape Data rows. This is disastrous for updating data values.

The user can also choose to get the Visio client to refresh the data every 1 to 60 minutes. This is not to be confused with the refresh period of Visio documents that are saved to SharePoint.

Excel documents can be stored in SharePoint, and they use Excel Services to refresh data. Visio documents can also be linked to Excel workbooks in SharePoint. When Visio documents are viewed in the Visio Web Access control in a SharePoint web page, they can be set to refresh from the data source periodically. This ensures that the viewer is seeing the latest state of the data... that is, almost. Office365 has a fixed 5 minute data refresh task going on in the background, so it could take that long to see changes in the Visio diagram viewed in a SharePoint web page.

**Switching a data source from local to SharePoint services**

If the original workbook was stored locally and saved to SharePoint, then the data source can be safely changed to the new location.

The **Overwrite user changes to shape data** option should be ticked if the data source is where the data should be edited.

## Using Excel as an intermediary source

Excel contains an increasingly large list of data sources that it can consume and reform. The following screenshot of Excel 2016 displays the current list of **Data | Get & Transform | New Query | Other** sources that are available in addition to **From File, From Database**, and **From Azure**:

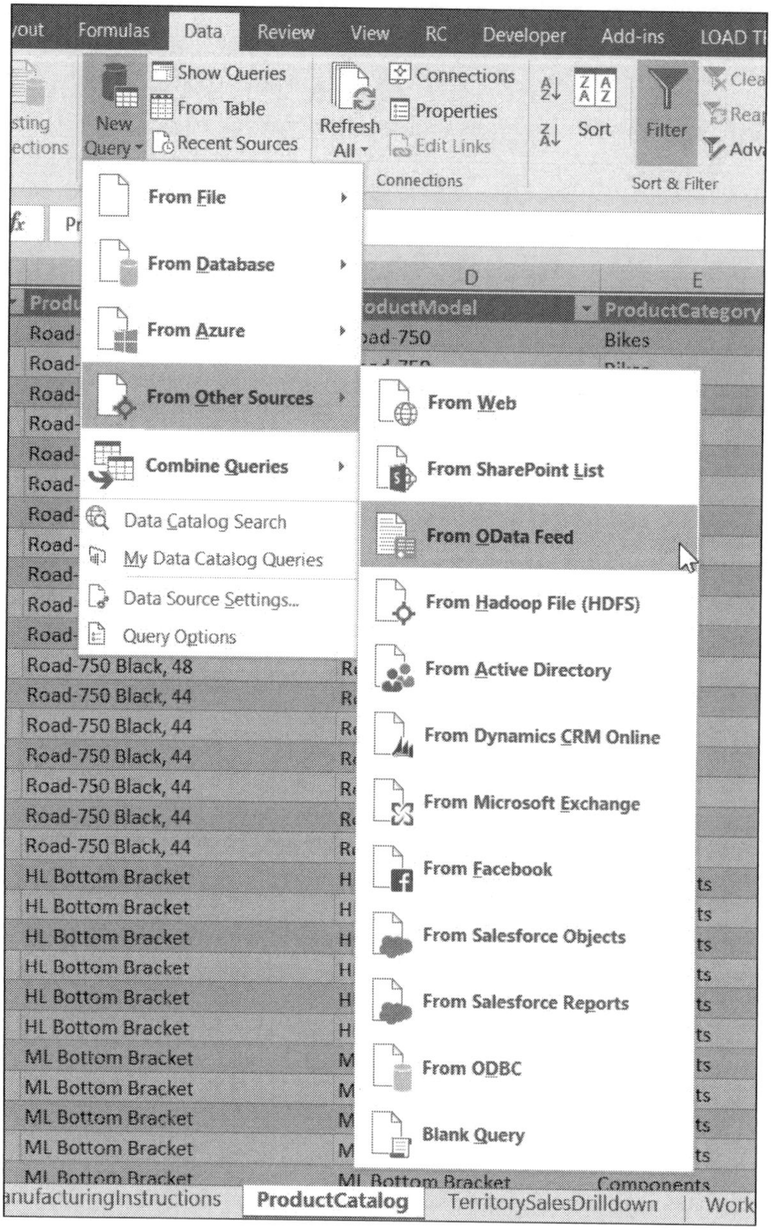

For example, once an OData feed is in Excel, it is available to link to Visio shapes using the methods described earlier.

> There is a sample OData feed described in the following blog post: `http://blogs.msdn.com/b/derrick_vanarnams_blog/archive/2012/09/06/announcing-the-adventureworks-odata-feed-sample.aspx`

The only caveat is that these data sources must be refreshed before the linked data can be refreshed.

## Handling conflicts when data changes

The **Personnel** organization chart shown previously is good for updates to information about each person. For example, the title, department, e-mail, telephone, and related hyperlinks will all update automatically if the Visio document linked data recordset is refreshed.

As the **Name** column has been used for the primary key, then any changes to the name will cause a conflict that needs to be resolved.

It will not move shapes within the chart, nor will it delete shapes or add new shapes.

In the following example, **Carol Philips** has left and been replaced by **Charlie Cooke**. This has caused two issues:

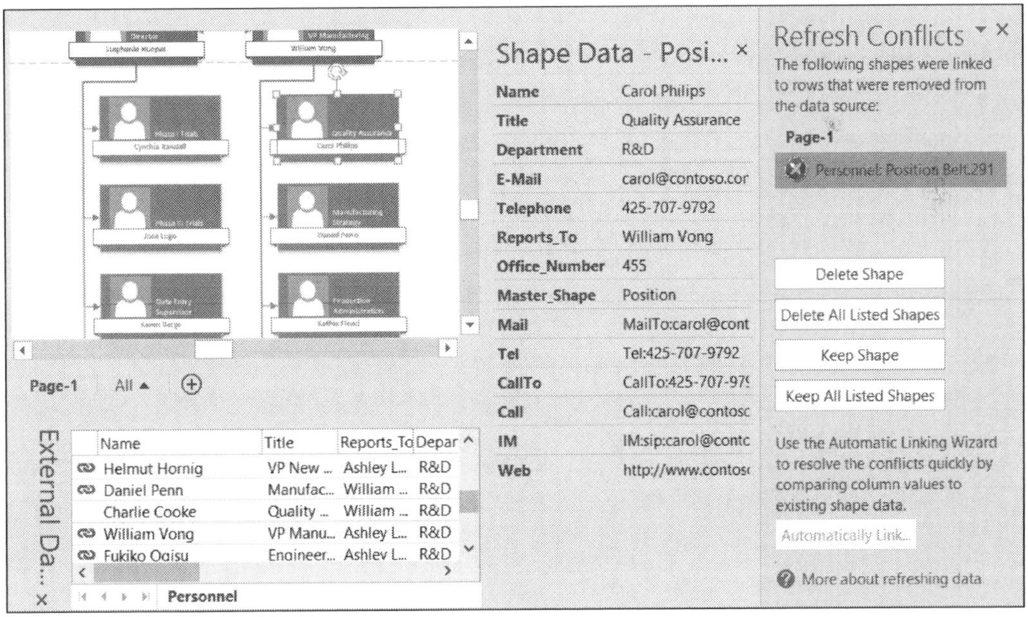

# Importing from Microsoft Access databases

Microsoft Access has been an extremely popular desktop database tool for many years despite many rumors of its demise. It also remains a useful application for combining data from many sources, and presenting them for reports. The following screenshot shows an example query in Access that joins several tables together and has some custom columns to create hyperlinks:

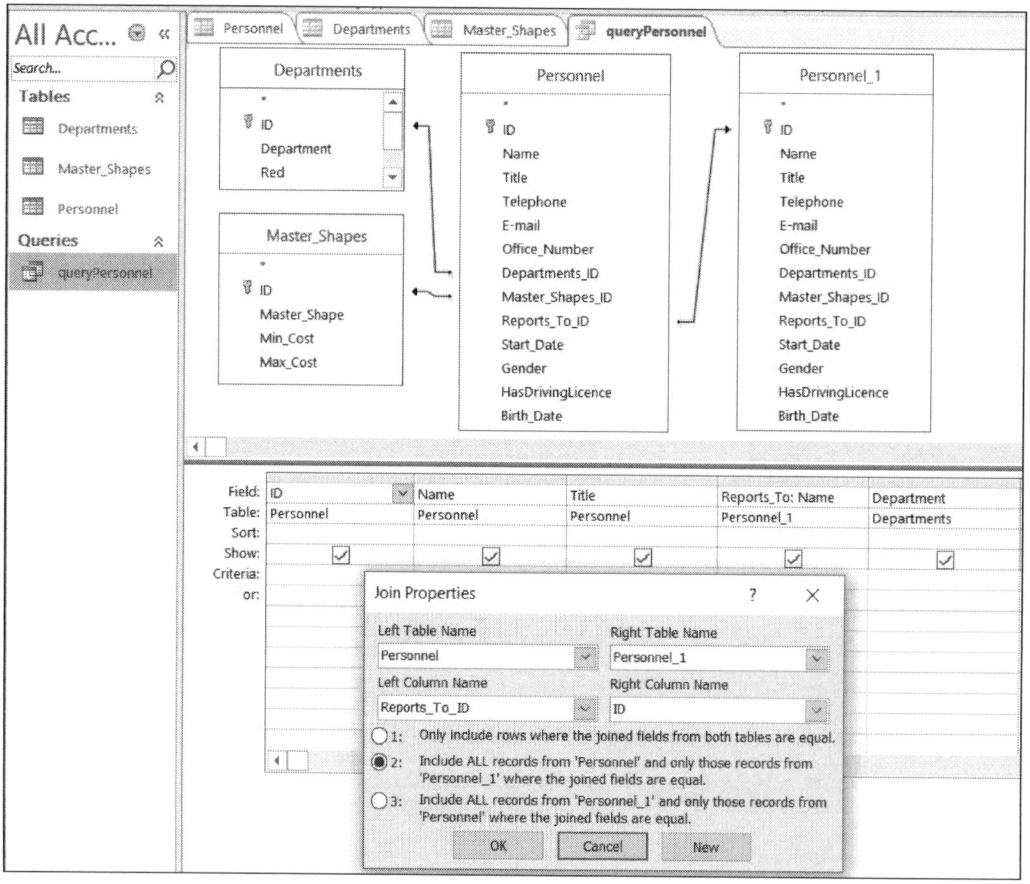

There is a slight difference in the formula for the hyperlink columns because Access (and SQL Server) expects a plus sign rather than an ampersand:

```
MailTo: "MailTo:"+[Personnel].[E-mail]
```

In Visio, the **Data Selector** dialog that is offered when an Access database is selected allows the full file path of the file to be entered or browsed. Then the user selects the query or table to import, as shown in the following screenshot:

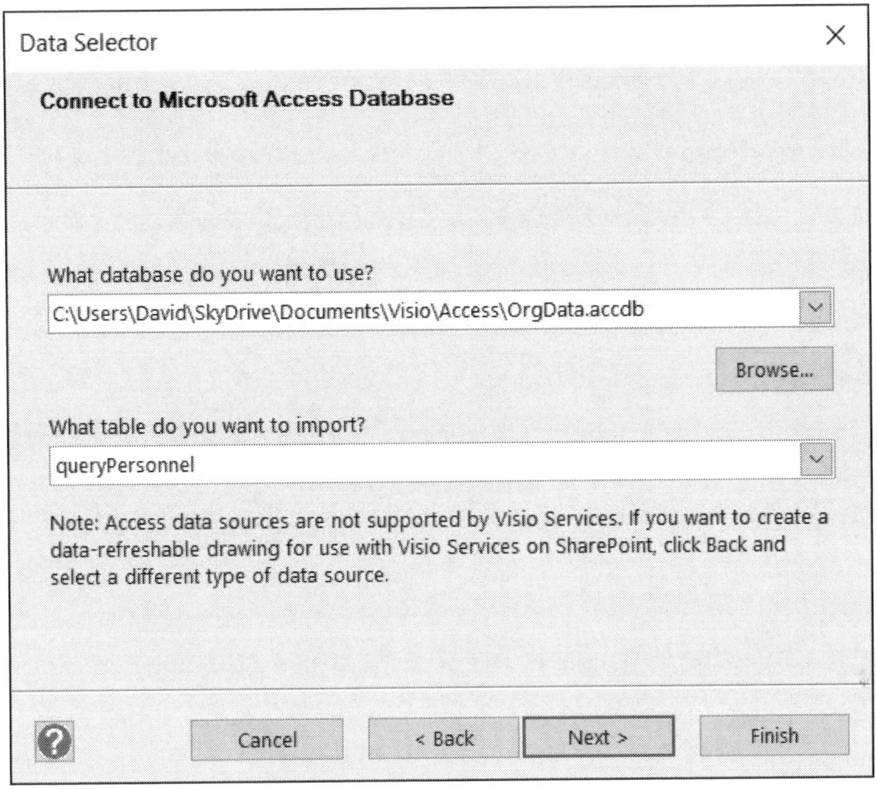

The user can then select the columns to display along with any filter, as for the Excel worksheet option previously. The unique identifier can then be confirmed or chosen, as before.

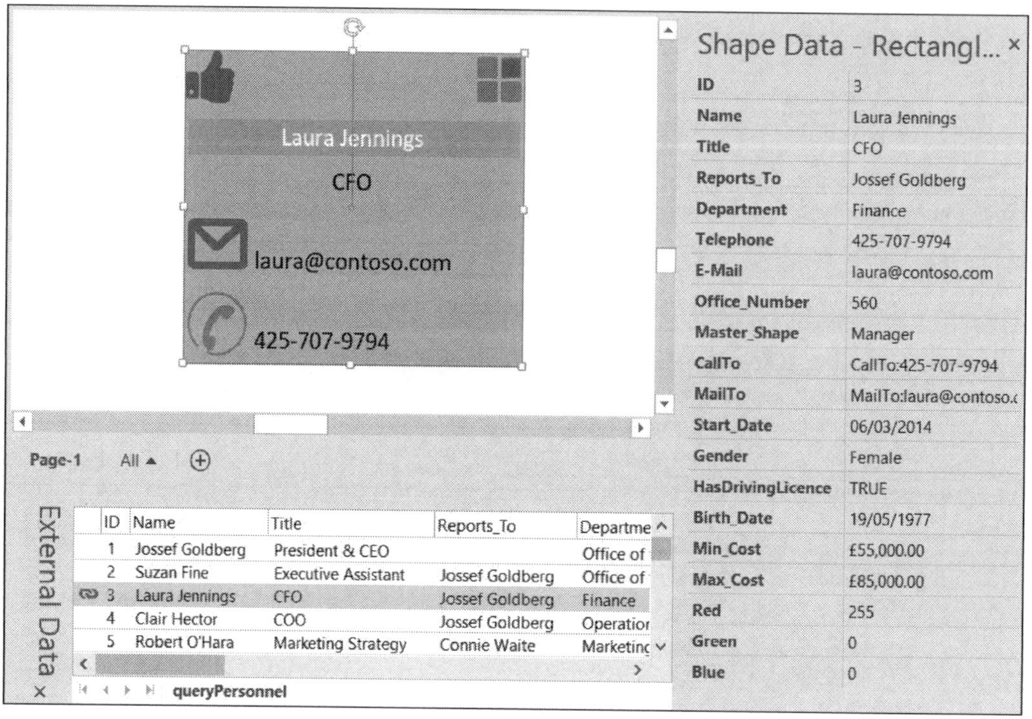


## Doing the same import from the Access database with code

The same data import process can be achieved with the following `ImportPersonnelFromAccess()` VBA sub-function:

```
Const accessFileName as String = "<access file path>"

Public Sub ImportPersonnelFromAccess()
```

```
Dim doc As Visio.Document
Set doc = ActiveDocument

Dim cmd As String
Dim conString As String
Dim drs As Visio.DataRecordset
conString = "Provider=Microsoft.ACE.OLEDB.12.0;" & _
            "User ID=Admin;" & _
            "Data Source=" & accessFileName & ";" & _
            "Mode=Read;" & _
            "Extended Properties="""";" & _
            "Jet OLEDB:System database="""";" & _
            "Jet OLEDB:Engine Type=6;" & _
            "Jet OLEDB:Database Locking Mode=0;"

cmd = "select * from `Personnel`"
Set drs = doc.DataRecordsets.Add(conString, cmd, 0, "Personnel")

Dim pKeys(1 To 1) As String
pKeys(1) = "ID"
drs.SetPrimaryKey VisPrimaryKeySettings.visKeySingle, pKeys

End Sub
```

The Access Web databases actually use SQL Azure databases behind the scenes. Take a look at `http://blog.bvisual.net/2015/09/16/linking-an-access-web-database-to-visio/` for information about connecting to them.

# Importing from SharePoint lists

SharePoint provides the opportunity to provide lists and views. Views in SharePoint are similar to queries in Access. They provide the ability to limit the number of columns, or to extend columns, by adding the hyperlink protocols as previously described. In the following screenshot, the **E-Mail** column has been recognized by SharePoint as a hyperlink, but it is still necessary to provide an extra column for Visio:

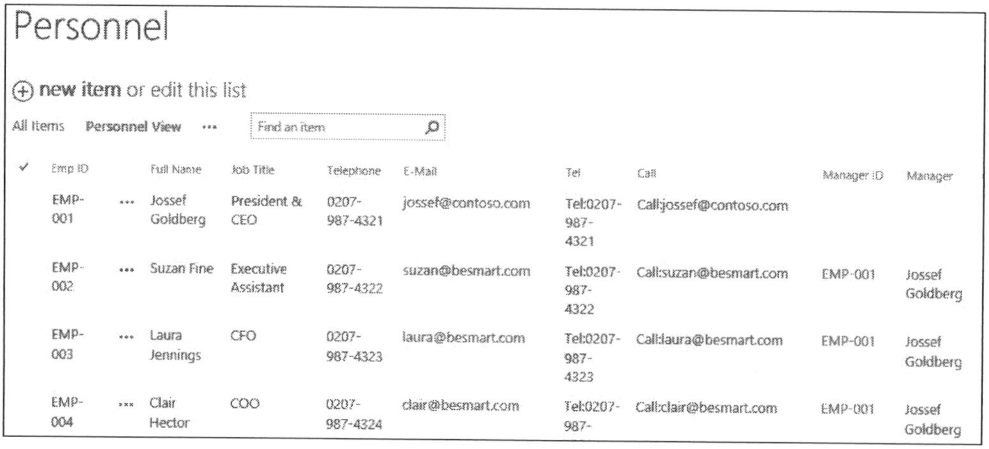


Fortunately, SharePoint provides the ability to add calculated columns, as shown in the following screenshot:

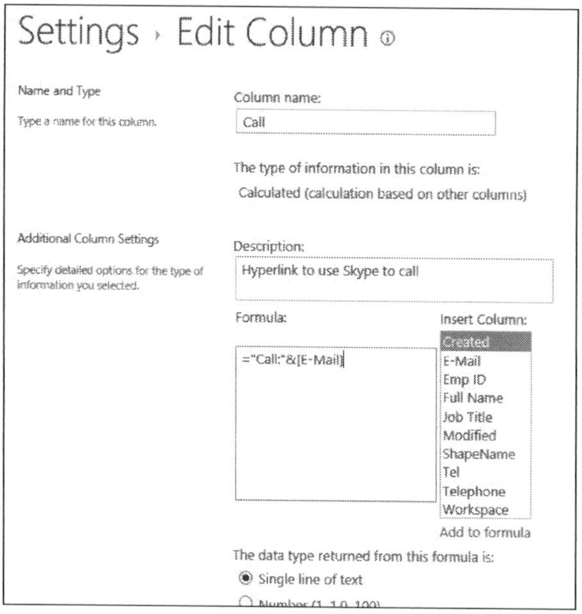

In Visio, when a **Microsoft SharePoint Foundation List** is selected as the data source, the **Data Selector** dialog requires a web URL to be entered:

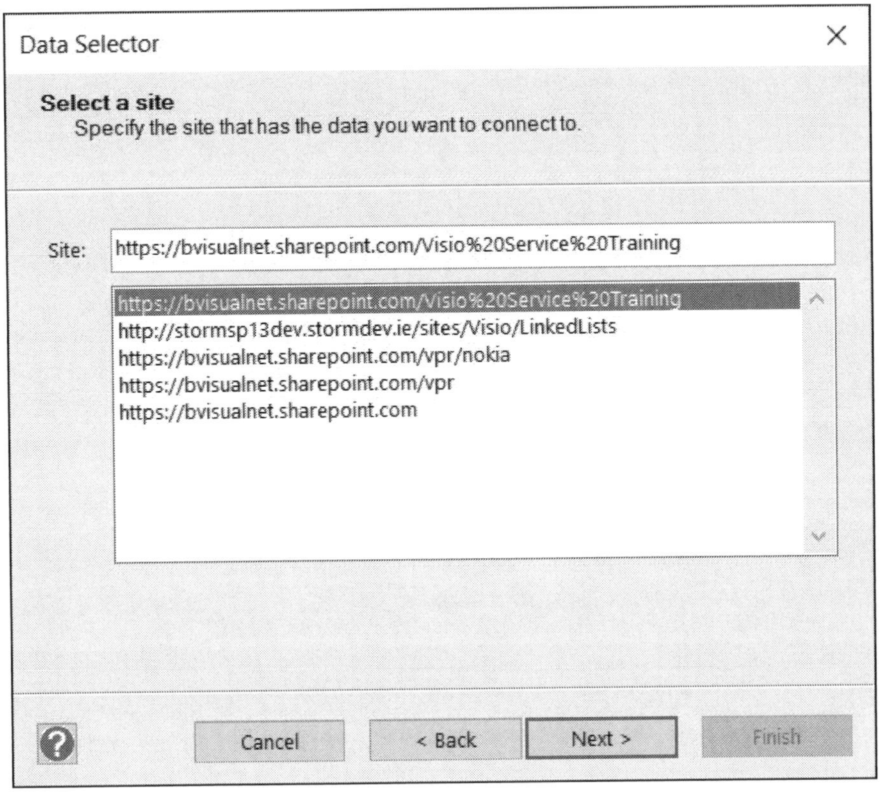

The **Data Selector** dialog will then offer a choice between accepting the basic list or selecting a view, as shown in the following dialog:

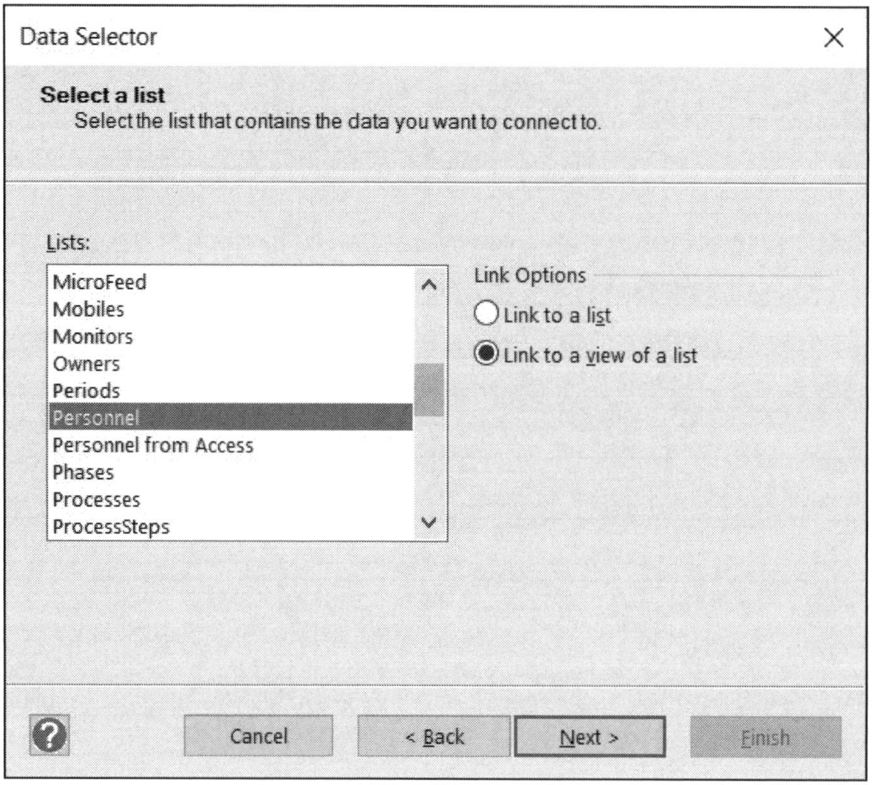

There is always one view available, which is normally called **All Items**, but there could be more. This is shown in the following screenshot where the custom **Personnel View** option is selected:

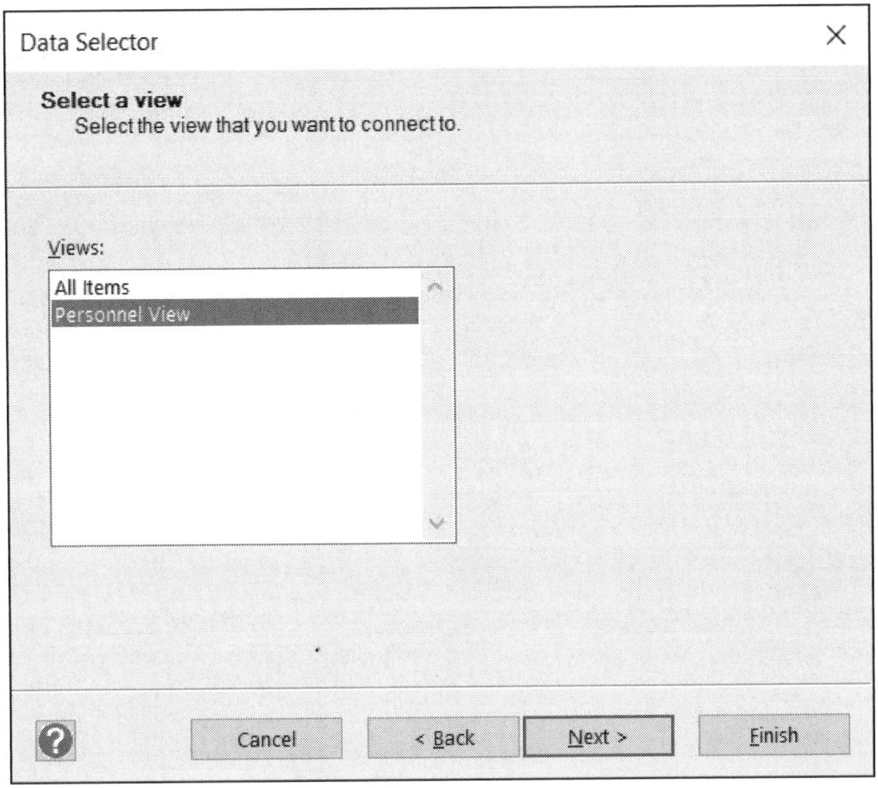

Once added, **External Data** is added to the Visio document; here, it is clear that there are more columns added than requested in the view. Therefore, these extra system columns can be unticked to make them invisible, as shown in the following screenshot. In addition, Visio does not recognize them:

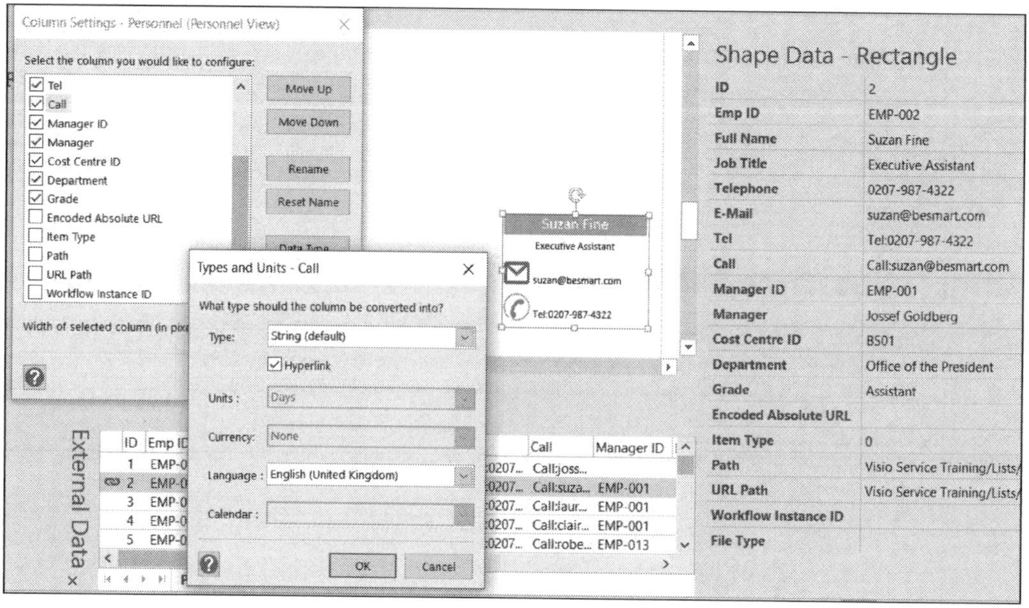


Once these changes are applied, then the extra columns are removed from the shapes too, and the hyperlinks are automatically created.

Of course, it can get boring making these changes every time, so a productivity macro in VBA can be useful.

SharePoint lists can have a column defined as a hyperlink type, and these are correctly recognized by Visio. However, they cannot be calculated columns.

## Doing the same import from a SharePoint view with code

The same data import process can be achieved with the following `ImportPersonelViewFromSharePoint()` VBA sub-function. Notice that the list and view GUIDs need to be provided along with the URL of the website:

```
Const sharePointWebSite as String = "<a SharePoint web url>"

Public Sub ImportPersonelViewFromSharePoint()

Dim doc As Visio.Document
Set doc = ActiveDocument
```

```
Dim cmd As String
Dim conString As String
Dim drs As Visio.DataRecordset

conString = "Provider=WSS;" & _
            "DATABASE=" & sharePointWebSite & ";" & _
            "LIST={99EC9D96-D705-49EA-A832-2D5723BC922C};" & _
            "VIEW={C3BB321C-4076-48F5-A2B8-DFE4A9EADCC2};"

cmd = "select * from [Personnel (Personnel View)]"
Set drs = doc.DataRecordsets.Add(conString, cmd, 0, _
    "Personnel (Personnel View)")

Dim pKeys(1 To 1) As String
pKeys(1) = "ID"
drs.SetPrimaryKey VisPrimaryKeySettings.visKeySingle, pKeys
drs.DataColumns.Item("Encoded Absolute URL").Visible = False
drs.DataColumns.Item("Item Type").Visible = False
drs.DataColumns.Item("Path").Visible = False
drs.DataColumns.Item("URL Path").Visible = False
drs.DataColumns.Item("Workflow Instance ID").Visible = False
drs.DataColumns.Item("File Type").Visible = False

drs.DataColumns.Item("Tel").Hyperlink = True
drs.DataColumns.Item("Call").Hyperlink = True

End Sub
```

> Take a look at `http://blog.bvisual.net/2014/09/26/linking-sql-database-on-azure-to-visio-via-sharepoint-online/` for a walkthrough of linking a SQL Azure database to Visio via SharePoint online.

# Importing from SQL Server data

The SQL Server is available in many different editions and can be available from a local installation, a network server, or even somewhere in the cloud.

> This section uses the sample `AdventueWorks2014` database available from `http://msftdbprodsamples.codeplex.com/`.

The following **Data Connection Wizard** is opened if a SQL Server data source is selected:

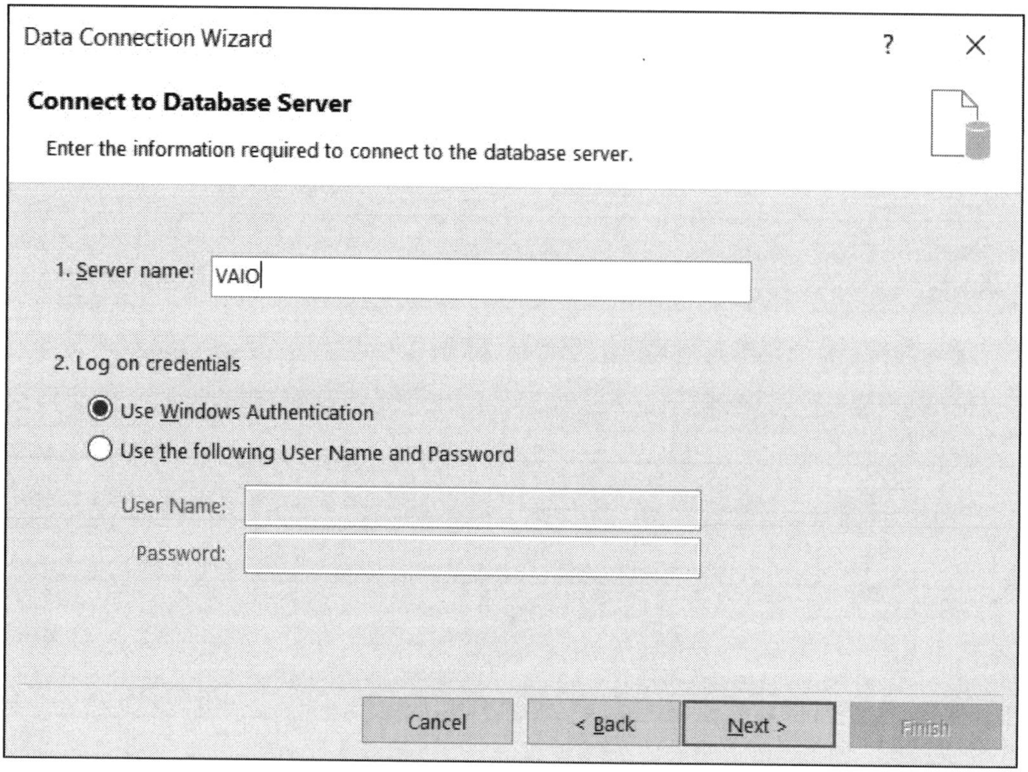

The Visio user is then prompted to select a specific database and then a view or table that they have permission to read data from:

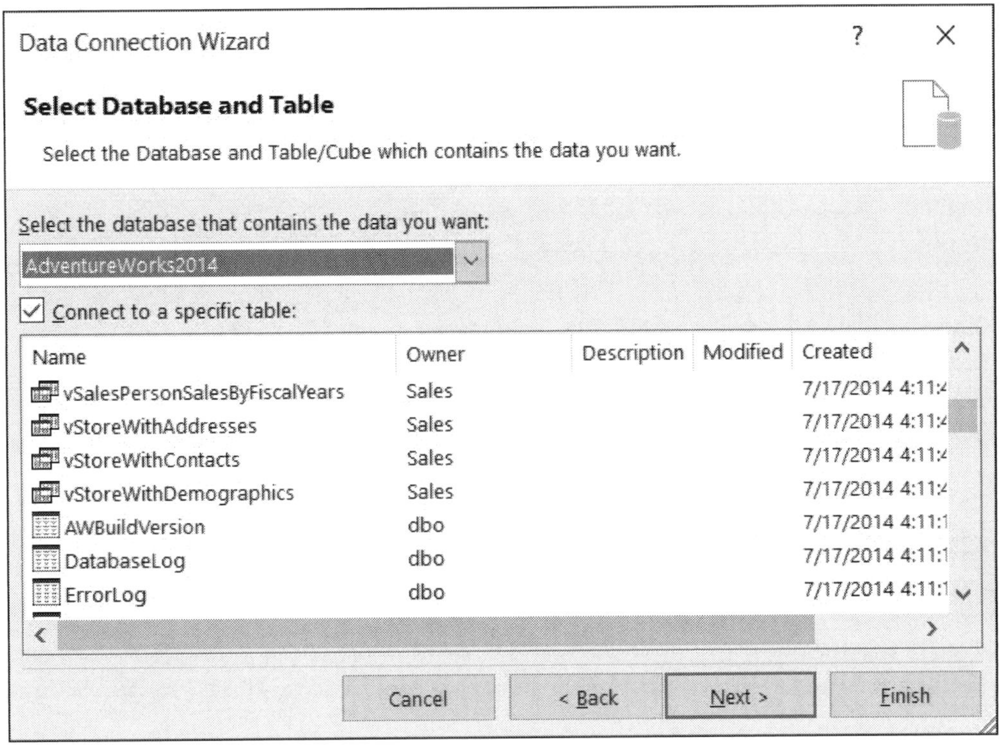

The Visio user is only able to see the databases, tables, and views that are allowed with the login account. The next panel of the **Data Connection Wizard** then provides the ability to save the connection file as a defined name, as shown in the next screenshot. This **Office Data Connection** (`*.odc`) file can contain the password, that is, if the user chose to log in with a SQL username rather than a Windows account:

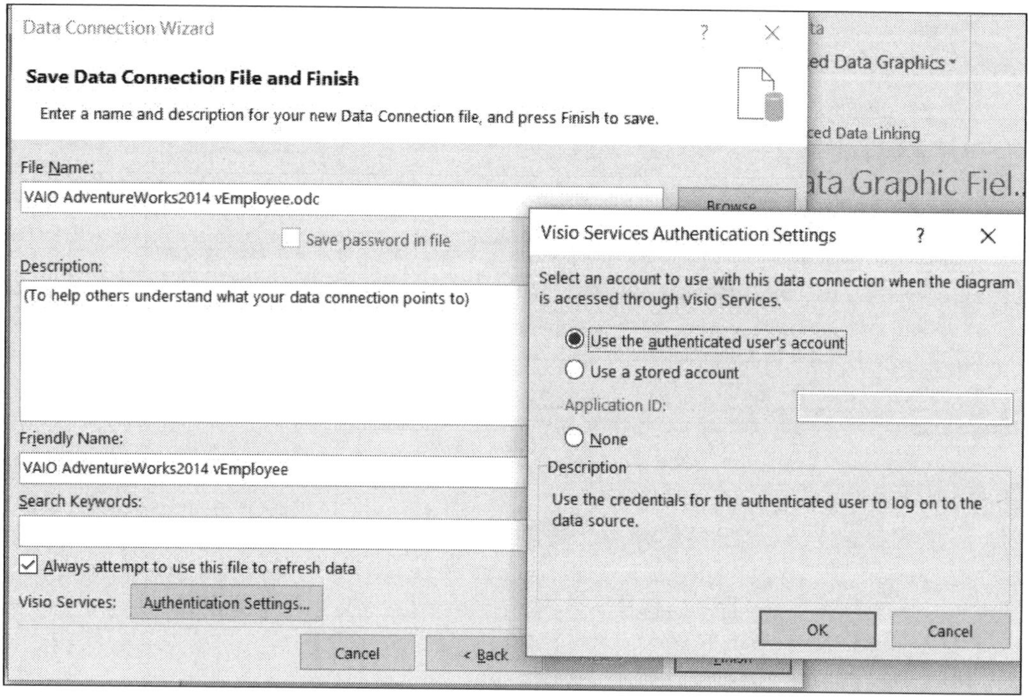


If the Visio document is to be stored in SharePoint, then the user can opt to specify a stored account that will be used by Visio Services to refresh the document data. This would also require SharePoint to have control of the connection to the SQL Server database.

The `SELECT` clause for the command string can then be modified by unticking unnecessary columns in the **Select Columns** dialog, as shown in the following screenshot:

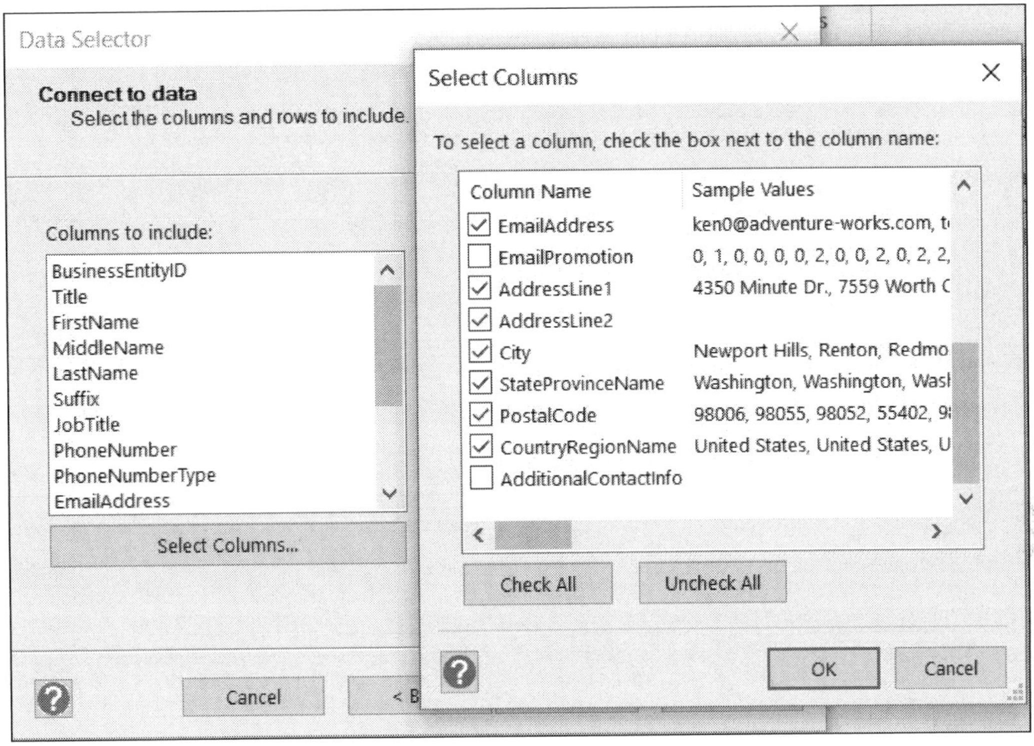

The rows can be filtered using the UI to build a SQL `WHERE` clause, as shown in the next screenshot, where a specific value for `CountryRegionName` is selected:

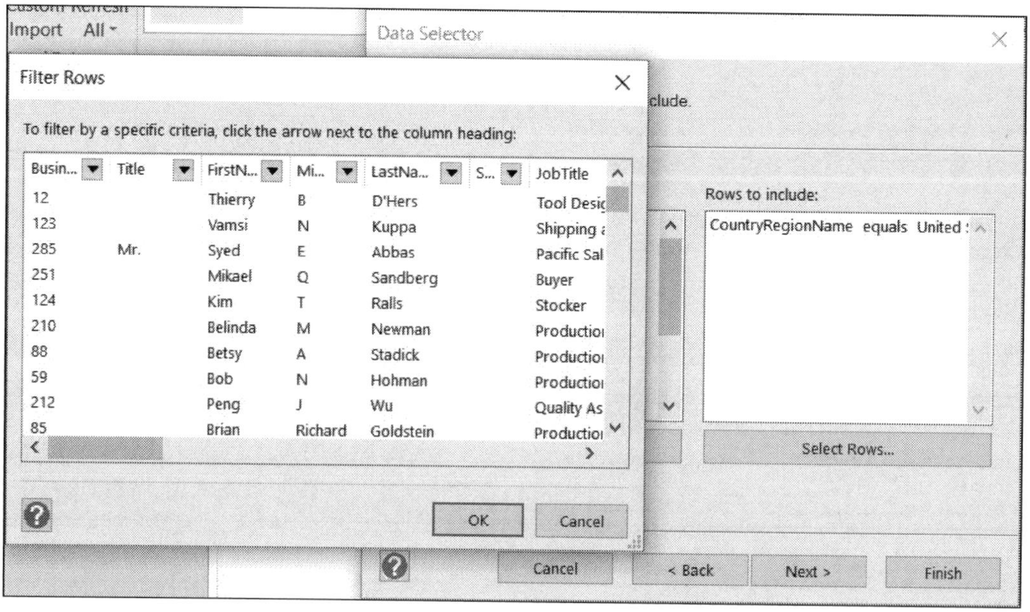

The recordset is then displayed in the **External Data** window, from where it can be linked to shapes, as shown in the following screenshot:

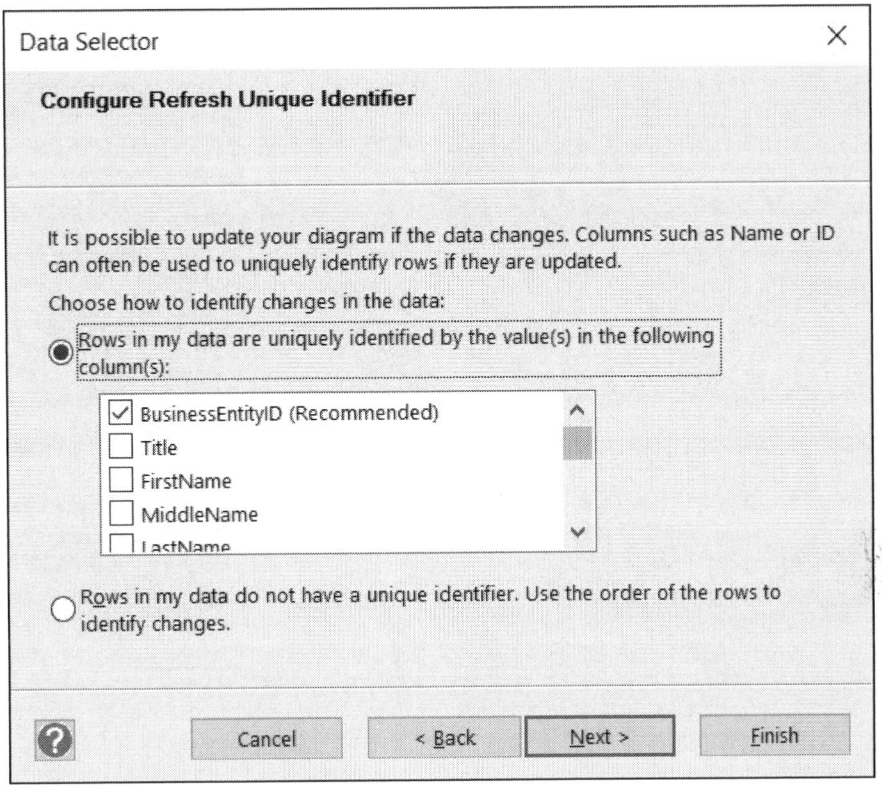

Finally, the recordset will be imported into Visio and will be available for linking to shapes, as shown in the following screenshot:

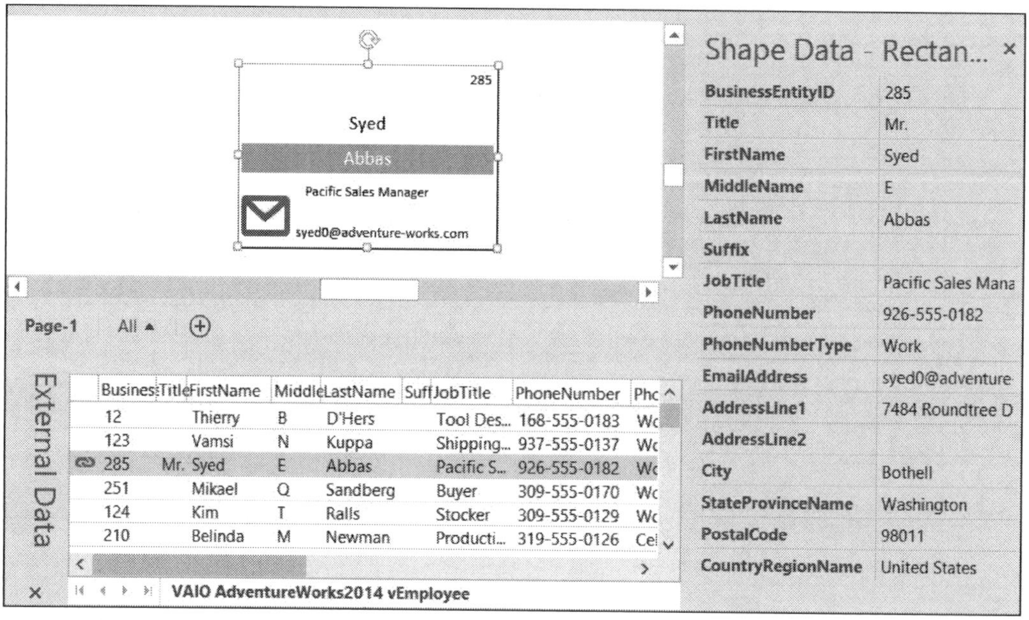


> Take a look at `http://blog.bvisual.net/2014/09/11/linking-sql-database-on-azure-to-visio/` for a walkthrough on linking the SQL Azure dataset to Visio.

## Using code to retrieve the SQL Server data

The previously described process to import the data from a specific table or view from the SQL Server database could have been achieved with the following `ImportSQLView()` VBA sub-function:

```
Const dbServer as string = "<a server name>"

Public Sub ImportSQLView()

Dim doc As Visio.Document
Set doc = ActiveDocument

Dim drs As Visio.DataRecordset  'The data recordset
Dim aryKeys() As String 'Array to hold the p key columns
Dim cmd As String   'The command string
Dim conString As String 'The connection string
```

```
Dim drsName As String    'The dataset name
Dim dbName As String     'The database name

dbName = "AdventureWorks2014"
conString = "Provider=SQLOLEDB.1;" & _
            "Integrated Security=SSPI;" & _
            "Persist Security Info=True;" & _
            "Data Source=" & dbServer & ";" & _
            "Initial Catalog=" & dbName & ";" & _
            "Use Procedure for Prepare=1"
cmd = "SELECT [BusinessEntityID],[Title]," & _
    "[FirstName],[MiddleName],[LastName],[Suffix]," & _
    "[JobTitle],[PhoneNumber],[PhoneNumberType]," & _
    "[EmailAddress],[AddressLine1],[AddressLine2]," & _
    "[City],[StateProvinceName],[PostalCode]," & _
    "[CountryRegionName] " & _
    "FROM [HumanResources].[vEmployee]" & _
    "WHERE [CountryRegionName] = N'United States'"
aryKeys() = Split("BusinessEntityID", ";")
drsName = "vEmployee"

Set drs = doc.DataRecordsets.Add(conString, cmd, _
    visDataRecordsetDelayQuery, drsName)

drs.SetPrimaryKey VisPrimaryKeySettings.visKeySingle, aryKeys()
drs.Refresh

Dim win As Visio.Window
Set win = ActiveWindow
win.Windows.ItemFromID(visWinIDExternalData).Visible = True

End Sub
```

The `DataRecordset.Refresh()` method can be used to refresh the data from the source subsequently.

## Getting data with stored procedures

It is sometimes more efficient, and compliant, to get data using a stored procedure. The following screenshot is from Microsoft SQL Server 2014 Management Studio and displays the `dbo.uspGetManagerEmployees` stored procedure in the `AdventureWorks2014` database:

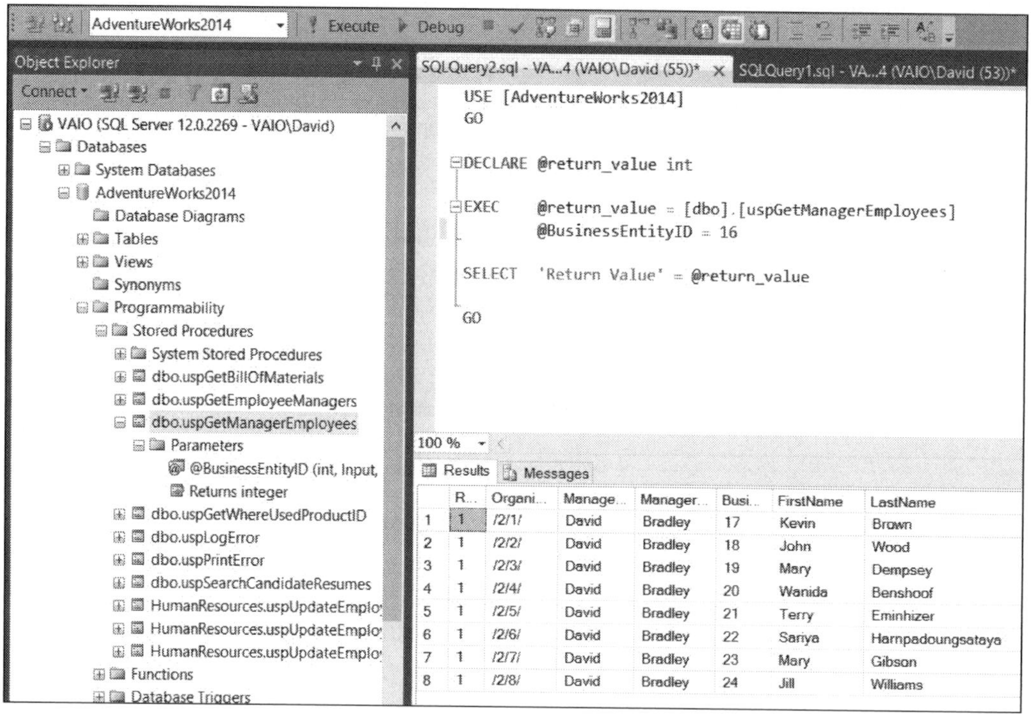


Although the **Data Selector** dialog offers SQL Server as an option, it is not possible to select a stored procedure. However, they can be used in code, as shown in the following sample `ImportSQLSP()` sub-function. Note that constants are declared at the start of VBA files:

```
Const dbServer as string = "<a server name>"

Public Sub ImportSQLSP()
```

```
Dim doc As Visio.Document
Set doc = ActiveDocument

Dim drs As Visio.DataRecordset  'The data recordset
Dim aryKeys() As String 'Array to hold the p key columns
Dim cmd As String   'The command string
Dim conString As String 'The connection string
Dim drsName As String   'The dataset name
Dim dbName As String    'The database name

dbName = "AdventureWorks2014"
conString = "Provider=SQLOLEDB.1;" & _
            "Integrated Security=SSPI;" & _
            "Persist Security Info=True;" & _
            "Data Source=" & dbServer & ";" & _
            "Initial Catalog=" & dbName & ";" & _
            "Use Procedure for Prepare=1"
cmd = "EXEC [dbo].[uspGetManagerEmployees] 16"
aryKeys() = Split("BusinessEntityID", ";")
drsName = "Employees for Manager 16"

Set drs = doc.DataRecordsets.Add(conString, cmd, _
    VisDataRecordsetAddOptions.visDataRecordsetDelayQuery, _
        drsName)

drs.SetPrimaryKey VisPrimaryKeySettings.visKeySingle, aryKeys()
drs.Refresh

Dim win As Visio.Window
Set win = ActiveWindow
win.Windows.ItemFromID(visWinIDExternalData).Visible = True

End Sub
```

Running this code will add a recordset to the **External Data** window, as shown in the following screenshot. The rows will then be available for linking as normal:

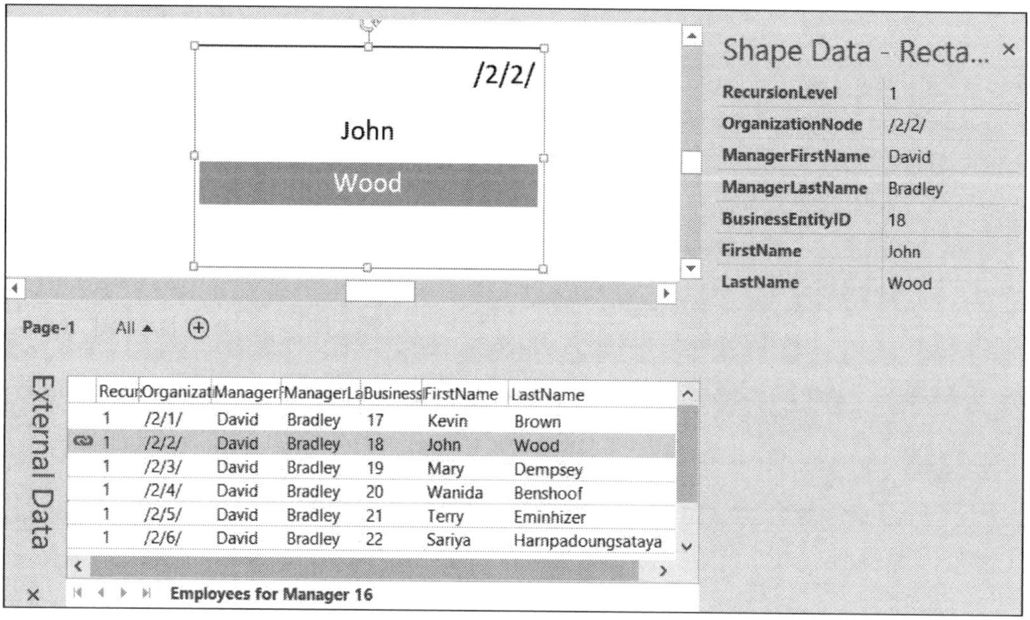

# Importing data with OLEDB and ODBC

There may be times when the data source is not covered by the previous options. In this case, there is a fall-back: using the OLEDB or ODBC **Data Connection Wizard**. This offers the opportunity to select from a variety of data sources, as shown in the following screenshot:

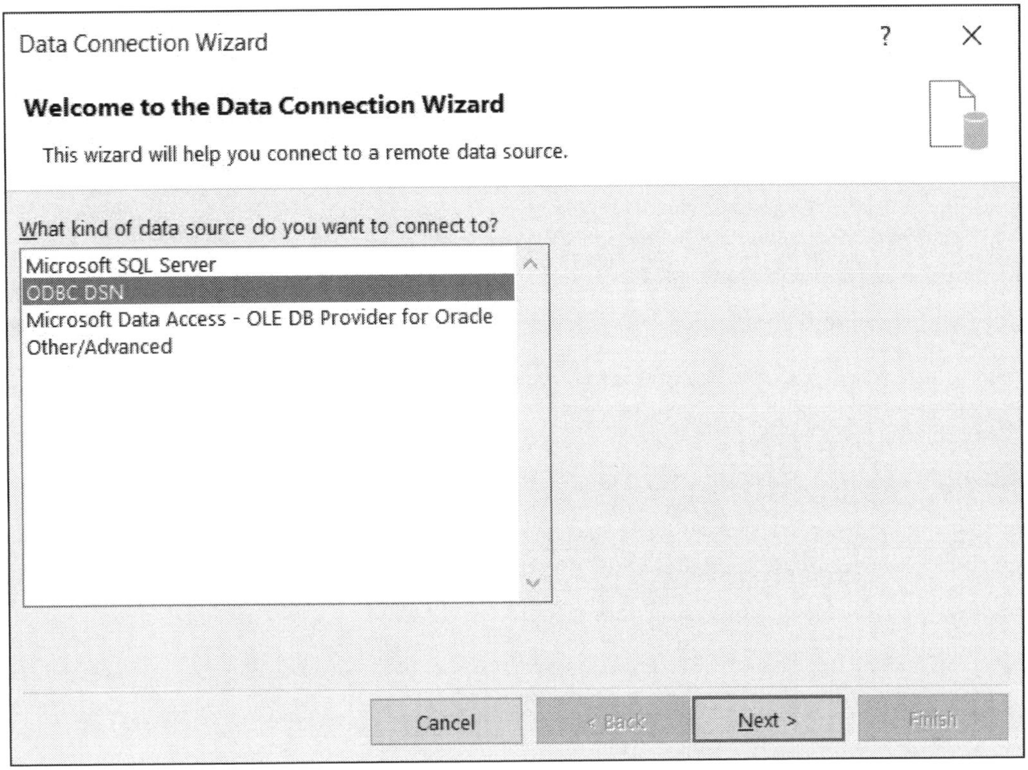

Microsoft Visio installs a sample Access database, cunningly called **Visio Database Samples**, that contains many tables and views.

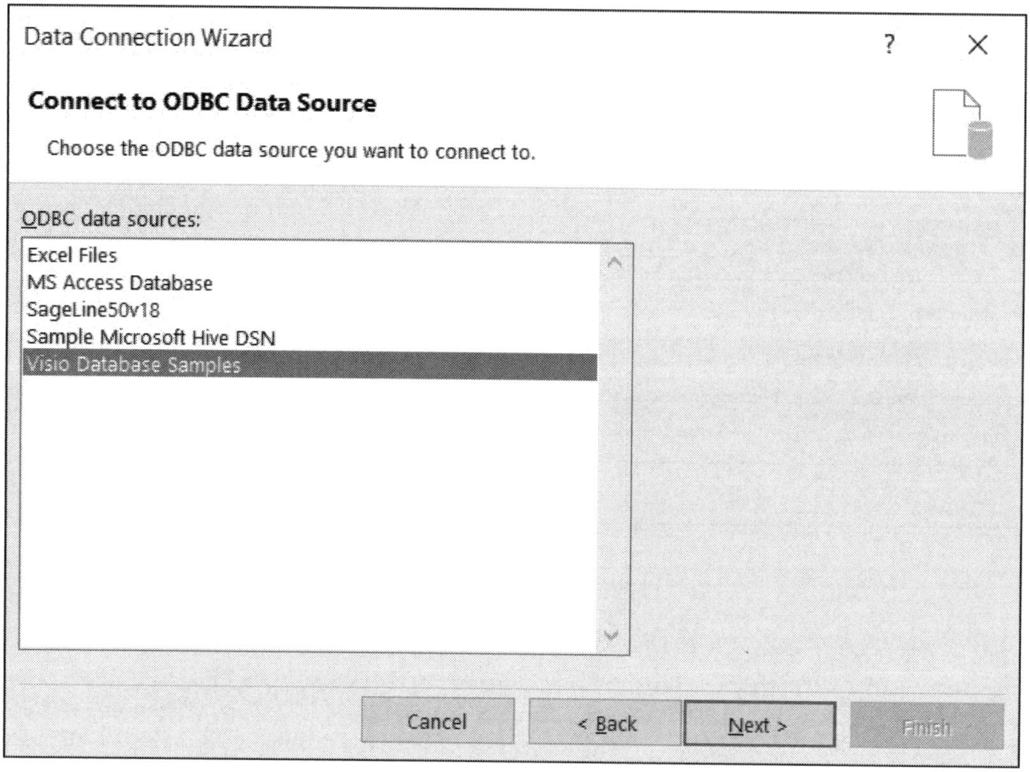

The Visio user is offered a choice of tables and views and given the opportunity to select a specific column or filter the data before the connection is saved into an ODC file:

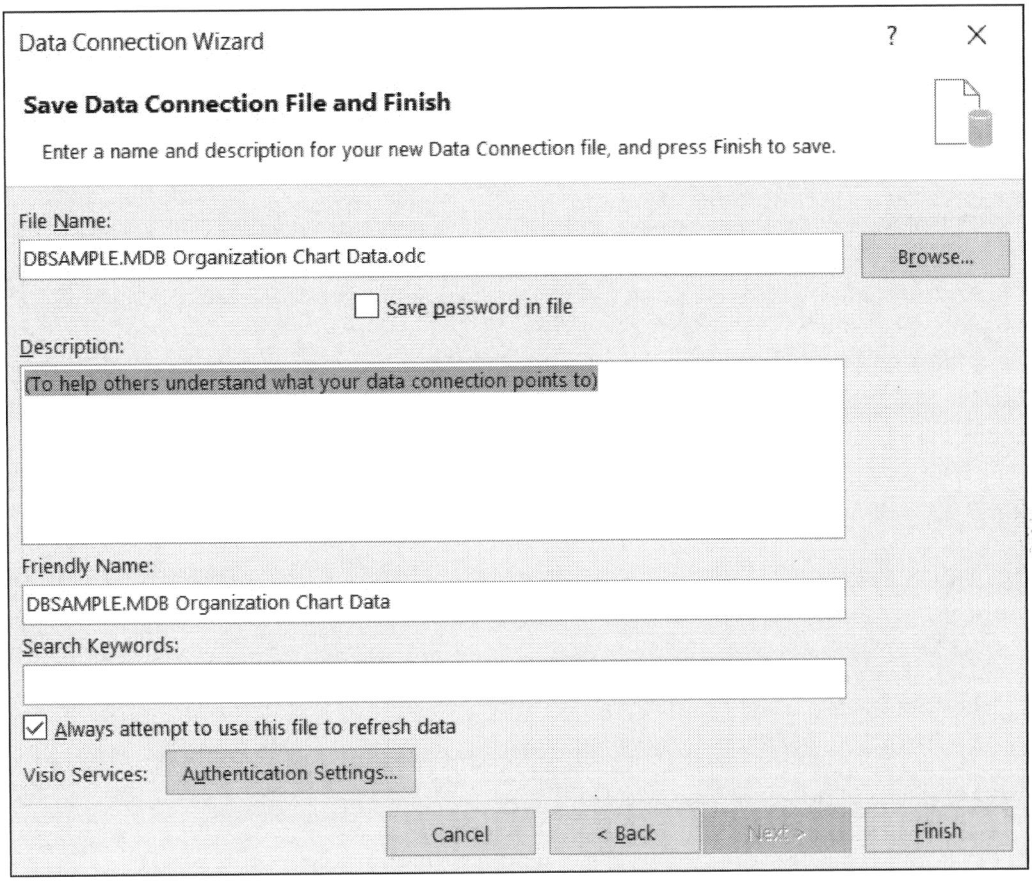


The rest of the process is like all of the other sources.

## Connecting the Visio Samples via ODBC in code

The following `ImportOrgDataFromDsnAccess()` sub-function uses ODBC to import data from a table in the Access database that is installed with Visio. Again, a constant is declared before the actual sub-function:

```
Const dsnVisioSamples As String = "DSN=Visio Database Samples;" & _
    "DriverId=25;FIL=MS Access;MaxBufferSize=2048;PageTimeout=5;"

Public Sub ImportOrgDataFromDsnAccess()
Dim doc As Visio.Document
Set doc = ActiveDocument

Dim cmd As String
Dim conString As String
Dim drs As Visio.DataRecordset

conString = "Provider=MSDASQL.1;" & _
            "Persist Security Info=True;" & _
            "Mode=Read;" & _
            "Extended Properties=""" & dsnVisioSamples & """;"

cmd = "select * from `Organization Chart Data`"
Set drs = doc.DataRecordsets.Add(conString, cmd, 0, "Organization
Chart Data")

Dim pKeys(1 To 1) As String
pKeys(1) = "Name"
drs.SetPrimaryKey VisPrimaryKeySettings.visKeySingle, pKeys

End Sub
```

# Using previously created connections

The SQL Server and OLEDB\ODBC connection options mentioned earlier in this chapter created an **Office Data Connection** (**ODC**) file and then used that to import the data. Therefore, on subsequent uses, this ODC file can be used instead, as shown in the following screenshot:

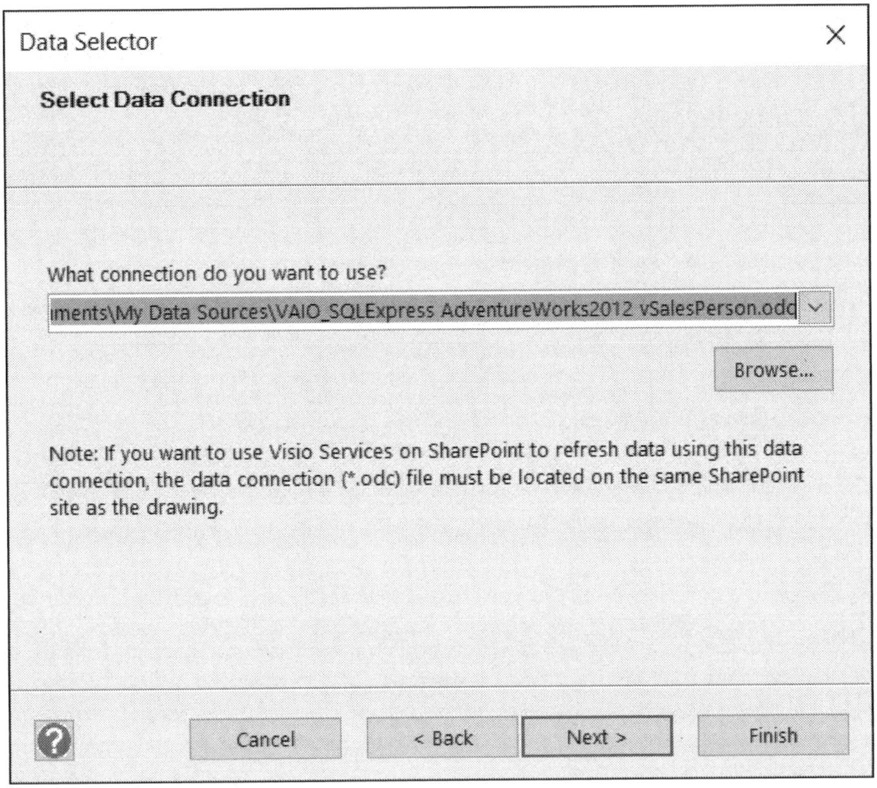


The user is then prompted to select the columns and filter the rows, as done earlier.

The ODC files are stored in the `My Data Sources` folder by default, but they can be copied and moved to other locations (including within SharePoint if the Visio document is to be saved to the same SharePoint site). It can then be used for refresh activities using **Visio Services**. Of course, the data source specified within the ODC file must be accessible from SharePoint.

Other applications, such as Microsoft Excel, can also create ODC files, but this does not mean that they will be compatible for use with Visio. For example, Excel supports creating ODC files for multiple tables and views in a single file, but Visio only supports a single one.

Once an ODC file has been created and tested, it is very easy to use it to import the data using code, as shown in the following `ImportFromODCFile()` sub-function:

```
Const odcFile As String = "<odc file name>"

Public Sub ImportFromODCFile()

Dim doc As Visio.Document
Set doc = ActiveDocument
Dim drs As Visio.DataRecordset

Set drs = doc.DataRecordsets.AddFromConnectionFile(odcFile, _
    0, "Data from ODC")

End Sub
```

The second argument for the `DataRecordsets.AddFromConnectionFile(...)` method is the same as for the `DataRecordsets.Add(...)` method listed previously.

# Using XML data

Visio can also import data from XML files, but they must be in the classic ADO schema format. The following screenshot displays the contents of the XML file that can be copied from `https://msdn.microsoft.com/en-us/library/ms676547(v=vs.85).aspx`:

```
  <?xml version="1.0"?>
- <xml xmlns:z="#RowsetSchema" xmlns:rs="urn:schemas-microsoft-com:rowset"
  xmlns:dt="uuid:C2F41010-65B3-11d1-A29F-00AA00C14882" xmlns:s="uuid:BDC6E3F0-
  6DA3-11d1-A2A3-00AA00C14882">
  - <s:Schema id="RowsetSchema">
    - <s:ElementType rs:updatable="true" rs:CommandTimeout="30" content="eltOnly"
      name="row">
      - <s:AttributeType name="ShipperID" rs:basecolumn="ShipperID"
        rs:basetable="Shippers" rs:basecatalog="Northwind" rs:writeunknown="true"
        rs:number="1">
          <s:datatype rs:maybenull="false" rs:fixedlength="true" rs:precision="5"
            dt:maxLength="2" dt:type="i2"/>
        </s:AttributeType>
      - <s:AttributeType name="CompanyName" rs:basecolumn="CompanyName"
        rs:basetable="Shippers" rs:basecatalog="Northwind" rs:writeunknown="true"
        rs:number="2">
          <s:datatype rs:maybenull="false" dt:maxLength="40" dt:type="string"
            rs:dbtype="str"/>
        </s:AttributeType>
      - <s:AttributeType name="Phone" rs:basecolumn="Phone" rs:basetable="Shippers"
        rs:basecatalog="Northwind" rs:writeunknown="true" rs:number="3"
        rs:nullable="true">
          <s:datatype rs:fixedlength="true" dt:maxLength="24" dt:type="string"
            rs:dbtype="str"/>
        </s:AttributeType>
        <s:extends type="rs:rowbase"/>
      </s:ElementType>
    </s:Schema>
  - <rs:data>
      <z:row Phone="(503) 555-9831 " CompanyName="Speedy Express" ShipperID="1"/>
      <z:row Phone="(503) 555-3199 " CompanyName="United Package" ShipperID="2"/>
      <z:row Phone="(503) 555-9931 " CompanyName="Federal Shipping" ShipperID="3"/>
    </rs:data>
  </xml>
```


The following `ImportXml()` VBA sub-function requires a reference to Microsoft XML, v6.0. It will import the correctly formatted data in a file path defined in the `xmlFileName` constant:

```
Const xmlFileName as String = "<xml file path>"

Public Sub ImportXml()
Dim doc As Visio.Document
Dim drs As Visio.DataRecordset
Dim dom As New MSXML2.DOMDocument60

Set doc = Visio.ActiveDocument
If dom.Load(xmlFileName) Then
    Set drs = doc.DataRecordsets.AddFromXML( _
       dom.XML, 0, "Shippers")
End If

End Sub
```

The second argument for the `AddFromXML(...)` function allows various options apart from the default `0`, except for the refresh options:

| **VisDataRecordsetAddOptions enum Constant** | **Value** | **Description** |
|---|---|---|
| `visDataRecordsetNoExternalDataUI` | 1 | This prevents data in the new data recordset from being displayed in the External Data window. |
| `visDataRecordsetNoAdvConfig` | 4 | This prevents the data recordset from being displayed in the Configure Refresh dialog box. |
| `visDataRecordsetDontCopyLinks` | 16 | This adds a data recordset, but Shape Data links are not cut or copied. |

This code will then import the XML data into the Visio document, where it can be used to link to shapes, as shown in the following screenshot:

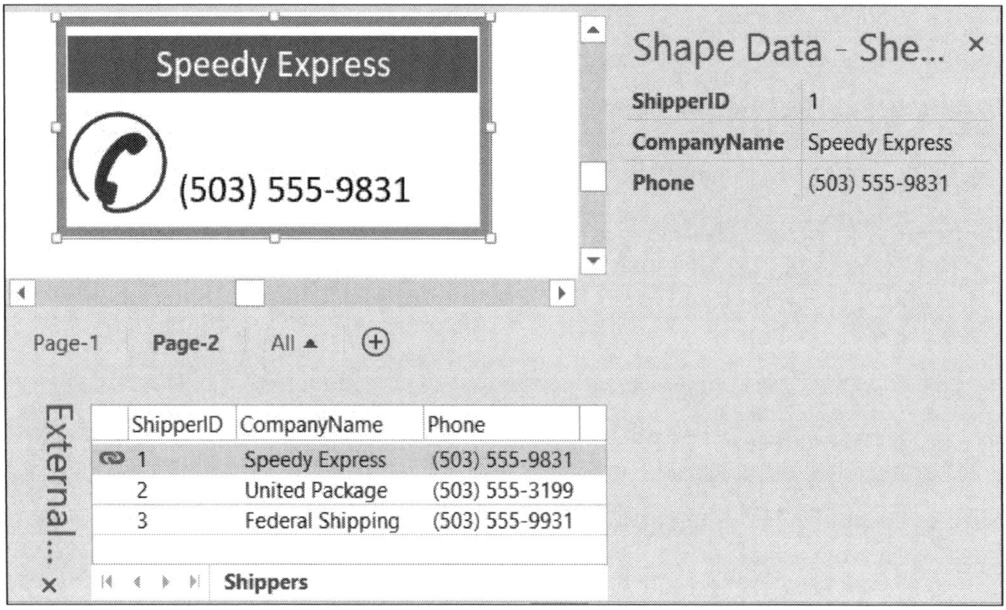

There may be times when it is necessary to refresh the XML data in the Visio document. The following `RefreshXml()` sub-function will refresh for a given `xmlFileName`, but the `DataRecordset.Name` is also required because there is no `DataConnection` object created by the XML file imports:

```
Public Sub RefreshXml()
Dim doc As Visio.Document
Dim drs As Visio.DataRecordset
Dim dom As New MSXML2.DOMDocument60

Set doc = Visio.ActiveDocument
If dom.Load(xmlFileName) Then
    For Each drs In doc.DataRecordsets
        If drs.Name = "Shippers" And _
            drs.DataConnection Is Nothing Then
            drs.RefreshUsingXML dom.XML
            Exit For
        End If
    Next
End If

End Sub
```

> There is more information about this XML format at `https://msdn.microsoft.com/en-us/library/ms676547(v=vs.85).aspx`.

# Removing external data connections for privacy and efficiency

The data import feature described in this chapter will cache the data as XML within the document as well as within each linked shape. The shapes may contain less than the cached XML because not all rows need to be linked, and some columns may have been marked as invisible. It may be necessary to remove this cached XML from the Visio document because it may contain sensitive data, or just to reduce the file size.

The user can go to each recordset in the **External Data** window and select **Remove** from the right-click menu, but this can be tedious if there are many recordsets.

Fortunately, there is an option, **Remove data from external sources stored in the document**, in the **File** | **Info** | **Remove Hidden Information** dialog to do this:

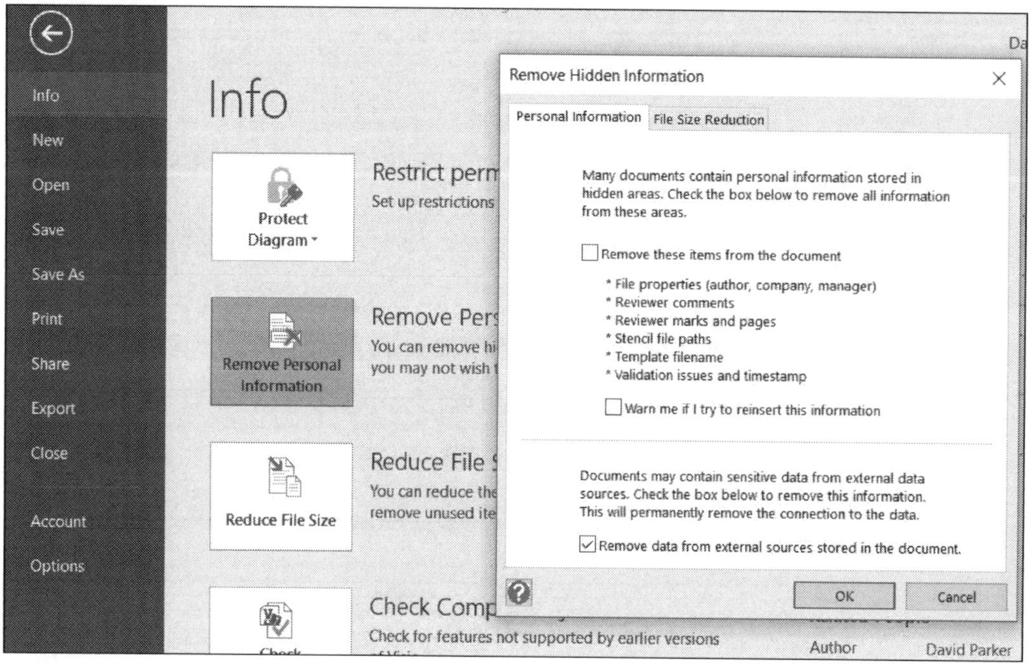


The same task can be done in code using the `Document.RemoveHiddenInformation (visRHIDataRecordsets)` method.

# Creating data links to the shapes

Most of this chapter has dealt with importing data into the Visio document, and very little has been about actually linking the data to the shapes. More will be discussed in *Chapter 9, Automating Structured Diagrams*, but a few simple methods are introduced here. The beauty of having the `Document.DataRecordsets` available in code is that it provides a consistent method for automating any data links to shapes, regardless of the origin of the data.

## Linking data to shapes manually

The Visio user interface presents several methods for linking data to shapes. The first is to just drag a row from the **External Data** window onto an existing shape. This will just add the data to the shape, which is the technique that has been used throughout this chapter.

There are times when it is impossible to drag the data row onto a shape, such as when the shape is a List or Container. Therefore, the method is to select the shape first, then the data row, and **Link to Selected Shapes** from the right-click menu of the **External Data** window.

Another manual method is to select a master shape in the **Shapes** panel, then drag and drop one or more rows onto the page but not onto an existing shape. This will add a linked shape instance of the master for each selected row in the **External Data** window, as shown in the following screenshot:

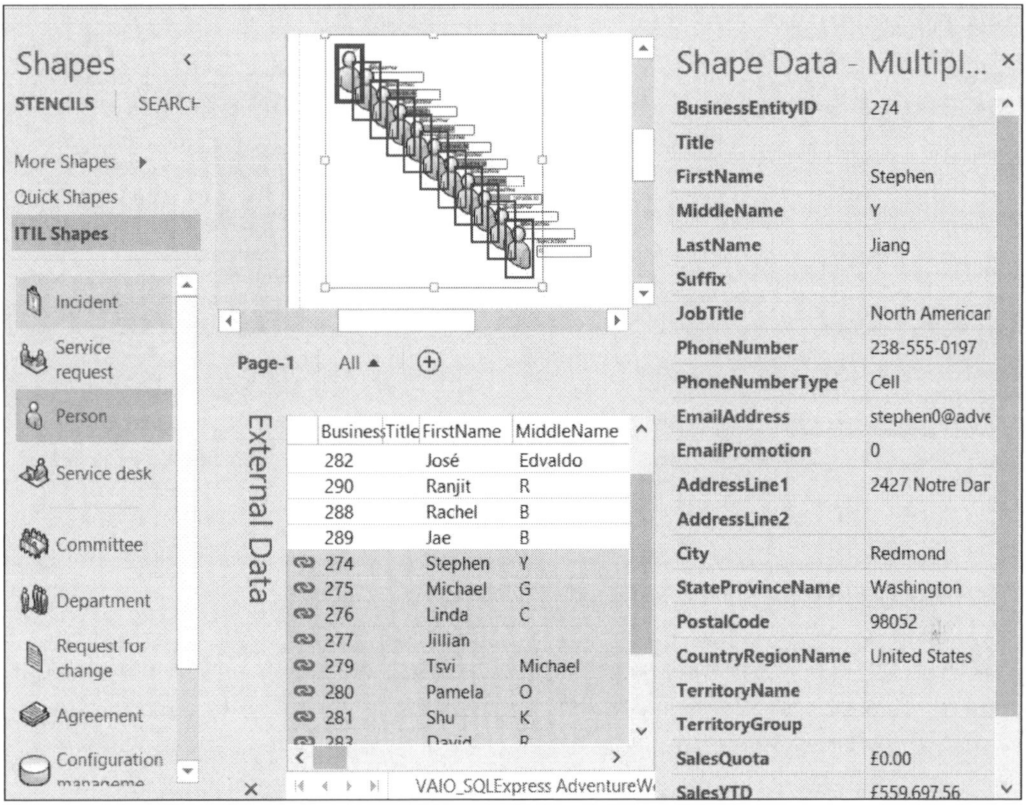


This operation is often done because a different master is required for different rows in the recordset, but it can end up with many shapes on top of each other, as shown in the previous example.

Automation can arrange the dropped shapes in an ordered manner, and it can apply suitable Data Graphics at the same time.

# Linking data to shapes automatically

One automatic method for linking data to shapes was used earlier in this chapter, with the `ImportPersonnelFromExcel()` sub-function when the existing `Name` Shape Data value on a shape was matched to the **Name** column in the data recordset.

## Linking shapes to a single data row

If a single `Shape` or `Selection` is referenced in code, and the ID of a row in a `DataRecordset`, then the `Shape.LinkToData(..)` method is used. There are three parameters for this method, as listed in the following table:

| Name | Required/ Optional | Data Type | Description |
|---|---|---|---|
| `DataRecordsetID` | Required | Long | This is the ID of the data recordset containing the data to link to. |
| `RowID` | Required | Long | This is the ID of the row in the data recordset containing the particular data record to link to. |
| `AutoApplyDataGraphics` | Optional | Boolean | This takes care of whether to automatically apply a data graphic to the linked shapes. |

## Linking multiple shapes to separate data rows

If many shapes are available in code, then they can each be linked to separate rows of data in the `DataRecordset` using the `Page.LinkShapesToDataRows(...)` method. This method has four parameters, with an optional fifth for Data Graphics:

| Name | Required/ Optional | Data Type | Description |
|---|---|---|---|
| `DataRecordsetID` | Required | Long | This is the ID of a data recordset contained in the current document, which contains the data to link to. |

| Name | Required/ Optional | Data Type | Description |
|---|---|---|---|
| `DataRowIDs()` | Required | Long | An array of type Long of data row IDs of rows in the data recordset specified in `DataRecordsetID` to be linked to the shapes specified in `ShapeIDs()`. |
| `ShapeIDs()` | Required | Long | An array of type Long of shape IDs of shapes on the page to be linked to the data rows specified in `DataRowIDs()` in the data recordset specified in `DataRecordsetID`. |
| `ApplyDataGraphicAfterLink` | Optional | Boolean | This takes care of whether to apply the current data graphic to the linked shapes. |

## Linking a new shape to a data row

It is often necessary to drop a new shape onto a page and to link it to a specific row of data. This can be done with the `Page.DropLinked(...)` method, which has the following six parameters:

| Name | Required/ Optional | Data Type | Description |
|---|---|---|---|
| `ObjectToDrop` | Required | [UNKNOWN] | This is the object that is to be dropped. While this is typically a Visio object, such as a Master, Shape, or Selection object, it can be any OLE object that provides an `IDataObject` interface. |

| Name | Required/ Optional | Data Type | Description |
|---|---|---|---|
| `x` | Required | Double | This is the *x* coordinate at which to place the center of the shape's width or `PinX`. |
| `y` | Required | Double | This is the *y* coordinate at which to place the center of the shape's height or `PinY`. |
| `DataRecordsetID` | Required | Long | This is the ID of the data recordset that contains the data to link to. |
| `DataRowID` | Required | Long | This is the ID of the data row that contains the data to link to. |
| `ApplyDataGraphicAfterLink` | Required | Boolean | This takes care of whether to apply the current data graphic to the linked shape. The default is not to apply a data graphic. |

As an example, the following `DropLinkAPerson()` VBA sub-function will find the row for a `Michael Blythe` in the data recordset named `Data From ODC`. It will link this row to a new **Person** shape that is dropped at the *x, y* coordinate 2,2 on the page. If there happens to be more than one `Michael Blythe`, then there will be multiple shapes spaced out horizontally:

```
Public Sub DropLinkAPerson()

Dim doc As Visio.Document
Set doc = Visio.ActiveDocument

Dim pag As Visio.Page
Set pag = Visio.ActivePage
```

```
Dim shp As Visio.Shape
Dim mst As Visio.Master
Dim dX As Double
Dim dY As Double
Dim drs As Visio.DataRecordset
'Assume that the recordset exists in the document
For Each drs In doc.DataRecordsets
    If drs.Name = "Data from ODC" Then
        Exit For
    End If
Next
'Assume this master exists in the document
Set mst = doc.Masters("Person")

Dim rowIDs() As Long
Dim lRow As Long
Dim criteria As String

criteria = "[FirstName] = 'Michael' AND [LastName] = 'Blythe'"
'Get the row IDs of all the rows in the data recordset
rowIDs = drs.GetDataRowIDs(criteria)

'Iterate through all the records in the data recordset.
For lRow = LBound(rowIDs) To UBound(rowIDs)
    'Increment position if more than one row matches
    dX = 2 + (lRow * mst.Shapes(1).Cells("Width").ResultIU)
    dY = 2
    Set shp = pag.DropLinked(mst, dX, dY, drs.ID, rowIDs(lRow), True)
Next lRow

End Sub
```

When the code is run on a page in a document where the `Person` master and the **Data from ODC** data recordset exits, then a `Person` shape is added to the page, already linked to the data row. In the following screenshot, the shape is dropped 2 inches across and up from the bottom-left corner of the page:

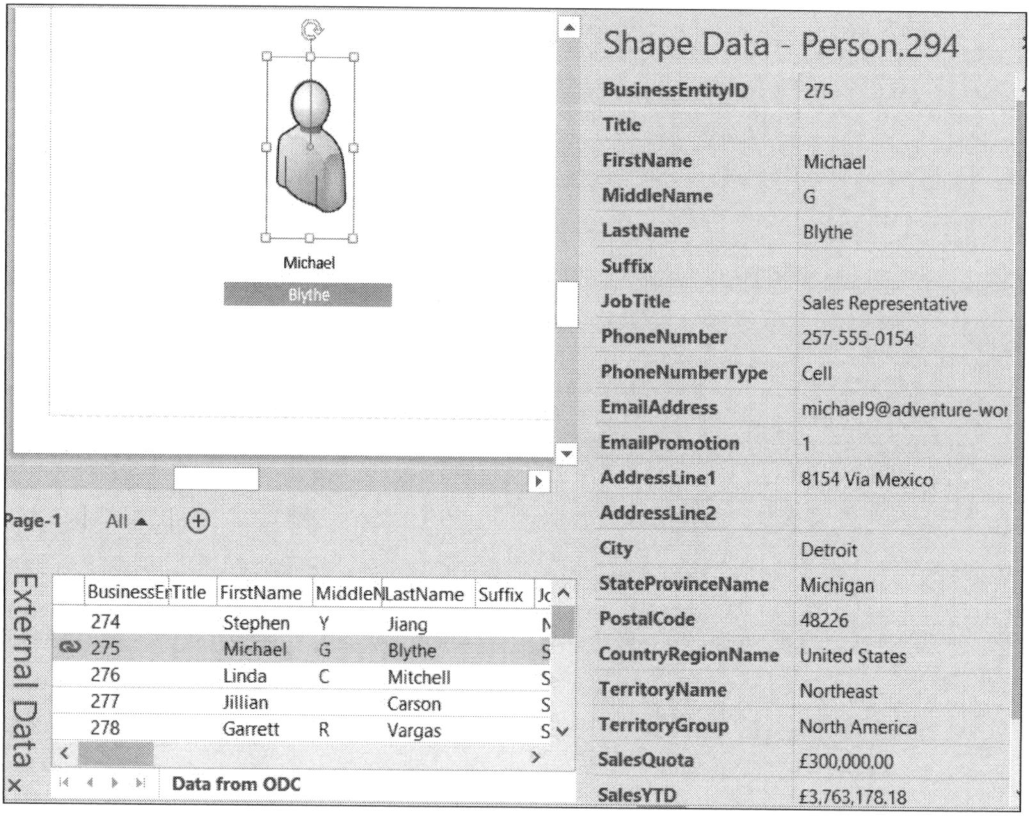


## Linking multiple new shapes to data rows

There is also a `Page.DropManyLinkedU(...)` method, which provides the ability to drop and link multiple shapes in one action. This is more efficient than walking from each one to drop and link them individually. This method takes the following six parameters:

| Name | Required/ Optional | Data Type | Description |
|---|---|---|---|
| `ObjectsToInstance()` | Required | Variant | This is an array of type Variant of objects to create instances of. |

| Name | Required/ Optional | Data Type | Description |
|---|---|---|---|
| `XYs()` | Required | Double | This is an array of the type Double. |
| `DataRecordsetID` | Required | Long | This is the ID of the data recordset containing the data rows to link to. |
| `DataRowIDs()` | Required | Long | This is an array of the type Long of IDs of the data rows, containing the data to link to. |
| `ApplyDataGraphicAfterLink` | Required | Boolean | This deals with whether to apply the current data graphic to the linked shapes. |
| `ShapeIDs()` | Required | Long | This is the out parameter; an array of type Long of shapes created and linked to. |

The following example of the `DropLinkUSPersonnel()` VBA function will find all of the personnel from the United States in the `Data from ODC` data recordset and drop a linked shape for each row horizontally across the page:

```
Public Sub DropLinkUSPersonnel()
Dim doc As Visio.Document
Set doc = Visio.ActiveDocument

Dim pag As Visio.Page
Set pag = Visio.ActivePage

Dim shp As Visio.Shape
Dim mst As Visio.Master
Dim dX As Double
Dim dY As Double
Dim drs As Visio.DataRecordset
'Assume that the recordset exists in the document
For Each drs In doc.DataRecordsets
    If drs.Name = "Data from ODC" Then
        Exit For
    End If
Next
```

```
'Assume this master exists in the document
Set mst = doc.Masters("Person")

Dim rowIDs() As Long
Dim lRow As Long
Dim criteria As String

criteria = "[CountryRegionName] = 'United States'"
'Get the row IDs of all the rows in the data recordset
rowIDs = drs.GetDataRowIDs(criteria)

Dim avObjects() As Variant
Dim adXYs() As Double
Dim alDataRowIDs() As Long

ReDim avObjects(LBound(rowIDs) To UBound(rowIDs))
ReDim adXYs(LBound(rowIDs) To ((2 * UBound(rowIDs)) + 1))
ReDim alDataRowIDs(LBound(rowIDs) To UBound(rowIDs))

'Iterate through all the records in the data recordset.
For lRow = LBound(rowIDs) To UBound(rowIDs)
    avObjects(lRow) = mst
    'Increment position if more than one row matches
    adXYs(lRow * 2) = 2 + _
        (lRow * mst.Shapes(1).Cells("Width").ResultIU)
    adXYs((lRow * 2) + 1) = 2
    alDataRowIDs(lRow) = rowIDs(lRow)
Next lRow

Dim alShapeIDs() As Long
Dim lReturned As Long
lReturned = pag.DropManyLinkedU(avObjects, adXYs, _
    drs.ID, alDataRowIDs, True, alShapeIDs)

End Sub
```

Each shape has its own link back to the data recordset, as shown in the following screenshot:

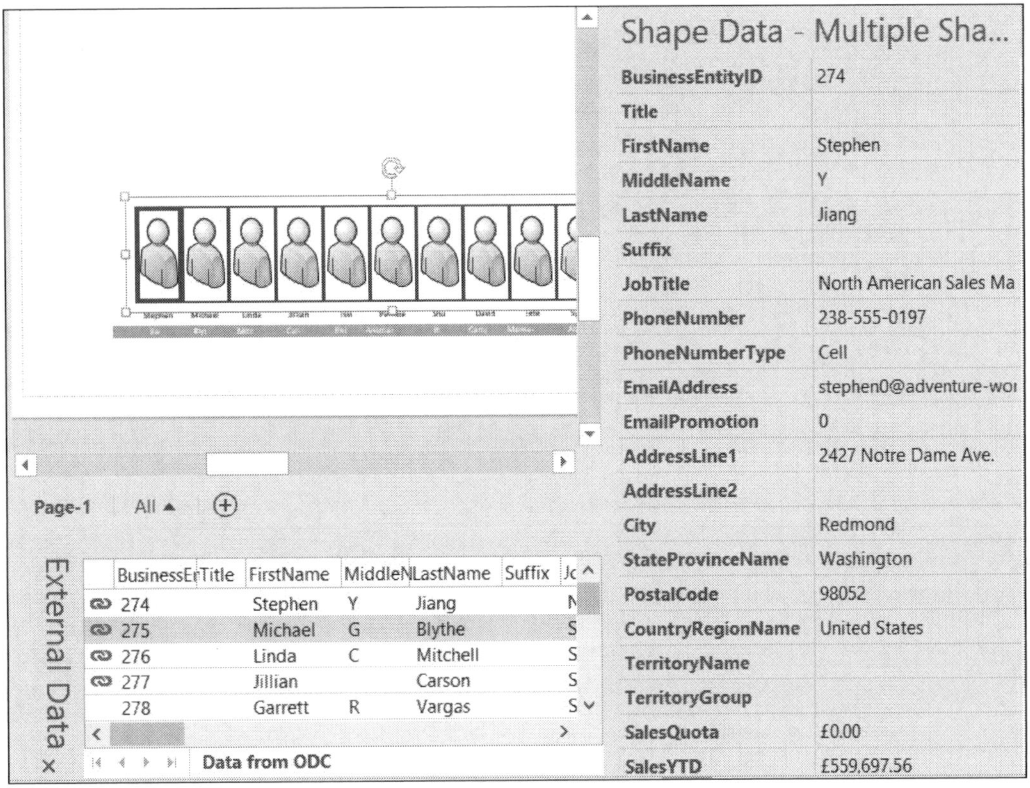


# Summary

This chapter has gone through the many different sources for importing data into Visio and has shown how each can be done manually or with code. This was followed by examples of linking rows of this data to shapes on the drawing page (again, manually and in code).

The next chapter will go into more detail about displaying this data on the shapes using the Data Graphics feature, whether it be simple text, icons, data bars, or color by value.

# 4
# Using the Built-In Data Graphics

The previous chapter presented the different sources that can be used to import data into Visio Professional documents, and then how rows of data can be linked to shapes. This data surfaced as Data Graphics in many cases without any explanation of this feature. So, this chapter will discuss all the different Data Graphics items that are provided with Visio Professional.

**Data Graphics** make data diagrams alive with information because they are automatically updated when the data they are linked to changes. They turn a static picture into an information dashboard that can used to present operational intelligence accurately.

In this chapter, we shall cover the following topics:

- Understanding the different Data Graphics types:
    - Text Callout
    - Icon Set
    - Data Bar
    - Color By Value
- Configuring Data Graphics quickly
- Using the advanced configuration of Data Graphics
- Learning how to insert and edit Legends

# Displaying data with graphics

The following screenshot from Visio Professional 2016 shows default **Data Graphics** being applied to a simple rectangle when the row from the **External Data** window is dragged and dropped on to it:

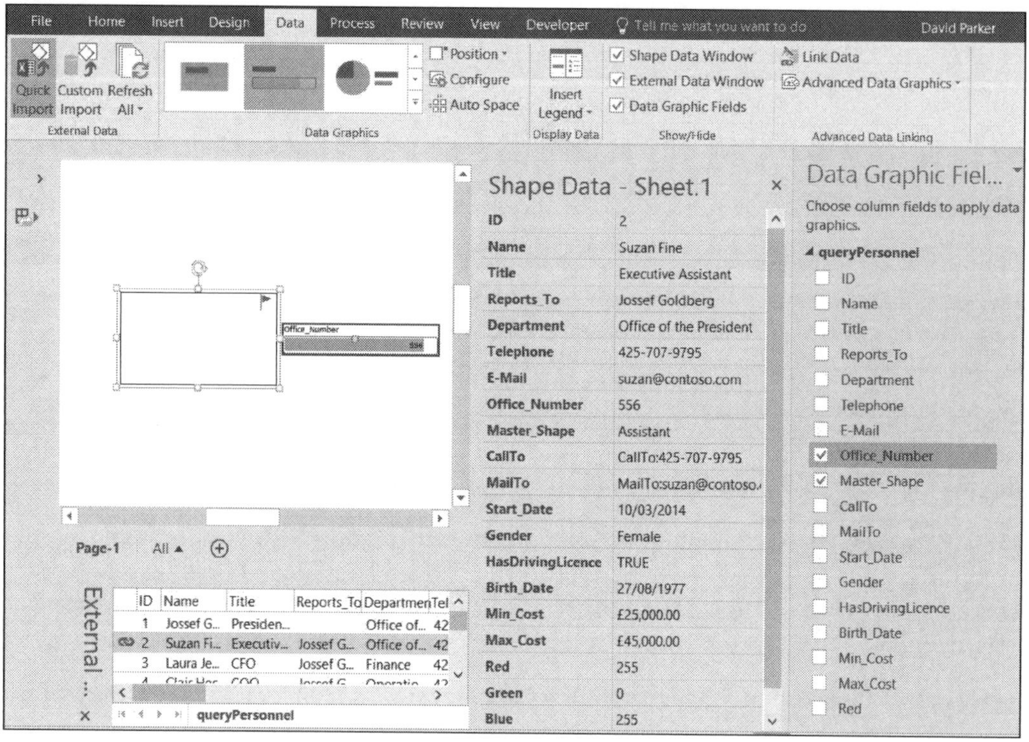


Visio Professional 2016 added the **Data Graphics** group to the **Data** ribbon tab. Apart from the **Auto Space** button, everything on this ribbon group has been available in all Professional (and Premium) editions since Visio 2007 on the **Data Graphics** button. This button has now been renamed **Advanced Data Graphics**, made smaller, and pushed into the **Advanced Data Linking** group.

The **Data Graphic Fields** panel, on the far right in the previous screenshot, is also new in Visio 2016. It lists all of the visible `DataRecordsets` that are in the document, with a checkable list of each visible field/column.

The **Data Graphics** drop-down gallery, also new in Visio 2016, provides the ability to easily apply a graphic item from one of the four types, as shown in the following screenshot, to the selected **Data Graphic Field**:

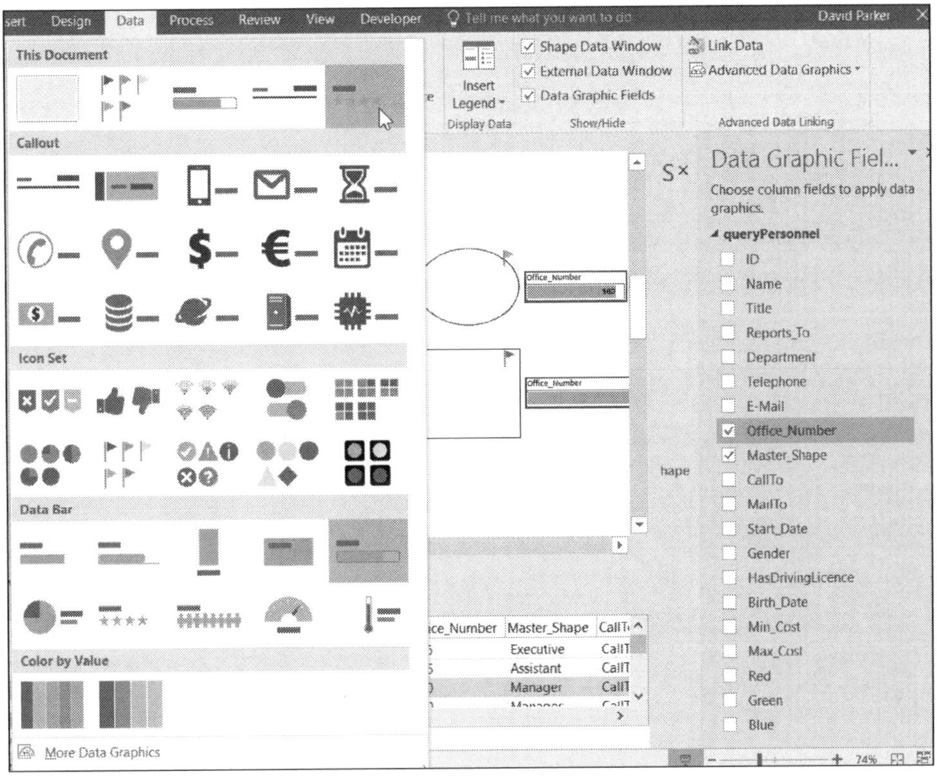


The gallery does not present all of the possible styles of each type. The full choice is made available by the **Configure** button.

# Changing the position of a graphic item

A graphic item can be located in one of 49 different positions in and around each shape. The positions can range from **Above shape, left** to **Top, right**. The **Position** dropdown provides quick access to six variations, and further dropdowns are available for all of the **Horizontal** and **Vertical** positions, as shown in the following screenshot:

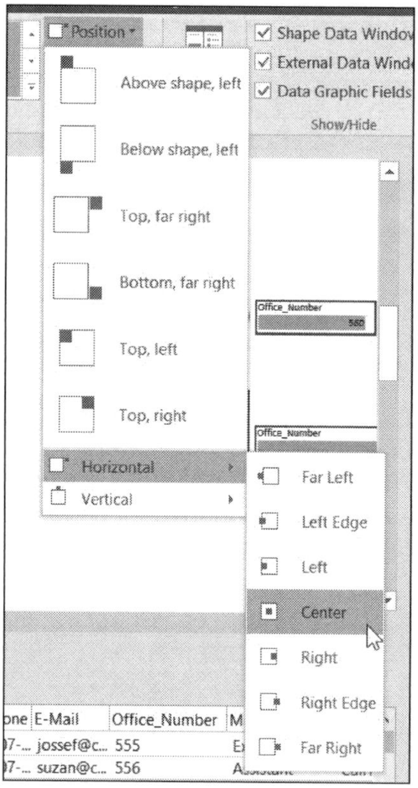


The position can also be changed using the **Configure** button.

# Configuring the graphic item

The position of a graphic item can also be changed in the **Edit Item** dialog that can be opened with the **Data** | **Data Graphics** | **Configure** button. This dialog also allows the type and style of the graphic item to be changed, and for more configuration of the item, as shown in the following screenshot:

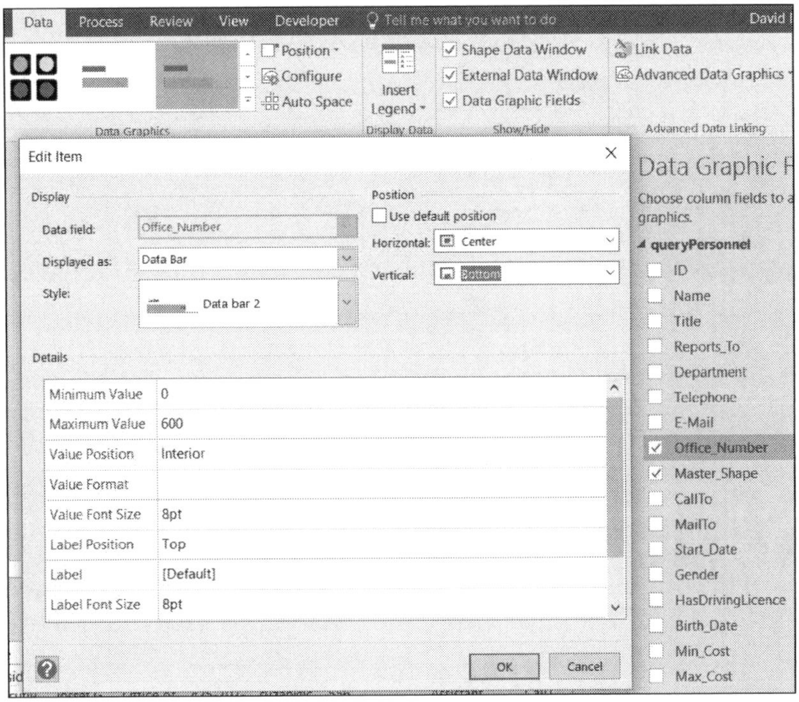


Notice that the **Data field** dropdown is disabled in this screenshot. This is because the **Edit Item** dialog was opened from the **Data** | **Data Graphics** | **Configure** button for a ticked **Data Graphic Field**.

# Using the Advanced Data Graphics dialog

The **Advanced Data Graphics** drop-down gallery provides the ability to create and edit Data Graphics, or apply them to or remove them from selected shapes:

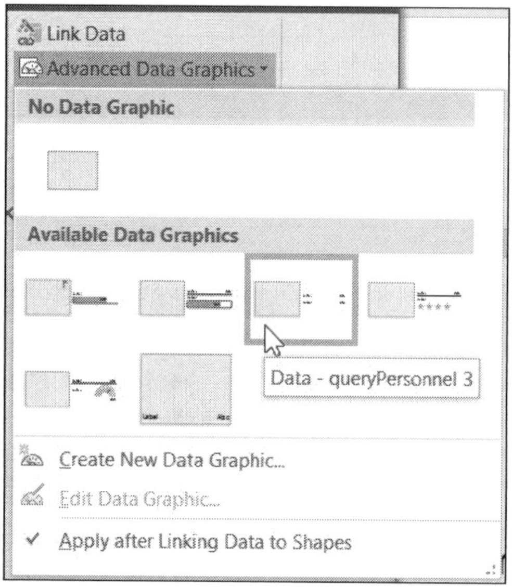


Notice that the tooltip for each of the **Available Data Graphics** displays a name. This is the name of the Data Graphic Master, and it can be edited by the **Rename...** option in the right-click menu of each item, as shown on the following screenshot:

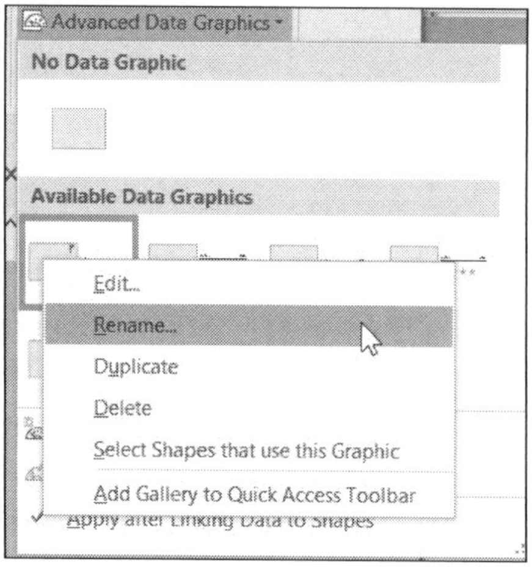


This right-click menu also provides options to **Edit...**, **Duplicate**, **Delete**, and **Select Shapes that use this Graphic**.

# Understanding the Graphic Item types

A Data Graphics is a collection of graphic items with specific configurations. The graphic items are each one of four types, Text Callout, Icon Set, Data Bar, or Color By Value. There can be multiple instances of the first three types simultaneously, but there can be only one active Color By Value.

> Take a look at the following article to get a stencil for each type: `http://blog.bvisual.net/2015/12/24/using-visio-professional-2016-text-callouts-icon-sets-and-data-bars-to-display-data-directly/`

# Using Text Callouts

Visio 2016 introduced some new Text Callouts that include an icon along with the text. This has caused a new setting to be added called **Show Value**, which gives the option to make the text value invisible. There are a number of these new styles available, as seen in the following screenshot:

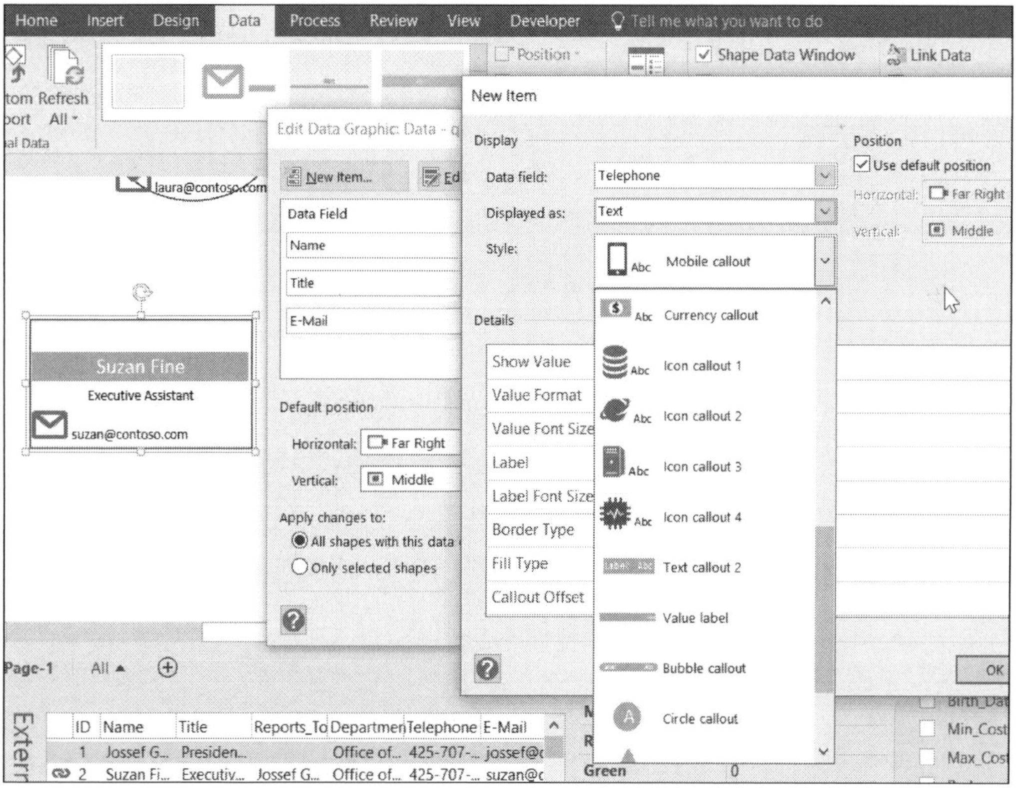

There are a number of configuration settings available for Text Callouts; they are listed in the following table:

| Setting | Comment |
|---|---|
| **Show Value** | Select from **Yes** or **No**. |
| **Value Format** | Enter a format string, or select via the **Data Format** dialog opened with button. |
| **Value Font Size** | The default is **8 pt**. |
| **Label Position** | Select from **Not Shown**, **Above**, and **Below Value**. |
| **Label** | The default will use the **Shape Data** label, or you can enter any other text. |
| **Label Font Size** | The default is **8 pt**. |
| **Border Type** | Select from **None**, **Bottom**, and **Outline**. |
| **Fill Type** | Select from **None** and **Filled**. |
| **Callout Offset** | Select from **Left**, **None**, and **Right**. |
| **Callout Width** | The default is **0**, which refers to the width of the shape. You can use units such as in, mm, or pt. |

The following screenshot displays each of the built-in Text Callouts:

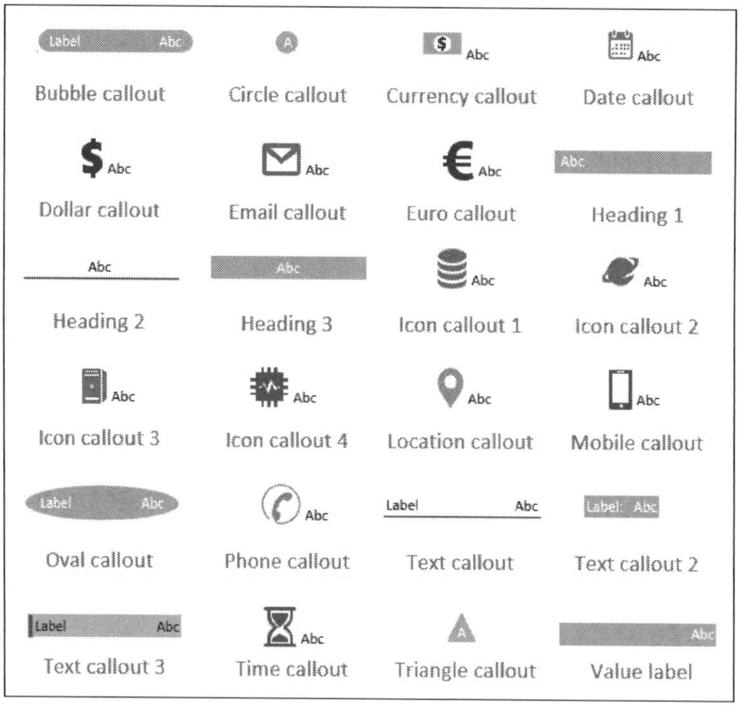

# Using Icon Sets

There are a number of Icon Sets provided, and all but one have five different icons available to match the specified criteria. The following screenshot shows how the rules for an Icon Set can be edited to match an icon with criteria:

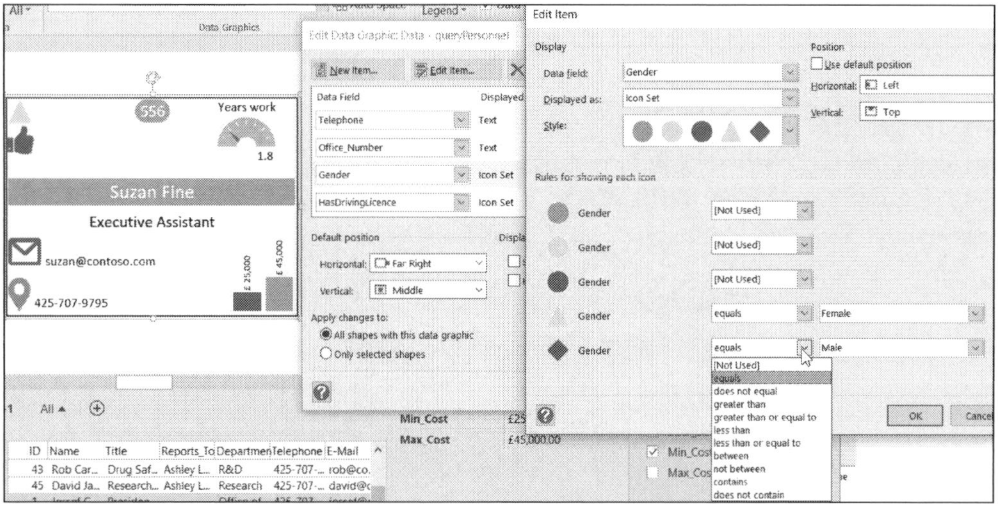


The following screenshot lists the different icons within each Icon Set:

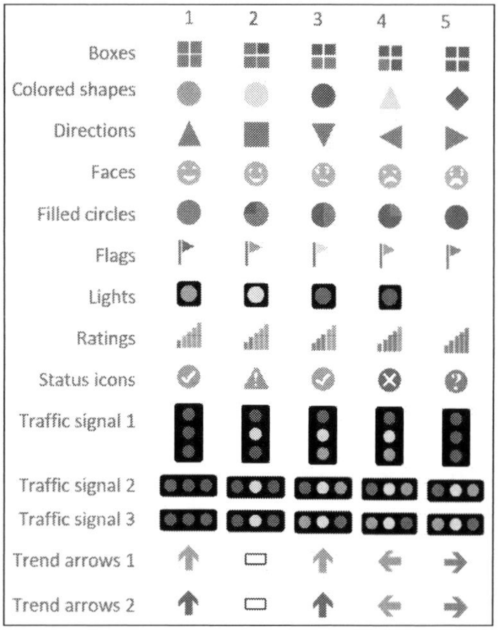

Notice that **Lights** has only four icons available.

> Take a look at the following article to learn how to add a sixth default icon: `http://blog.bvisual.net/2012/04/11/how-to-have-six-icons-in-a-visio-data-graphic-icon-set/`

# Using Data Bars

The **Data Bar** type is particularly useful for numeric values because it can display the relative quantity between a **Minimum Value** and **Maximum Value**, as shown in the following screenshot:

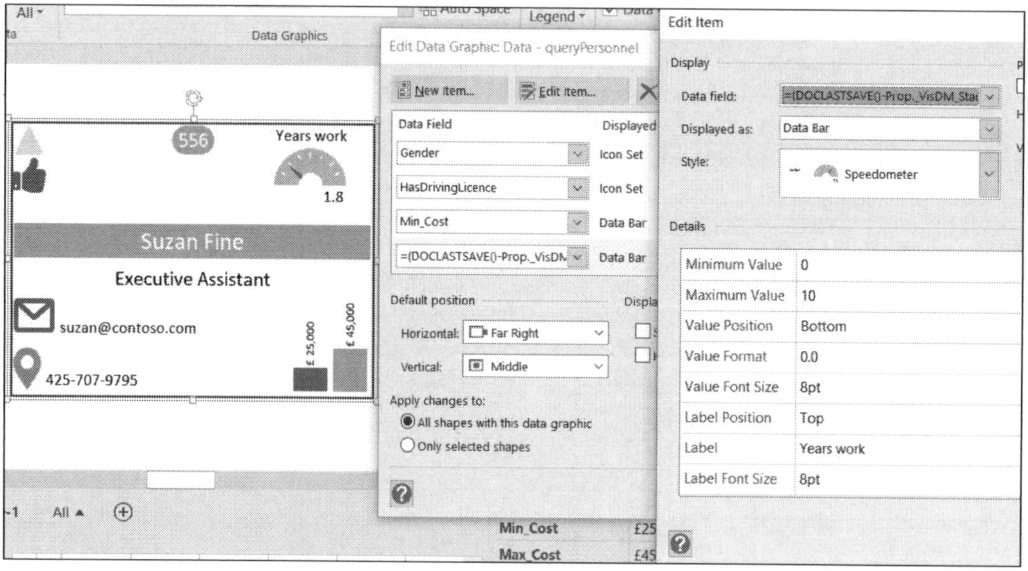


Notice that the `= (DOCLASTSAVE () -Prop._VisDM_Start_Date)/365 ed` formula has been used to calculate the number of years that each person has been with the organization.

There are a number of different styles; some are horizontal, some are vertical, and three allow up to five different shape data row values to be displayed in the same graphic, as displayed in the following screenshot:

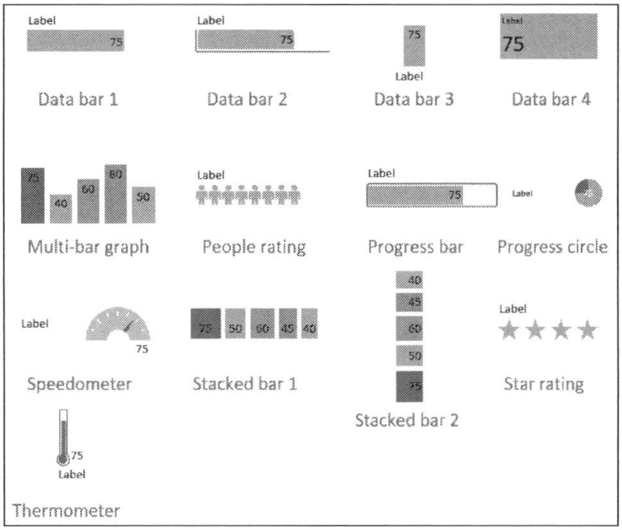


The following table lists the settings that can be configured for each Data Bar:

| Setting | Comment |
|---|---|
| **Minimum Value** | The default is **0**. |
| **Maximum Value** | The default is **100**, but enter at least the maximum value expected. |
| **Value Format** | Enter a format string, or select via the **Data Format** dialog opened with button. |
| **Value Font Size** | The default is **8 pt**. |
| **Label Position** | Select from **Not Shown**, **Top**, **Bottom**, **Interior**, and **Interior-Rotated**. |
| **Label** | By default, this will use the **Shape Data** label, or you can enter any other text. |
| **Label Font Size** | The default is **8 pt**. |
| **Value Position** | Select from **Not Shown**, **Top**, **Bottom**, and **Bottom-Rotated**. |
| **Callout Offset** | Select from **Left**, **None**, and **Right** to provide a slight offset. |
| **Callout Width** | This is only for horizontal oriented databars. The default is **0**, which refers to the width of the shape. It can use units such as in, mm, or pt. |
| **Callout Height** | This only for vertical oriented data-bars. The default is **0**, which refers to the height of the shape. It can use units such as in, mm, or pt. |
| **Label 1** | This is applicable to multi-data types. By default, it will use the **Shape Data** label, or you can enter any other text. |
| **Field 2 ( to 5)** | This is applicable to multi-data types. The default is **[Not Used]**, but select any other data row, or enter a formula via **More fields...**. |
| **Label 2 ( to 5)** | This is applicable to multi-data types. By default, it will use the **Shape Data** label, or you can enter any other text. |

# Applying Color By Value

The Color by Value type is different from the others because it is achieved purely by setting the formulas in a few ShapeSheet cells. After a **Data field** is set, and the **Displayed as** value is changed to **Color by Value**, then **Color assignments** are proposed for each of the distinct values in the `DataRecordset`, as shown in the following screenshot:

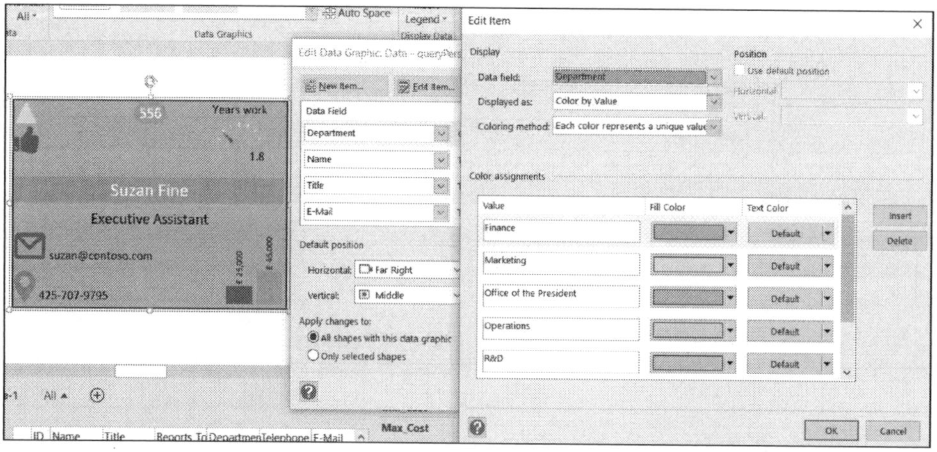


If there is no `DataRecordset` associated with the selected shapes, then it may be necessary to type in all of the matching values.

There are 16 different **Fill Colors** proposed, so they will be reused if there are more values. However, these colors are usually not the most desirable ones, so editing is normally required. The **Text Color** value can also be customized if required.

If the selected **Data field** is of a numeric or datetime data type, then there is a second coloring method available, as shown in the following screenshot:

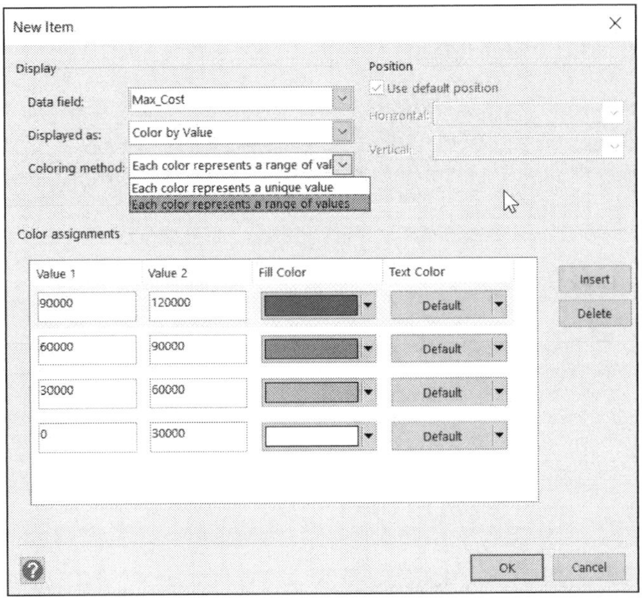


This allows ranges to be redefined, and within them a specified color will be applied.

A Data Graphic Master can have more than one Color By Value setting configured, as shown in the following screenshot, but only the first Color by Value setting will be applied to the shapes. The up and down arrows can be used to change the order of the graphic items:

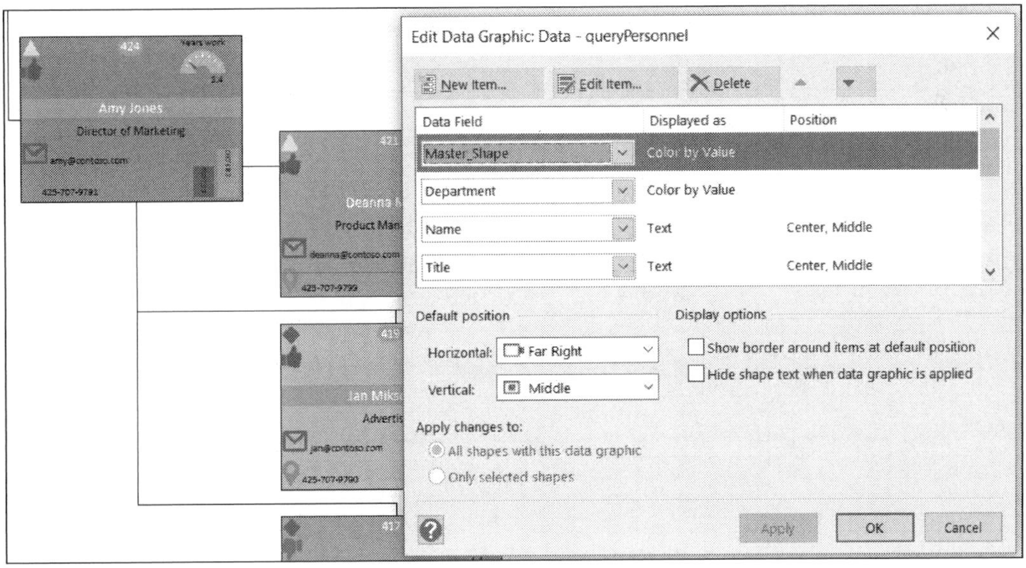

The position of any graphic item can be changed with the up and down arrows on the **Edit Data Graphic: Data** dialog.

Since the Color By Value type always lists the unique values in the dialog, it can be useful to switch the **Displayed as** setting temporarily in order to check on these values. This is especially useful when trying to remember the text to match for the icons.

# Adding a legend

Once Data Graphics have been applied to the shapes, it can be difficult to remember the meaning of the different colors, icons, and data bars, as shown in this following screenshot:

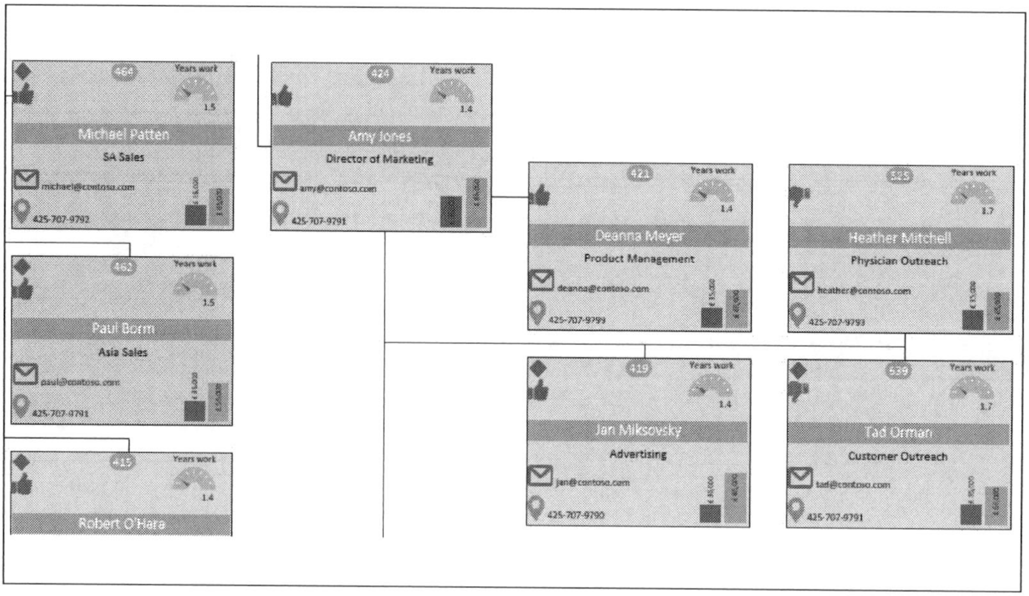


Fortunately, Visio Professional provides a **Data | Display Data | Insert Legend** function that will drop a legend, built either horizontally or vertically, in the top-right corner of the page, as shown in the following screenshot:

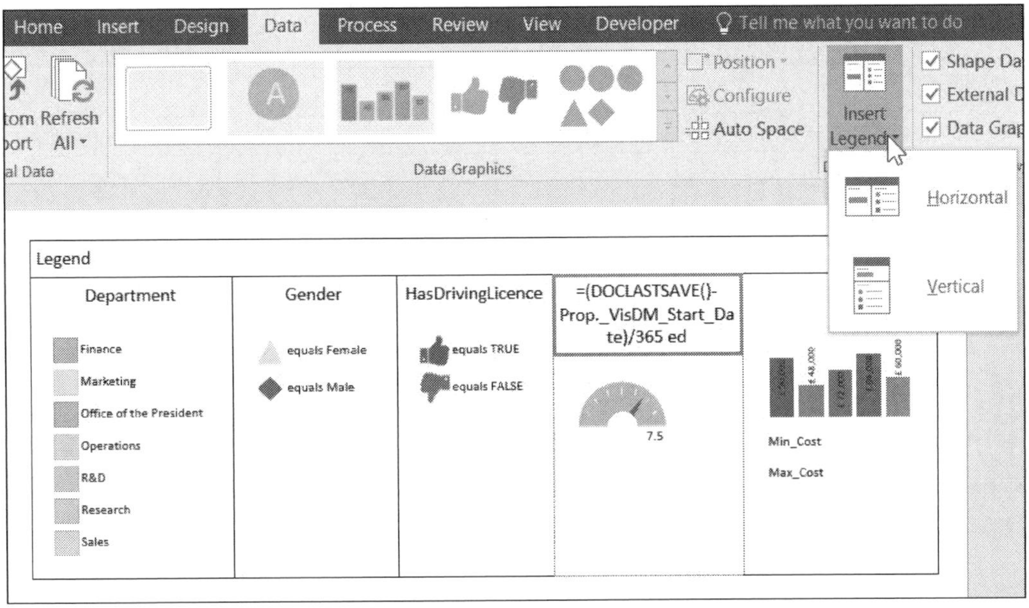


Once the legend has been dropped onto the page, it can be edited to make the headings and text more readable. In fact, the legend is a special list shape, so through it, each list item could be moved or deleted easily.

> Take a look at the following article about the legend with multi-data graphic items: `http://blog.bvisual.net/2015/12/24/improving-the-legend-of-multi-data-data-graphic-items-in-visio`

# Analyzing the composition of a Data Graphic

A Data Graphic is actually stored as a special type of `Master` in a stencil. The `Master` contains a reference to each of the graphic items within it along with their configurations. The graphic items are also special masters, except for Color By Value, which is stored as a formula in user-defined cells.

The Data Graphic and Graphic Item masters do not appear in the **Document Stencil** list, but they are visible in the **Drawing Explorer** window, as can be seen in the following screenshot:

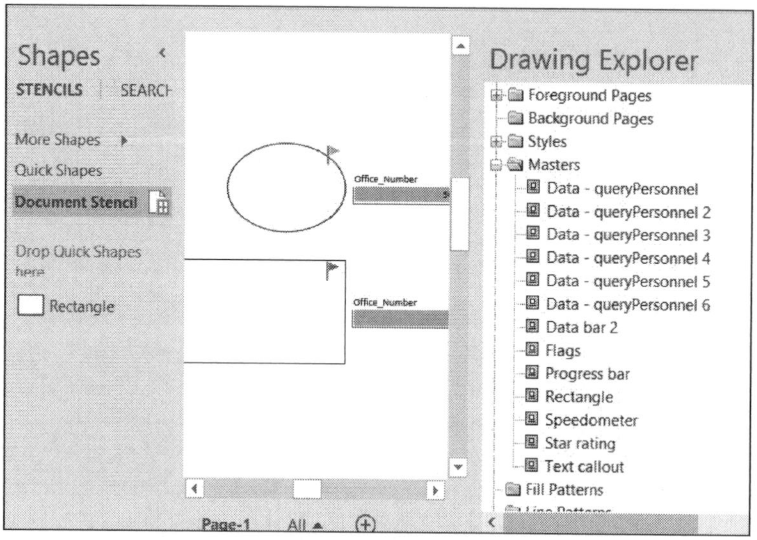


The following `ListDataGraphicMasters()` VBA macros simply produces a list of the data graphics in the active **Document Stencil**:

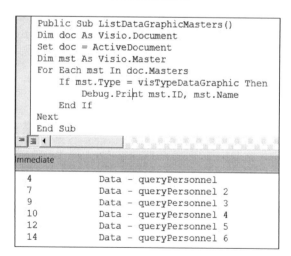

```
Public Sub ListDataGraphicMasters()
Dim doc As Visio.Document
Set doc = ActiveDocument
Dim mst As Visio.Master
For Each mst In doc.Masters
    If mst.Type = visTypeDataGraphic Then
        Debug.Print mst.ID, mst.Name
    End If
Next
End Sub
```

Immediate

```
4             Data - queryPersonnel
7             Data - queryPersonnel 2
9             Data - queryPersonnel 3
10            Data - queryPersonnel 4
12            Data - queryPersonnel 5
14            Data - queryPersonnel 6
```

Listing the graphic item masters is a bit more involved because the necessary information is stored in specific user-defined cells of the group shape. So, the `ListGraphicItemMasters()` VBA macro, which is displayed in the following screenshot, checks the contents of the `User.msvCalloutType` cell, if it exists:

```
Public Sub ListGraphicItemMasters()
Dim doc As Visio.Document
Set doc = ActiveDocument
Dim mst As Visio.Master
Dim shp As Visio.Shape

For Each mst In doc.Masters
    Set shp = mst.Shapes(1)
    If shp.CellExists("User.msvCalloutType", _
        VisExistsFlags.visExistsAnywhere) <> 0 Then
        Debug.Print mst.ID, _
            shp.Cells("User.msvCalloutType").ResultStr(""), _
            mst.Name
    End If
Next
End Sub
```

```
Immediate
5           Data Bar      Progress bar
6           Icon Set      Flags
8           Text Callout  Text callout
11          Data Bar      Star rating
13          Data Bar      Speedometer
28          Data Bar      Data bar 2
```

A Data Graphic Master is a collection of Graphic Item Masters, so the `ListDataGraphicMastersAndItems()` VBA macro displayed in the following screenshot also lists the graphic items:

```
Public Sub ListDataGraphicMastersAndItems()
Dim doc As Visio.Document
Set doc = ActiveDocument
Dim mst As Visio.Master
Dim shp As Visio.Shape

For Each mst In doc.Masters
    If mst.Type = visTypeDataGraphic Then
        Debug.Print mst.ID, mst.Name
        For Each shp In mst.Shapes(1).Shapes
            If shp.CellExists("User.msvCalloutType", _
                VisExistsFlags.visExistsAnywhere) <> 0 Then
                Debug.Print , shp.ID, _
                    shp.Cells("User.msvCalloutType").Formula, _
                    shp.Cells("User.visDGUseMaster").Formula
            End If
        Next
    End If
Next
End Sub
```

```
Immediate
4             Data - queryPersonnel
               11            "Data Bar"    USE("Data bar 2")
               9             "Icon Set"    USE("Flags")
7             Data - queryPersonnel 2
               6             "Data Bar"    USE("Progress bar")
               9             "Text Callout"              USE("Text callout")
9             Data - queryPersonnel 3
               6             "Text Callout"              USE("Text callout")
               8             "Text Callout"              USE("Text callout")
10            Data - queryPersonnel 4
```

When a Data Graphic is applied to a shape, then the configuration is used to insert the Graphic Item shapes into the target shape. Therefore, using Data Graphics will convert a shape into a group shape, if it is not one already. Consequently, it is advisable to ensure that master shapes are groups already, as we will see in *Chapter 6, Creating Custom Master Shapes*.

# Summary

In this chapter, you learned about the different types and styles of Data Graphics that are available out of the box in Visio Professional 2016. We have seen that most Graphic Items are configurable, and that they are inserted in shapes when Data Graphics are applied.

We have seen how Data Graphics can turn a static diagram into an operational intelligence dashboard.

In the next chapter, you will learn how the Pivot Diagram can be used to form the structure of a visual data diagram.

# 5

# Using the Pivot Diagram Add-On

Most Microsoft Excel users are familiar with Pivot Tables and Pivot Charts. These features provide the ability to group and aggregate data numerically and visually. Visio provides a similar ability with the Pivot Diagram add-on, through which data can be grouped and aggregated with connected shapes. The shapes can then be enhanced with Data Graphics to provide a rich representation of the information in them.

The Pivot Diagram is an add-on, so there is no programmable interface for it, but it does provide a nice way of producing a breakdown diagram. It shares some features with the Link Data feature and can optionally be mashed together with it, thus turning it into a semi-refreshable information dashboard.

In this chapter, we shall cover the following topics:

- Learning how to use the Pivot Diagram add-on
- Configuring the diagrams
- Understanding how to overlay data using Link Data

# Choosing a data source

A Pivot Diagram can be started from the **Business** | **PivotDiagram** template or from the **Insert PivotDiagram** ribbon button, which can be added using the **Customize the Ribbon...** tool. The **Data Selector** dialog that is presented is almost identical to the one opened by **Data** | **Custom Import**, except for the additional **Microsoft SQL Server Analysis Services** option, as seen in the following screenshot:

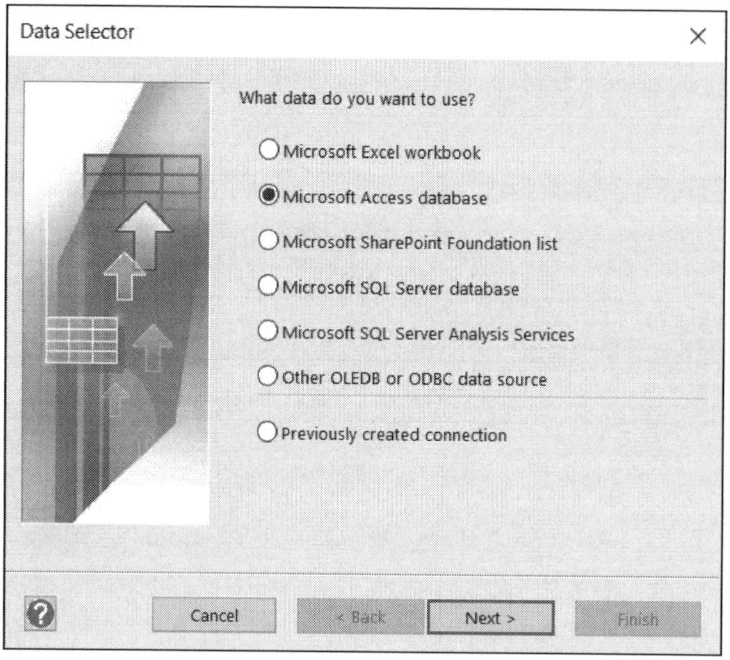


The `queryPersonnel` query from the Microsoft Access database, `OrgData.accdb`, that was used in *Chapter 3, Linking Data to Shapes*, has been used for the following example. The next screenshot demonstrates how any numerical and date columns are automatically presented as options in the **Add Total** box in the **PivotDiagram** window:

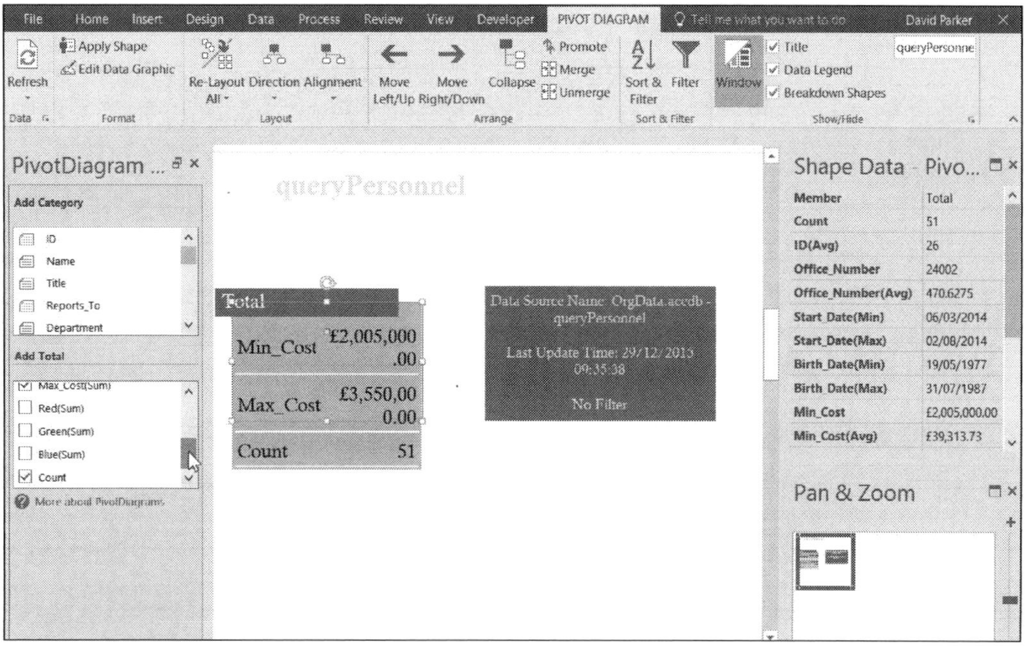


Ticking and unticking columns in the **Add Total** box will cause the Data Graphics on the **Total** shape to change. This shape is actually an instance of a master called **Pivot Node**, which is present in the document stencil.

The add-on has its own ribbon tab labeled **PIVOT DIAGRAM**, as can be seen in the previous screenshot. This provides access to many functions that are useful for working with this type of diagram.

The **Show/Hide** group on this ribbon tab enables the visibility of the **PivotDiagram** window, the **Title** text, the **Data Legend** shape, and the **Breakdown Shapes** to be toggled. In addition, the text for the **Title** text can be edited using the textbox on this ribbon group.

# Using SQL Server Analysis Services

Analysis Services is an online analytical data engine that is used in decision support and can be built as either an OLAP or tabular data model. The Pivot Diagram add-on can support either type of model, and the following screenshot shows the selection of a tabular model:

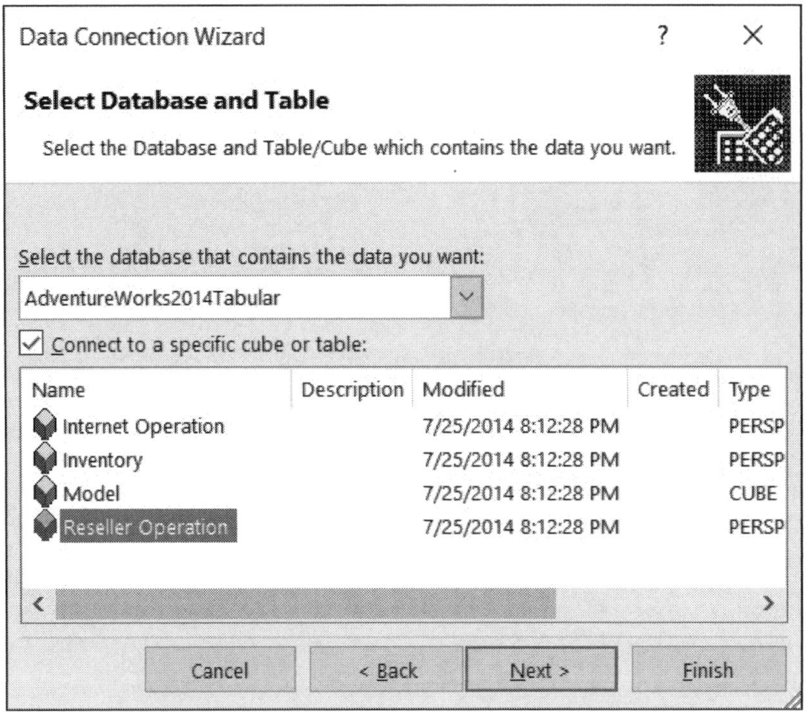


The Pivot Diagram add-on performs some similar types of computations and aggregations as Analysis Services, but it does this in the client. Therefore, it is good practice to have as much of the computation as possible in Analysis Services, and to filter the number of records required by the Visio Pivot Diagram add-on as much as possible.

# Looking behind the data

Running the `ListDataRecordsets()` function from *Chapter 2, Understanding How Data Is Stored within Visio*, would result in the following output:

```
Immediate
 1          queryPersonnel              SELECT distinct  COUNT(*) AS [Member],  COUNT(*) AS [Count],
            Provider=Microsoft.ACE.OLEDB.12.0;User ID=Admin;Data Source=C:\Users\David\SkyDrive\Docum

 1          True          2             Member          Member
 2          True          2             Count           Count
 3          True          2             ID(Avg)         ID(Avg)
 4          True          2             Office_Number  Office_Number
 5          True          2             Office_Number(Avg)             Office_Number(Avg)
 6          True          5             Start_Date(Min)                Start_Date(Min)
 7          True          5             Start_Date(Max)                Start_Date(Max)
 8          True          5             Birth_Date(Min)                Birth_Date(Min)
 9          True          5             Birth_Date(Max)                Birth_Date(Max)
 10         True          7             Min_Cost        Min_Cost
 11         True          7             Min_Cost(Avg)  Min_Cost(Avg)
 12         True          7             Max_Cost        Max_Cost
 13         True          7             Max_Cost(Avg)  Max_Cost(Avg)
 14         True          2             Red             Red
 15         True          2             Red(Avg)        Red(Avg)
 16         True          2             Green           Green
 17         True          2             Green(Avg)      Green(Avg)
 18         True          2             Blue            Blue
 19         True          2             Blue(Avg)       Blue(Avg)
```

This reveals that Pivot Diagram is using the same feature, but the `DataRecordsets` are not visible in the **External Data** window.

A closer look at the SQL statement that is automatically constructed by the add-on shows how the values are derived:

```
SELECT distinct
COUNT(*) AS [Member],
COUNT(*) AS [Count],
AVG([ID]) as [ID(Avg)],
SUM([Office_Number]) as [Office_Number],
AVG([Office_Number]) as [Office_Number(Avg)],
MIN([Start_Date]) as [Start_Date(Min)],
MAX([Start_Date]) as [Start_Date(Max)],
MIN([Birth_Date]) as [Birth_Date(Min)],
MAX([Birth_Date]) as [Birth_Date(Max)],
SUM([Min_Cost]) as [Min_Cost],
AVG([Min_Cost]) as [Min_Cost(Avg)],
SUM([Max_Cost]) as [Max_Cost],
AVG([Max_Cost]) as [Max_Cost(Avg)],
SUM([Red]) as [Red],
AVG([Red]) as [Red(Avg)],
SUM([Green]) as [Green],
AVG([Green]) as [Green(Avg)],
SUM([Blue]) as [Blue],
AVG([Blue]) as [Blue(Avg)]
FROM `queryPersonnel`
```

In fact, the first two `COUNT(*)` columns are always present, but the rest depend upon the types of data in the fields in the underlying table, query, or view.

In fact, there is no completely reliable method currently available for only listing Pivot Diagram recordsets, of which there may be many in a single diagram.

The `DataRecordset.RefreshSetting` is always equal to `VisRefreshSettings.visRefreshNoReconcilationUI`, and the `CommandString` always contains the phrase `AS [Member], COUNT(*) AS [Count]`. However, it is possible, though unlikely, that a non-Pivot Diagram `DataRecordset.CommandString` value contains the same phrase.

# Configuring the default Data Graphics

The Pivot Node shapes just use the normal Data Graphics features that were described in *Chapter 4*, *Using the Built-In Data Graphics*, so they can be configured in just the same way, as shown in the following screenshot:

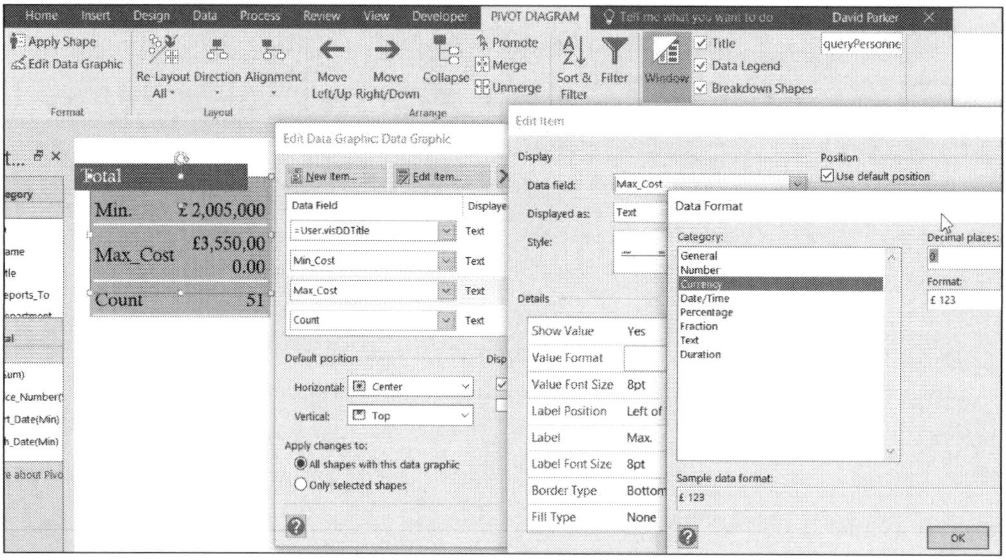


# Breaking down by category

Of course, it would be pretty pointless to just show a single shape on the page, and the Pivot Diagram add-on provides the ability to break down by a selected category from either the **Add Category** box on the **Pivot Diagram** window, or from the right-click menu option, **Add Category**, on a Pivot Node shape, as shown in the next screenshot:

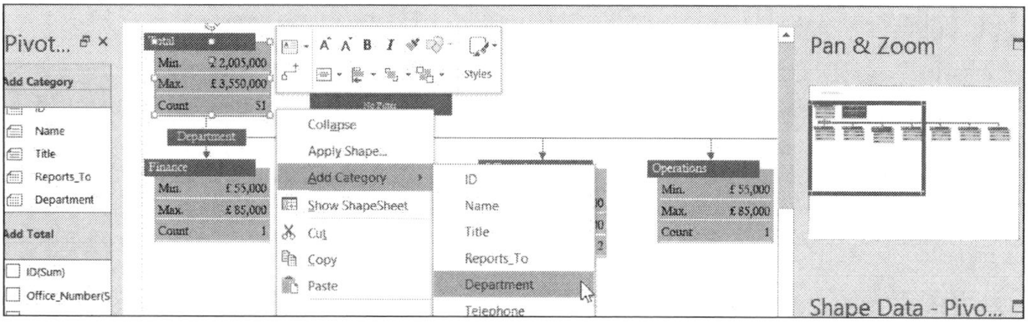


By default, a Pivot Breakdown shape labeled **Department** (in the screenshot) is added between the initial Pivot Node shape and the new Pivot Node shapes. These Breakdown Shapes can be hidden with the option on the **Show\Hide** group, but they also have a right-click menu option that can be useful.

The first option in this menu, **Collapse**, will remove the Breakdown Shape, the child Pivot Connector shapes, and the child Pivot Node shapes.

# Sorting Pivot Nodes

The second option, **Sort...**, on the right-click menu of the Breakdown Shapes, opens the **Breakdown Options** dialog. This can be used to sort the child nodes by a Shape Data row that is available from the drop-down list, as seen in the following screenshot:

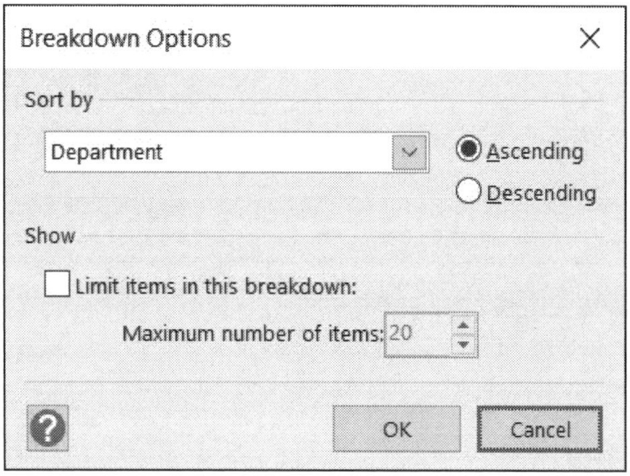


The Pivot Node shapes can also be moved using the **PIVOT DIAGRAM** | **Arrange** | **Move Left/Up** and **Move Right/Down** ribbon buttons.

# Editing Data Graphics of child nodes

The third option, **Edit Data Graphic...**, opens up the **Edit Data Graphic** dialog as described in *Chapter 4, Using the Built-In Data Graphics*. However, it only selects the child nodes of the Breakdown Shape. This can be useful because merely canceling this dialog, after it has opened, will leave them in the active selection. This can be very useful at times.

# Selecting Pivot Nodes

It is also often necessary to select Pivot Nodes that have the same `Member` value in the Shape Data row. The following VBA macro, `SelectSameMember()`, will cause Visio to select all the Pivot Node shapes in the active page that have the same `Member` value as the first one selected:

```
Public Sub SelectSameMember()
Dim shp As Visio.Shape
If ActiveWindow.Selection.Count = 0 Then Exit Sub
Set shp = ActiveWindow.Selection.PrimaryItem
If shp.CellExistsU("Prop._VisDM_Member", visExistsAnywhere) = 0 Then Exit Sub

Dim member As String
member = shp.Cells("Prop._VisDM_Member").ResultStr("")

Dim mst As Visio.Master
Set mst = ActiveDocument.Masters("Pivot Node")
Dim sel As Visio.Selection
Set sel = ActivePage.CreateSelection(visSelTypeByMaster, 0, mst)
Dim i As Integer
For i = sel.Count To 1 Step -1
    Set shp = sel(i)
    If member <> shp.Cells("Prop._VisDM_Member").ResultStr("") Then
        sel.Select shp, VisSelectArgs.visDeselect
    End If
Next

ActiveWindow.Selection = sel

End Sub
```

The code is almost self-explanatory, except, perhaps, for the need to loop backwards through the selection when deselecting some of them.

> Read more about selecting nodes in my article at `http://blog.bvisual.net/2012/07/11/selecting-nodes-in-visio-pivotdiagrams`.

# Configuring columns

The fourth and final right-click menu option, **Configure Column...**, opens the dialog shown in the next screenshot. The label for the Breakdown Shape can be edited here, as can a filter for the child shapes that are displayed:

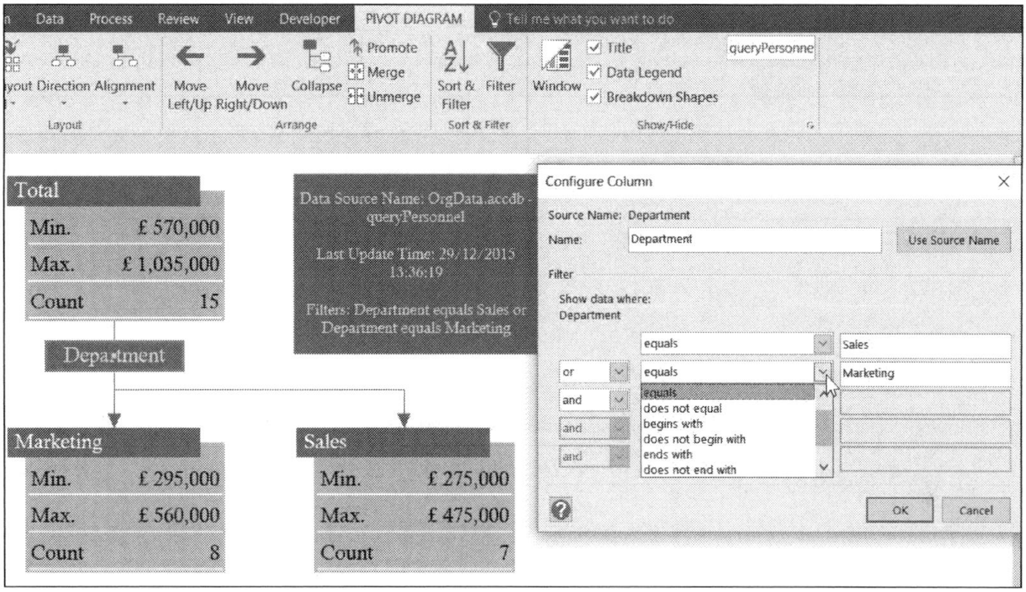


Behind the scenes, the `WHERE` clause of the SQL statement for the displayed filter is changed to the following:

```
WHERE ([Department] = 'Sales' OR [Department] = 'Marketing')
```

# Merging nodes

There are times when a breakdown will result in very uneven child nodes. In this example, there are only a few personnel in three of the departments, so the **Merge** button can be pressed with them already selected, as shown in the following screenshot:

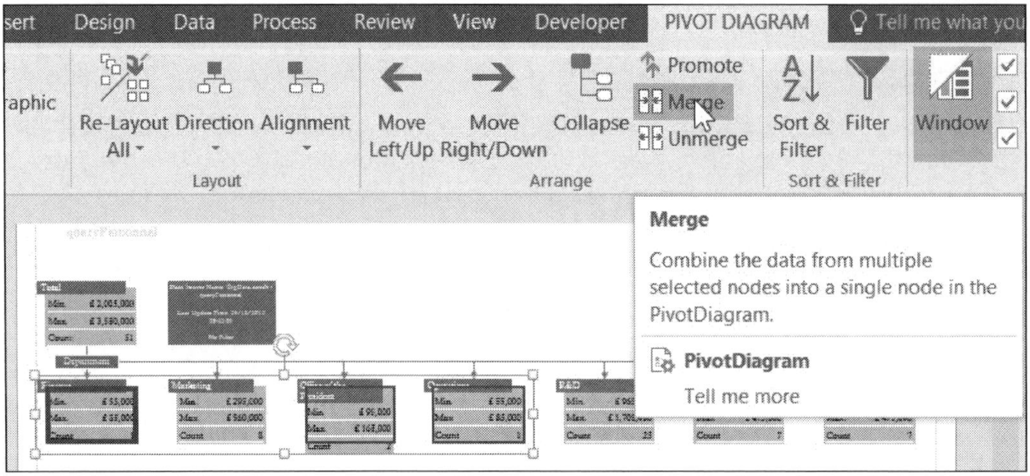


This results in the Shape Data of the three nodes being merged into one, as shown next:

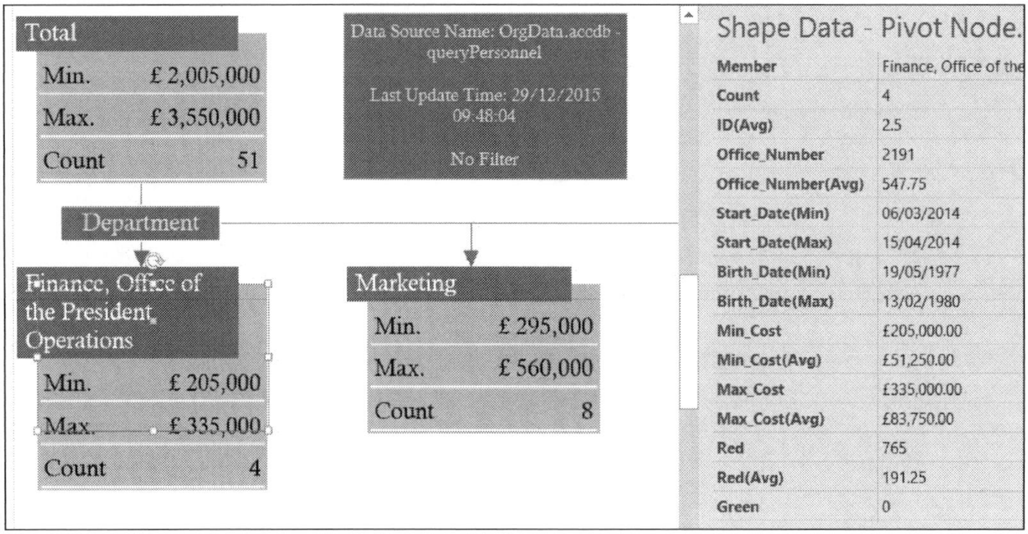

Behind the scenes, the `WHERE` clause of the SQL statement has been changed to the following:

```
WHERE ([Department] = 'Finance'  OR [Department] = 'Office of the
President'  OR [Department] = 'Operations' )
```

# Applying shapes to enhance legibility

There are times when it is useful to add a graphic to Pivot Node shapes, so as to better represent their meaning. The **PIVOT DIAGRAM** | **Format** | **Apply Shape** button opens the **Apply Shape** dialog. This dialog, as shown next, presents the open stencils (apart from the **PivotDiagram Shapes** one) to be selected with the **Stencil** drop-down list. The masters on the selected stencil are displayed:

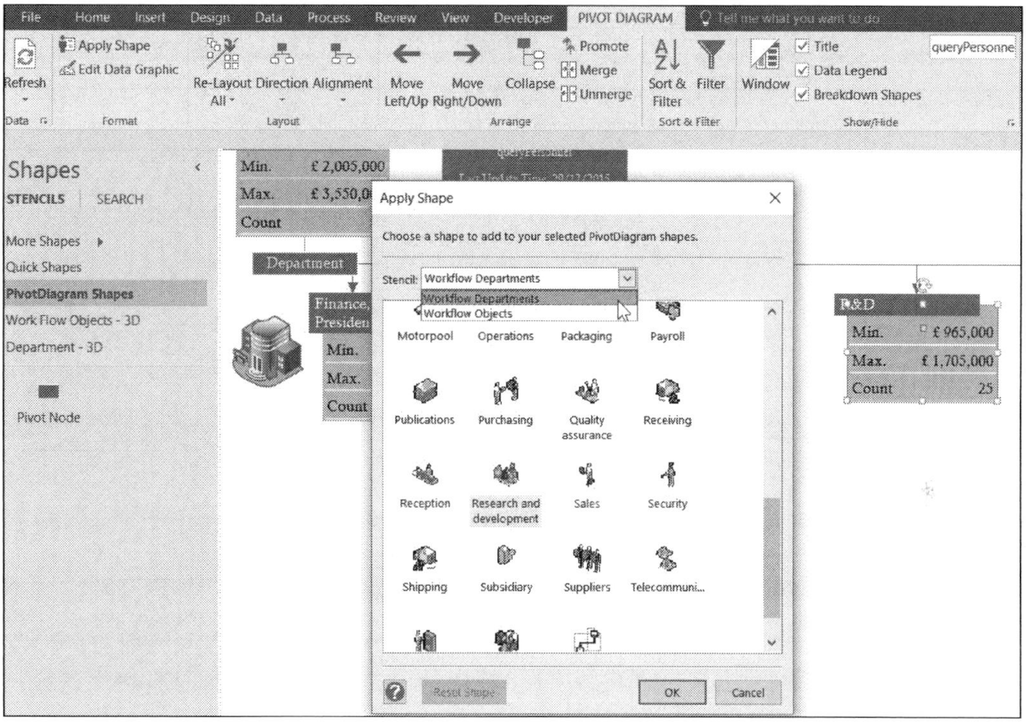


When a master is selected and the **OK** button is pressed, the shape is inserted into the selected Pivot Node shapes.

# Configuring the PivotDiagram options

There are a few options that can be configured for the whole diagram using the **PivotDiagram Options** dialog, as shown in the next screenshot. This can be opened from the **PIVOT DIAGRAM | Data | Data Options** button:

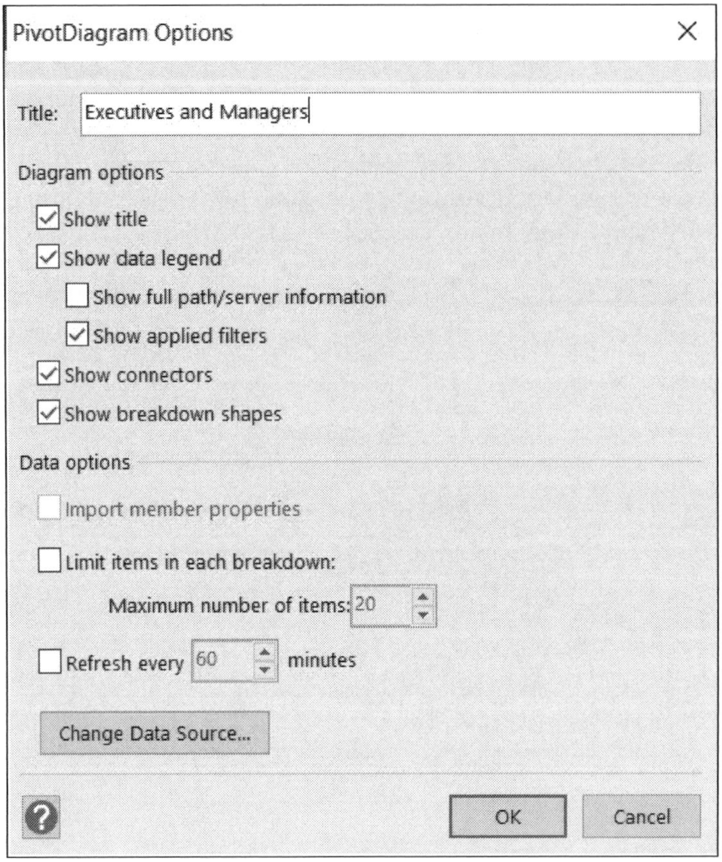


This dialog contains some options that were already in the **Show/Hide** group, but it contains more items that can have their visibility toggled with, such as the Pivot Connector shapes.

It also allows a refresh period to be set to fire every time between 1 and 60 minutes. The data sources can be refreshed manually using the **Data** | **Refresh** button, or it can fire periodically using this dialog.

Unlike the **Link Data** feature described in *Chapter 3, Linking Data to Shapes*, the data source of **PivotDiagrams** cannot be configured in SharePoint to automatically refresh periodically without being open in the Visio client.

# Laying the nodes out

There are some useful buttons available in the **PIVOT DIAGRAM** | **Layout** ribbon group. The actions apply to the immediate child nodes of the selected Pivot Node shape or shapes. So, in the next screenshot, the child nodes are shown with the **Alignment** | **Left** option, but they are about to be changed to **Alignment** | **Top**. This will cause them to rearrange vertically:

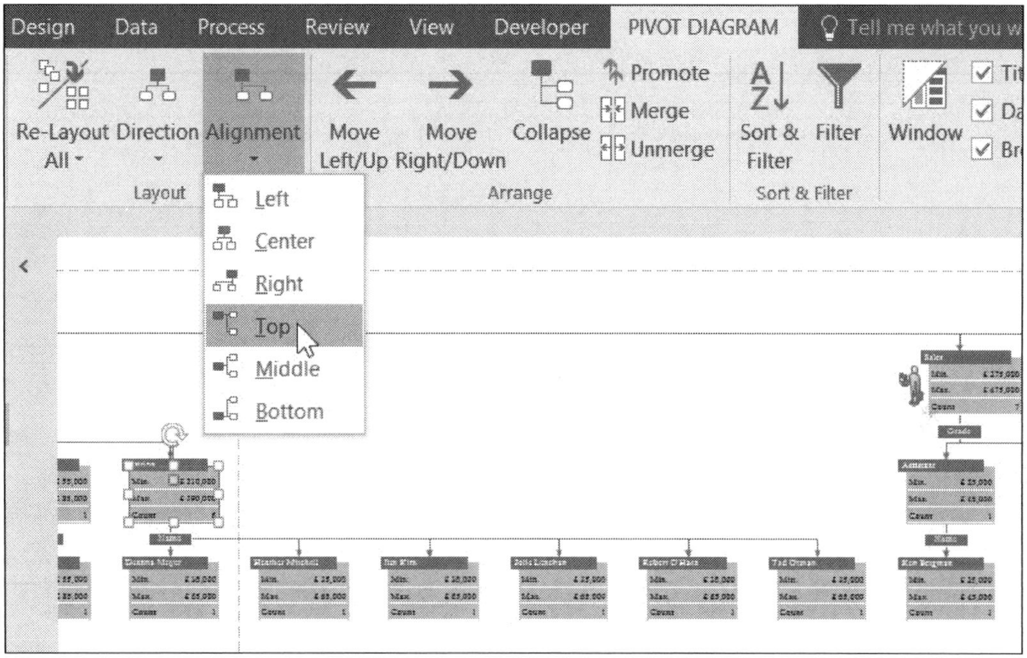

The direction of all the child nodes of a selected Pivot Node shape can also be changed, as shown in the next screenshot where the whole diagram was changed from **Top-to-Bottom** to **Left-to-Right**:

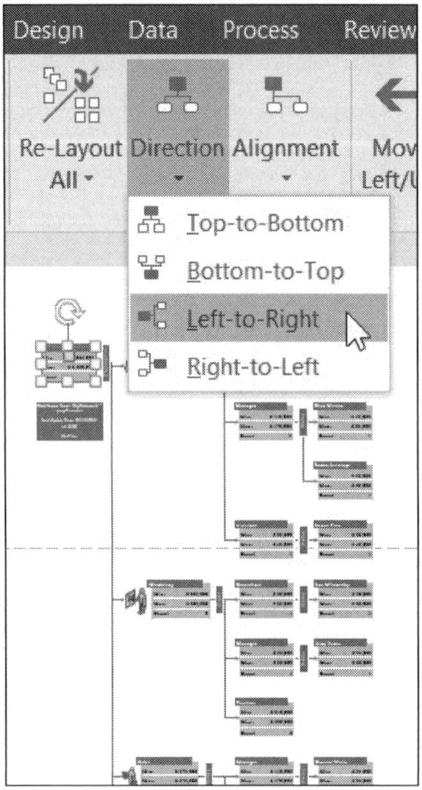


# Overlaying linked data

The data source for the Pivot Diagram structure may not be refreshable in SharePoint, but there is nothing to prevent some of the displayed data from being refreshable by using the **Link Data** feature. In the following example, the same `queryPersonnel` query that was used to generate the Pivot Diagram has been imported using the **Data** | **External Data** | **Custom Import** button. The values in the **Name Data Column** field are matched with the values in the **Shape Field Member**:

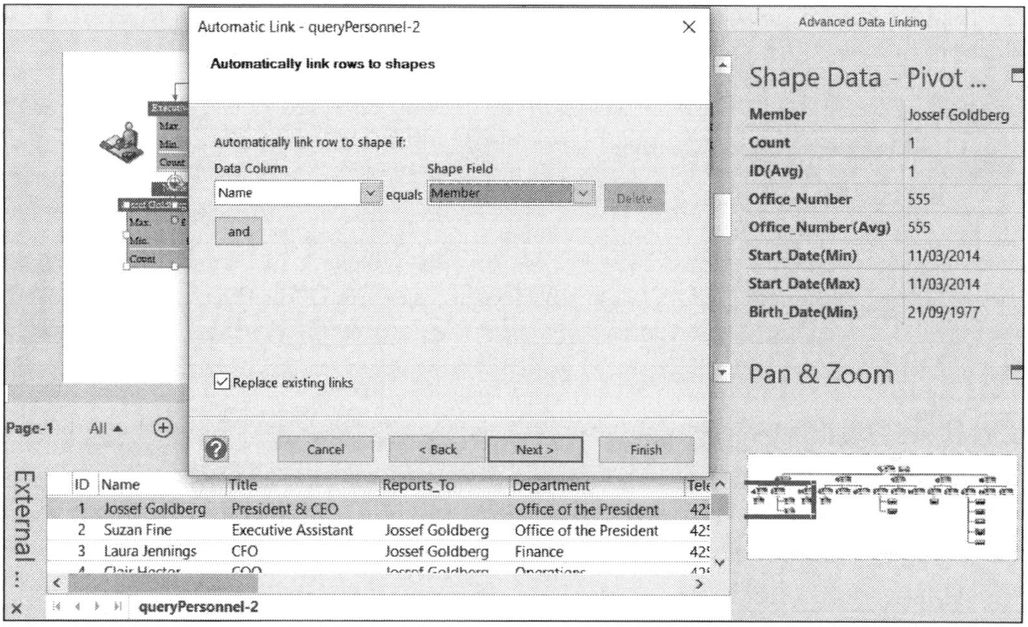


This will add the data from the matching rows to the Pivot Node shapes. These can then have a new Data Graphic applied to them, as shown in the following screenshot:

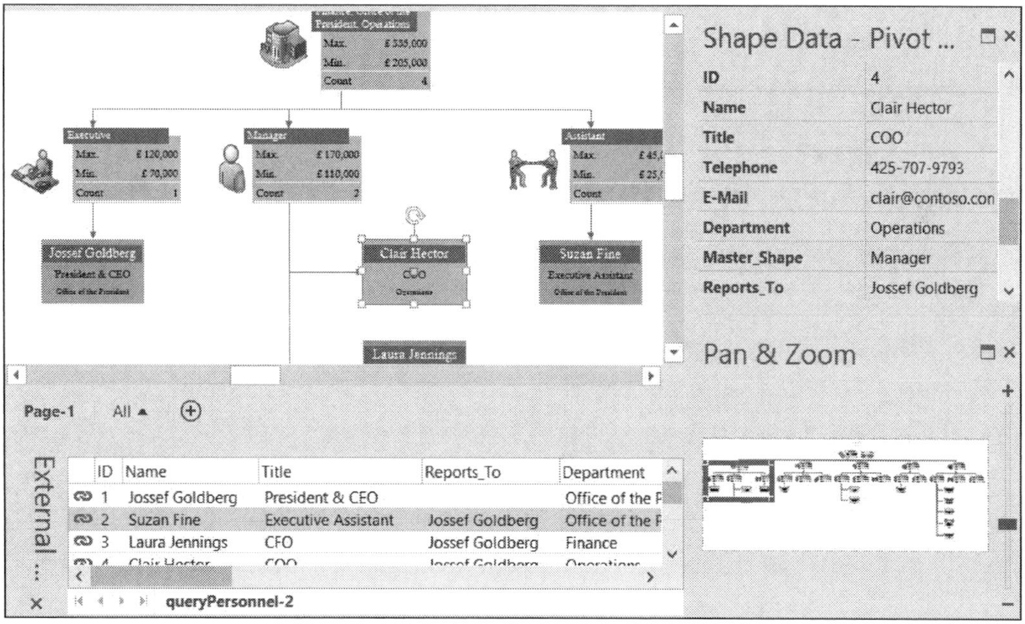

So, the Pivot Diagram add-on can be used to create the framework for a refreshable dashboard in addition to providing roll-up and aggregation of data.

Since the Pivot Breakdown and Pivot Connector shapes do not need to be displayed, the diagram does not need to look hierarchical either. The Pivot Node shapes can be arranged to suit, for example, the view over a geographical map.

> Visit `http://blog.bvisual.net/2012/09/03/using-visio-stacked-bar-charts/` for more ideas for the Pivot Diagram.

# Summary

In this chapter, we learned about the Pivot Diagram add-on, and how it uses some of the same technology as the **Custom Import** feature. We have seen how to configure the options of a diagram, and how to overlay data using **Custom Import**.

In the next chapter, we will learn about creating custom masters for use with **Link Data**. This will increase the reusability and efficiency, and it will reduce the maintenance required.

# 6

# Creating Custom Master Shapes

In the previous chapters, we learned about importing data into Visio, how to link data to shapes, and how to use the built-in Data Graphics. These are all necessary skills, but there are more ways that Visio can take advantage of linked shape data. Shapes can be made to resize, move, change appearance, and much more. The secret is to make Master shapes that respond to data values.

In this chapter, we will learn the following topics:

- How to enhance built-in Masters
- How to create custom Masters
- How to make shapes react to Shape Data value changes
- How to share custom templates and stencils with others
- Understanding a Master and Shape instance

The normal Visio user creates a diagram by selecting a template, which opens a blank page with one or more docked stencils. Often, a shape is created by dragging and dropping a **Master** shape from one of these stencils onto the page. In fact, in *Chapter 3, Linking Data to Shapes*, multiple copies of the **Person** Master from the **Business | Business Process | ITIL** Shapes stencil were created by dragging and dropping multiple rows from the **External Data** window.

The shapes on the page appear to be copies of the **Master** shape that was dragged and dropped from the **ITIL Shapes** stencil, but they are actually instances of a copy of the **Master** shape (which is first copied to the **Document Stencil**), and then all of the **Person** shapes on the page are Shape instances of the Master in the **Document Stencil**, as shown in the following screenshot:

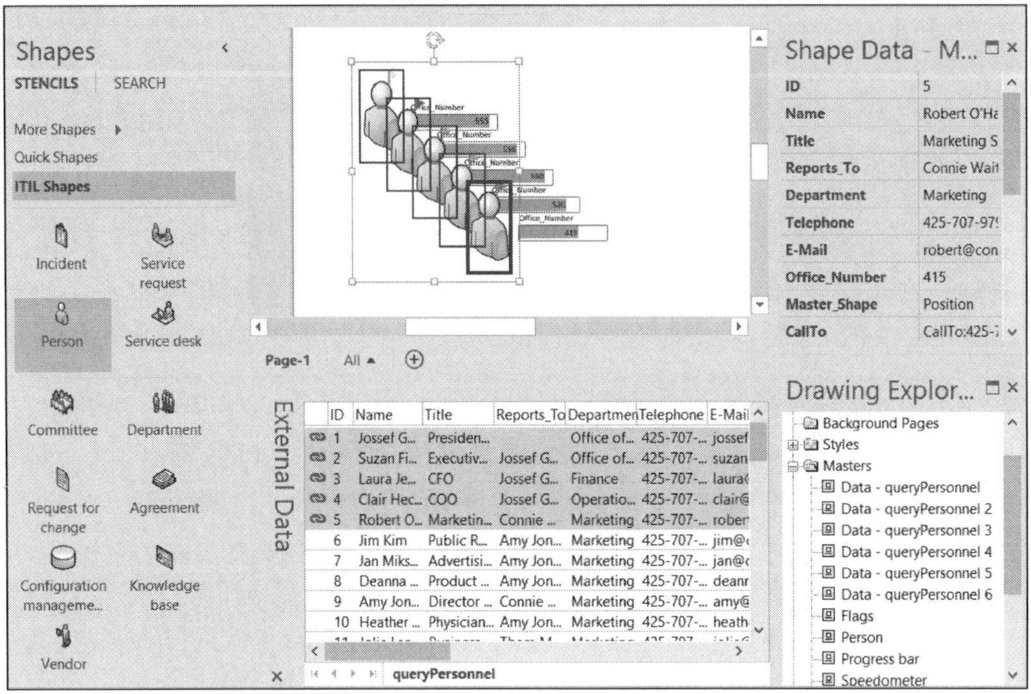


> If the data rows were dragged and dropped from the **External Data** window without a Master selected in a stencil, then Visio would automatically create a Master called **Rectangle**. It will then drop Shape instances of this Master onto the page.

Every Visio document has a Document Stencil, which often does not contain any **Master** shapes until a Master is dropped from a global stencil. Indeed, in the previous screenshot, there were no Masters either, until the **Person** Master shape was copied by the action of dragging the data rows onto the page. The copy of the **Person** Master can be seen in the **Masters** node of the **Drawing Explorer** window, and all of the other Masters that can be seen there are either Data Graphic or Graphic Item Masters. None of these other Masters are visible in the **More Shapes | Document Stencil**, but they are there. This is shown in the following screenshot:

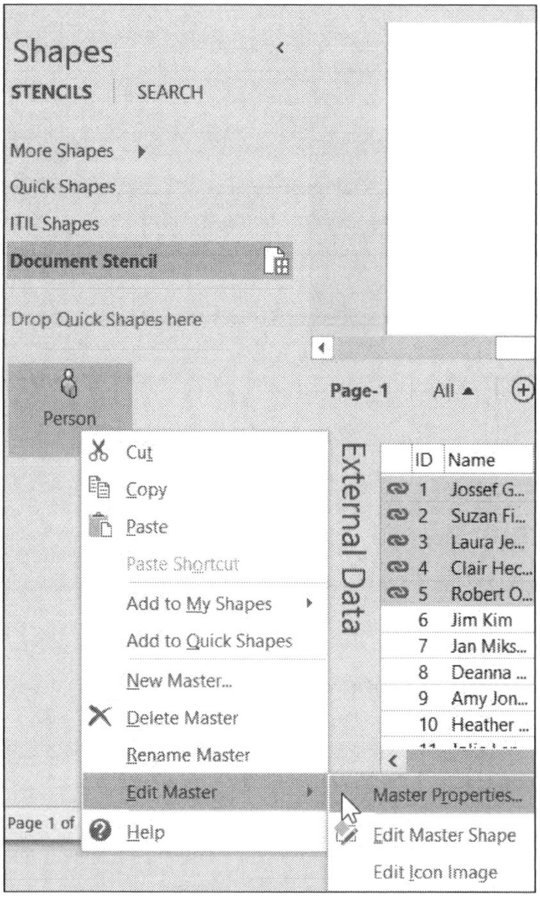


Notice that the **Master Properties...** are available on the right-click menu of the **Person** Master in the **Document Stencil**.

There are several stencils that have a Master named **Person**, but there can only be one Master named **Person** in a single stencil. So, if a second or third Master named **Person** was dragged from another stencil, then Visio would have to automatically rename them by appending the **ID** (separated with a full-stop) to the **Name**, as shown in the following screenshot:

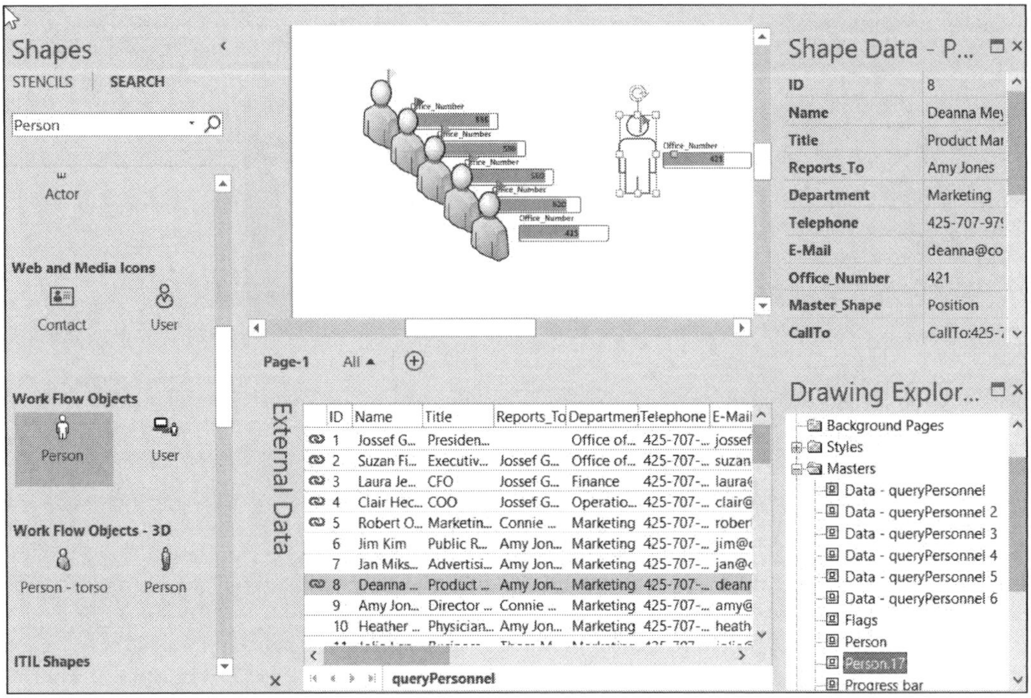


However, it is not always desirable to have multiple **Person** Masters, and this can be prevented by ticking the **Match master by name on drop** setting on the **Master Properties** dialog, as shown in the following screenshot:

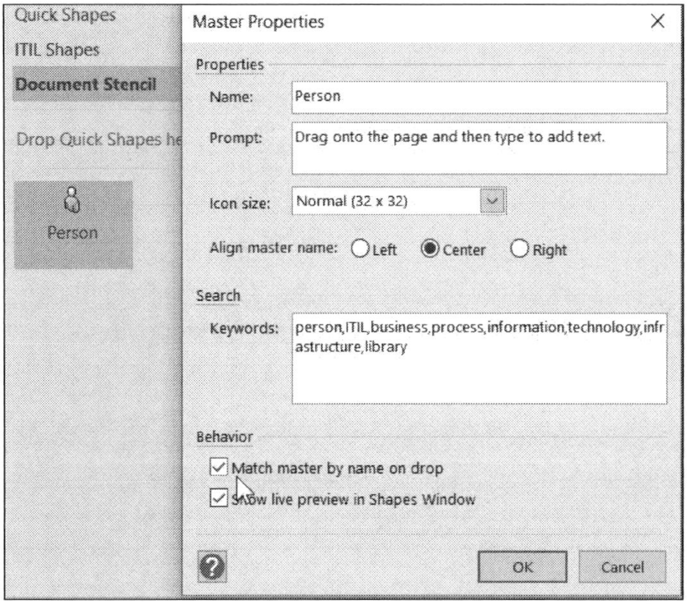


Now, with only one **Person** Master in the **Document Stencil**, dragging and dropping a different **Person** Master from another stencil appears, at first, to be dragging the wrong Master because the image of the shape is shown under the cursor, as shown in the following screenshot:

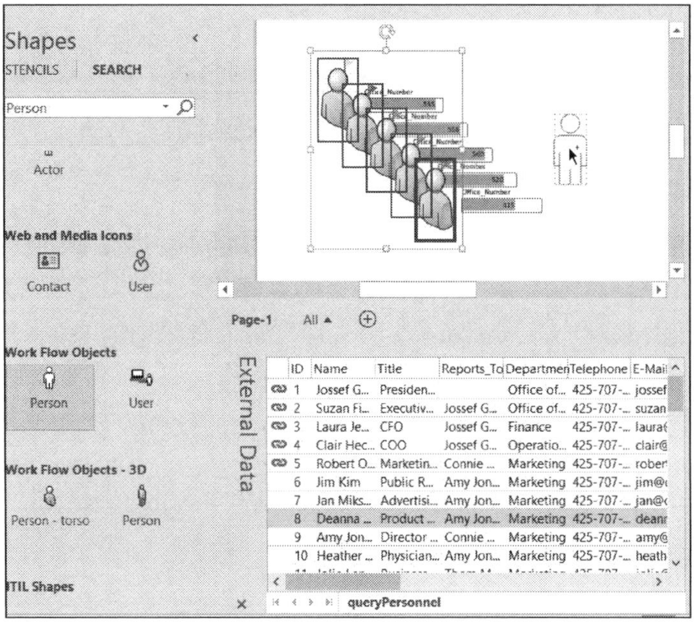

However, when the mouse button is released, the **Person** Master in the **Document Stencil** is actually dropped, as can be seen in the following screenshot:

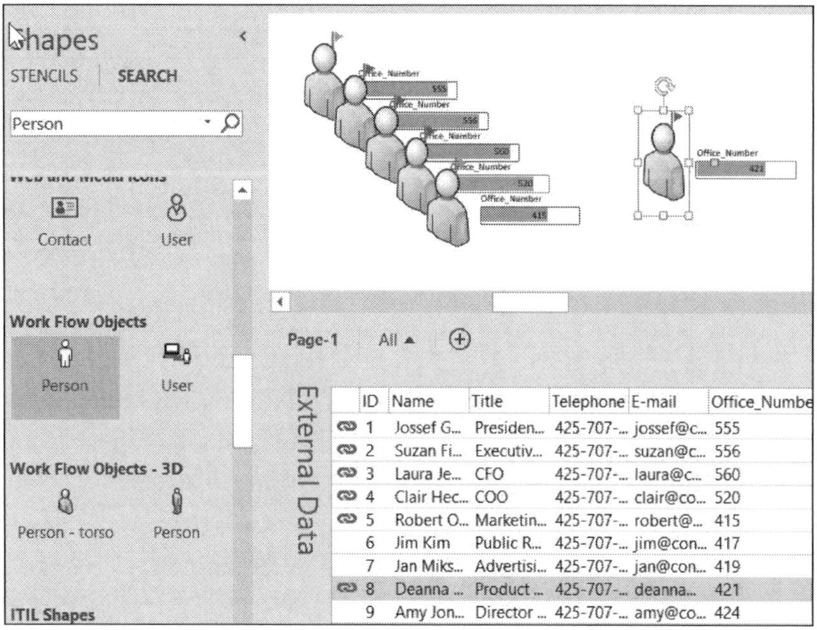


By the same rule, if the **Person** Master shape is modified, then it also needs to have the **Match master by name on drop** setting ticked. Otherwise, Visio will automatically assume that it is a different Master, and a normal user could end up creating many duplicate Masters in the **Document Stencil**.

This is the most important fact to grasp because this is the key to providing custom versions of Masters in the built-in stencils.

> Even some of the built-in templates contain Masters in their **Document Stencil** in order to provide a custom version of a Master. For example, the **Dynamic connector** Master already exists in the **Software and Database | Crow's Foot Database Notation** template.

# Modifying the ribbon

Microsoft created the ribbon to bring order into the UI, but that meant that they decided to leave some buttons out that were previously in the command bars. Some of these buttons were extremely useful, and fortunately, they can be easily added back into the ribbon. The following screenshot shows a few added to a new group called **Extras** in the **Developer** tab. The one called **Edit Object** is extremely useful because it will open a group shape in edit mode, allowing the sub-shapes to be selected and modified. This dialog can be opened from the right-click menu option, **Customize the Ribbon...**, from any blank area in the ribbon:

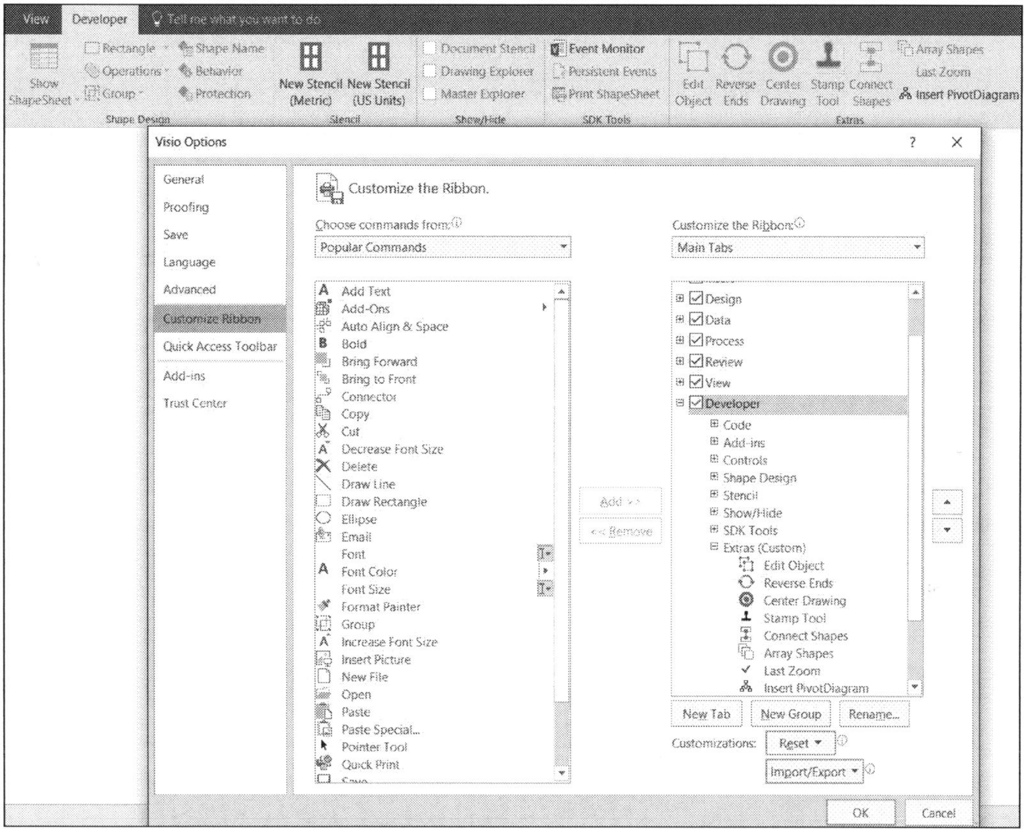

# Preparing shapes for data linking

When it comes to preparing shapes for linking to data, then the most vital part of the shape is the **Shape Data** section, and Data Graphics will add three User-defined Cells rows plus one **Controls** row. In the following screenshot (which is part of the ShapeSheet of one of the **Person** Shape instances), the **PinX** and **PinY** values are colored *blue*, whereas the rest of the **Shape Transform** cell values are colored *black*. This *black* font color indicates that the value is inherited from a **Master** shape, and the *blue* font color indicates that the value is stored within the Shape itself. All of the values in the other three sections in this screenshot are colored *blue* because each of these sections have had rows inserted by data linking or by Data Graphics:

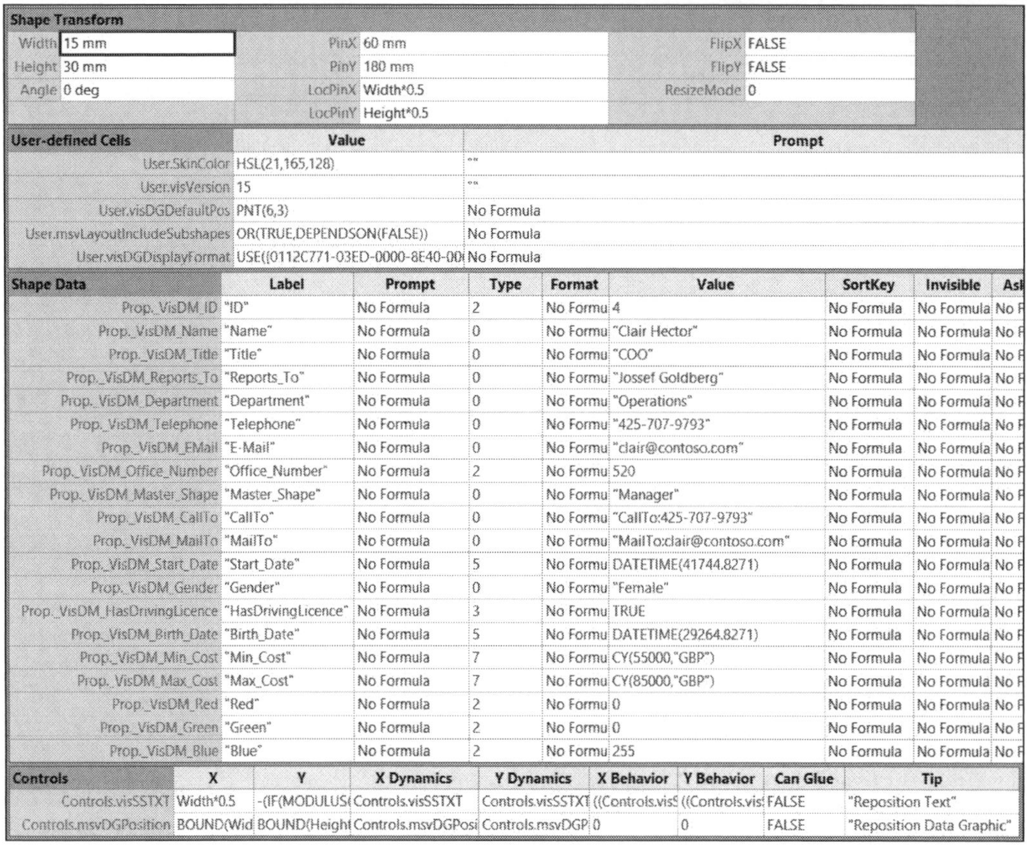

| Shape Transform | | | | | |
|---|---|---|---|---|---|
| Width | 15 mm | PinX | 60 mm | FlipX | FALSE |
| Height | 30 mm | PinY | 180 mm | FlipY | FALSE |
| Angle | 0 deg | LocPinX | Width*0.5 | ResizeMode | 0 |
| | | LocPinY | Height*0.5 | | |

| User-defined Cells | Value | Prompt |
|---|---|---|
| User.SkinColor | HSL(21,165,128) | "" |
| User.visVersion | 15 | "" |
| User.visDGDefaultPos | PNT(6,3) | No Formula |
| User.msvLayoutIncludeSubshapes | OR(TRUE,DEPENDSON(FALSE)) | No Formula |
| User.visDGDisplayFormat | USE({0112C771-03ED-0000-8E40-00 | No Formula |

| Shape Data | Label | Prompt | Type | Format | Value | SortKey | Invisible | Ask |
|---|---|---|---|---|---|---|---|---|
| Prop._VisDM_ID | "ID" | No Formula | 2 | No Formu | 4 | No Formula | No Formula | No F |
| Prop._VisDM_Name | "Name" | No Formula | 0 | No Formu | "Clair Hector" | No Formula | No Formula | No F |
| Prop._VisDM_Title | "Title" | No Formula | 0 | No Formu | "COO" | No Formula | No Formula | No F |
| Prop._VisDM_Reports_To | "Reports_To" | No Formula | 0 | No Formu | "Jossef Goldberg" | No Formula | No Formula | No F |
| Prop._VisDM_Department | "Department" | No Formula | 0 | No Formu | "Operations" | No Formula | No Formula | No F |
| Prop._VisDM_Telephone | "Telephone" | No Formula | 0 | No Formu | "425-707-9793" | No Formula | No Formula | No F |
| Prop._VisDM_EMail | "E-Mail" | No Formula | 0 | No Formu | "clair@contoso.com" | No Formula | No Formula | No F |
| Prop._VisDM_Office_Number | "Office_Number" | No Formula | 2 | No Formu | 520 | No Formula | No Formula | No F |
| Prop._VisDM_Master_Shape | "Master_Shape" | No Formula | 0 | No Formu | "Manager" | No Formula | No Formula | No F |
| Prop._VisDM_CallTo | "CallTo" | No Formula | 0 | No Formu | "CallTo:425-707-9793" | No Formula | No Formula | No F |
| Prop._VisDM_MailTo | "MailTo" | No Formula | 0 | No Formu | "MailTo:clair@contoso.com" | No Formula | No Formula | No F |
| Prop._VisDM_Start_Date | "Start_Date" | No Formula | 5 | No Formu | DATETIME(41744.8271) | No Formula | No Formula | No F |
| Prop._VisDM_Gender | "Gender" | No Formula | 0 | No Formu | "Female" | No Formula | No Formula | No F |
| Prop._VisDM_HasDrivingLicence | "HasDrivingLicence" | No Formula | 3 | No Formu | TRUE | No Formula | No Formula | No F |
| Prop._VisDM_Birth_Date | "Birth_Date" | No Formula | 5 | No Formu | DATETIME(29264.8271) | No Formula | No Formula | No F |
| Prop._VisDM_Min_Cost | "Min_Cost" | No Formula | 7 | No Formu | CY(55000,"GBP") | No Formula | No Formula | No F |
| Prop._VisDM_Max_Cost | "Max_Cost" | No Formula | 7 | No Formu | CY(85000,"GBP") | No Formula | No Formula | No F |
| Prop._VisDM_Red | "Red" | No Formula | 2 | No Formu | 0 | No Formula | No Formula | No F |
| Prop._VisDM_Green | "Green" | No Formula | 2 | No Formu | 0 | No Formula | No Formula | No F |
| Prop._VisDM_Blue | "Blue" | No Formula | 2 | No Formu | 255 | No Formula | No Formula | No F |

| Controls | X | Y | X Dynamics | Y Dynamics | X Behavior | Y Behavior | Can Glue | Tip |
|---|---|---|---|---|---|---|---|---|
| Controls.visSSTXT | Width*0.5 | -(IF(MODULUS( | Controls.visSSTXT | Controls.visSSTXT | ((Controls.vis | ((Controls.vis | FALSE | "Reposition Text" |
| Controls.msvDGPosition | BOUND(Wid | BOUND(Height | Controls.msvDGPosi | Controls.msvDGP | 0 | 0 | FALSE | "Reposition Data Graphic" |

There are three very good reasons for preparing Master shapes for data linking and Data Graphics:

- Enhancements can be made to the shape to respond to data value changes
- Edits made to the Master Shape are propagated to inherited sections of Shape instances
- The Visio document will be smaller in size because less information has to be stored within each shape instance

Therefore, whenever possible, it is good practice to enhance the **Master** shape using the **Edit Master | Edit Master Shape** action from the right mouse menu of the Master in the **Document Stencil**. When the **Master** edit dialog opens, as shown in the following screenshot, then the **Master Explorer** window and **ShapeSheet** can be opened via their respective buttons on the **Developer** tab:

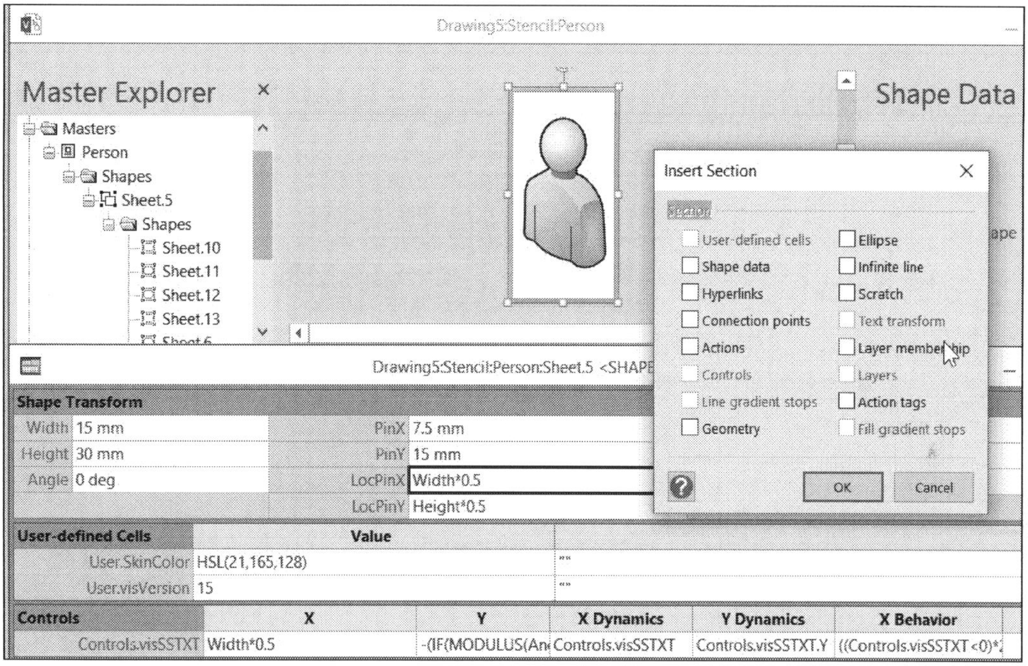


The **Design | Sections | Insert** ribbon button will open the **Insert Section** dialog, on which the **User-defined cells, Shape data**, and **Controls** sections can be inserted if necessary. Only the **Shape data** section needed to be inserted in the preceding example.

Then it is simply a matter of inserting the necessary rows into the **ShapeSheet** sections. In the following screenshot, the `_VisDM_` prefix, which was automatically created for the name of each **Shape Data** row, has been removed, and the **Label** cell value must be exactly the same as the column heading in the **External Data** recordset. The **Prompt** cells each have a suitable formula, and the values in the **Type** cells have been enclosed within the `GUARD(…)` function. This is because the data linking feature sometimes gets the **Type** wrong, or the developer wants to change the **Type**. In either case, the `GUARD(…)` function prevents the data linking feature from changing it subsequently. As can be seen in the following screenshot, the default formulas for the **Value** cells are mostly empty:

| User-defined Cells | Value | |
|---|---|---|
| User.SkinColor | HSL(21,165,128) | "" |
| User.visVersion | 15 | "" |
| User.visDGDefaultPos | PNT(6,3) | No Formula |
| User.msvLayoutIncludeSubshapes | OR(TRUE,DEPENDSON(FALSE)) | No Formula |
| User.visDGDisplayFormat | "" | No Formula |
| User.visDGCBVFill | "" | "" |
| User.visDGOldColors | "" | "" |

| Shape Data | Label | Prompt | Type | Format | Value | SortKey | Invisible | Ask | LangID | Calendar |
|---|---|---|---|---|---|---|---|---|---|---|
| Prop.ID | "ID" | Prop.ID.Label&" (I | GUARD(2) | No Formu | No Formula | No Formula | No Formula | No For | 2057 | No Formu |
| Prop.Name | "Name" | Prop.Name.Label& | GUARD(0) | No Formu | "" | No Formula | No Formula | No For | 2057 | No Formu |
| Prop.Title | "Title" | Prop.Title.Label&" | GUARD(0) | No Formu | "" | No Formula | No Formula | No For | 2057 | No Formu |
| Prop.Reports_To | "Reports_To" | Prop.Reports_To.L | GUARD(0) | No Formu | "" | No Formula | No Formula | No For | 2057 | No Formu |
| Prop.Department | "Department" | Prop.Department. | GUARD(0) | No Formu | "" | No Formula | No Formula | No For | 2057 | No Formu |
| Prop.Telephone | "Telephone" | Prop.Telephone.La | GUARD(0) | No Formu | "" | No Formula | No Formula | No For | 2057 | No Formu |
| Prop.EMail | "E-Mail" | Prop.EMail.Label& | GUARD(0) | No Formu | "" | No Formula | No Formula | No For | 2057 | No Formu |
| Prop.Office_Number | "Office_Number" | Prop.Office_Numb | GUARD(2) | No Formu | No Formula | No Formula | No Formula | No For | 2057 | No Formu |
| Prop.Master_Shape | "Master_Shape" | Prop.Master_Shap | GUARD(0) | No Formu | "" | No Formula | No Formula | No For | 2057 | No Formu |
| Prop.CallTo | "CallTo" | Prop.CallTo.Label | GUARD(0) | No Formu | "" | No Formula | No Formula | No For | 2057 | No Formu |
| Prop.MailTo | "MailTo" | Prop.MailTo.Label | GUARD(0) | No Formu | "" | No Formula | No Formula | No For | 2057 | No Formu |
| Prop.Start_Date | "Start_Date" | Prop.Start_Date.La | GUARD(5) | No Formu | No Formula | No Formula | No Formula | No For | 2057 | No Formu |
| Prop.Gender | "Gender" | Prop.Gender.Labe | GUARD(0) | No Formu | "" | No Formula | No Formula | No For | 2057 | No Formu |
| Prop.HasDrivingLicence | "HasDrivingLicence" | Prop.HasDrivingLi | GUARD(3) | No Formu | TRUE | No Formula | No Formula | No For | 2057 | No Formu |
| Prop.Birth_Date | "Birth_Date" | Prop.Birth_Date.La | GUARD(5) | No Formu | No Formula | No Formula | No Formula | No For | 2057 | No Formu |
| Prop.Min_Cost | "Min_Cost" | Prop.Min_Cost.Lab | GUARD(7) | No Formu | CY(0,"GBP") | No Formula | No Formula | No For | 2057 | No Formu |
| Prop.Max_Cost | "Max_Cost" | Prop.Max_Cost.Lal | GUARD(7) | No Formu | CY(0,"GBP") | No Formula | No Formula | No For | 2057 | No Formu |
| Prop.Red | "Red" | Prop.Red.Label&" | GUARD(2) | No Formu | 0 | No Formula | No Formula | No For | 2057 | No Formu |
| Prop.Green | "Green" | Prop.Green.Label& | GUARD(2) | No Formu | 0 | No Formula | No Formula | No For | 2057 | No Formu |
| Prop.Blue | "Blue" | Prop.Blue.Label&" | GUARD(2) | No Formu | 0 | No Formula | No Formula | No For | 2057 | No Formu |

| Controls | X | Y | X Dynamics | Y Dynamics | X Behavior | Y Behavior | Can Glue | Tip |
|---|---|---|---|---|---|---|---|---|
| Controls.visSSTXT | Width*0.5 | -(IF(MODULUS( | Controls.visSSTXT | Controls.visSSTXT | ((Controls.visS | ((Controls.vis | FALSE | "Reposition Text" |
| Controls.msvDGPosition | BOUND(Wid | BOUND(Height | Controls.msvDGPosi | Controls.msvDGP | 0 | 0 | FALSE | "Reposition Data Graphic" |

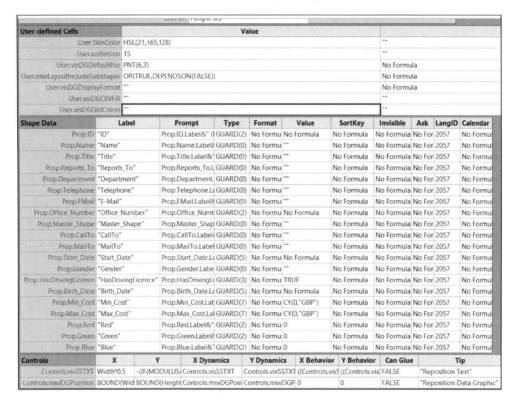

The **User-defined Cells** rows added by Data Graphics are named as follows:

- `visDGDefaultPos`
- `msvLayoutIncludeSubshapes`
- `visDGDisplayFormat`
- `visDGCBVFill`
- `visDGOldColors`

Note that the last two will be added or deleted automatically by the Visio application, depending upon Color By Value being included in the applied Data Graphics.

There is also one row added in the **Controls** section by the **Data Graphics** feature:

- `msvDGPosition`

> A `CopyAllFromShapeToMaster()` VBA macro is provided in this book's code download; it will copy the necessary rows to the **Master** shape from one of its **Shape** instances.

# Making graphics respond to data value changes

The following screenshot shows a triangular shape, named `DepartmentMarker`, added to the group shape of the **Person** master in the **Document Stencil**:

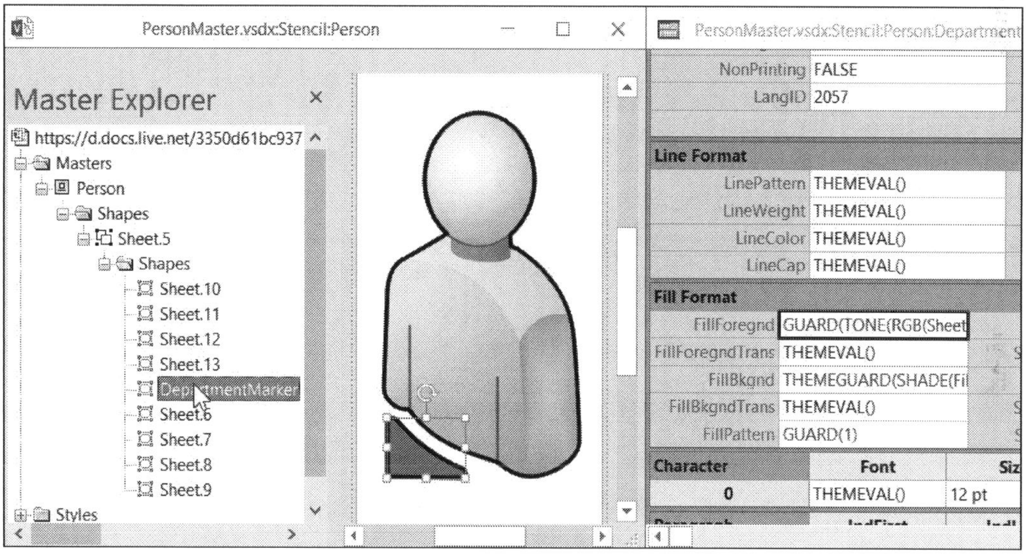

Notice that the top group shape is currently named `Sheet.5`. This is the default name, and it will remain as the `NameID` property even if the shape is renamed. In fact, 99% of Masters have the top group Shape with an ID of `5`. `NameID` is the ID of the shape preceded by sheet making it `Sheet.5`.

To make the color of the `DepartmentMarker` Shape change whenever the value of the **Department** Shape Data row changes, the following formulas were entered:

```
FillForegnd=GUARD(TONE(RGB(Sheet.5!Prop.Red,Sheet.5!Prop.
Green,Sheet.5!Prop.Blue),50))

FillPattern=GUARD(1)
```

The `RGB(r,g,b)` function takes three numbers between 0 and 255 for the red, green, and blue values. These are obtained from the respective Shape Data rows (`Prop.Red`, `Prop.Green`, and `Prop.Blue`) in the parent group Shape, `Sheet.5`. However, in order to mute the color a little, the `TONE(…)` function has been used. `FillPattern=1` means solid fill, and therefore the `FillBkgnd` formula is ignored.

So, whenever the enhanced **Person** shape is now used with data, then the `DepartmentMarker` shape will automatically display the color for the department, as shown in the following screenshot:

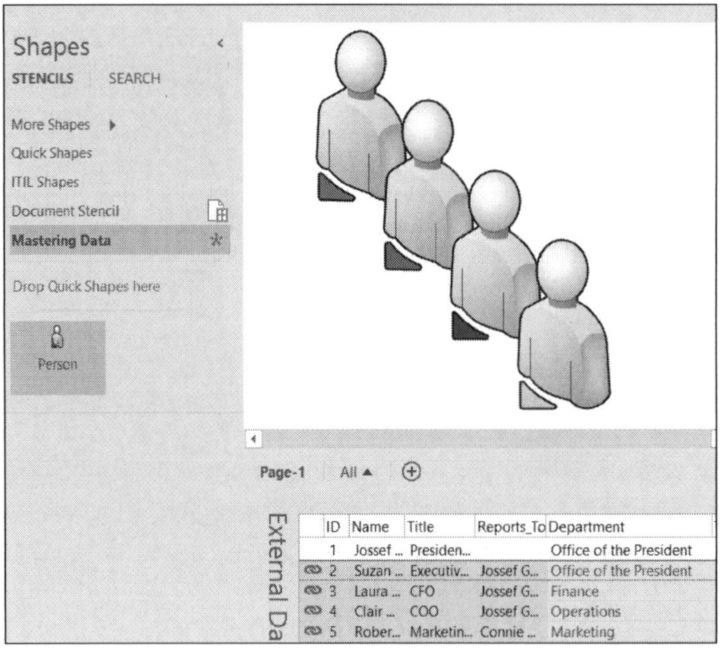

Next, a simple rectangle was added inside the **Person** Master Shape. **Insert | Field** was then used to add text. The **Custom Formula** option allows a formula to be typed in. This should start with an `=` symbol, just like in an Excel cell formula, followed by the `NameID` property of the group shape, `Sheet.5`, followed by a `!` symbol. Then, the cell name, `Prop.Name`, is entered, as can be seen in the following screenshot:

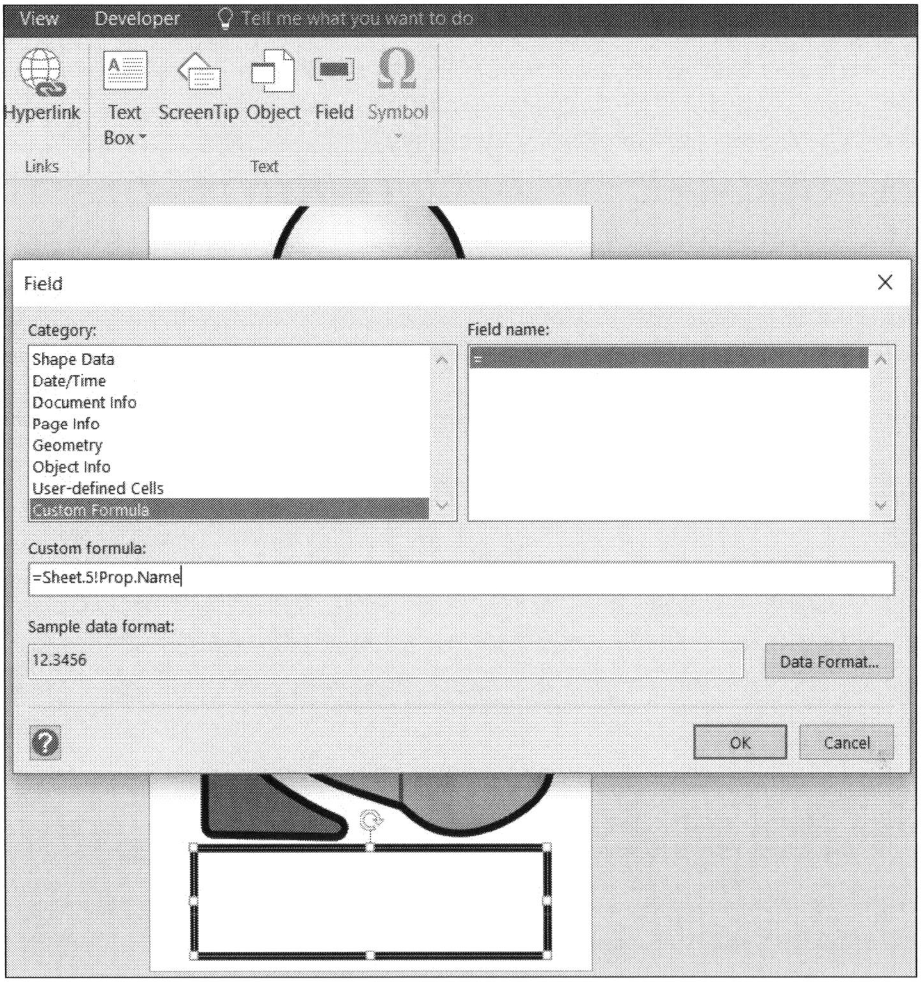

The rectangle is then rotated, formatted, and renamed `NameBlock`, as shown in the following screenshot:

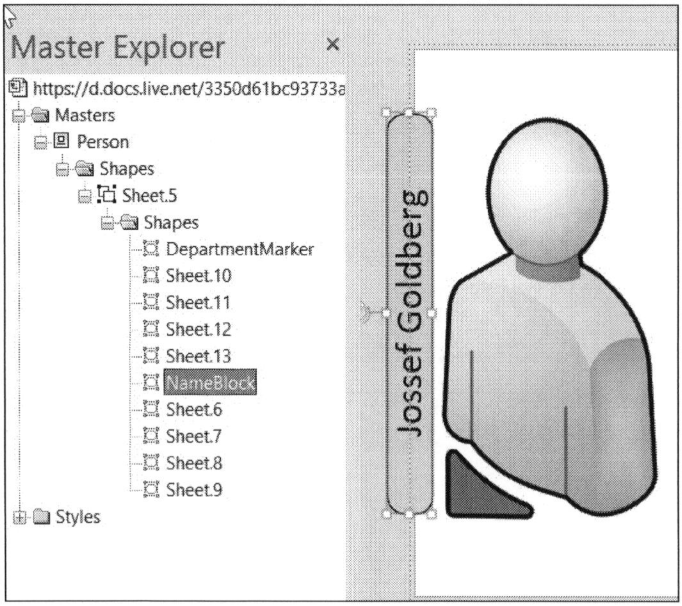


Again, the color cell formulas were edited, but the `TINT(...)` function was used rather than `TONE(...)` in order to get a much lighter background behind the text:

```
FillForegnd=GUARD(TINT(RGB(Sheet.5!Prop.Red,Sheet.5!Prop.
Green,Sheet.5!Prop.Blue),100))

FillPattern=GUARD(1)
```

In this example, the `Prop.Master_Shape` Shape Data can only have a one of five choices, or six if no value is counted. Therefore, the following formulas were added:

```
Prop.Master_Shape.Type=GUARD(1)
Prop.Master_Shape.Format=";Executive;Manager;Position;Assistant;Consu
ltant"
```

A value of 1 for the `Type` cell means it is a fixed list, and this list is entered as a choice, separated by semicolons in the `Format` cell. Note that the first choice is empty before the first semicolon.

It is usually best to reference the index value of the chosen value, rather than the value itself, so a new User-defined cell was added, named `Master_ShapeIdx`, to hold a `LOOKUP(...)` function that returns the index position of a value in a list:

```
User.Master_ShapeIdx
=LOOKUP(Prop.Master_Shape,Prop.Master_Shape.Format)
```

These formulas can be seen in the following screenshot:

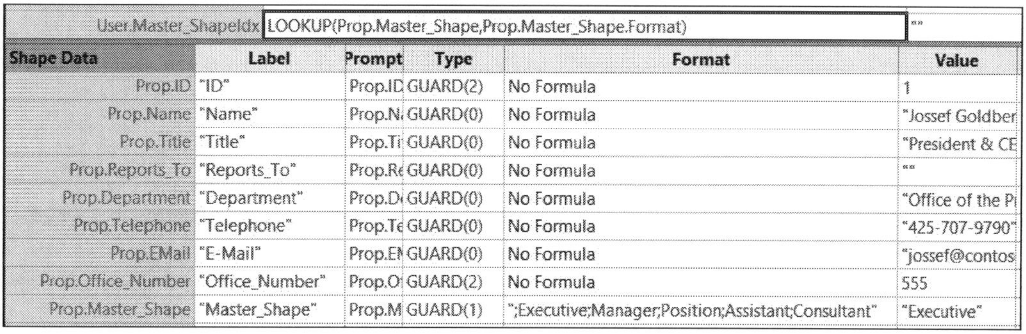

| User.Master_ShapeIdx | LOOKUP(Prop.Master_Shape,Prop.Master_Shape.Format) | | | | "" |
|---|---|---|---|---|---|
| **Shape Data** | **Label** | **Prompt** | **Type** | **Format** | **Value** |
| Prop.ID | "ID" | Prop.ID | GUARD(2) | No Formula | 1 |
| Prop.Name | "Name" | Prop.N | GUARD(0) | No Formula | "Jossef Goldber |
| Prop.Title | "Title" | Prop.Ti | GUARD(0) | No Formula | "President & CE |
| Prop.Reports_To | "Reports_To" | Prop.Re | GUARD(0) | No Formula | "" |
| Prop.Department | "Department" | Prop.D | GUARD(0) | No Formula | "Office of the Pi |
| Prop.Telephone | "Telephone" | Prop.Te | GUARD(0) | No Formula | "425-707-9790" |
| Prop.EMail | "E-Mail" | Prop.EN | GUARD(0) | No Formula | "jossef@contos |
| Prop.Office_Number | "Office_Number" | Prop.O | GUARD(2) | No Formula | 555 |
| Prop.Master_Shape | "Master_Shape" | Prop.M | GUARD(1) | ";Executive;Manager;Position;Assistant;Consultant" | "Executive" |

Then a new shape called `ShoulderPips` was added, which contained five ellipse shapes. A formula was added into each `NoShow` cell of the corresponding **Geometry** sections in order to change the visibility of the section dependent upon the value of the `User.MasterShapeIdx.Value` cell:

```
Geometry1.NoShow=OR(Sheet.5!User.Master_ShapeIdx=0,Sheet.5!User.
Master_ShapeIdx>1)
Geometry2.NoShow =OR(Sheet.5!User.Master_ShapeIdx=0,Sheet.5!User.
Master_ShapeIdx>2)
Geometry3.NoShow =OR(Sheet.5!User.Master_ShapeIdx=0,Sheet.5!User.
Master_ShapeIdx>3)
Geometry4.NoShow =OR(Sheet.5!User.Master_ShapeIdx=0,Sheet.5!User.
Master_ShapeIdx>4)
Geometry5.NoShow =Sheet.5!User.Master_ShapeIdx=0
```

These formulas are shown in the following screenshot:

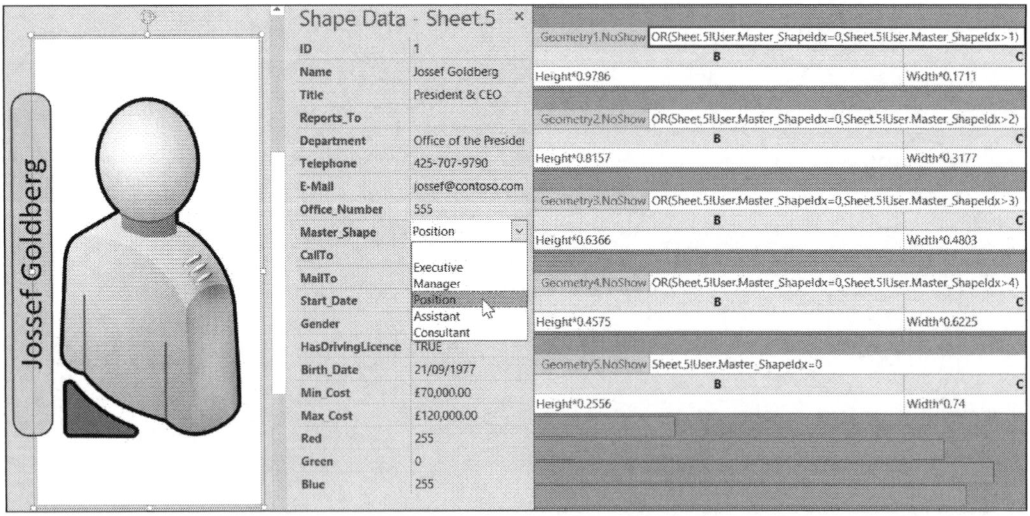


This will cause the number of pips on the shoulder to change according to the value of the `Prop.Master_Shape.Value` cell, as displayed in the following screenshot:

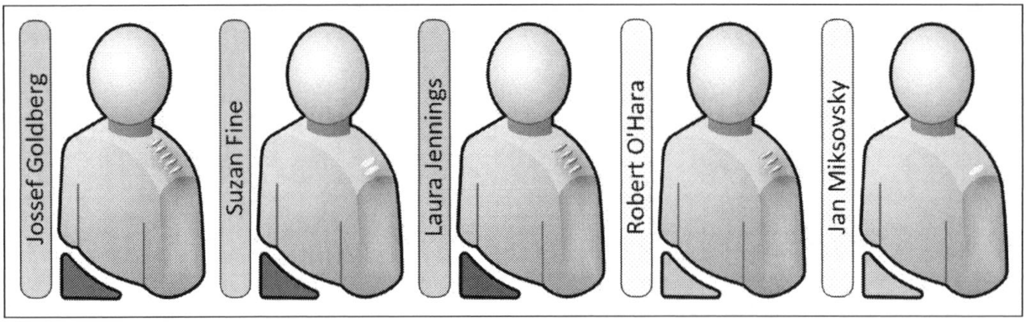

# Using elapsed days to size and position shapes

Another approach might be to change the size, color, and text according to the values. Indeed, Visio pages could have the **Measurement Units** field set to elapsed time, as shown in the following screenshot of the **Page Setup** dialog:

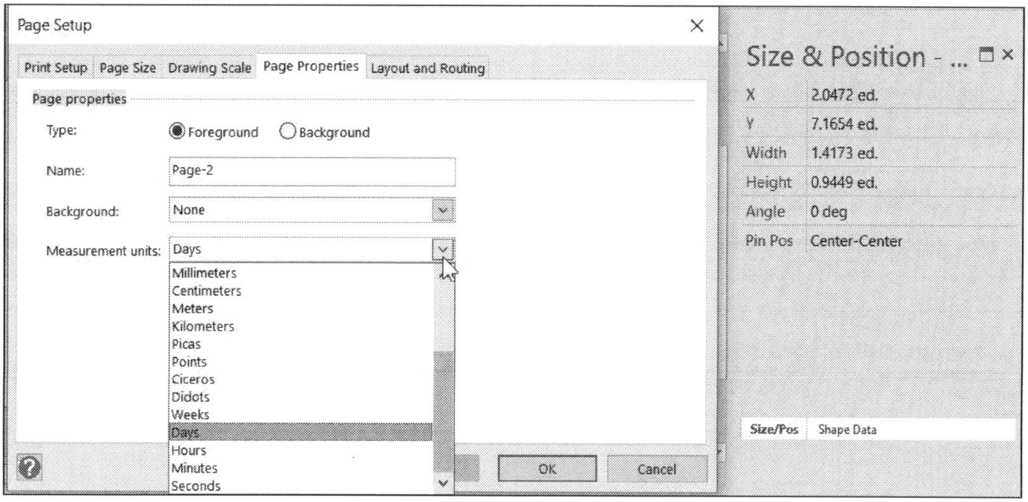


However, this would mean that both axes represent elapsed time. So, in a case where only one axis (say the horizontal axis) needs to be elapsed time, a different approach can be taken. This following technique has been used many times for road map diagrams, for example.

Two properties were added to the page, one for the **Begin Date**, along the left margin of the page, and the other for the **End Date**, along the right margin of the page. Therefore, the space between the left and right margins represents the number of days between the **Begin** and **End Dates**. The following User-defined cells were added to the page:

```
PageElapsedDays=Prop.EndDate-Prop.BeginDate
PageDaysWidth= (PageWidth-PageLeftMargin-PageRightMargin)
PageDaysPerUnit =User.PageElapsedDays/(User.PageDaysWidth/
DrawingScale)
```

These can be seen in the following screenshot:

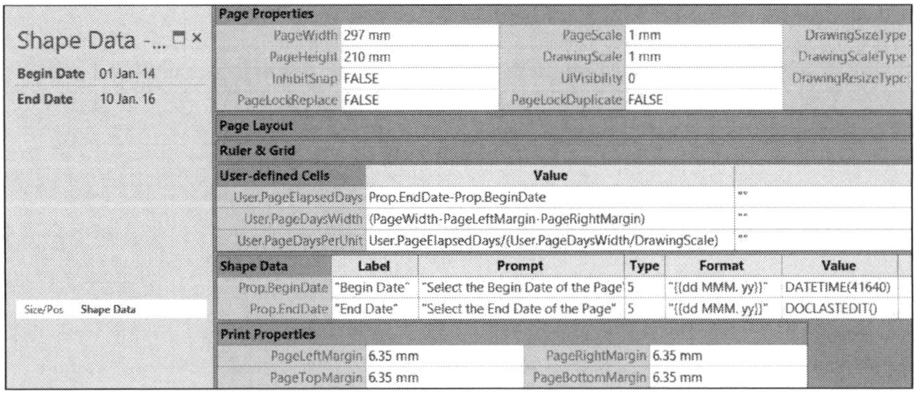


Then, a new rectangular Shape was created, and the following cells were updated:

```
Width=GUARD((ThePage!DrawingScale*(ThePage!Prop.EndDate-Prop._VisDM_
Start_Date))/ThePage!User.PageDaysPerUnit)
Height=GUARD(32 mm*(1/User.Master_ShapeIdx))
PinX=(GUARD(ThePage!PageWidth-ThePage!PageRightMargin))
PinY=(ThePage!PageHeight-ThePage!PageTopMargin)-(Height*(Prop.ID-1))
```

These formulas along with the User-defined cell, `Master_ShapeIdx` (as described for the **Person** Master), can be seen in the following screenshot:

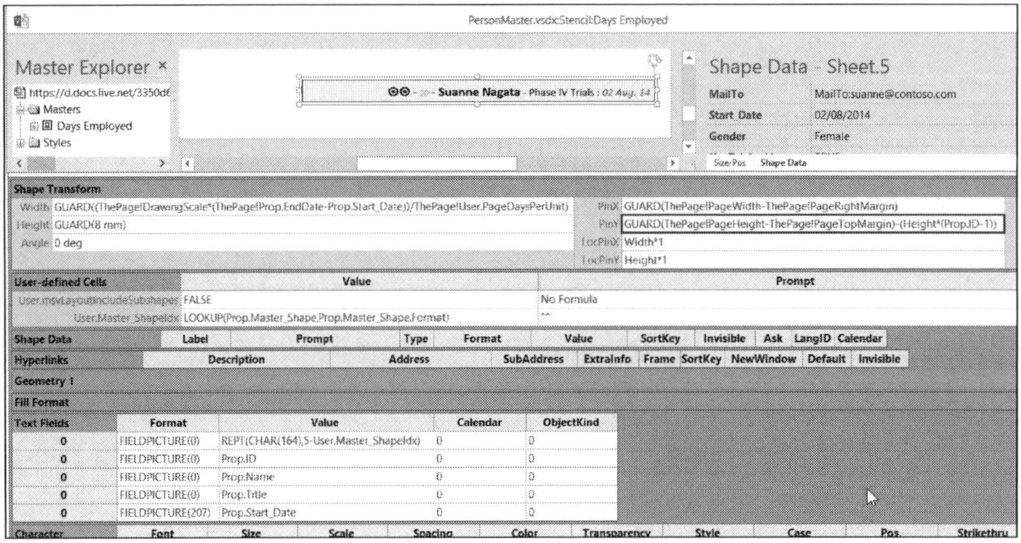

These formulas ensure that the left edge of the rectangle is at the horizontal position that represents the **Prop.Start_Date** value of the **Person** Master, and the right edge is at the **Prop.End_Date** of the page.

The vertical position, **PinY,** is set relative to the **Prop.ID** values in order to spread them out.

The color was set to the **Prop.Department** value, as in the **Person** Master, and the text displayed various values. Then, once these shapes are dropped data-linked onto the page, they automatically position themselves vertically and horizontally, as shown in the following screenshot:

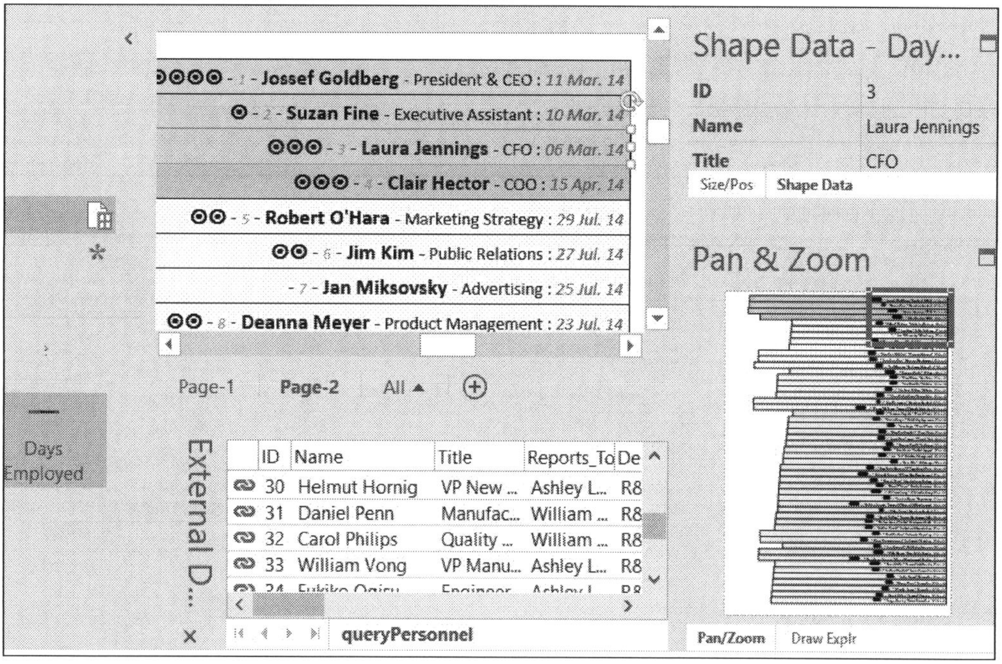


A similar technique could be used to distribute shapes in an X/Y fashion. Take a look at the following article to learn how shapes can be distributed on a map underlay using the longitude and latitude values: `http://blog.bvisual.net/2015/05/27/distributing-data-points-automatically-on-maps-in-visio/`

# Sharing custom Templates, Stencils, and Masters

Custom Masters are delivered in a custom Stencil. Stencils can be deployed individually or along with a custom Template that they are docked with. A Visio installation creates a <Documents>\My Shapes folder. If Visio Stencils are placed into this folder, or in a sub-folder, then they will become available in **More Shapes | My Shapes** in the Visio UI.

Alternatively, a folder path, or multiple folder paths separated by semicolons, can be entered into the **Stencils** option of the **File Locations** dialog opened from the **Visio Options | Advanced** panel, as shown in the following screenshot:

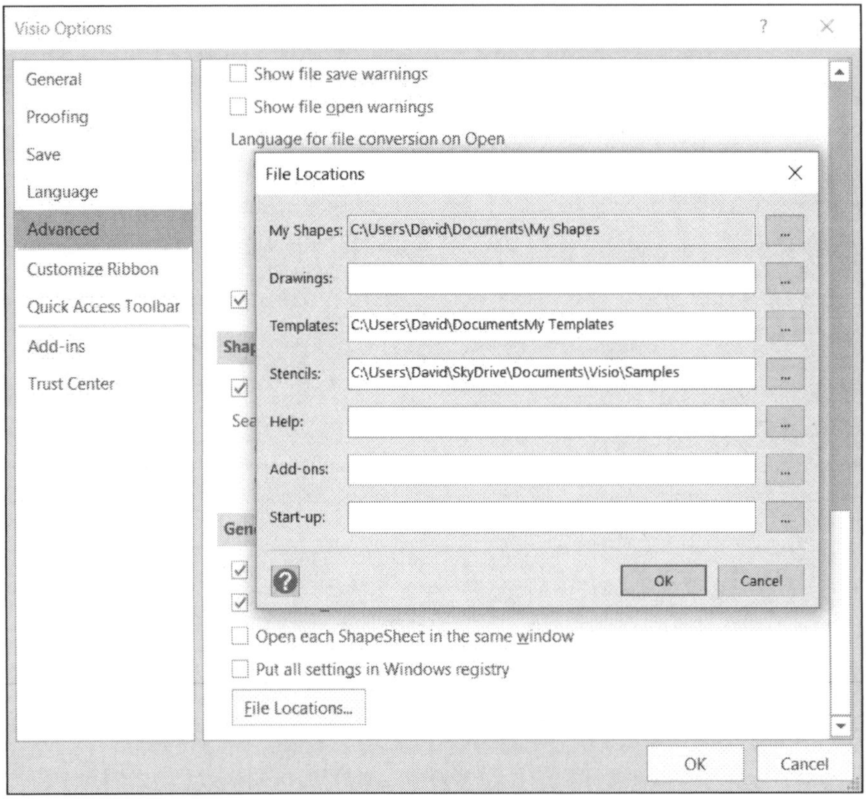

Similarly, the **Templates** option allows multiple folder paths for custom Templates. The Visio UI will display any template in the **CATEGORIES** panel, and any sub-folder that contains a template will be shown with a folder icon, as shown in the following screenshot:

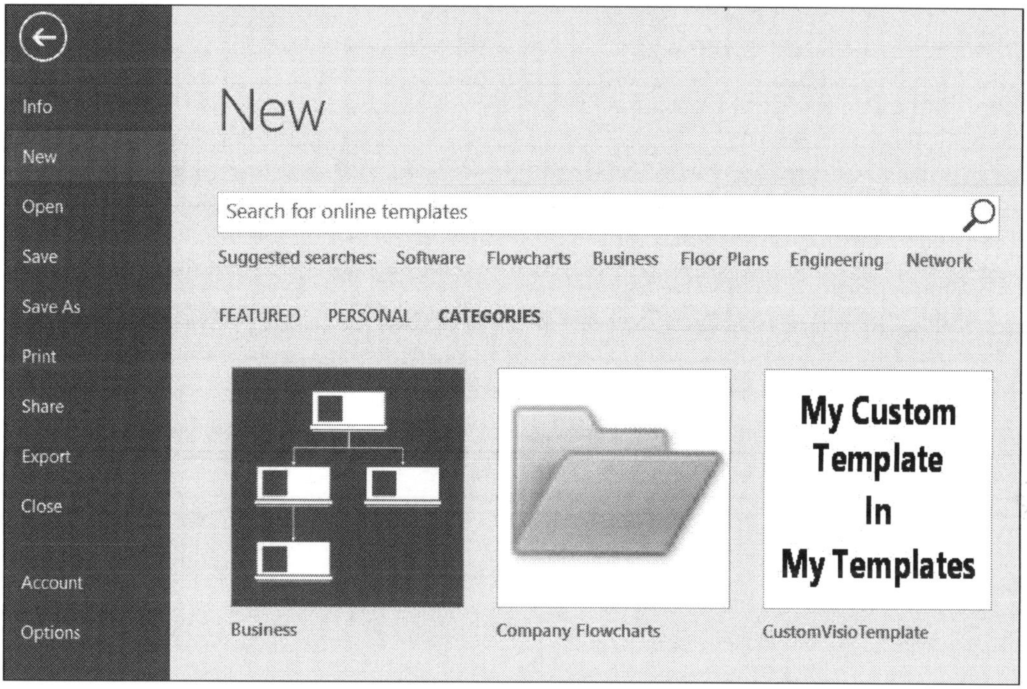


There is no way currently of updating the default image for a sub-folder that appears as a category. By default, the template preview image is created from the contents of the first page, but this can be fixed with any suitable image.

> Take a look at this article to learn more about improved template preview images: `http://blogs.msdn.com/b/chhopkin/archive/2008/10/29/create-perfect-previews-for-your-templates.aspx`

# Including in a custom template

A custom template can be saved with Microsoft stencils docked, just like the Microsoft templates. If the template document contains Masters with the same name as the Masters on the Microsoft stencils, then the custom Master should be substituted for the Microsoft Master, provided that the **Match master by name on drop** setting is ticked. It is possible that the differences between the custom Master and the Microsoft Master are so great that Visio cannot reconcile them as being the same. In this case, a duplicate Master will be created automatically.

The main Microsoft Office applications all have a **Default personal templates location** field automatically set to `<Documents>\Custom Office Templates\`. The **Visio Options** dialog can be opened by selecting **File** | **Options** | **Save**. It appears blank by default for Visio installations, so perhaps setting it to the same folder as the other programs could be considered convenient, as shown in the following screenshot:

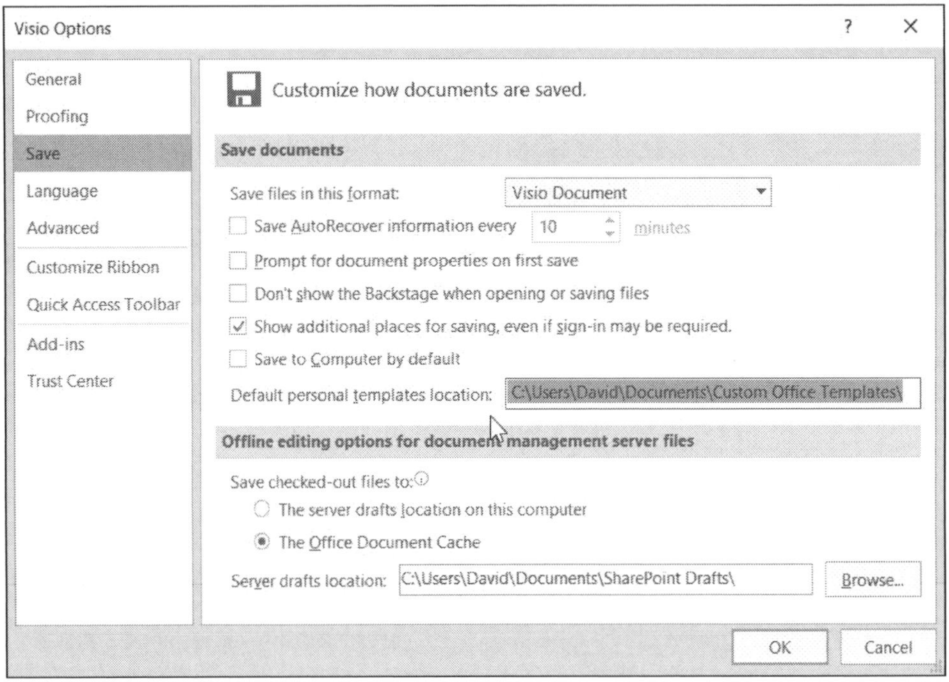

Then a Visio document template can be saved in this folder, or in a sub-folder, as shown in the following screenshot:

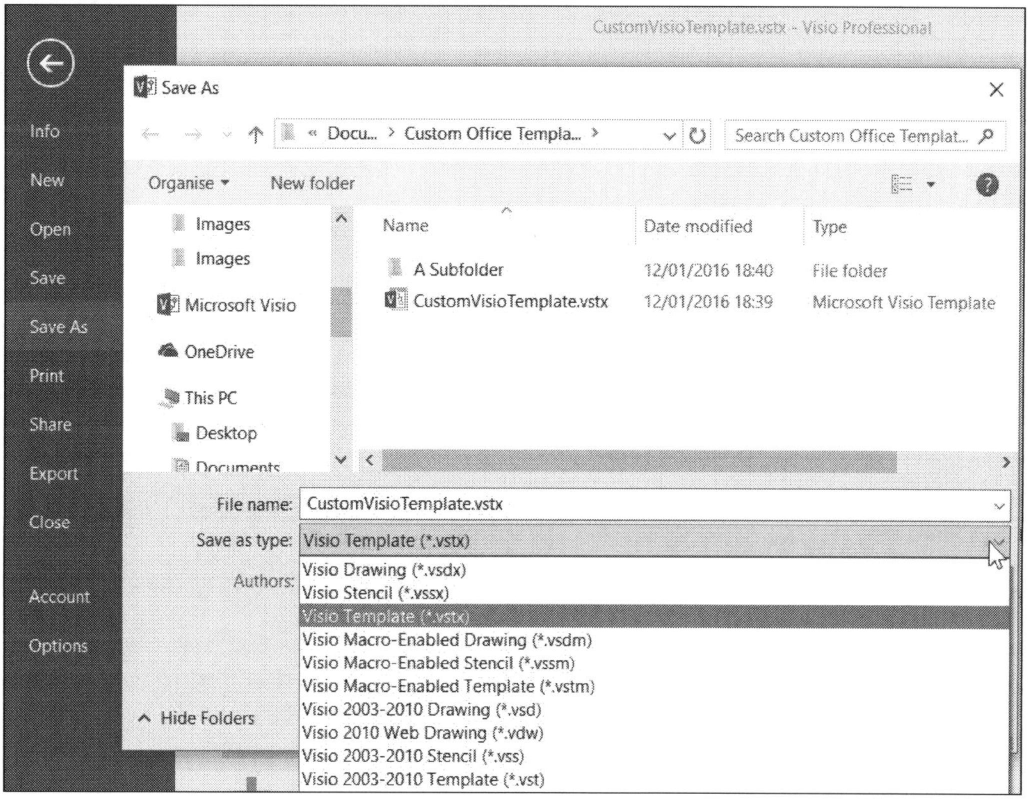

If Visio detects a template in the personal templates location, then **PERSONAL** appears to the left of **CATEGORIES** in the UI, as shown in the following screenshot. Also, if there are sub-folders with templates in them, then they appear too:

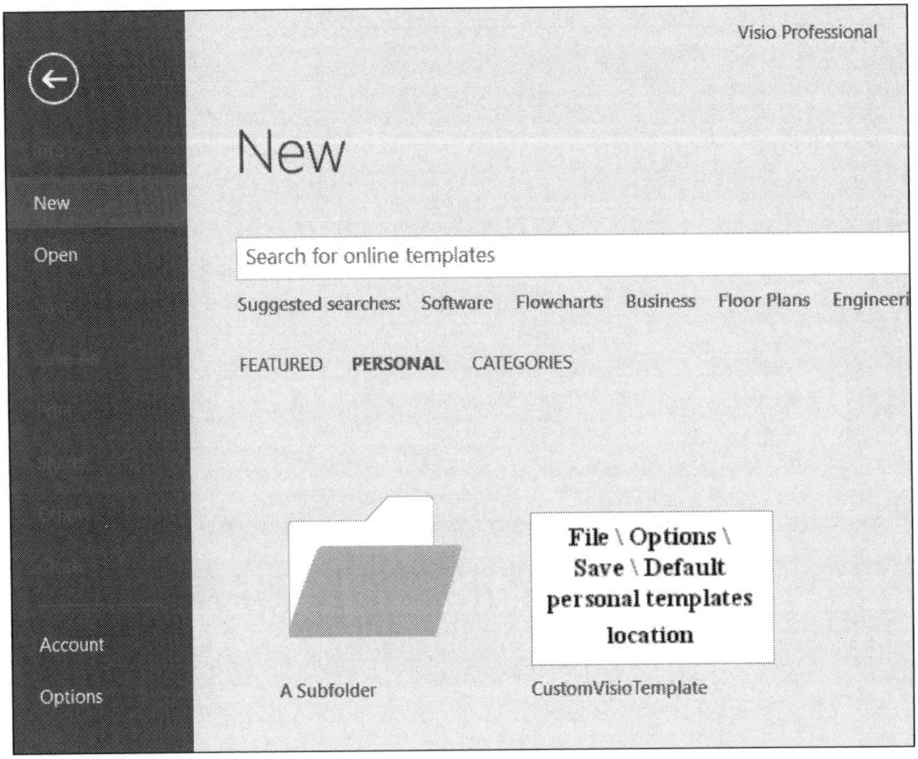


Again, by default, the template preview image is created from the contents of the first page.

# Delivering Templates and Stencils with SharePoint

Visio Templates can be set as a **Content Type** for any Document Library in SharePoint. This is covered in detail in *Chapter 12, Integrating Validated Diagrams with SharePoint 2013 and Office365*, from my previous book, *Microsoft Visio 2013 Business Process Diagramming and Validation*.

Take a look at `https://www.packtpub.com/hardware-and-creative/microsoft-visio-2013-business-process-diagramming-and-validation` for details.

# Creating installation packages

A development application, such as Microsoft Visual Studio, can create **MSI** (**Microsoft Installation**) packages. This can include the templates and stencils in a single package and provide the user with an interface to select where these files are to be installed on the PC, as shown in the following screenshot of a Visual Studio Installer project:

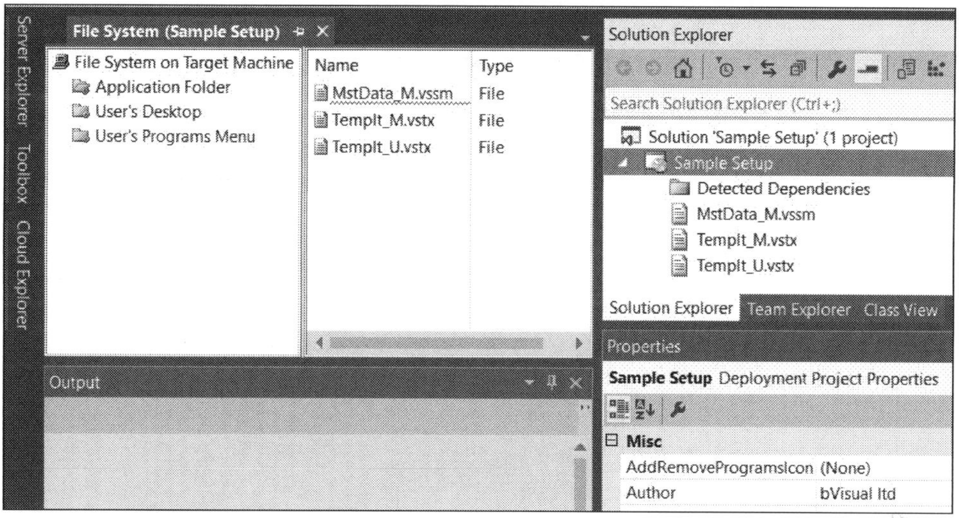

These templates and stencils will not be discovered by the Visio UI unless they are installed in the specific directories discussed earlier in this chapter. However, the MSI file can be enhanced by the Visio Solution Publishing Tool that comes with the Microsoft Visio Software Development Kit (SDK). This provides the ability of defining the **Visio Version** language (**LCID**) and the **Menu path**, as shown in the following screenshot:

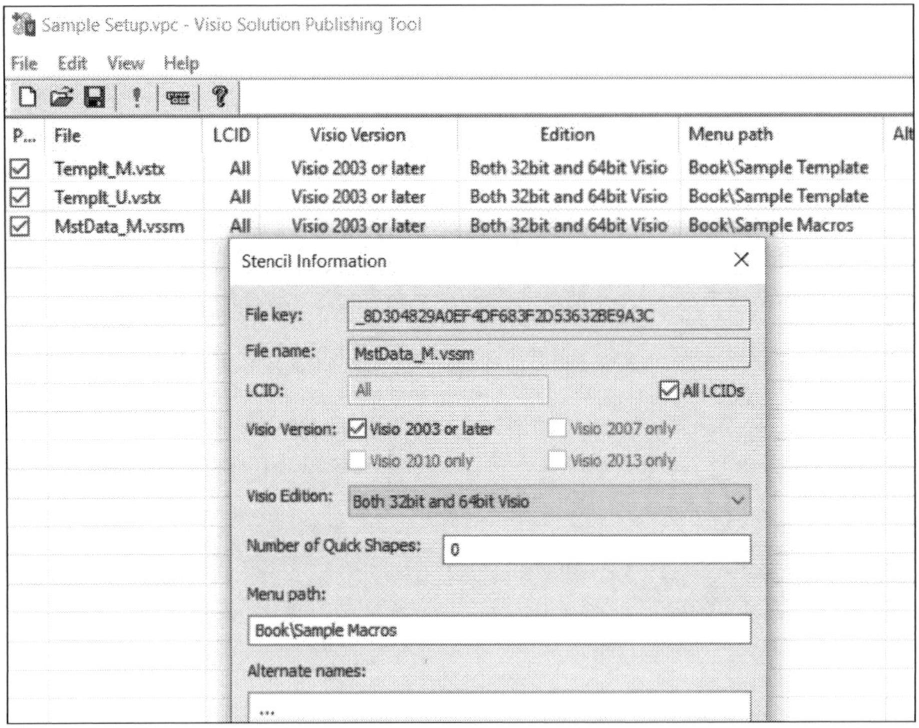


The **Menu path** field defines a category before the backslash, and the stencil or template name after it. This presents the template with a **Book** category, as shown in the following screenshot:

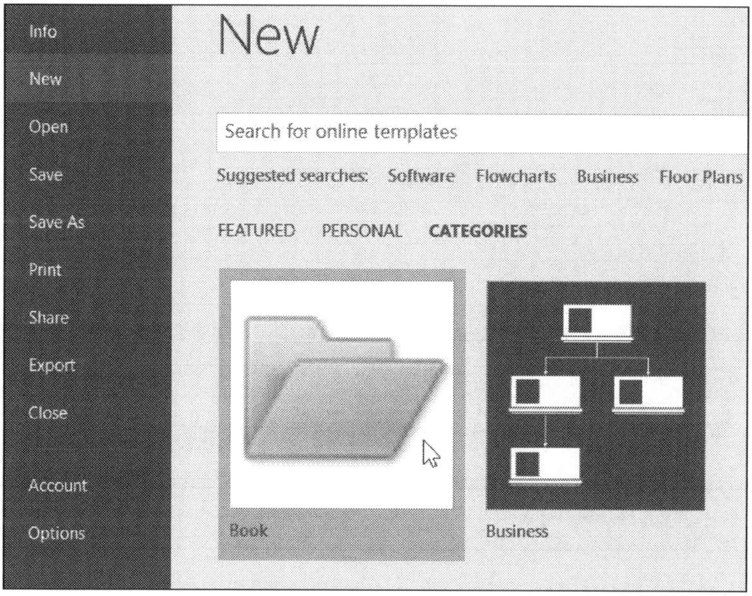


There is just one template displayed inside the **Book** category, but there are two options for **Units** provided, as shown in the following screenshot:

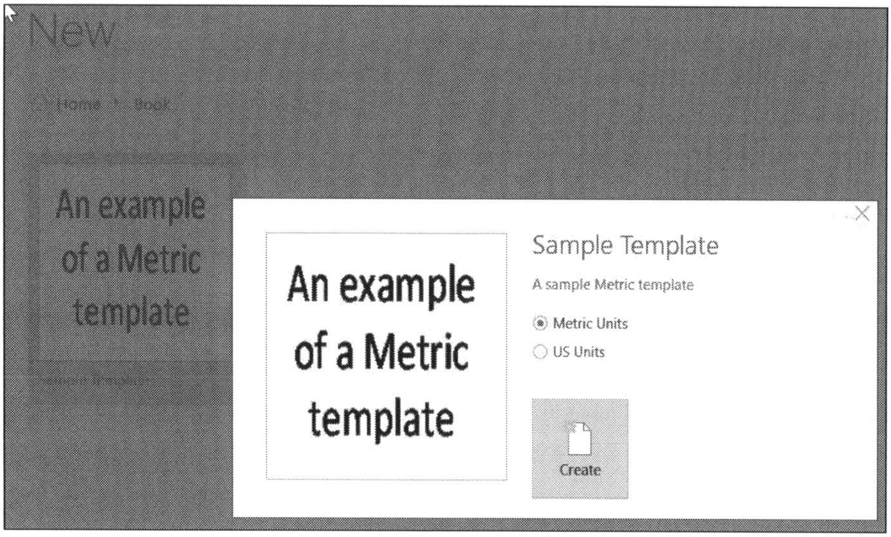

This is because the source files were similarly named but with a suffix of `_M` for **Metric Units** and `_U` for **US Units**. The Visio Solution Publishing Tool was used to provide them both with the same name, that is, **Sample Template**.

The **Sample Macros** stencil is displayed in the Visio UI under a **Book** category, as shown in the following screenshot:

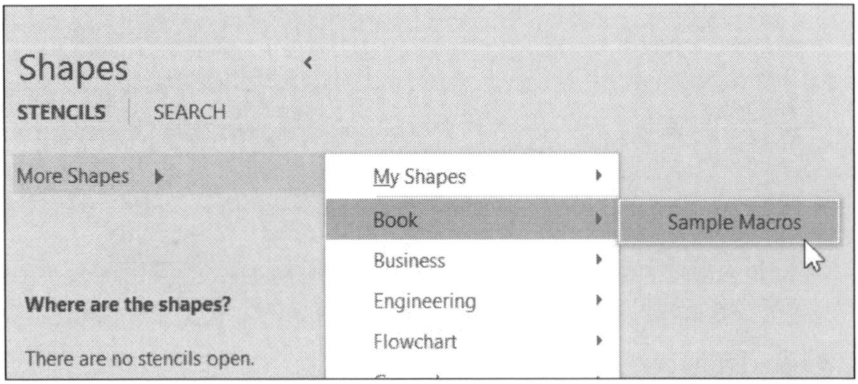


Only one stencil was included in this installation package, and it was saved as a metric document. It will not be displayed if the drawing document is **US Units**. Therefore, installations that require Stencils to be visible in both units will need to include duplicates with the `_M` and `_U` prefixes, but with the same **Menu path** in the tool.

> Find out more about the Visio Solution Publishing Tool at `https://msdn.microsoft.com/en-us/library/bb677166(v=office.12).aspx#Vis2007Publishing_UsingtheVisioSolutionPublishingTool`.

There is a WiX Setup Project alternative to using the MSI and Visio Solution Publishing Tool method. This was documented in *Chapter 11, A Worked Example for Data Flow Model Diagrams – Part 3*, in my previous book, *Microsoft Visio 2013 Business Process Diagramming and Validation.*

> Download the latest Visio SDK from `https://www.microsoft.com/en-us/search/result.aspx?q=Visio+SDK&form=dlc`.

# Summary

In this chapter, we learned how to create enhanced versions of Microsoft Visio Master shapes, and how to create our own Stencils and Masters. We then learned how we can share these customizations with others.

In the next chapter, we will learn how to create custom Text Callouts, Icon Sets, and Data Bars graphic items for use in Data Graphics.

# 7

# Creating Custom Data Graphics

In *Chapter 4, Using the Built-In Data Graphics*, we learned how to use the built-in Data Graphics. There are three types of graphic items to display data values: text callouts, icons, and data bars. In addition, there is the ability to color by value, but this does not require any new shapes.

This chapter covers enhancing existing data graphic items, and the creation of new Text Callouts, Icon Sets, and Data Bars.

In this chapter, we will learn the following topics:

- How graphic item Masters are structured
- How custom Icon Sets are created
- How custom Data Bars are created
- How custom Text Callouts are created

# Understanding the structure of graphic item Masters

Each of the three types of graphic item master (Text Callout, Icon Set, and Data Bar) have their own special ShapeSheet cells. These cells provide the information for Visio to present in the **Data Graphic** dialogs and for the application to add the graphic items to each shape. The following screenshot shows a Text Callout (with the letter symbol and the e-mail address), an Icon Set (with a thumbs up or down), and a Data Bar (displaying the salary range for the grade):

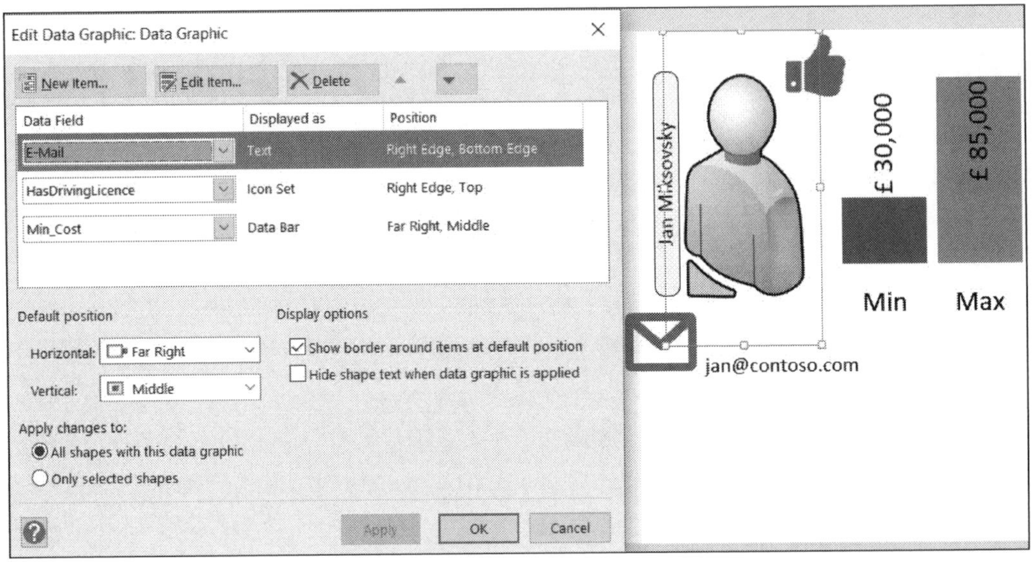


The configuration of these graphic items is contained within a Data Graphic Master. When a Data Graphic is applied to a shape, each Graphic Item Master is inserted into it. Of course, this cannot happen if the target shape is not a group shape, so it must first be converted into a group if it is not one already.

If the Data Graphic configuration is changed, then each of the shapes that have it applied on them must be re-configured.

Each graphic item Master contains a shape that has a number of User-defined Cells and Shape Data rows that are used to configure the shape. The Shape Data rows are marked as invisible, but they have particular row names and cell values that are recognized by the Visio engine. Similarly, there are a number of reserved row names for User-defined Cells.

The developer may add other Shape Data rows, but they will not be surfaced in the UI. The developer may also add other User-defined Cells to enhance the Graphic Item shapes.

The naming of the reserved User-defined Cells appears to be inconsistent because some are given the prefix of `msv` or `vis`, but others have no prefix at all.

# Knowing which Data Graphic is applied

There are times when it may be necessary to know which Data Graphic is applied to which shape. The following macro, `ListShapesDataGraphic()`, will list the name of each shape that has a Data Graphic, along with the name of the Data Graphic:

```
Public Sub ListShapesDataGraphic()
Dim pag As Visio.Page
Set pag = ActivePage
Dim shp As Visio.Shape
Dim dgGuid As String

For Each shp In pag.Shapes
    If shp.CellExists("User.visDGDisplayFormat", _
            VisExistsFlags.visExistsAnywhere) <> 0 Then
        dgGuid = Replace(Replace( _
            shp.Cells("User.visDGDisplayFormat").FormulaU, _
            "USE(", ""), ")", "")
        Debug.Print shp.Name, pag.Document.Masters(dgGuid).Name
    End If
Next

End Sub
```

Immediate

```
Person.763    Data Graphic
Person        Data Graphic
Person.820    Data Graphic
Person.843    Data Graphic
Person.866    Data Graphic
Person.933    Data Graphic
Person.967    Data Graphic
```

This is useful for integrity checking, but it is even more useful to force a Data Graphic to be re-applied. This is done by first removing and then re-applying the Data Graphic to a shape, as shown in the following `ReApplyShapesDataGraphic()` macro:

```
Public Sub ReApplyShapesDataGraphic()
Dim pag As Visio.Page
Set pag = ActivePage
Dim shp As Visio.Shape
Dim dgGuid As String

For Each shp In pag.Shapes
    If shp.CellExists("User.visDGDisplayFormat", _
            VisExistsFlags.visExistsAnywhere) <> 0 Then
        dgGuid = Replace(Replace( _
            shp.Cells("User.visDGDisplayFormat").FormulaU, _
            "USE(", ""), ")", "")
        If Len(dgGuid) > 0 Then
            shp.DataGraphic = Nothing
            shp.DataGraphic = pag.Document.Masters(dgGuid)
        End If
        Debug.Print shp.Name, pag.Document.Masters(dgGuid).Name
    End If
Next

End Sub
```

Immediate

```
Person.763    Data Graphic
Person        Data Graphic
Person.820    Data Graphic
Person.843    Data Graphic
Person.866    Data Graphic
Person.933    Data Graphic
Person.967    Data Graphic
```

Both of these macros work by extracting the GUID of the Data Graphic applied from the `User.visDGDisplayFormat` cell. This GUID can then be used to reference the Data Graphic Master in the document.

# Reviewing a Text Callout graphic item Master

Visio 2016 introduced a new type of Text Callout Graphic Item that includes an icon to the left of the optional label and value text. For example, the following screenshot shows the Microsoft-provided `Email callout` Master:

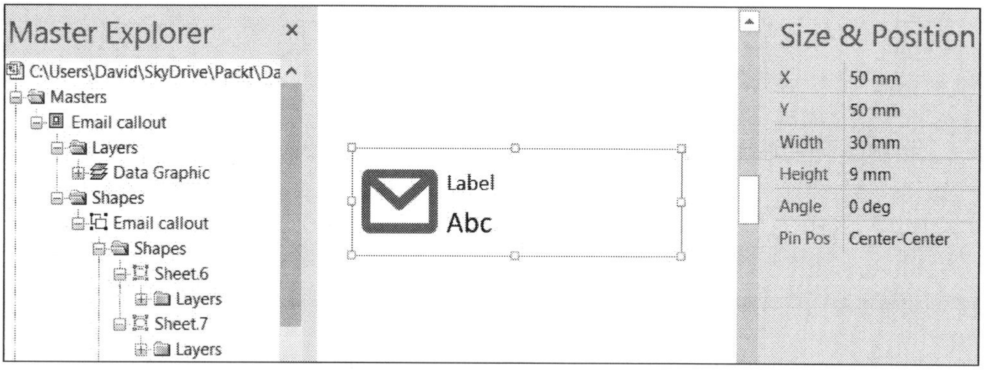


An inspection of the ShapeSheet of the shape shows that there are a lot of User-defined Cells that control the behavior of the shape. For example, the **Height** cell contains a formula that sums up the values from three User-defined Cells, as shown in the following screenshot:

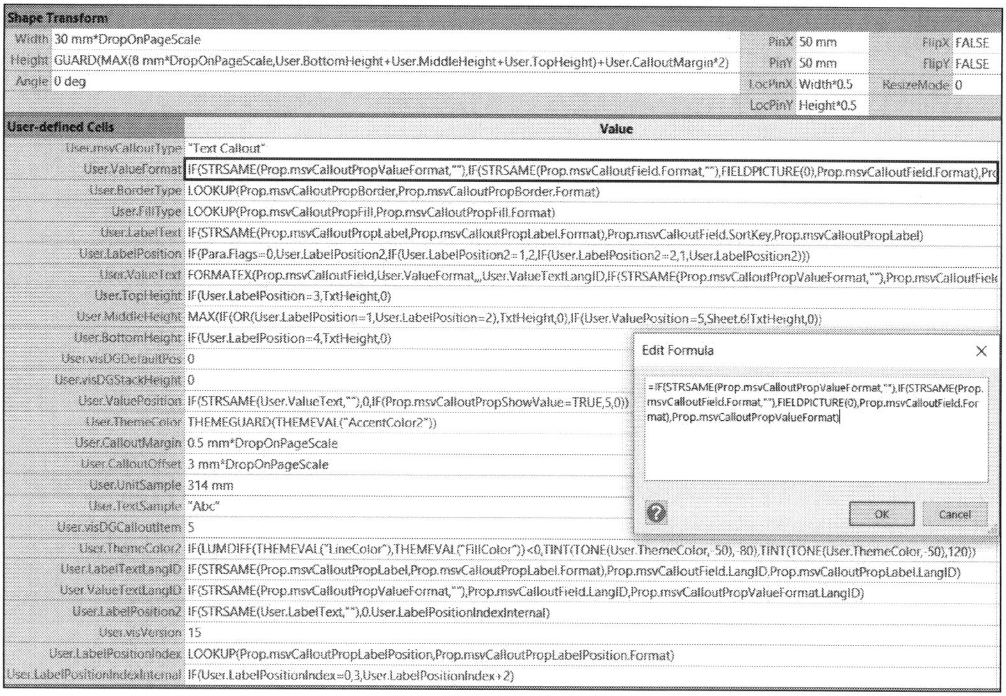

A similar inspection of the Shape Data rows, as shown next, reveals the information that is presented in the Data Graphic **Edit Item** dialog:

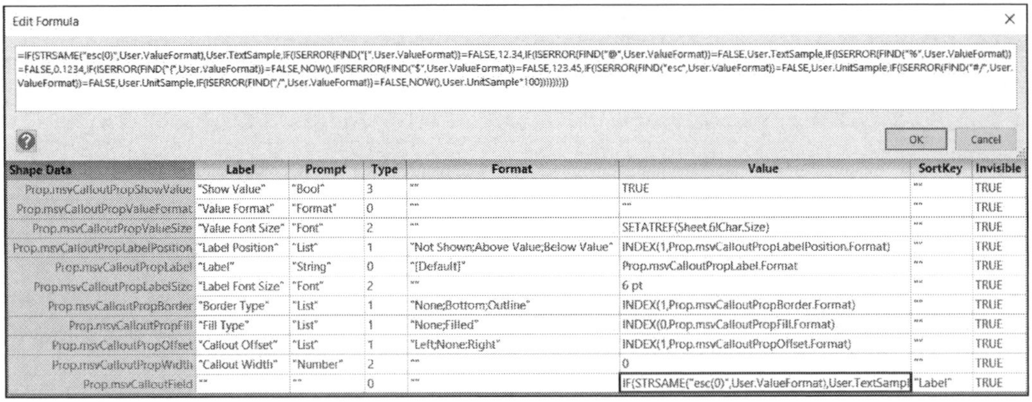


One of these rows, **Prop.msvCalloutPropShowValue**, has been introduced in Visio 2016 because it may not be necessary to show the label or value if there is a symbol present.

The following table lists the special Shape Data rows utilized by Text Callout Masters:

| Row Name | Label | Prompt | Type | Format |
|---|---|---|---|---|
| msvCalloutPropShowValue | "Show Value" | "Bool" | 3 | "" |
| msvCalloutPropValueFormat | "Value Format" | "Format" | 0 | "" |
| msvCalloutPropValueSize | "Value Font Size" | "Font" | 2 | c |
| msvCalloutPropLabelPosition | "Label Position" | "List" | 1 | "Not Shown;Left of Value;Right of Value;Above Value;Below Value" |
| msvCalloutPropLabel | "Label" | "String" | 0 | "[Default]" |
| msvCalloutPropLabelSize | "Label Font Size" | "Font" | 2 | "" |
| msvCalloutPropBorder | "Border Type" | "List" | 1 | "None;Bottom;Outline" |
| msvCalloutPropFill | "Fill Type" | "List" | 1 | "None;Filled" |
| msvCalloutPropOffset | "Callout Offset" | "List" | 1 | "Left;None;Right" |
| msvCalloutPropWidth | "Callout Width" | "Number" | 2 | "" |
| msvCalloutField | "" | "" | 0 | "" |

The `msvCalloutField` row stores a reference to the **Data field** that is assigned to the Text Callout, and the rest of them are presented in the **Edit Item** dialog.

The three label rows (`msvCalloutPropLabelPosition`, `msvCalloutPropLabel`, and `msvCalloutPropLabelSize`) are not required if the Text Callout is a heading type. This is because there is usually no label text present in the shape.

The `msvCalloutField` row has an interesting formula in the **Value** cell, which attempts to ascertain the data type and format required:

```
=IF(STRSAME("esc(0)",User.ValueFormat),User.TextSample,IF(ISERROR(
FIND("[",User.ValueFormat))=FALSE,12.34,IF(ISERROR(FIND("@",User.
ValueFormat))=FALSE,User.TextSample,IF(ISERROR(FIND("%",User.ValueFo
rmat))=FALSE,0.1234,IF(ISERROR(FIND("{",User.ValueFormat))=FALSE,NOW
(),IF(ISERROR(FIND("$",User.ValueFormat))=FALSE,123.45,IF(ISERROR(FIN
D("esc",User.ValueFormat))=FALSE,User.UnitSample,IF(ISERROR(FIND("#/
",User.ValueFormat))=FALSE,User.UnitSample,IF(ISERROR(FIND("/",User.
ValueFormat))=FALSE,NOW(),User.UnitSample*100))))))))
```

The following table lists the User-defined Cells that are found in the **Email callout** Master:

| Row Name | Value |
|---|---|
| msvCalloutType | "Text Callout" |
| ValueFormat | IF(STRSAME(Prop.msvCalloutPropValueFormat,""),IF(STRSAME(Prop.msvCalloutField.Format,""),FIELDPICTURE(0),Prop.msvCalloutField.Format),Prop.msvCalloutPropValueFormat) |
| BorderType | LOOKUP(Prop.msvCalloutPropBorder,Prop.msvCalloutPropBorder.Format) |
| FillType | LOOKUP(Prop.msvCalloutPropFill,Prop.msvCalloutPropFill.Format) |
| LabelText | IF(STRSAME(Prop.msvCalloutPropLabel,Prop.msvCalloutPropLabel.Format),Prop.msvCalloutField.SortKey,Prop.msvCalloutPropLabel) |
| LabelPosition | IF(Para.Flags=0,User.LabelPosition2,IF(User.LabelPosition2=1,2,IF(User.LabelPosition2=2,1,User.LabelPosition2))) |
| ValueText | FORMATEX(Prop.msvCalloutField,User.ValueFormat,,,User.ValueTextLangID,IF(STRSAME(Prop.msvCalloutPropValueFormat,""),Prop.msvCalloutField.Calendar,Prop.msvCalloutPropValueFormat.Calendar)) |
| TopHeight | IF(User.LabelPositionIndex=1,TxtHeight,0) |
| MiddleHeight | MAX(IF(OR(User.LabelPosition=1,User.LabelPosition=2),TxtHeight,0),IF(User.ValuePosition=5,Sheet.6!TxtHeight,0)) |
| BottomHeight | IF(User.LabelPosition=4,TxtHeight,0) |

| Row Name | Value |
|---|---|
| visDGDefaultPos | 0 |
| visDGStackHeight | 0 |
| ValuePosition | IF(STRSAME(User.ValueText,""),0,IF(Prop.msvCalloutPropShowValue=TRUE,5,0)) |
| ThemeColor | THEMEGUARD(THEMEVAL("AccentColor2")) |
| CalloutMargin | 0.5 mm*DropOnPageScale |
| CalloutOffset | 3 mm*DropOnPageScale |
| UnitSample | 314 mm |
| TextSample | "Abc" |
| visDGCalloutItem | 5 |
| ThemeColor2 | IF(LUMDIFF(THEMEVAL("LineColor"),THEMEVAL("FillColor"))<0,TINT(TONE(User.ThemeColor,-50),-80),TINT(TONE(User.ThemeColor,-50),120)) |
| LabelTextLangID | IF(STRSAME(Prop.msvCalloutPropLabel,Prop.msvCalloutPropLabel.Format),Prop.msvCalloutField.LangID,Prop.msvCalloutPropLabel.LangID) |
| ValueTextLangID | IF(STRSAME(Prop.msvCalloutPropValueFormat,""),Prop.msvCalloutField.LangID,Prop.msvCalloutPropValueFormat.LangID) |
| LabelPosition2 | IF(STRSAME(User.LabelText,""),0,User.LabelPositionIndexInternal) |
| visVersion | 15 |
| LabelPositionIndex | LOOKUP(Prop.msvCalloutPropLabelPosition,Prop.msvCalloutPropLabelPosition.Format) |
| LabelPositionIndexInternal | IF(User.LabelPositionIndex=0,3,User.LabelPositionIndex+2) |

The `msvCalloutType` row has the `Heading` formula in the **Text Callout** Masters that do not have a label defined.

**How to create spacer rows in a Data Graphic**

Sometimes it is useful to add blank rows between graphic items. To do this, simply use a Text Callout and choose not to show either the label or the value.

# Reviewing an Icon Set graphic item Master

All of the Icon Sets provided by Microsoft are 6 mm/0.25 in square. Some of them achieve different graphical representations with simple color and geometry changes. However, some of them require sub-shapes because they need more than one color, such as the **Flags** Master displayed in the next screenshot:

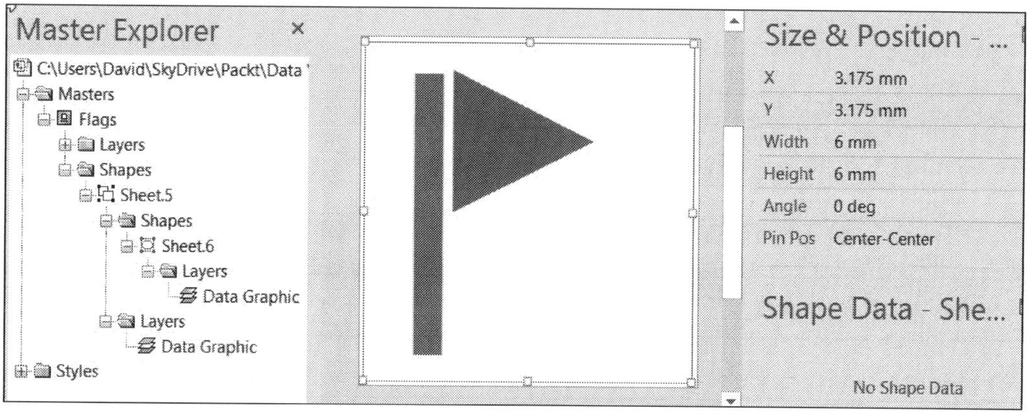

An inspection of the ShapeSheet reveals that Icon Sets are less complicated than Text Callouts, as shown in the following screenshot:

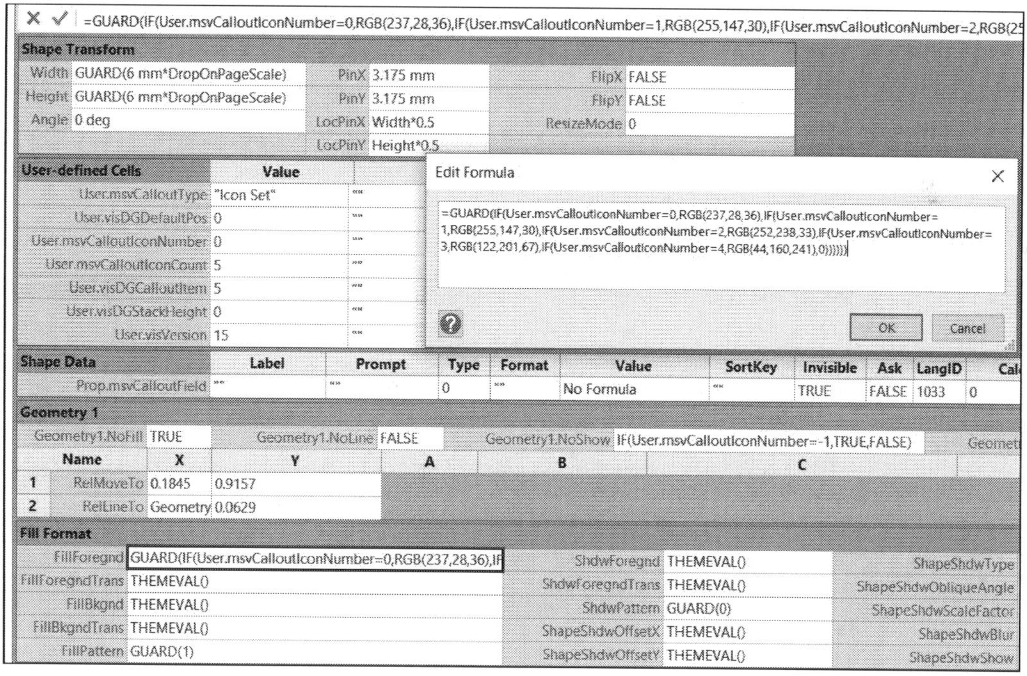

There is very little required in the **Shape Data** section because there is no other configuration possible for an Icon Set. This is the table of the Shape Data rows required for an Icon Set:

| Row Name | Label | Prompt | Type | Format |
|---|---|---|---|---|
| `msvCalloutField` | | | 0 | |

The `msvCalloutField` row is displayed as the data field in the UI.

The following table lists the User-defined Cells necessary for an Icon Set:

| Row Name | Value |
|---|---|
| msvCalloutType | "Icon Set" |
| visDGDefaultPos | 0 |
| msvCalloutIconNumber | 0 |
| msvCalloutIconCount | 5 |
| visDGCalloutItem | 5 |
| visDGStackHeight | 0 |
| visVersion | 15 |

An Icon Set can have no more than five icons because that is the maximum number of rows displayable in the UI. However, it is possible to have a sixth one displayed as the default, instead of having no icon.

> Take a look at the following article to see how to include a sixth icon: `http://blog.bvisual.net/2012/04/22/adding-the-sixth-legend-icon-in-visio-2010/`.

# Reviewing a Data Bar graphic item Master

The Data Bar graphic items are very complex because they invariably require multiple sub-shapes. Indeed, some Data Bars even allow for multiple data fields to be assigned to them, such as the **Multi-bar graph** graphic item shown in the following screenshot:

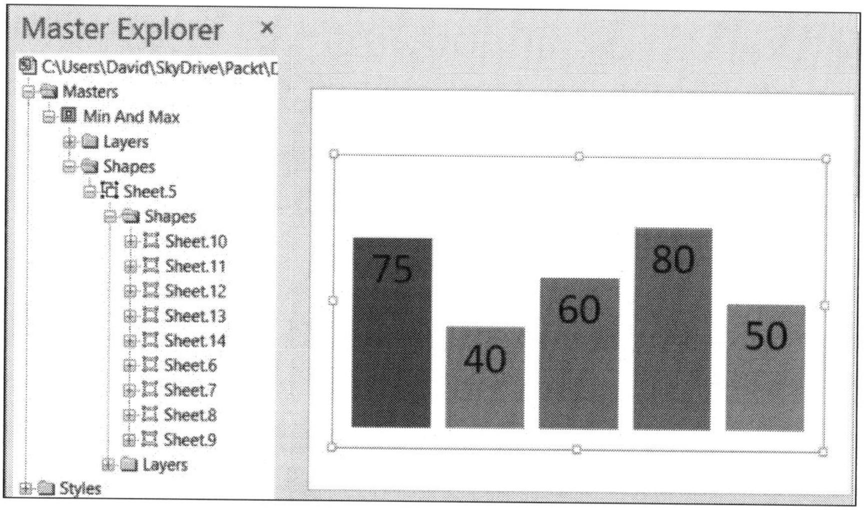


The **Shape Data** section is quite interesting, as shown in this screenshot:

| Shape Data | Label | Prompt | Type | Format | Value | SortKey |
|---|---|---|---|---|---|---|
| Prop.msvCalloutPropMin | "Minimum Value" | "Number" | 2 | "" | 0 | "" |
| Prop.msvCalloutPropMax | "Maximum Value" | "Number" | 2 | "" | 100 | "" |
| Prop.msvCalloutPropValuePosition | "Value Position" | "List" | 1 | "Not Shown;Top;Bo | INDEX(3,Prop.msvCalloutPropVa | "" |
| Prop.msvCalloutPropValueFormat | "Value Format" | "Format" | 0 | "" | "" | "" |
| Prop.msvCalloutPropValueSize | "Value Font Size" | "Font" | 2 | "" | SETATREF(Sheet.10!Char.Size) | "" |
| Prop.msvCalloutPropLabelPosition | "Label Position" | "List" | 1 | "Not Shown;Top;Bo | INDEX(0,Prop.msvCalloutPropLa | "" |
| Prop.msvCalloutPropLabelSize | "Label Font Size" | "Font" | 2 | "" | SETATREF(Char.Size) | "" |
| Prop.msvCalloutPropOffset | "Callout Offset" | "List" | 1 | "Left;None;Right" | INDEX(1,Prop.msvCalloutPropOf | "" |
| Prop.msvCalloutPropHeight | "Callout Height" | "Number" | 2 | "" | 0 | "" |
| Prop.msvCalloutPropLabel1 | "Label 1" | "String" | 0 | "[Default]" | Prop.msvCalloutPropLabel1.Forr | "" |
| Prop.msvCalloutPropField2 | "Field 2" | "Field" | 0 | "" | 0.4*(Prop.msvCalloutPropMax-Pi | "Label 2" |
| Prop.msvCalloutPropLabel2 | "Label 2" | "String" | 0 | "[Default]" | Prop.msvCalloutPropLabel2.Forr | "" |
| Prop.msvCalloutPropField3 | "Field 3" | "Field" | 0 | "" | 0.6*(Prop.msvCalloutPropMax-Pi | "Label 3" |
| Prop.msvCalloutPropLabel3 | "Label 3" | "String" | 0 | "[Default]" | Prop.msvCalloutPropLabel3.Forr | "" |
| Prop.msvCalloutPropField4 | "Field 4" | "Field" | 0 | "" | 0.8*(Prop.msvCalloutPropMax-Pi | "Label 4" |
| Prop.msvCalloutPropLabel4 | "Label 4" | "String" | 0 | "[Default]" | Prop.msvCalloutPropLabel4.Forr | "" |
| Prop.msvCalloutPropField5 | "Field 5" | "Field" | 0 | "" | 0.5*(Prop.msvCalloutPropMax-Pi | "Label 5" |
| Prop.msvCalloutPropLabel5 | "Label 5" | "String" | 0 | "[Default]" | Prop.msvCalloutPropLabel5.Forr | "" |
| Prop.msvCalloutField | "" | "" | 0 | "" | 0.75*(Prop.msvCalloutPropMax-I | "Label 1" |

As for the other graphic items, the `Prop.msvCalloutField` is used for the data field in the UI. However, because this particular Data Bar allows for up to four further data fields to be assigned, they are named `Prop.msvCalloutPropFieldn`, where `n` is from `2` to `5`. The associated labels are named `Prop.msvCalloutPropLabeln`, where `n` is from `1` to `5`:

| **Row Name** | **Label** | **Prompt** | **Type** | **Format** |
|---|---|---|---|---|
| msvCalloutPropMin | Minimum Value | Number | 2 | |
| msvCalloutPropMax | Maximum Value | Number | 2 | |
| msvCalloutPropValuePosition | Value Position | List | 1 | Not Shown;Top;Bottom;Interior;Interior-Rotated |
| msvCalloutPropValueFormat | Value Format | Format | 0 | |
| msvCalloutPropValueSize | Value Font Size | Font | 2 | |
| msvCalloutPropLabelPosition | Label Position | List | 1 | Not Shown;Top;Bottom;Bottom-Rotated |
| msvCalloutPropLabelSize | Label Font Size | Font | 2 | |
| msvCalloutPropOffset | Callout Offset | List | 1 | Left;None;Right |
| msvCalloutPropHeight | Callout Height | Number | 2 | |
| msvCalloutPropLabel1 | Label 1 | String | 0 | [Default] |
| msvCalloutPropField2 | Field 2 | Field | 0 | |
| msvCalloutPropLabel2 | Label 2 | String | 0 | [Default] |
| msvCalloutPropField3 | Field 3 | Field | 0 | |
| msvCalloutPropLabel3 | Label 3 | String | 0 | [Default] |
| msvCalloutPropField4 | Field 4 | Field | 0 | |
| msvCalloutPropLabel4 | Label 4 | String | 0 | [Default] |
| msvCalloutPropField5 | Field 5 | Field | 0 | |
| msvCalloutPropLabel5 | Label 5 | String | 0 | [Default] |
| msvCalloutField | | | 0 | |

If there was only one data field, then its label row would be named just `Prop.msvCalloutPropLabel`.

Indeed, it is possible to have more or less than five data fields with a Data Bar. The only requirement is that the appropriately named rows be present.

The following table lists the User-defined Cells in the **Multi-bar graph** Master:

| Row Name | Value |
|---|---|
| msvCalloutType | "Data Bar" |
| visDGDefaultPos | 0 |
| LabelPos | LOOKUP(Prop.msvCalloutPropLabelPosition,Prop.msvCalloutPropLabelPosition.Format) |
| ValuePos | LOOKUP(Prop.msvCalloutPropValuePosition,Prop.msvCalloutPropValuePosition.Format) |
| Margin | 1 mm*DropOnPageScale |
| CalloutOffset | 3 mm*DropOnPageScale |
| FullBarWidth | Height*0.285 |
| FullBarHeight | IF(User.LabelPos=0,IF(AND(User.ValuePos<>1,User.ValuePos<>2),Height*1-User.Margin*2,Height*0.75-User.Margin),IF(User.LabelPos=3,IF(User.ValuePos=1,Height*0.5,Height*0.5-User.Margin),IF(AND(User.ValuePos<>1,User.ValuePos<>2),Height*0.75-User.Margin,IF(User.LabelPos=User.ValuePos,Height*0.5-User.Margin,Height*0.5)))) |
| BarBottom | IF(User.LabelPos=3,IF(User.ValuePos=1,Height*0.375,Height*0.5),IF(User.LabelPos=2,IF(User.ValuePos=2,Height*0.5,Height*0.25),IF(User.ValuePos=2,Height*0.25,User.Margin))) |
| BarLeft | User.Margin |
| PercentFilled | (Prop.msvCalloutField-Prop.msvCalloutPropMin)/(Prop.msvCalloutPropMax-Prop.msvCalloutPropMin) |
| BarLength | IF(ISERR(User.PercentFilled),0,IF(User.PercentFilled<0,0,IF(User.PercentFilled>1,1,User.PercentFilled)))*User.FullBarHeight |
| LabelText | IF(STRSAME(Prop.msvCalloutPropLabel1,Prop.msvCalloutPropLabel1.Format),Prop.msvCalloutField.SortKey,Prop.msvCalloutPropLabel1) |
| ThemeColor | THEMEGUARD(THEMEVAL("AccentColor")) |
| BarCount | 1+IF(ISERRNA(Prop.msvCalloutPropField2),0,1)+IF(ISERRNA(Prop.msvCalloutPropField3),0,1)+IF(ISERRNA(Prop.msvCalloutPropField4),0,1)+IF(ISERRNA(Prop.msvCalloutPropField5),0,1) |
| visDGCalloutItem | 5 |
| ThemeColor2 | IF(LUMDIFF(THEMEVAL("LineColor"),THEMEVAL("FillColor"))<0,TINT(TONE(User.ThemeColor,-50),-80),TINT(TONE(User.ThemeColor,-50),120)) |
| visDGStackHeight | 0 |

| Row Name | Value |
|---|---|
| LabelTextLangID | IF(STRSAME(Prop.msvCalloutPropLabel1,Prop.msvCalloutPropLabel1.Format),Prop.msvCalloutField.LangID,Prop.msvCalloutPropLabel1.LangID) |
| visVersion | 15 |

# Reviewing a Color by Value graphic item

A Data Graphic Master can store multiple Color by Value configurations, but only one can be applied at any time. The first one encountered from the top of the list in the **Edit Data Graphic** dialog is the one that gets used.

The Color by Value graphic item can assign **Fill Colors** and **Text Colors** to specific values, or (in the case of numerical and date values) it applies them to ranges of values, as shown in the following screenshot:

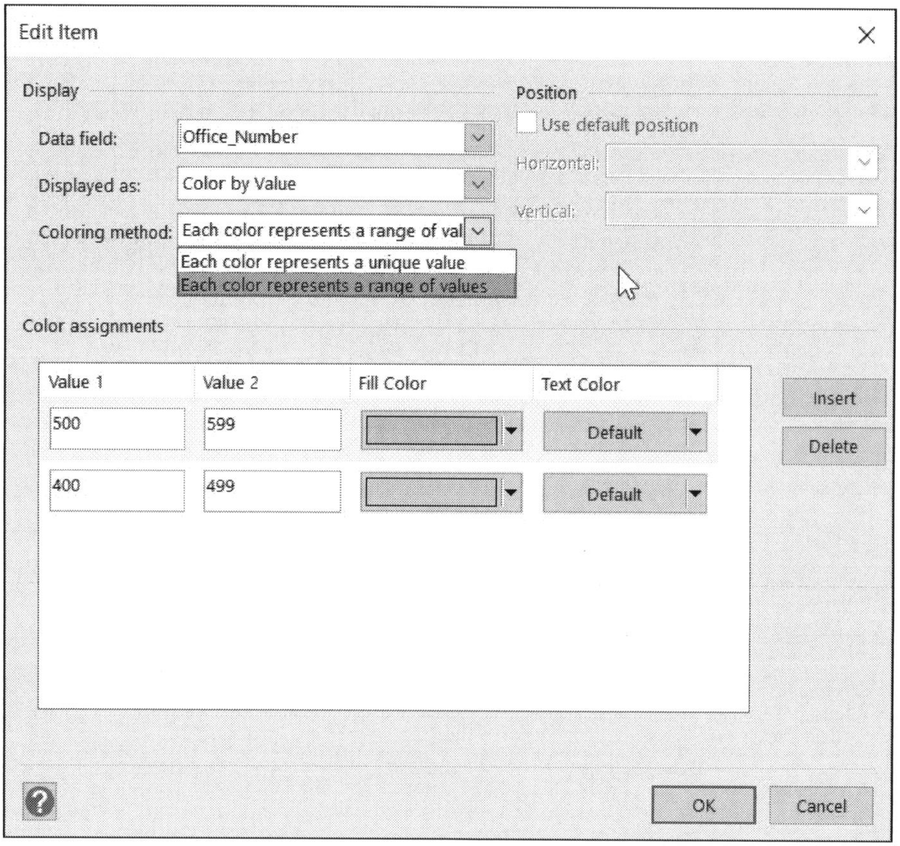

An examination of the ShapeSheet of the data graphic item shown in the following screenshot reveals that these color assignments are set in a potentially very long formula in a User-defined Cells row named `User.visDGColorItemBB`:

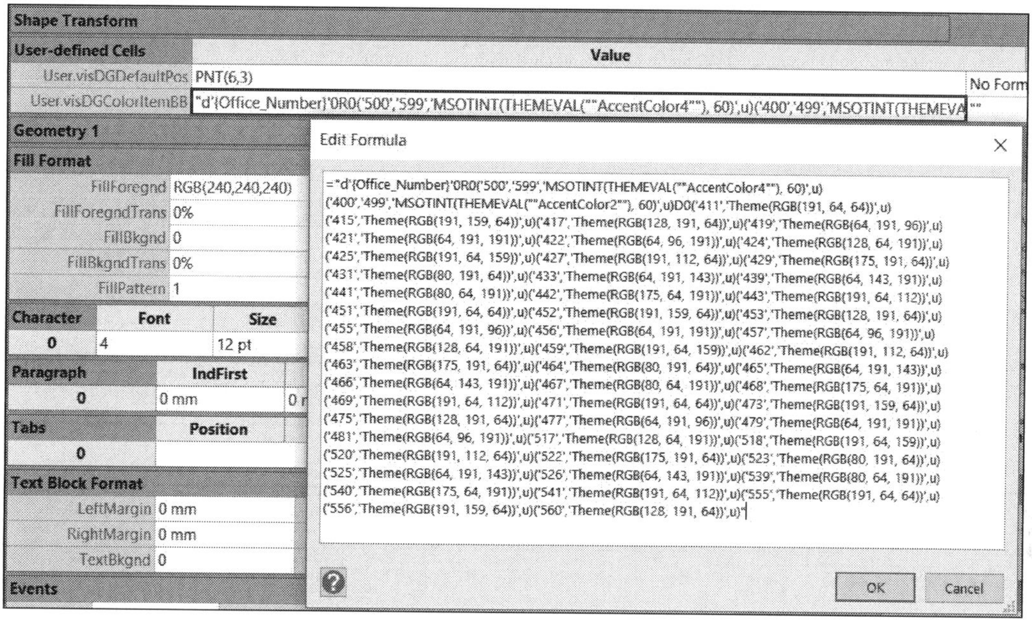


In fact, the row name just needs to start with `visDGColorItem` because Visio then appends a two-character suffix, such as `BB`.

Examination of the formula shows that the range and unique value alternatives are both present, but the version to be applied appears first.

# Modifying graphic items

The easiest way to create a Text callout, Icon Set, or Data Bar graphic item is to duplicate an existing one and then modify it. This is best done in the **Drawing Explorer** window because these graphic item masters are not visible in the Document Stencil. The **Duplicate** command is available on the right-click menu of the source Master. If the desired built-in graphic item is not in the **Drawing Explorer** window, then simply add it to a temporary Data Graphic for a shape in the document. This will bring a copy of the graphic item master into the Document Stencil.

The **Match master name on drop** property should be ticked in the local document stencil version of the Master.

The following screenshot shows the **Protection** section of the ShapeSheet of the graphic item Master. There are several cells that have `1` as a value in them, and they may need to be temporarily changed to `0` in order to unlock them.

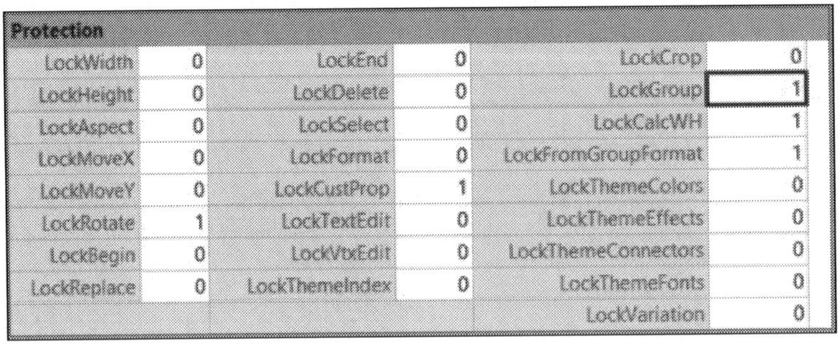

| Protection | | | | | |
|---|---|---|---|---|---|
| LockWidth | 0 | LockEnd | 0 | LockCrop | 0 |
| LockHeight | 0 | LockDelete | 0 | LockGroup | 1 |
| LockAspect | 0 | LockSelect | 0 | LockCalcWH | 1 |
| LockMoveX | 0 | LockFormat | 0 | LockFromGroupFormat | 1 |
| LockMoveY | 0 | LockCustProp | 1 | LockThemeColors | 0 |
| LockRotate | 1 | LockTextEdit | 0 | LockThemeEffects | 0 |
| LockBegin | 0 | LockVtxEdit | 0 | LockThemeConnectors | 0 |
| LockReplace | 0 | LockThemeIndex | 0 | LockThemeFonts | 0 |
| | | | | LockVariation | 0 |

These values should then be returned back to `1` or locked when the edits are complete.

# Modifying a Text Callout graphic item

There are many reasons for amending an existing graphic item, or for a new one to be created.

## Changing the symbol height

The new Text Callouts with built-in symbols are great, but it is a waste of space to keep the symbol the same height even if the label is not displayed. It leaves an empty space above or below the value. One such Master is the **Email callout** Master that was used on the **Person** Shapes, as shown in the following screenshot:

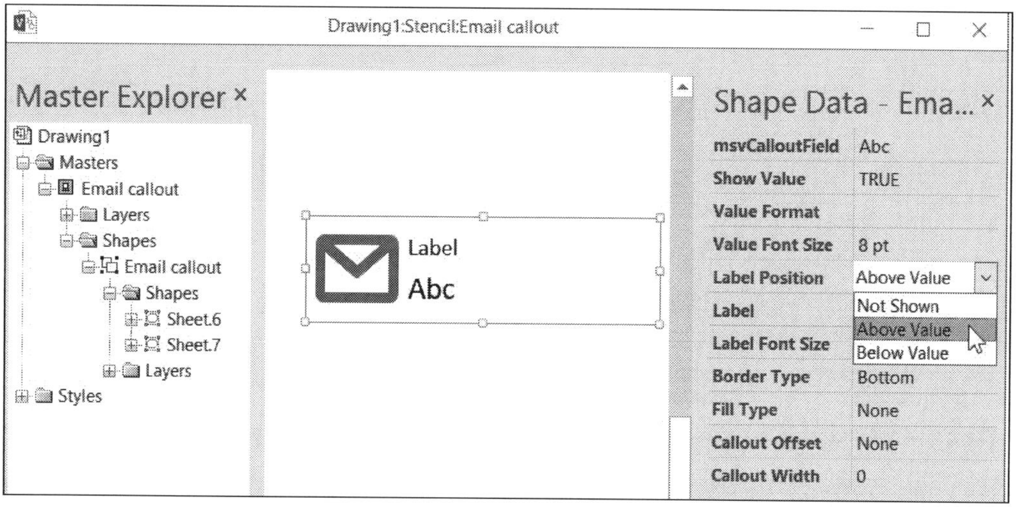


Note that the Shape Data rows have been made temporarily visible for the purpose of this explanation.

An examination of the `Height` formula in the ShapeSheet of the **Email callout Master** reveals the following:

```
=GUARD(MAX(8
mm*DropOnPageScale,User.BottomHeight+User.MiddleHeight+User
.TopHeight)+User.CalloutMargin*2)
```

This formula will force the shape to be a minimum of `8mm` high, regardless of whether the user has chosen to display the label and value or not.

This warranted a further analysis of the referenced User-defined cells, which are extracted in the following table:

| Row Name | Value |
|---|---|
| LabelPosition | IF(Para.Flags=0,User.LabelPosition2,IF(User.LabelPosition2=1,2,IF(User.LabelPosition2=2,1,User.LabelPosition2))) |
| TopHeight | IF(User.LabelPosition=3,TxtHeight,0) |
| MiddleHeight | MAX(IF(OR(User.LabelPosition=1,User.LabelPosition=2),TxtHeight,0),IF(User.ValuePosition=5,Sheet.6!TxtHeight,0)) |

| Row Name | Value |
|---|---|
| BottomHeight | IF(User.LabelPosition=4,TxtHeight,0) |
| ValuePosition | IF(STRSAME(User.ValueText,""),0,IF(Prop.msvCalloutPropShowValue=TRUE,5,0)) |
| ThemeColor | THEMEGUARD(THEMEVAL("AccentColor2")) |
| CalloutMargin | 0.5 mm*DropOnPageScale |
| CalloutOffset | 3 mm*DropOnPageScale |
| LabelPosition2 | IF(STRSAME(User.LabelText,""),0,User.LabelPositionIndexInternal) |
| LabelPositionIndex | LOOKUP(Prop.msvCalloutPropLabelPosition,Prop.msvCalloutPropLabelPosition.Format) |
| LabelPositionIndexInternal | IF(User.LabelPositionIndex=0,3,User.LabelPositionIndex+2) |

The desired appearance is for the symbol to be half size if there is no label displayed, that is, when `User.LabelPositionIndex=0`.

The shape height formula can be modified thus:

```
=GUARD(IF(User.LabelPositionIndex>0,1,0.5)*MAX(8 mm*
DropOnPageScale,User.BottomHeight+User.MiddleHeight+User
.TopHeight)+User.CalloutMargin*2)
```

However, this does not change the height of the symbol, which is defined in the `Sheet.7` sub-shape. This shape is controlled by the formula in its `Width` cell:

```
=GUARD(30 mm*Sheet.5!DropOnPageScale*0.24)
```

This is modified to reduce the size if the parent group shape has no label shown:

```
=GUARD(30
mm*Sheet.5!
DropOnPageScale*0.24*IF(Sheet.5!User.LabelPositionIndex>0,1,0.5))
```

The top-level shape in a Master is almost always `Sheet.5`.

Now the symbol is shown correctly, as can be seen in the following screenshot:

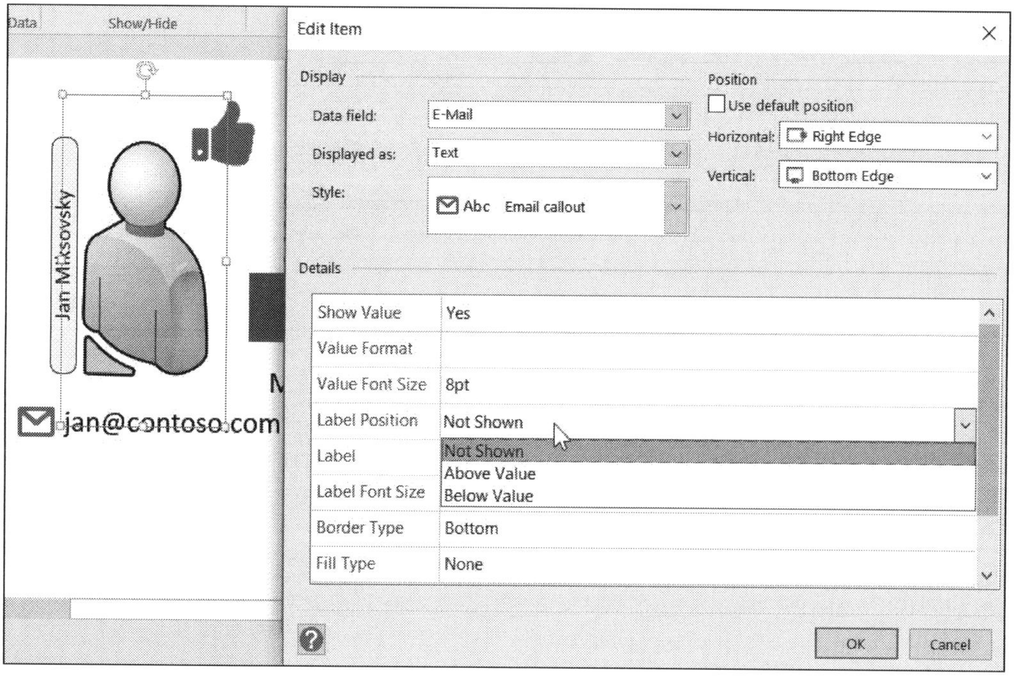

# Using Text Callouts to display symbols

Microsoft Office programs come with several fonts that include a myriad of symbols, as shown in the following diagram of the first few characters in some of these fonts:

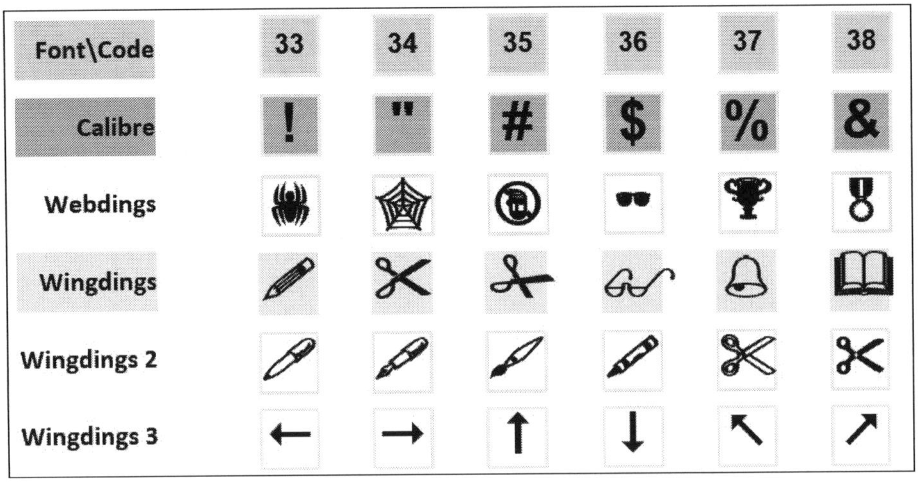


The Webdings font contains over 200 symbols, which can be useful as Data Graphics. The Heading 2 graphic item master has been duplicated in the **Drawing Explorer** window, and the copy has been renamed as `Heading Webdings`. This Master Shape was then edited to change its color and font to Webdings, as shown in the following screenshot:

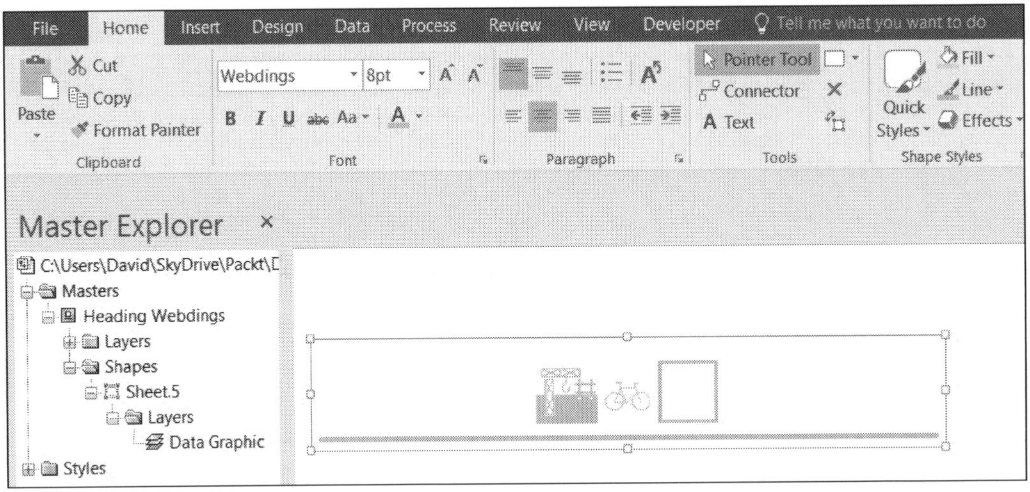

This new graphic item Master can then be used to display symbols. In this case, the following formula will display the `&` character, which happens to be a medal in the Webdings font, whenever a person has a driving licence:

```
=IF({HasDrivingLicence},"&","")
```

This can be seen in use in the following screenshot:

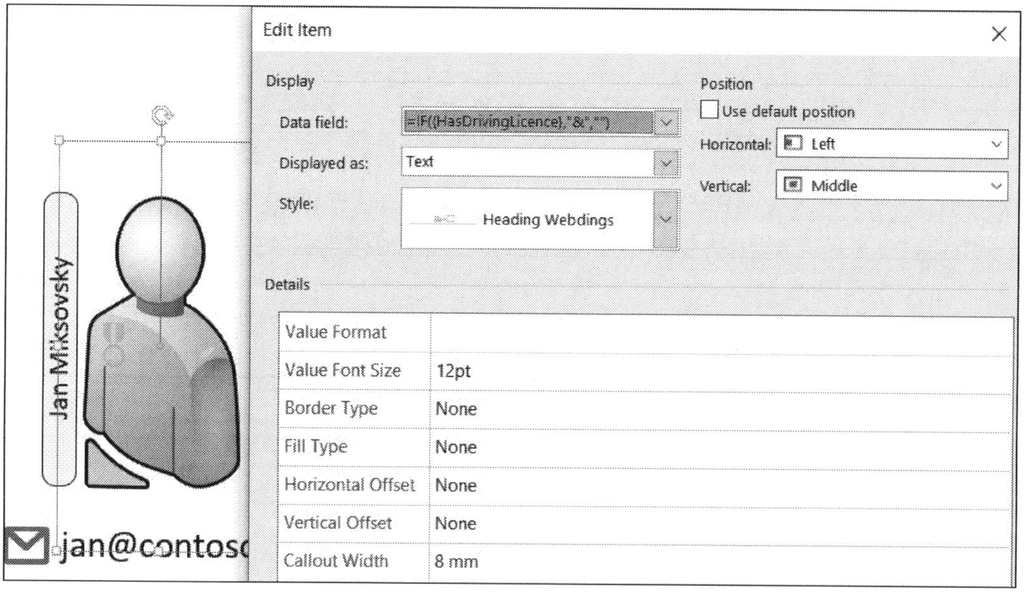


Note that the same result could have been achieved using the `CHAR(...)` function, as shown as follows:

```
=IF({HasDrivingLicence},Char(38),"")
```

This technique is useful in using characters that are not on the keyboard.

The sample download also shows the use of the Windings font to display the correct sign of the Zodiac for any given birth date:

# Modifying an Icon Set

There may be occasions when the built-in icon sets do not provide suitable symbology. For example, it may be useful to indicate gender with internationally recognized signs. The following image is taken from the Wikipedia page at `https://en.wikipedia.org/wiki/Gender_symbol`:

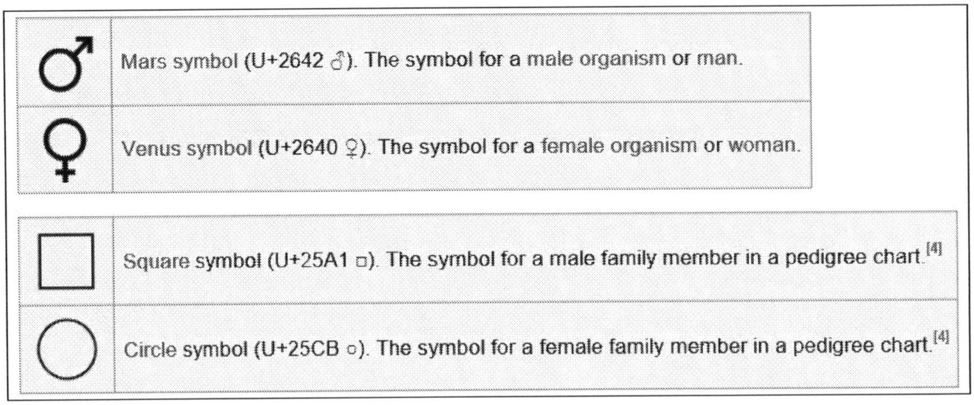


The four symbols displayed are in the order of the `User.msvCalloutIconNumber` values in the User-defined Cell section, from `0` to `3`. The gender is restricted to a Boolean state purely because the data defines it in that way.

Any of the built-in Icon Set Masters can be duplicated and modified. Some of them have sub-shapes that can be deleted, and some just have **Geometry** sections, which can also be deleted.

An **Ellipse** section was added to the ShapeSheet, and then its **NoShow** formula was edited to be invisible with the `=User.msvCalloutIconNumber=2` formula, as shown in the following screenshot:

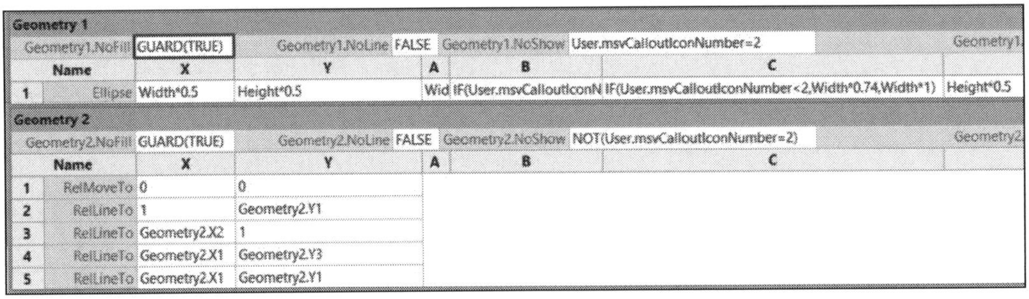


The **NoShow** formula was reversed for the second **Geometry** section with the `NOT(...)` function because the square is only displayed for the third symbol.

Finally, a third **Geometry** section was added to provide the arrow and cross for the normal male and female symbols, as shown in the following screenshot:

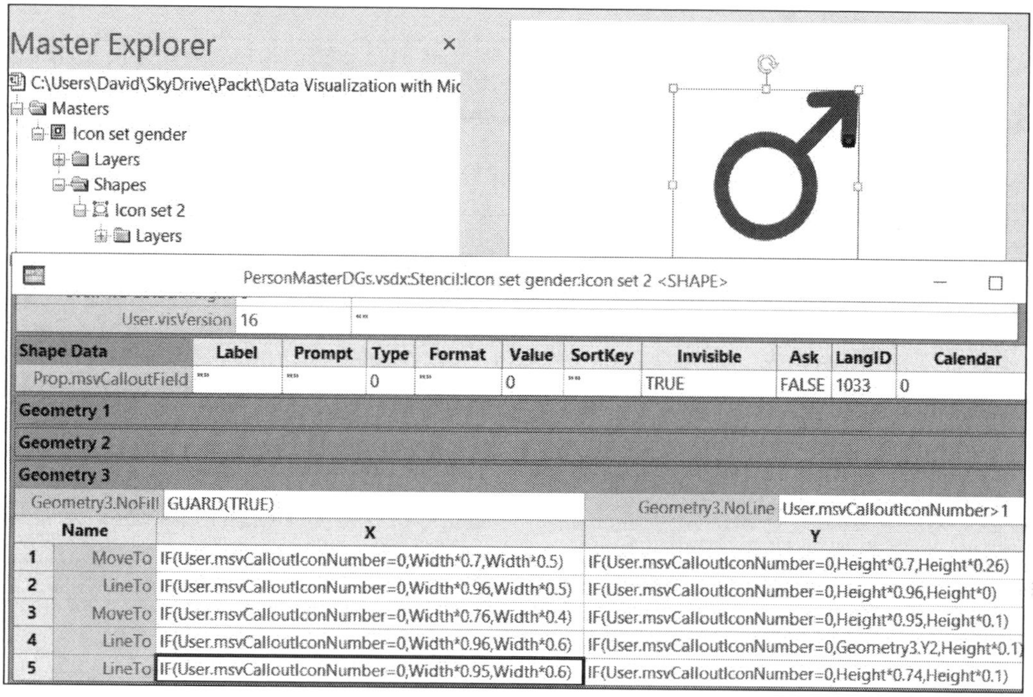


The **LineColor** formula was edited as red for the female symbols and blue for the male ones. This was achieved with the `MODULUS(...)` function because the female symbols are index `1` and `3`; therefore using 2 as the divisor would cause a non-zero value for these values. Then a simple `IF(...)` statement allows for the relevant `RGB(...)` values to be assigned, as shown in the following screenshot:

Line Format
LinePattern GUARD(1)
LineWeight GUARD(Width*0.08)
LineColor GUARD(IF(MODULUS(User.msvCalloutIconNumber,2),RGB(200,30,30),RGB(30,30,200)))
LineCap THEMEVAL()

The Master is named `Icon Set Gender` and becomes available in the **Edit Item** dialog to be assigned to any data field. Only two of the icons need to be matched with values, as shown in the following screenshot:

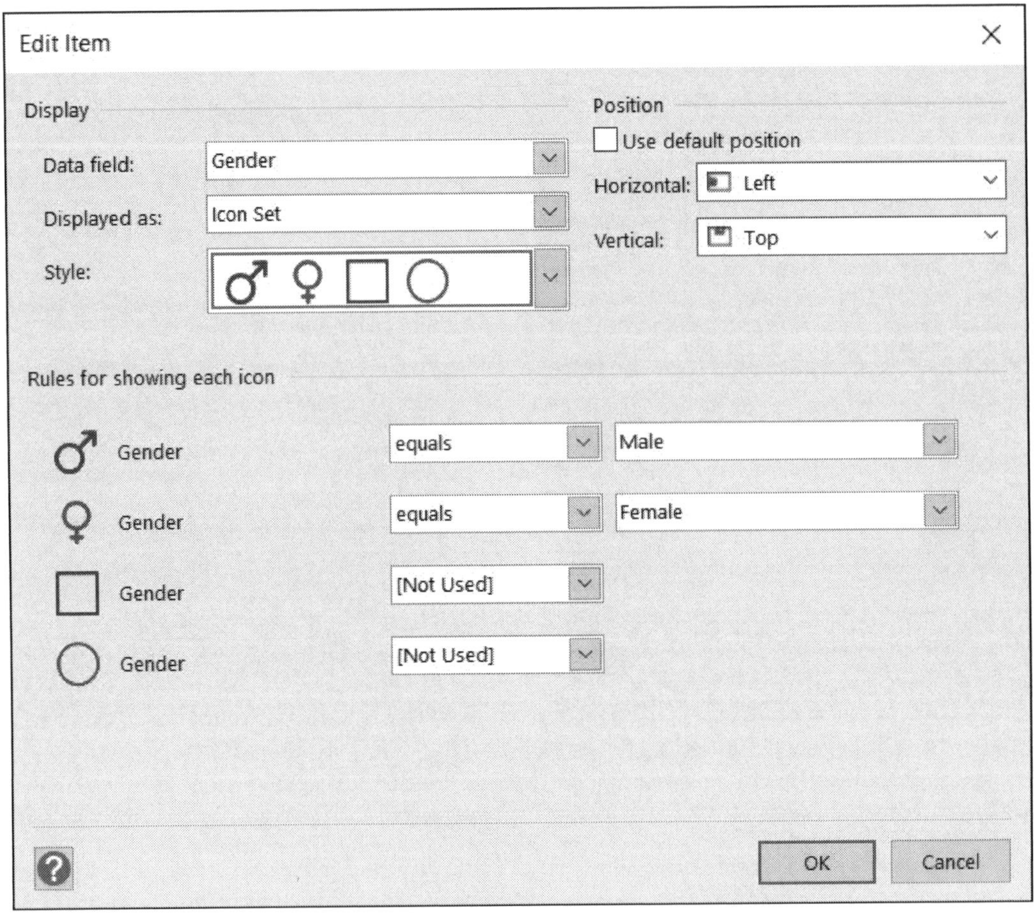


[ The following article describes how to make Icon Sets from any group of shapes or images: `http://blog.bvisual.net/2012/04/19/make-your-own-visio-data-graphic-icons-sets-automatically/`. ]

# Modifying a Data Bar

As stated earlier, Data Bars are more complex, and it is easiest to duplicate an existing Graphic Item master and adapt it. So, for this example, the **Multi-bar graph** Master was duplicated and renamed as `Data Range bar`.

The purpose is to easily display the relative size and position of any range within minimum and maximum values. All but two of the sub-shapes were deleted along with the Shape Data rows that controlled them, as can be seen in the following screenshot:

Fortunately, the sub-shapes only contain the value text.

The following rows were added to the User-defined Cells section:

| Row Name | Value |
|---|---|
| PercentStart | (Prop.msvCalloutPropField2-Prop.msvCalloutPropMin)/(Prop.msvCalloutPropMax-Prop.msvCalloutPropMin) |
| BarStart | IF(ISERR(User.PercentStart),0,IF(User.PercentStart<0,0,IF(User.PercentStart>User.PercentFilled,User.PercentFilled,User.PercentStart)))*User.FullBarHeight |
| ValueText2 | FORMATEX(Prop.msvCalloutPropField2,User.ValueFormat,,,User.ValueTextLangID,IF(STRSAME(Prop.msvCalloutPropValueFormat,""),Prop.msvCalloutField.Calendar,Prop.msvCalloutPropValueFormat.Calendar)) |

Two **Geometry** sections were added to the group shape to remove the fill color from the minimum value to the start of the value in the second data field, and to create a rectangle from the top of the first data field value to the maximum possible.

The following screenshot shows the formulas entered for these **Geometry** sections:

**Geometry 1**

| Geometry1.NoFill | FALSE | Geometry1.NoLine | FALSE |
|---|---|---|---|

| | Name | X | Y |
|---|---|---|---|
| 1 | MoveTo | User.BarLeft | User.BarBottom |
| 2 | LineTo | User.BarLeft+User.FullBarWidth | Geometry1.Y1 |
| 3 | LineTo | Geometry1.X2 | User.BarBottom+User.BarLength |
| 4 | LineTo | Geometry1.X1 | Geometry1.Y3 |
| 5 | LineTo | Geometry1.X1 | Geometry1.Y1 |

**Geometry 2**

| Geometry2.NoFill | FALSE | Geometry2.NoLine | FALSE |
|---|---|---|---|

| | Name | X | Y |
|---|---|---|---|
| 1 | MoveTo | User.BarLeft | User.BarBottom |
| 2 | LineTo | User.BarLeft+User.FullBarWidth | Geometry2.Y1 |
| 3 | LineTo | Geometry2.X2 | User.BarBottom+User.BarStart |
| 4 | LineTo | Geometry2.X1 | Geometry2.Y3 |
| 5 | LineTo | Geometry2.X1 | Geometry2.Y1 |

**Geometry 3**

| Geometry3.NoFill | TRUE | Geometry3.NoLine | FALSE |
|---|---|---|---|

| | Name | X | Y |
|---|---|---|---|
| 1 | MoveTo | User.BarLeft | User.BarBottom+User.BarLength |
| 2 | LineTo | User.BarLeft+User.FullBarWidth | Geometry3.Y1 |
| 3 | LineTo | Geometry3.X2 | Height*1 |
| 4 | LineTo | Geometry3.X1 | Geometry3.Y3 |
| 5 | LineTo | Geometry3.X1 | Geometry3.Y1 |

When this **Data Range bar** graphic item is selected, the user can input the **Minimum Value** and **Maximum Value** for the whole data set. The upper value of the range, **Max_Cost**, is selected for the data field, as shown in the following screenshot:

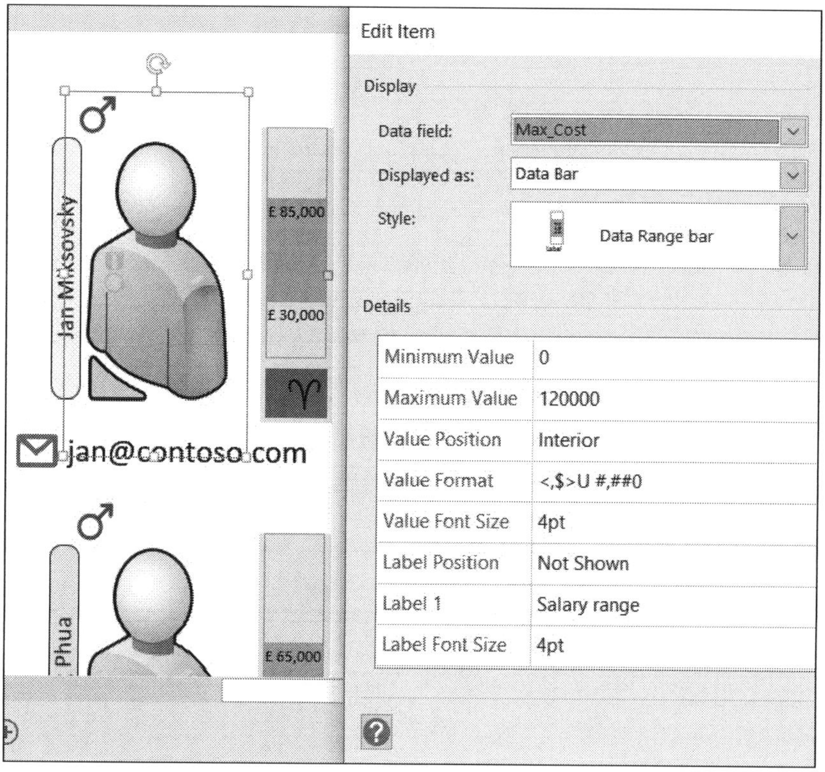


Then the user can scroll down to select the lower part of the range, **Min_Cost**, for **Field 2**.

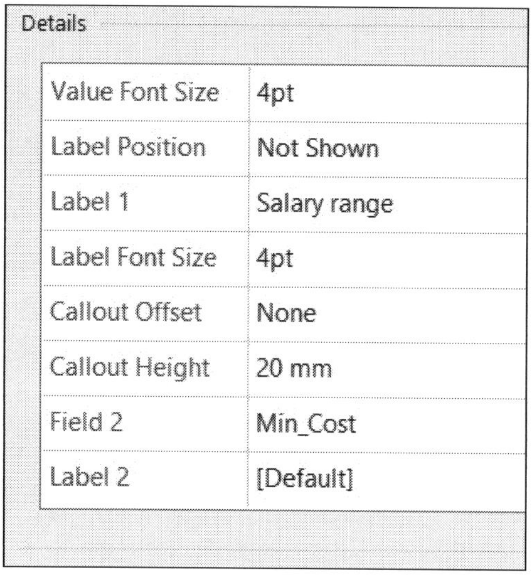

Details
Value Font Size
4pt
Label Position
Not Shown
Label 1
Salary range
Label Font Size
4pt
Callout Offset
None
Callout Height
20 mm
Field 2
Min_Cost
Label 2
[Default]

When all of these modifications are used, then the Person shapes look like the following screenshot:

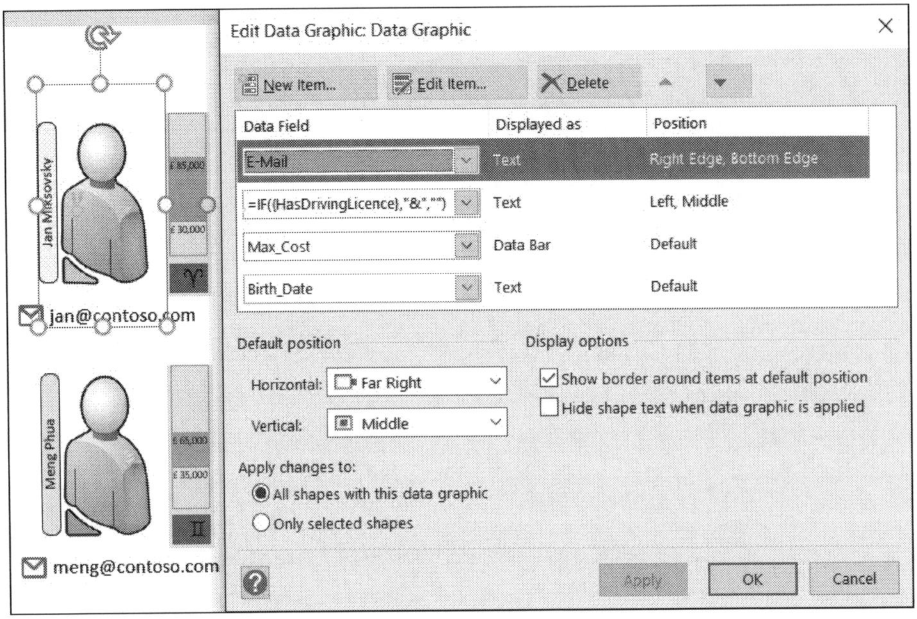


# Summary

In this chapter, you learned how to create enhanced versions of Microsoft Visio Graphic Item Master shapes. We created custom Text callouts, Icon Sets, and Data Bars. We recognized that it is easiest to copy, adapt, and reuse existing Graphic Item Masters.

In the next chapter, you will learn how validation rules can be used to check conformance to corporate standards. You will also learn about the built-in reports tool, and how to extract useful information from structured diagrams.

# 8

# Validating and Extracting Information

In previous chapters, we learnt how to import data and display information graphically. However, Visio can be used to generate data too, so in this chapter we will learn a little about validation rules and the Shape Reports tool. We will learn how to retrieve values from Shape Data and the User-defined Cell rows. We will also learn how to navigate connections between shapes, and whether a shape is inside a container or a list.

In this chapter, we will learn:

- What validation rules are
- How to use the Shape Reports tool
- How to write code to extract information from structured diagrams

## Introducing validation rules

So far, most of this book has dealt with importing data into a Visio diagram, keeping it synchronized with the data source, and displaying the data visually for easy interpretation. However, Visio can also be used to generate data. This data can be Shape Data, but it can also be derived from the connections between shapes, the particular connection point, and the direction of the connector. Data can be generated from the container or list a shape is within, or even the index position within a list.

Data can be exported from Visio to create a report on the contents, or it can be exported to another system. In either case, it is important that the data is correctly structured and formulated because businesses might rely upon its veracity. An example of this is Microsoft SharePoint Workflows. There are templates for both SharePoint 2010 and 2013/2016 workflows in Visio Professional. There are two versions because there are two different SharePoint Workflow engines. It is possible to generate workflows from the Visio diagrams created from these templates. It could be catastrophic if, for example, a never-ending workflow loop was accidentally created. Therefore it is necessary for the diagrams to be validated against a set of rules, as in the following screenshot:

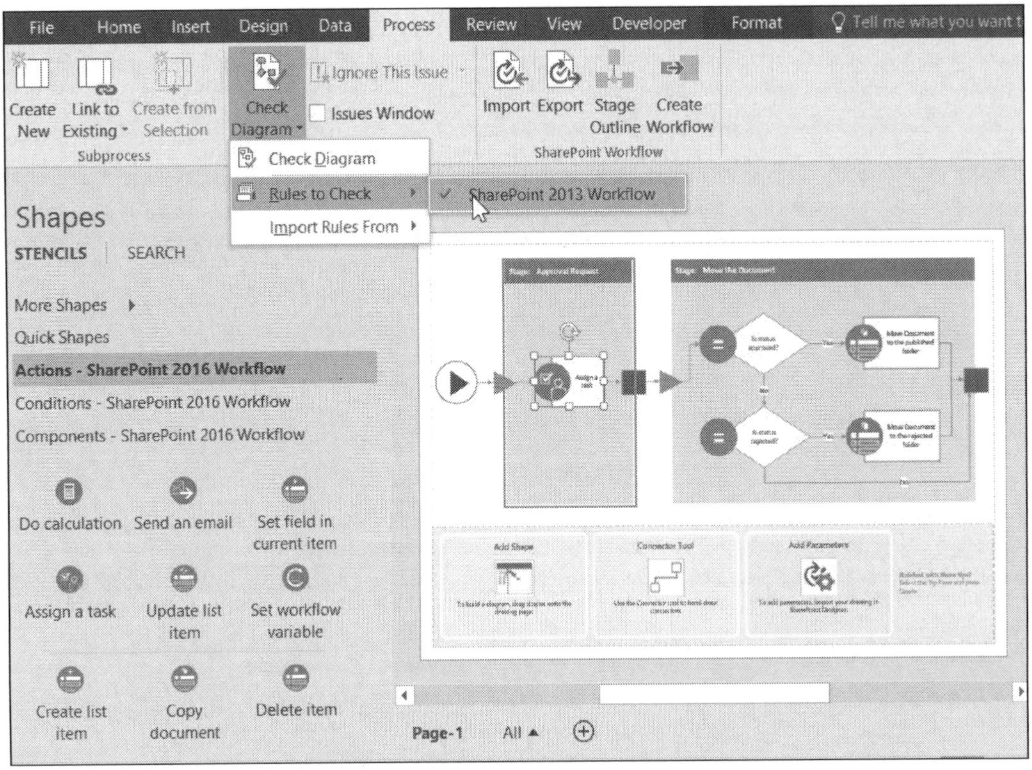


This is done with validation rules, which is part of Visio Professional. These rules can be written in code, such as C# or C++, but can also be written using pseudo-ShapeSheet formulas contained in XML snippets. Microsoft wrote the rules for SharePoint Workflows in code because they are extremely complex, but have provided examples of the XML rules for flowcharts and for BPMN 2.0. The following example is from a small BPMN diagram, where the validation discovers that there is an issue with the process:

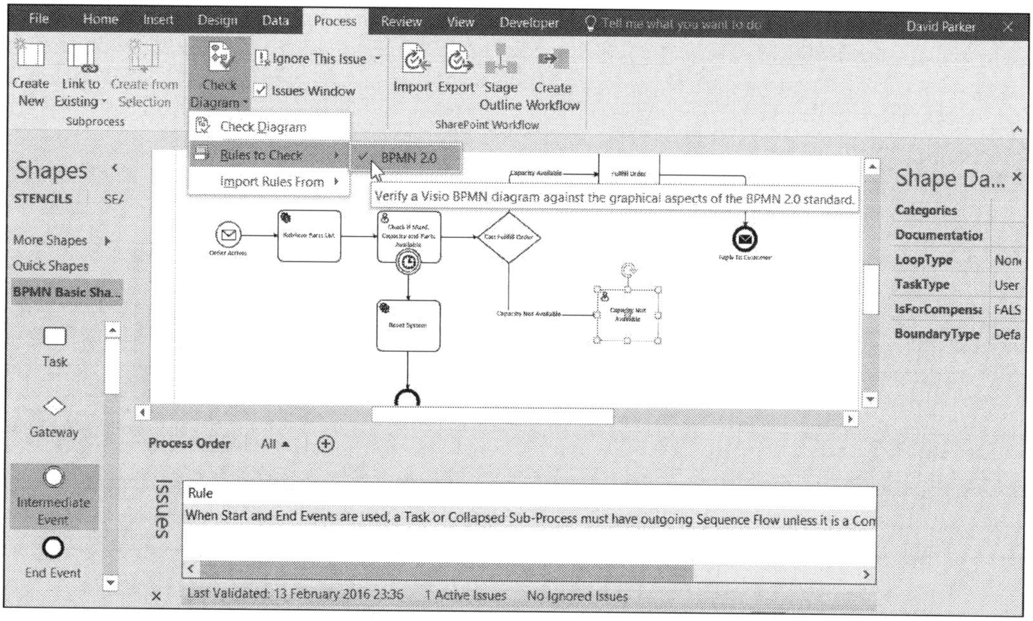


The **Issues** window lists the infringement with a description of the rule that has been transgressed. There is no out-of-the-box interface for viewing the content of these rules, but you can view the rule sets with a little code, as in the following `EnumerateRuleSets()` macro:

```
Public Sub EnumerateRuleSets()
Dim doc As Visio.Document
Dim ruleSet As Visio.ValidationRuleSet
Set doc = Visio.ActiveDocument
Debug.Print "EnumerateRuleSets : Count =", doc.Validation.RuleSets.Count

For Each ruleSet In doc.Validation.RuleSets
    With ruleSet
        Debug.Print "ID :", .ID
        Debug.Print "Enabled :", .Enabled
        Debug.Print "RuleSetFlags :", .RuleSetFlags
        Debug.Print "Count of Rules :", .Rules.Count
        Debug.Print "NameU :", .nameU
        Debug.Print "Description :", .Description
    End With
Next
End Sub
```

Immediate

```
EnumerateRuleSets : Count =  1
ID :            1
Enabled :      True
RuleSetFlags :              0
Count of Rules :            76
NameU :        BPMN 2.0
Description : Verify a Visio BPMN diagram against the graphical aspects of the BPMN 2.0 standard.
```

The following code, `EnumerateRulesSets()`, lists all the rules within the active document:

```
Public Sub EnumerateRules()
Dim doc As Visio.Document
Dim ruleSet As Visio.ValidationRuleSet
Dim rule As Visio.ValidationRule
Set doc = Visio.ActiveDocument
For Each ruleSet In doc.Validation.RuleSets
    If ruleSet.Enabled Then
        Debug.Print "EnumerateRules for RuleSet : " & _
            ruleSet.nameU & " : Count = " & _
            ruleSet.Rules.Count
        For Each rule In ruleSet.Rules
            With rule
                Debug.Print "ID :"; .ID
                Debug.Print "NameU :", .nameU
                Debug.Print "Category :", .Category
                Debug.Print "TargetType :", .TargetType
                Debug.Print "Description :", .Description
                Debug.Print "FilterExpression :", .FilterExpression
                Debug.Print "TestExpression :", .TestExpression
                Debug.Print
            End With
        Next
    End If
Next
End Sub

Private Function getRuleSet(ByVal doc As Visio.Document, _
ByVal nameU As String) As Visio.ValidationRuleSet
Dim retVal As Visio.ValidationRuleSet
Dim ruleSet As Visio.ValidationRuleSet
Set retVal = Nothing
For Each ruleSet In doc.Validation.RuleSets
    If UCase(ruleSet.nameU) = UCase(nameU) Then
        Set retVal = ruleSet
        Exit For
    End If
Next
Set getRuleSet = retVal
End Function
```

This code outputs all the rules in all `RuleSets` in the active Visio document, so the following table displays just the rule that was an issue in the earlier example. Note that the Test Expression has been abbreviated for clarity.

| | |
|---|---|
| **NameU** | `SequenceFlowFromActivities` |
| **Category** | Activities |
| **Target Type** | `visRuleTargetShape` |
| **Description** | When start and end events are used, a task or collapsed sub-process must have outgoing sequence flow unless it is a compensation activity. |
| **Filter Expression** | AND(NOT(Prop.BpmnIsForCompensation),NOT(HASCATEGORY("Expanded Sub-Process"))) |
| **Test Expression** | `IF(AGGCOUNT(FILTERSET(GLUEDSHAPES(2),"Actions.SequenceFlow.Checked"))=0,`<br>`IF(AGGCOUNT(FILTERSET(PARENTCONTAINERS(),"HASCATEGORY(""Expanded Sub-Process"")"))=0, AGGCOUNT(FILTERSET(ThePage!SHAPESONPAGE(),"AND(HASCATEGORY(""Event""),OR(Actions.Start.Checked,Actions.StartNonInterrupting.Checked,Actions.End.Checked), AGGCOUNT(FILTERSET(PARENTCONTAINERS(),""HASCATEGORY(""""Expanded Sub-Process"""")""))=0)"))=0,`<br>`IF(…,`<br>`IF(…,`<br>`IF(…)))),TRUE)` |

If the macro was run on a document created with SharePoint Workflows then there will be `Rules`, but they do not have any values for `FilterExpression` or `TestExpression` because these are written in code.

`Rule` can be targeted at `Shape`, `Page`, or `Document`, and `FilterExpression` ensures that all irrelevant targets are ignored before they are tested with `TestExpression`. As can be seen previously, this expression can be quite complicated, and an examination of it will reveal that some of the functions used, such as `HASCATEGORY()`, are ShapeSheet functions. However, other functions, such as `AGGCOUNT()` and `FILTERSET()`, are only available in `Rule`. Some of the functions available in rules have a close equivalent in a ShapeSheet. For example, `FILTERSET(PARENTCONTAINERS(), <filter>)` is similar to the ShapeSheet function `CONTAINERSHEETREF()`.

> Refer to my previous book for an in-depth look into Visio's validation rules: `https://www.packtpub.com/hardware-and-creative/microsoft-visio-2013-business-process-diagramming-and-validation`.

# Getting information from data diagrams

Visio documents are data diagrams, and Visio can be used to generate data just as easily as it can consume and represent data. Some of the built-in Visio add-ons have custom export features, such as Gantt Chart, which can export a Microsoft Project file. There is also a general tool, Shape Reports, that can be used to export specific shapes and their data. Often, though, it is necessary to write custom extracts with code.

## Using Shape Reports

Visio includes a Shape Reports feature on the **Review** ribbon tab. This can be used to create simple reports of shapes and their data from Visio. It is not a fully featured report writer, but nonetheless it can be very useful at times. Some reports are provided out-of-the box and become available within documents, depending upon the type of shapes found within it. However, it is easy to create custom reports that can be stored as separate files (with a `*.vrd` extension) or within the Visio document. These definitions are written in XML and can be edited directly, but it is more normal to use the UI provided.

The following screenshot shows how a report can be filtered to be on all pages, the active page, or just the selected shapes. The **Advanced...** button opens a dialog that allows the shapes to be further refined by creating criteria that they must match. For example, the screenshot specifies that the `User.msvShapeCatrgories` row must exist, and that the value of it must not be **Connecting Object**. This will have the effect of ignoring all connectors in a BPMN diagram, but including the other shape categories, such as Task, Event, and Gateway.

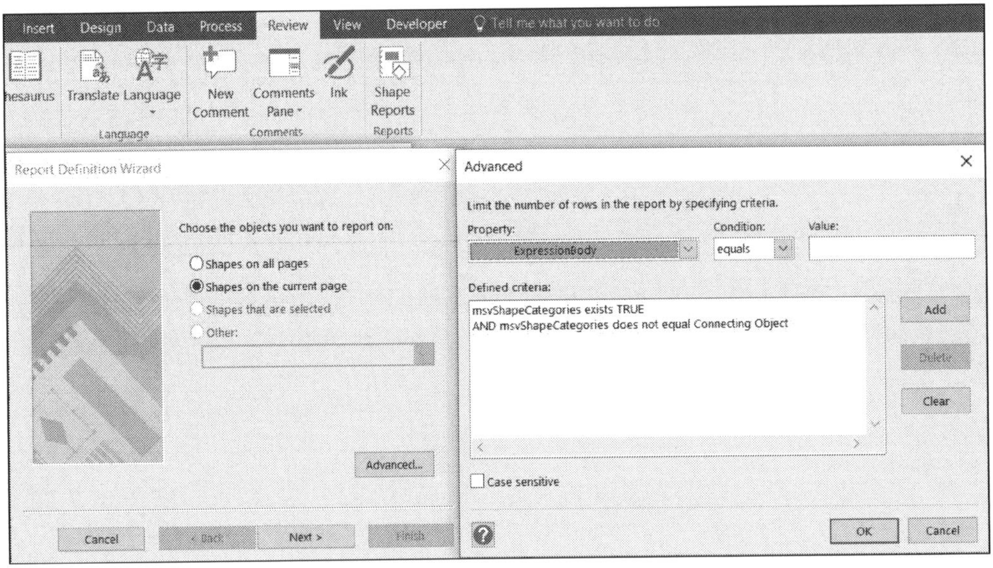

The report definition can be titled, and the tabular contents can be optionally grouped by a selected property. The next screen allows for Shape Data, User-defined Cells, and some other special properties to be selected for the report:

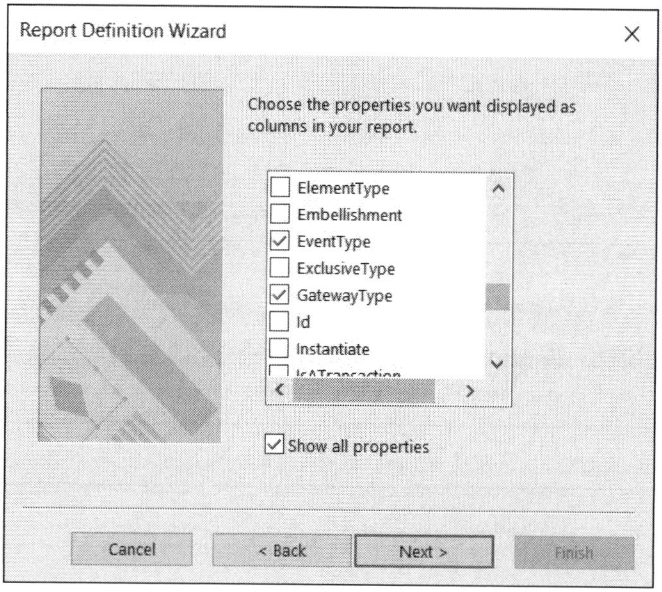


If any of the other properties are numeric, then they can have aggregation functions (`TOTAL`, `AVG`, `MAX`, `MIN`, and `MEDIAN`) calculated, otherwise they can be simply counted. Any numeric values can have a format applied, as seen in the following screenshot:

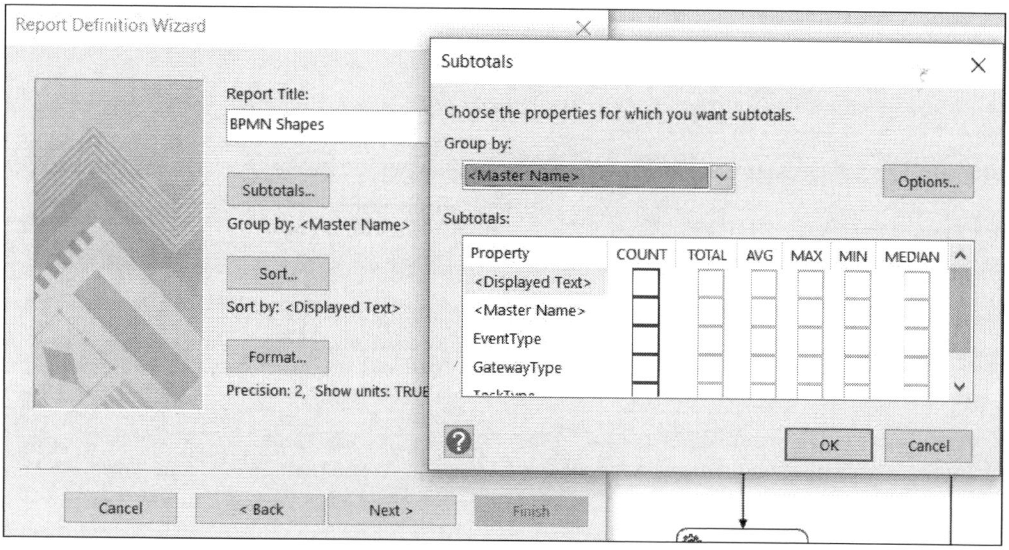

Additionally, the **Sort...** button opens the following dialog to define the column order and row sorting:

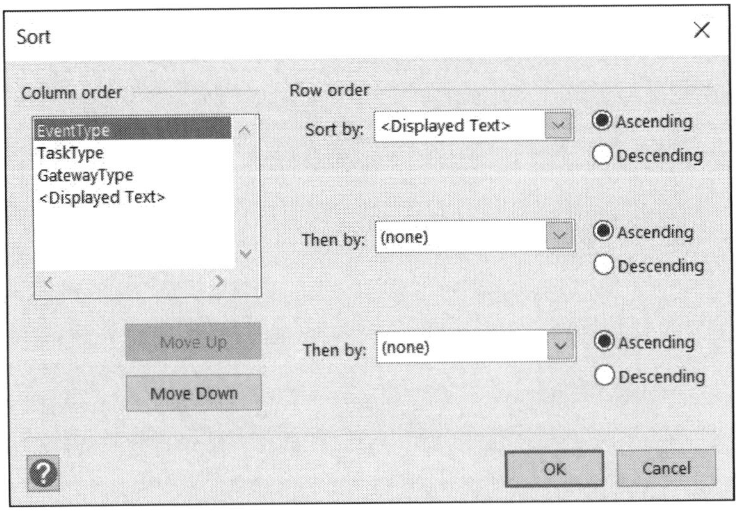


Finally, the report can be saved with **Name** and **Description**, either within the document or as an external file, as seen in the following screenshot:

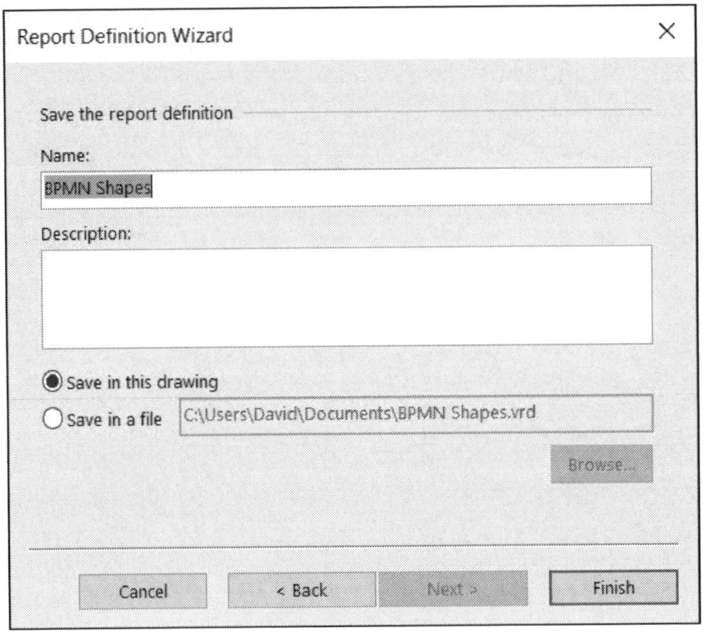

Any report can then be output into an Excel workbook, an HTML file, a Visio shape (which is actually an embedded Excel worksheet), or an XML file, as shown in the following image:

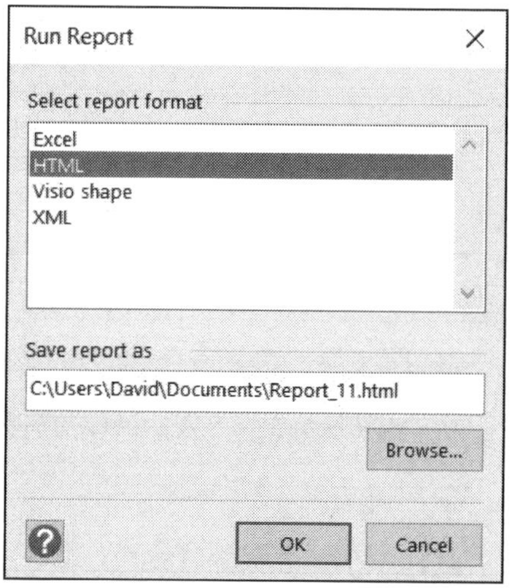


The following screenshot shows an output to an HTML file:

**BPMN Shapes**

| Master Name | EventType | TaskType | GatewayType | Displayed Text |
|---|---|---|---|---|
| End Event | End | - | - | Reply To Customer |
| Gateway | - | - | Exclusive | Can Fulfil Order? |
| Intermediate Event | End | - | - | - |
| Intermediate Event | Intermediate | - | - | - |
| Price Tag | - | - | - | 2 ways |
| Price Tag | - | - | - | 2 ways |
| Start Event | Start | - | - | Start Event |
| Task | - | User | - | Capacity Not Available |
| Task | - | User | - | Check if Manf. Capacity and Parts Available |
| Task | - | Service | - | Fulfil Order |
| Task | - | Service | - | Reset System |
| Task | - | Service | - | Retrieve Parts List |

Note that there is a header row containing the report title. This is also true of the Excel-formatted report.

> **Creating Excel tables to become linked lists**
>
> If shape data is extracted into an Excel workbook using the Shape Reports feature, then, if the title row is deleted, the remaining table can be linked back to the shapes, as described in *Chapter 3, Linking Data to Shapes.*

# Reading Shape Data

Visio shapes can contain a lot of information in the form of values in the Shape Data rows. These values can be of various types of data and can be extremely long, despite the built-in Visio interface only providing a single row to enter the data in. In fact, each row can hold millions of characters, even though a VBA string can only hold 308,894 characters. Some custom interfaces do display multiple lines of text contained within a Shape Data row, and of course some data sources can import large data into each row.

The Shape Reports feature is a simple tool and cannot handle connections, containment, or even shapes with different Shape Data rows.

When it comes to reading the data from shapes then there are some factors to consider, such as the data type and the visibility. For example, the following screenshot just shows the visible data from a single **Task** shape in a BPMN diagram:

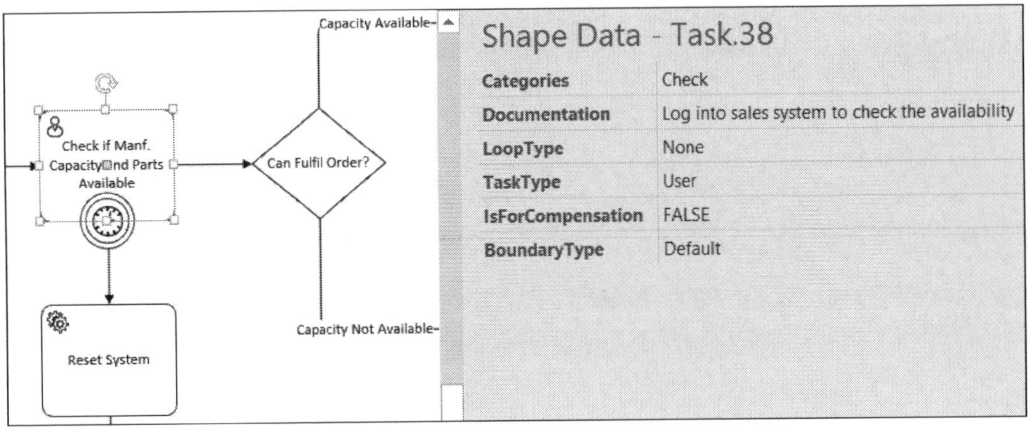

To the Visio user, there appear to be six Shape Data rows, some text, and a unique name. In fact, there are seventeen Shape Data rows in this shape, but eleven are invisible.

The following VBA macro, `EnumerateShapePropRows()`, simply loops through each Shape Data row and outputs the row number, the invisible cell value, the row name, and the label:

```
Public Sub EnumerateShapePropRows()
If Application.ActiveWindow.Selection.Count = 0 Then
    Exit Sub
End If

Dim shp As Visio.Shape
Dim iRow As Integer
Dim cel As Visio.Cell
Dim iSect As Integer
iSect = VisSectionIndices.visSectionProp

Set shp = Application.ActiveWindow.Selection.PrimaryItem
Debug.Print "EnumerateShapePropRows : " & shp.Name
If Not shp.SectionExists(iSect, _
    VisExistsFlags.visExistsAnywhere) Then
    Debug.Print , "Does not contain any Shape Data rows"
    Exit Sub
End If

With shp
    Debug.Print "Shape Data row count : ", .RowCount(iSect)
    Debug.Print "Row", "InVis", "RowName", "Label"
    For iRow = 0 To .RowCount(iSect) - 1
        Set cel = .CellsSRC(iSect, iRow, 0)
        Debug.Print cel.row, .CellsSRC(iSect, iRow, _
            VisCellIndices.visCustPropsInvis).ResultStr(""), _
            cel.rowName, _
            .CellsSRC(iSect, iRow, _
            VisCellIndices.visCustPropsLabel).ResultStr("")
    Next iRow
End With
End Sub
```

This macro outputs the following for the selected **Task** shape:

```
EnumerateShapePropRows : Task.38
Shape Data row count :        17
Row            InVis          RowName        Label
 0             TRUE           BpmnId         Id
 1             FALSE          BpmnCategories                Categories
 2             FALSE          BpmnDocumentation             Documentation
 3             TRUE           BpmnName       Name
 4             TRUE           BpmnActivityType              ActivityType
 5             FALSE          BpmnLoopType   LoopType
 6             FALSE          BpmnTaskType   TaskType
 7             TRUE           BpmnScript     Script
 8             TRUE           BpmnInstantiate               Instantiate
 9             TRUE           BpmnSubProcessType            SubProcessType
 10            TRUE           BpmnIsCollapsed               IsCollapsed
 11            TRUE           BpmnIsATransaction            IsATransaction
 12            FALSE          BpmnIsForCompensation         IsForCompensation
 13            TRUE           BpmnElementType               ElementType
 14            TRUE           BpmnAdHoc      AdHoc
 15            TRUE           BpmnAdHocOrdering             AdHocOrdering
 16            FALSE          BpmnBoundaryType              BoundaryType
```

It is clear that there is a lot of unnecessary information available for this particular shape. Therefore, the following macro, `EnumerateVisibleShapePropRows()`, only lists the values of the visible rows:

```
Public Sub EnumerateVisibleShapePropRows()
If Application.ActiveWindow.Selection.Count = 0 Then
    Exit Sub
End If

Dim shp As Visio.Shape
Dim iRow As Integer
Dim cel As Visio.Cell
Dim iSect As Integer
iSect = VisSectionIndices.visSectionProp

Set shp = Application.ActiveWindow.Selection.PrimaryItem
Debug.Print "EnumerateVisibleShapePropRows : " & shp.Name
If Not shp.SectionExists(iSect, _
    VisExistsFlags.visExistsAnywhere) Then
    Debug.Print , "Does not contain any Shape Data rows"
    Exit Sub
End If
Dim iVisible As Integer
With shp
    Debug.Print "Shape Data row count : ", .RowCount(iSect)
    Debug.Print "Row", "SortKey", "Type", "RowName", "Label", "Value"
    For iRow = 0 To .RowCount(iSect) - 1
        Set cel = .CellsSRC(iSect, iRow, 0)
        If .CellsSRC(iSect, iRow, VisCellIndices.visCustPropsInvis).ResultIU = 0 Then
            iVisible = iVisible + 1
            Debug.Print cel.row, _
                .CellsSRC(iSect, iRow, VisCellIndices.visCustPropsSortKey).ResultStr(""), _
                .CellsSRC(iSect, iRow, VisCellIndices.visCustPropsType).ResultIU, _
                cel.rowName, _
                .CellsSRC(iSect, iRow, VisCellIndices.visCustPropsLabel).ResultStr(""), _
                .CellsSRC(iSect, iRow, VisCellIndices.visCustPropsValue).ResultStr("")
        End If
    Next iRow
    Debug.Print "Visible Shape Data row count : ", iVisible
End With
End Sub
```

For clarity, the output has been formatted as the following table:

| EnumerateVisibleShapePropRows: | | | | Task.38 | |
|---|---|---|---|---|---|
| **Shape Data row count:** | | | | 17 | |
| **Row** | **SortKey** | **Type** | **RowName** | **Label** | **Value** |
| 1 | | 0 | BpmnCategories | Categories | Check |
| 2 | | 0 | BpmnDocumentation | Documentation | Log into sales system to check the availability |
| 5 | | 1 | BpmnLoopType | LoopType | None |
| 6 | | 1 | BpmnTaskType | TaskType | User |
| 12 | | 3 | BpmnIsForCompensation | IsForCompensation | FALSE |
| 16 | | 1 | BpmnBoundaryType | BoundaryType | Default |
| **Visible Shape Data row count:** | | | | 6 | |

This output is similar to that seen by the user, who sees only the last two columns, **Label** and **Value**. If **SortKey** had values in them, then the UI would order them in alphanumeric order.

This **Task** shape would probably be referred to by the text it contains, **Check if Manf. Capacity and Parts Available**. This can be extracted in code with `Shape.Text`, or more safely with `Shape.Characters.Text`.

Alternatively, these particular shapes have a Shape Data row named `BpmnName`, which has the formula `GUARD(SHAPETEXT(TheText))` in the **Value** cell.

It is not always necessary, or desirable, to loop through all the rows in a section in order to get the value of just one or two rows whose names are already known. In this case, the values can be retrieved or set, using the row name; for example, `Shape.Cells("Prop.BpmnName").ResultStr("")`. However, it is important that the cell actually exists, otherwise an `"Unexpected end of file"` error will be generated. The existence of a cell can be checked with `Not Shape.CellExists("Prop.BpmnName", Visio.visExistsFlags.visExistsAnywhere) = 0`.

The following sub-function is specific to BPMN diagrams because it anticipates the particular categories that are within them. It returns the ID, shape type specific text, and the shape text for any given shape on a page. Note that some Shape Data rows can be called by name because they are known to exist, whilst one with the label `TriggerOrResult` must be found by looping through to find the visible row, as there are many with the same label.

```
Private Sub GetShapetext(ByVal pag As Visio.Page, ByVal shapeName As String, _
    ByRef id As Integer, ByRef shapeTxt As String, ByRef txt As String)
Dim shp As Visio.Shape
Dim iRow As Integer
Dim iSect As Integer
    iSect = Visio.visSectionProp
    Set shp = pag.Shapes.Item(shapeName)
    txt = shp.Characters.Text
    id = shp.id
    If shp.HasCategory("Event") Then
        shapeTxt = "( ) : " & shp.Cells("Prop.BpmnEventType").ResultStr("")
        For iRow = 0 To shp.RowCount(iSect) - 1
            If shp.CellsSRC(iSect, iRow, _
                VisCellIndices.visCustPropsLabel).ResultStr("") = "TriggerOrResult" And _
                shp.CellsSRC(iSect, iRow, VisCellIndices.visCustPropsInvis).ResultIU = 0 Then
                shapeTxt = shapeTxt & " - " & _
                    shp.CellsSRC(iSect, iRow, VisCellIndices.visCustPropsValue).ResultStr("")
                Exit For
            End If
        Next
    ElseIf shp.HasCategory("Task") Then
        shapeTxt = "[ ] : " & shp.Cells("Prop.BpmnTaskType").ResultStr("")
        shapeTxt = shapeTxt & " - " & shp.Cells("Prop.BpmnLoopType").ResultStr("")
    ElseIf shp.HasCategory("Collapsed Sub-Process") Then
        shapeTxt = "[+] : " & shp.Cells("Prop.BpmnTaskType").ResultStr("")
        shapeTxt = shapeTxt & " - " & shp.Cells("Prop.BpmnLoopType").ResultStr("")
    ElseIf shp.HasCategory("Gateway") Then
        shapeTxt = "< > : " & shp.Cells("Prop.BpmnGatewayType").ResultStr("")
    ElseIf shp.HasCategory("Connecting Object") Then
        shapeTxt = "--- "
    ElseIf Not shp.CellExists("User.msvShapeCategories", visExistsAnywhere) = 0 Then
        shapeTxt = shp.Cells("User.msvShapeCategories").ResultStr("")
    ElseIf Not shp.Master Is Nothing Then
        shapeTxt = shp.Master.Name
    Else
        shapeTxt = shp.Name
    End If
End Sub
```

`Rows`, like many objects within Visio, can have a different universal name to the local name, so there are also functions, `CellsU()` and `CellExistsU()`, for the occasions where it is different. This was a feature added to Visio with the intention of having a language-specific display of names but language-independent base names.

It is also possible that the Shape Data rows contain information that has been inserted via code as SolutionXML, but that feature is underused. Some of the built-in solutions do use SolutionXML, such as the Space Plan add-on, but this is stored at the document level rather than the shape cell level.

> **Visio Web Access shape info**
>
> Visio documents can be viewed in the Visio Web Access web-part, which contains a Shape Info panel for viewing selected shape data rows and hyperlinks. This panel displays the label and formatted value of the visible Shape Data rows.

# Reading User-defined Cells

The User-defined Cells section can also contain information that may be required. The following macro, `EnumerateShapeUserRows()`, lists the values in this section for the selected shape:

```
Public Sub EnumerateShapeUserRows()
If Application.ActiveWindow.Selection.Count = 0 Then
    Exit Sub
End If

Dim shp As Visio.Shape
Dim iRow As Integer
Dim cel As Visio.Cell
Dim iSect As Integer
iSect = VisSectionIndices.visSectionUser

Set shp = Application.ActiveWindow.Selection.PrimaryItem
Debug.Print "EnumerateShapeUserRows : " & shp.Name
If Not shp.SectionExists(iSect, _
    VisExistsFlags.visExistsAnywhere) Then
    Debug.Print , "Does not contain any User-defined cell rows"
    Exit Sub
End If

With shp
    Debug.Print "User-defined cell row count : ", .RowCount(iSect)
    Debug.Print "Row", "RowName", "Value"
    For iRow = 0 To .RowCount(iSect) - 1
        Set cel = .CellsSRC(iSect, iRow, 0)
        Debug.Print cel.row, _
            cel.rowName, _
            .CellsSRC(iSect, iRow, _
            VisCellIndices.visUserValue).ResultStr("")
    Next iRow
End With
End Sub
```

Again, for clarity, the output has been formatted into a table:

| **EnumerateShapeUserRows :** | | `Task.38` |
|---|---|---|
| User-defined cell row count: | | `13` |
| **Row** | **RowName** | **Value** |
| 0 | `BpmnNumIconsVisible` | `0.0000` |
| 1 | `BpmnIsExtendedSubProcess` | `FALSE` |
| 2 | `msvStructureType` | `0.0000` |
| 3 | `msvSDContainerResize` | `0.0000` |
| 4 | `visVersion` | `15.0000` |
| 5 | `msvShapeCategories` | `Task` |
| 6 | `BpmnIconHeight` | `4.0000 mm` |
| 7 | `BpmnIconPinY` | `3.0000 mm` |
| 8 | `BpmnBoundaryType` | `0.0000` |
| 9 | `DefaultWidth` | `25.0000 mm` |
| 10 | `DefaultHeight` | `20.0000 mm` |
| 11 | `ResizeTxtHeight` | `20.0000 mm` |
| 12 | `IsInstance` | `TRUE` |

Perhaps the only useful information in this section is the `User.msvShapeCategories` value, which, in the case of this particular **Task** shape, is **Task**. However, this cell contains a semi-colon-separated list of categories to which the shape belongs. As with the Shape Data rows earlier, it is important to test whether a cell actually exists before attempting to get its value, otherwise an `Unexpected end of file` error will be raised.

Fortunately, in the case of this particular User-defined Cell row, Microsoft has provided a safe function for testing if a shape belongs to a specific category. So, calling `Shape,HasCategory("Task")` will return `TRUE` if the row exists and the list contains `"Task"`, but will return `FALSE` if the row does not exist or it exists but does not contain `"Task"`. Be aware that this method is case-sensitive, so `Shape.HasCategory("task")` will return `FALSE` for the BPMN **Task** shapes.

There are more User-defined Cell rows used in other templates and solutions, but none have a specific Shape method provided to test the values like `HasCategory()`.

# Reading connections

Connections between shapes are often the most important way that data can be created more easily graphically than textually. However, the direction of flow between shapes is also important in structured diagrams. A lot of the connector shapes in Visio have an arrow that makes the direction of flow easy to understand, but even this can be misused because the end arrows of a connector shape can often be changed manually, to make it look as if the flow is reversed, without physically swapping the connector line around. Validation rules can spot this type of mistake, but prevention is the best cure.

A command (**Reverse Ends**) is available for the ribbon, but is not on any of the standard ribbon tabs. Therefore, it is recommended to add this useful command button as it swaps the direction of the flow of selected connector shapes.

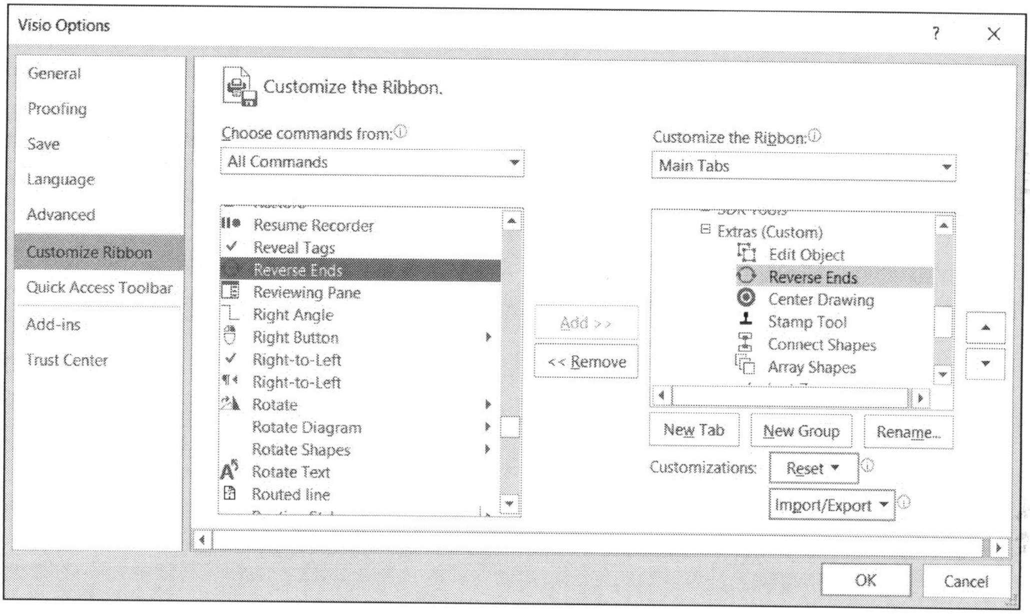


Consider a 1D connector shape which has a beginning and end, thus defining its flow direction. The begin point can be glued to one, and only one, cell on a shape. Similarly, the end point can be glued to one, and only one, cell on a shape. The cells that the connector is glued to are normally in a 2D shape. The two 2D shapes at either end are considered to be connected to each other, but they are glued to the connector.

The following BPMN diagram, created using the BPMN template in Visio 2016, is used as an example of reading connections in a structured diagram. It mostly has 2D shapes that are connected via a 1D connector shape; however, there is an **Event** shape glued directly to a **Task** shape too.

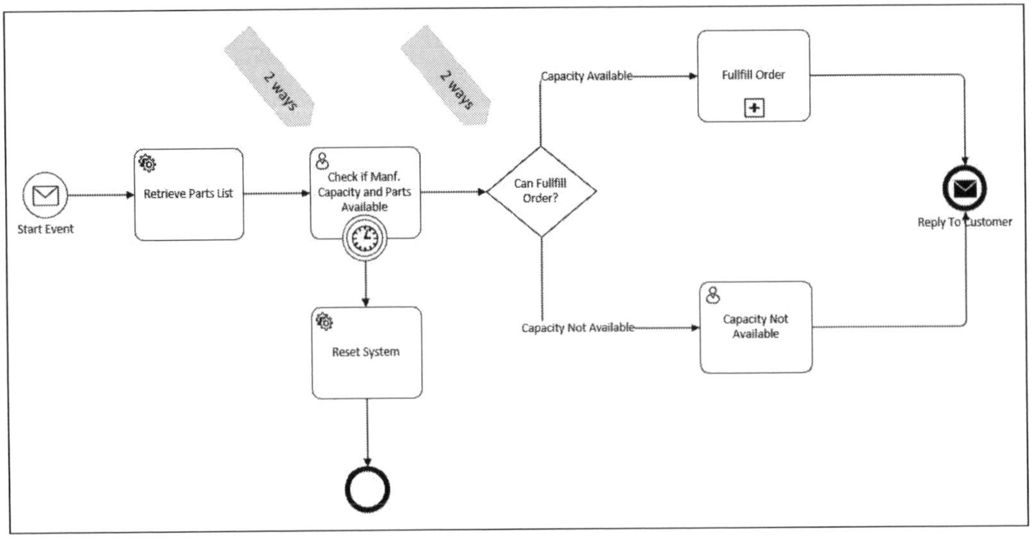


The two shapes with the **2 ways** text are actually Callout shapes, and as such are purely for annotation and not considered part of the diagram flows.

## Listing connected shapes

The Visio Connectivity API provides a method, `ConnectedShapes()`, on a `Shape` object that provides the ability to get an array of incoming, outgoing, or all connected shapes, optionally filtered by category. The following VBA macro, `ListConnectedShapes()`, uses this to simply list all the outgoing connections of every shape on the page:

```
Public Sub ListConnectedShapes()
If ActivePage Is Nothing Then
    Exit Sub
End If
Dim pag As Visio.Page
Set pag = ActivePage
Dim shp As Visio.Shape
Dim targetShape As Visio.Shape
Dim aryTargetIDs() As Long
Dim targetID As Long
Dim i As Integer
Debug.Print "ID", "Name", "Text", "To ID", "To Name", "To Text"
For Each shp In pag.Shapes
    If Not shp.OneD Then
        aryTargetIDs = shp.ConnectedShapes(visConnectedShapesOutgoingNodes, "")
        For i = 0 To UBound(aryTargetIDs)
            Set targetShape = pag.Shapes.ItemFromID(aryTargetIDs(i))
            Debug.Print shp.id, shp.Name, shp.Characters.Text, _
                targetShape.id, targetShape.Name, targetShape.Characters.Text
        Next
    End If
Next

End Sub
```

For clarity, the output for the sample BPMN diagram has been put into a table:

| ID | Name | Text | To ID | To Name | To Text |
|---|---|---|---|---|---|
| 1 | Start Event | Start Event | 14 | Task | Retrieve Parts List |
| 14 | Task | Retrieve Parts List | 38 | Task.38 | Check if Manf. Capacity and Parts Available |
| 38 | Task.38 | Check if Manf. Capacity and Parts Available | 113 | Gateway | Can Fulfil Order? |
| 62 | Task.62 | Reset System | 86 | Intermediate Event | |
| 100 | Intermediate Event.100 | | 62 | Task.62 | Reset System |
| 113 | Gateway | Can Fulfil Order? | 129 | Task.129 | Fulfil Order |
| 113 | Gateway | Can Fulfil Order? | 153 | Task.153 | Capacity Not Available |
| 129 | Task.129 | Fulfil Order | 193 | End Event | Reply To Customer |
| 153 | Task.153 | Capacity Not Available | 193 | End Event | Reply To Customer |

The `ConnectedShapes()` method assumes that there is a connector between the source and the target shapes. It does respect the direction of the connector shape but, with regard to this BPMN diagram, this list is not really complete because it does not find the link between the **Task** labeled **Check if the Manf. Capacity and Parts Available** and the **Timer Event** shape that is glued to it. Therefore, it is impossible to follow the complete flow of this process using just the `ConnectedShapes()` method. In addition, any text that is on a connector shape is unavailable.

## Listing glued shapes

The Visio Connectivity API also provides a method, `GluedShapes()`, on a `Shape` object that provides the ability to get an array of the incoming 1D/2D, outgoing 1D/2D, or all the glued shapes, optionally filtered by category. The following VBA macro, `ListGluedShapes()`, uses this to simply list all the outgoing glued shapes of every shape on the page:

```
Public Sub ListGluedShapes()
If ActivePage Is Nothing Then
    Exit Sub
End If
Dim pag As Visio.Page
Set pag = ActivePage
Dim shp As Visio.Shape
Dim targetShape As Visio.Shape
Dim aryTargetIDs() As Long
Dim targetID As Long
Dim i As Integer
Debug.Print "ID", "Name", "Text", "To ID", "To Name", "To Text"
For Each shp In pag.Shapes
    aryTargetIDs = shp.GluedShapes(visGluedShapesOutgoing1D, "")
    For i = 0 To UBound(aryTargetIDs)
        Set targetShape = pag.Shapes.ItemFromID(aryTargetIDs(i))
        Debug.Print shp.id, shp.Name, shp.Characters.Text, _
            targetShape.id, targetShape.Name, targetShape.Characters.Text
    Next
    aryTargetIDs = shp.GluedShapes(visGluedShapesOutgoing2D, "")
    For i = 0 To UBound(aryTargetIDs)
        Set targetShape = pag.Shapes.ItemFromID(aryTargetIDs(i))
        Debug.Print shp.id, shp.Name, shp.Characters.Text, _
            targetShape.id, targetShape.Name, targetShape.Characters.Text
    Next
Next

End Sub
```

For clarity, the output for the sample BPMN diagram has been put into a table:

| ID | Name | Text | To ID | To Name | To Text |
|---|---|---|---|---|---|
| 1 | Start Event | Start Event | 37 | Dynamic Connector | |
| 37 | Dynamic Connector | | 14 | Task | Retrieve Parts List |
| 14 | Task | Retrieve Parts List | 61 | Dynamic Connector.61 | |
| 61 | Dynamic Connector.61 | | 38 | Task.38 | Check if Manf. Capacity and Parts Available |
| 38 | Task.38 | Check if Manf. Capacity and Parts Available | 128 | Dynamic Connector.128 | |
| 85 | Dynamic Connector.85 | | 62 | Task.62 | Reset System |
| 62 | Task.62 | Reset System | 99 | Dynamic Connector.99 | |
| 99 | Dynamic Connector.99 | | 86 | Intermediate Event | |
| 100 | Intermediate Event.100 | | 85 | Dynamic Connector.85 | |
| 100 | Intermediate Event.100 | | 38 | Task.38 | Check if Manf. Capacity and Parts Available |
| 128 | Dynamic Connector.128 | | 113 | Gateway | Can Fulfil Order? |
| 113 | Gateway | Can Fulfil Order? | 152 | Dynamic Connector.152 | Capacity Available |
| 113 | Gateway | Can Fulfil Order? | 176 | Dynamic Connector.176 | Capacity Not Available |
| 152 | Dynamic Connector.152 | Capacity Available | 129 | Task.129 | Fulfil Order |
| 129 | Task.129 | Fulfil Order | 206 | Dynamic Connector.206 | |
| 176 | Dynamic Connector.176 | Capacity Not Available | 153 | Task.153 | Capacity Not Available |
| 153 | Task.153 | Capacity Not Available | 1000 | Dynamic Connector.1000 | |

| ID | Name | Text | To ID | To Name | To Text |
|---|---|---|---|---|---|
| 206 | Dynamic Connector.206 | | 193 | End Event | Reply To Customer |
| 1000 | Dynamic Connector.1000 | | 193 | End Event | Reply To Customer |

This gives us all required information, but the way that these glued connections actually flow is still unclear. In addition, there are some types of diagrams where the actual connection point that a connector is glued to is important. That information is just not available with the `GluedShapes()` method.

# Listing routes or pathways through a diagram

There is still another way of reading connections in a diagram. This was the way that it always had to be done before the `ConnectedShapes()` and `GlueShapes()` methods were introduced. It is a little more complicated because it uses the `Page` or `Shape Connects` and `FromConnects` collections.

The accompanying code includes a function named `ListPathways()`, which utilizes all three ways of retrieving the connection and glue information and builds up the list of pathways through a BPMN diagram.

The output, as shown next for the example BPMN diagram, could be the start of exporting data to another system. The first column is just an index number for this listing, but a < symbol means that there are multiple ways of flowing from this row; the > symbol means that this is the start of an alternate way, and the = sign means that the way has reached the end of its flow.

The second column is just the ID of each shape, which is, of course, unique within the page. The third column is a little pseudo shape denoting Event, Task, Gateway, and Connector followed by some text pulled from some of its Shape Data. The last column is the shape text. These values were returned by `GetShapetext()`, which was listed earlier in this chapter.

```
Pathways
1           1       ( ) : Start - Message        Start Event
2           37      ---
3           14      [ ] : Service - None         Retrieve Parts List
4           61      ---
5           38      [ ] : User - None            Check if Manf. Capacity and Parts Available
<
6 >         100     ( ) : Intermediate - Timer
7           85      ---
8           62      [ ] : Service - None         Reset System
9           99      ---
10          86      ( ) : End - None
=
6 >         128     ---
7           113     < > : Exclusive              Can Fullfill Order?
<
8 >         152     ---          Capacity Available
9           129     [+] : Service - None         Fullfill Order
10          206     ---
11          193     ( ) : End - Message          Reply To Customer
=
8 >         176     ---          Capacity Not Available
9           153     [ ] : User - None            Capacity Not Available
10          1000    ---
11          193     ( ) : End - Message          Reply To Customer
=
```

# Reading containment

One of the most structured out-of-the-box diagram types is the Cross-Functional Flowchart template, as shown in the following screenshot:

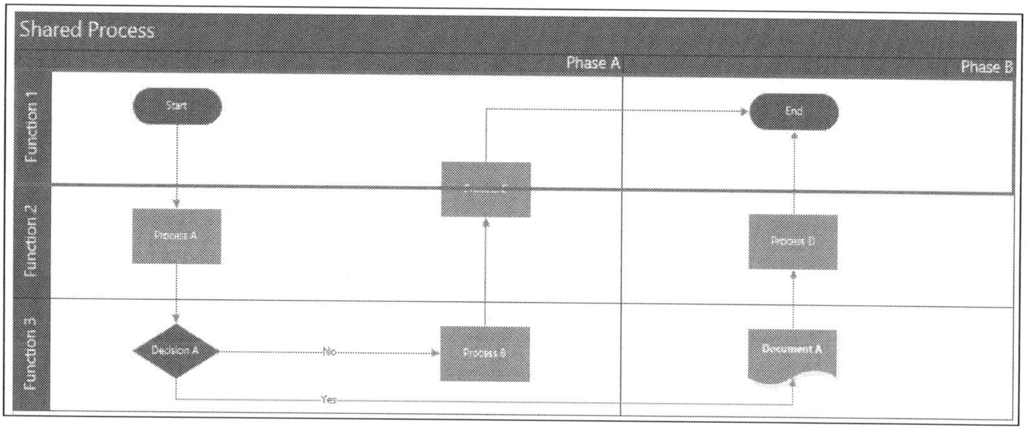


What makes this complicated is the use of horizontal swimlanes and vertical phases, within which flowchart shapes are placed. In fact, the swimlanes and phases are list items within their own list containers. Both these list containers are contained within an outer normal container.

The following VBA macro, `ListContainers()`, finds all the containers and lists in the previous example diagram and outputs them into a table:

```
Public Sub ListContainers()
If ActivePage Is Nothing Then
    Exit Sub
End If
Dim pag As Visio.Page
Set pag = ActivePage
Dim containerShape As Visio.Shape
Dim aryContainerIDs() As Long
Dim aryMemberIDs() As Long
Dim containerID As Long
Dim iCntr As Integer
Dim iMmbr As Integer
Dim memberID As Variant
Dim memberShape As Visio.Shape
Dim aryItemIDs() As Long
Dim iItm As Integer
Dim itemID As Variant
Dim itemShape As Visio.Shape

    aryContainerIDs = pag.GetContainers(visContainerExcludeNested)
    For iCntr = 0 To UBound(aryContainerIDs)
        Set containerShape = pag.Shapes.ItemFromID(aryContainerIDs(iCntr))
        aryMemberIDs = containerShape.ContainerProperties.GetMemberShapes( _
                visContainerFlagsExcludeListMembers + _
                visContainerFlagsExcludeConnectors)
        Debug.Print containerShape.id, containerShape.Name, containerShape.Text
        For iMmbr = 0 To UBound(aryMemberIDs)
            Set memberShape = pag.Shapes.ItemFromID(aryMemberIDs(iMmbr))
            Debug.Print containerShape.ContainerProperties.GetMemberState(memberShape), _
                memberShape.id, memberShape.Name, memberShape.Text
            aryItemIDs = memberShape.ContainerProperties.GetListMembers()
            For iItm = 0 To UBound(aryItemIDs)
                Set itemShape = pag.Shapes.ItemFromID(aryItemIDs(iItm))
                Debug.Print , memberShape.ContainerProperties.GetListMemberPosition(itemShape), _
                    itemShape.id, itemShape.Name, itemShape.Text
            Next
        Next
    Next
End Sub
```

The output clearly shows the nesting of the swimlane and separator (phase) list item shapes within their list containers, along with their list position. Both the list containers are nested within **CFF Container** with the text **Shared Process**.

```
31          CFF Container Shared Process
1            34           Swimlane List
             1             38           Swimlane.9     Function 1
             2             35           Swimlane       Function 2
             3             41           Swimlane.15    Function 3
1            44           Phase List
             1             1000         Separator.1000               Phase A
             2             45           Separator      Phase B
```

However, it is usually more necessary to get the containers (in this case, a swimlane and separator/phase) that a shape is within. The following macro, `ListItems()`, retrieves the list that a shape is within, and also indicates whether it is wholly contained or on the boundary (**iState**).

```
Public Sub ListItems()
If ActivePage Is Nothing Then
    Exit Sub
End If
Dim pag As Visio.Page
Set pag = ActivePage
Dim cntnrShp As Visio.Shape
Dim aryContainerIDs() As Long
Dim containerID As Long
Dim i As Integer
Dim shp As Visio.Shape
Dim sel As Visio.Selection
Dim iState As Integer

For Each shp In pag.Shapes
    If shp.OneD = 0 Then
        Set sel = pag.CreateSelection(visSelTypeEmpty)
        sel.Select shp, Visio.visSelect
        aryContainerIDs = sel.MemberOfContainersUnion()
        If UBound(aryContainerIDs) > 0 Then
            Debug.Print shp.id, shp.Name, shp.Characters.Text, UBound(aryContainerIDs)
            For i = 0 To UBound(aryContainerIDs)
                Set cntnrShp = pag.Shapes.ItemFromID(aryContainerIDs(i))
                iState = 0
                If cntnrShp.ContainerProperties.ContainerType = visContainerTypeNormal Then
                    iState = cntnrShp.ContainerProperties.GetMemberState(shp)
                    Debug.Print , iState, cntnrShp.id, cntnrShp.Name, cntnrShp.Text
                End If
            Next
        End If
    End If
Next
End Sub
```

This will output the following table, where it can be seen that **Process C** is on the boundary of one swimlane:

| | | | | | |
|---|---|---|---|---|---|
| 48 | Start/End | Start | 2 | | |
| | 1 | 38 | Swimlane.9 | Function 1 | |
| | 1 | 1000 | Separator.1000 | | Phase A |
| 50 | Start/End.35 | End | 2 | | |
| | 1 | 38 | Swimlane.9 | Function 1 | |
| | 1 | 45 | Separator | Phase B | |
| 51 | Process | Process C | 2 | | |
| | 2 | 38 | Swimlane.9 | Function 1 | |
| | 1 | 1000 | Separator.1000 | | Phase A |
| 52 | Process.37 | Process B | 2 | | |
| | 1 | 41 | Swimlane.15 | Function 3 | |
| | 1 | 1000 | Separator.1000 | | Phase A |
| 53 | Process.38 | Process A | 2 | | |
| | 1 | 35 | Swimlane | Function 2 | |
| | 1 | 1000 | Separator.1000 | | Phase A |
| 54 | Decision | Decision A | 2 | | |
| | 1 | 41 | Swimlane.15 | Function 3 | |
| | 1 | 1000 | Separator.1000 | | Phase A |
| 55 | Process.45 | Process D | 2 | | |
| | 1 | 35 | Swimlane | Function 2 | |
| | 1 | 45 | Separator | Phase B | |
| 61 | Document | Document A | 2 | | |
| | 1 | 41 | Swimlane.15 | Function 3 | |
| | 1 | 45 | Separator | Phase B | |

[ The following article describes how flowchart shapes can be enhanced to include the phase as a Shape Data row : `http://blog.bvisual.net/2015/11/13/using-the-cross-functional-flowchart-phases-in-visio/`. ]

# Summary

In this chapter, we learnt how to read the information contained within structure diagrams. This involved Shape Data, User-defined Cells, connectivity, and containers. We were also introduced to Validation Rules and the Shape Report tool.

In the next chapter, we will learn how to generate structured diagrams with code.

# 9

# Automating Structured Diagrams

In the previous chapters, we learnt how to import data and display information graphically, and even how to validate the structure of a diagram. However, there are many scenarios when generating all or part of a diagram from data can save hours of manual layout work. In this chapter, we will look into ways of generating structured diagrams from data. This will include dropping specific shapes for specific data values, connecting shapes together, and placing them into containers and lists. Finally, we will learn how to associate callouts with shapes.

This chapter includes copious VBA macros, which contain the principles for actions in any other coding language.

In this chapter, we will learn the following:

- Using a specific Master shape
- Dropping and linking shapes to data
- Connecting shapes from data
- Adding data-linked shapes to containers
- Adding data-linked shapes to lists
- Adding callouts to shapes

# Structuring diagrams overview

The Structured Diagram API was introduced in Visio 2010 to provide programmatic access to new features and shape types. The Structured Diagram API classes, properties, and methods are italicized in the following partial Visio API object model:

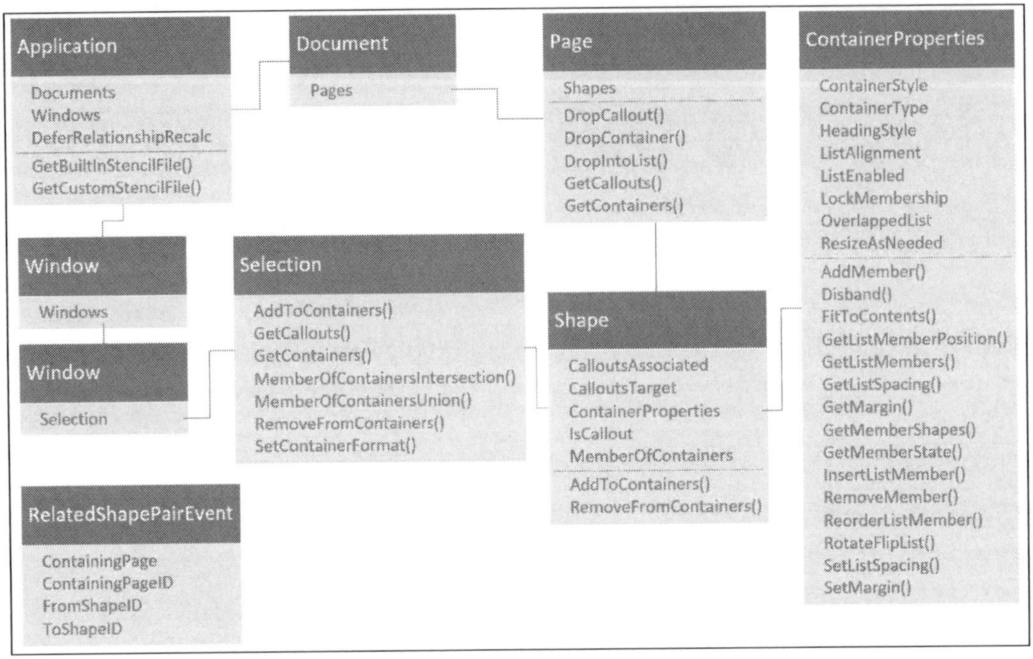


This chapter includes example code of some of the most useful parts of the Structured Diagram API, but, for brevity, does not include thorough error checking.

> For more information about the Structured Diagram API, see `https://blogs.msdn.microsoft.com/visio/2010/01/27/container-list-and-callout-api-in-visio-2010/`.

# Enabling diagram services

Using Visio manually always triggers the structured diagram behaviors, where applicable. However, it may not always be desirable via automation code, so the default is for no structured diagramming behaviors. Fortunately, they can be selectively enabled using Structured Diagram API. Therefore, most of the code examples in this chapter are, or should be, topped and tailed with the following snippet, which is similar to a recorded macro:

```
Dim dsEnabled As Long
    dsEnabled = doc.DiagramServicesEnabled
    doc.DiagramServicesEnabled = VisDiagramServices.visServiceAll

<do something>

    doc.DiagramServicesEnabled = dsEnabled
```

The last line ensures that the state is returned to the original setting.

> See `https://msdn.microsoft.com/en-us/library/office/ff765437.aspx` for more information about the `DiagramServicesEnabled` property.

# Setting undo scopes

In a similar vein to the enabling of diagram services, it is a good idea to encompass multiple actions that affect the diagram structure within undo scope. This groups a number of events together, so that they can be undone in one simple action, if necessary. The following snippet is also similar to the code produced by recording a macro:

```
Dim scopeID As Long
    scopeID = Application.BeginUndoScope("Move Shapes into
    Container")
<do something>
    Application.EndUndoScope scopeID, True
```

# Selecting a Master shape to drop

A Master object must be obtained before it can be dropped onto a page using code. Simply knowing the name of a desired Master is not enough because the Master may not exist in the Document Stencil yet. Also, there may be more than one Master with the same name on any opened stencil, so the stencil name may also be required. In fact, the active Document may have a number of docked stencils, so they should be checked first. Then, the Visio Application may have a number of different stencil documents open. Lastly, the stencil may not even be open in Visio, so the stencil may need to be opened, but that is left for the accompanying code for this book.

The caption that appears on the header bar of a stencil is either the mapped long name or title of the stencil, if there is one, otherwise it displays the name without the file extension. All the built-in stencils have terse filenames that are mapped to longer names that are displayed in the UI. These mappings are stored in `PublishComponent` table of installer database. Developers can also create installation sets with these mappings using a number of techniques that will be covered in *Chapter 11, Choosing a Deployment Methodology*. The following function, `GetDocMaster()`, returns a Master with a given name, having ensured that the stencil matches an optional specified name:

```
Public Function GetDocMaster(ByVal doc As Visio.Document, _
    ByVal name As String, ByVal stencilName As String) As Visio.Master

    If Len(stencilName) > 0 And Not _
        (doc.name = stencilName Or _
            doc.Title = stencilName Or _
            StripExt(doc.name) = stencilName) Then
        Set GetDocMaster = Nothing
        Exit Function
    End If

Dim aryMasterNames() As String
    doc.Masters.GetNames aryMasterNames
Dim iMaster As Integer
    For iMaster = LBound(aryMasterNames) To UBound(aryMasterNames)
        If aryMasterNames(iMaster) = name Then
            Set GetDocMaster = doc.Masters.Item(name)
            Exit Function
        End If
    Next iMaster
    Set GetDocMaster = Nothing
End Function
```

There is a naming convention used by the Visio UI for recognizing the Metric and US Units stencils (and templates). If the terse name, before the extension, ends with `_U`, then it is a US Units document, and if it ends with `_M`, then it is a Metric document.

For example, the Work Flow Objects stencil in the Flowchart category is `WFOBME_M.VSSX` or `WFOBME_U.VSSX`, file in the Visio installation folder. The Flowchart category is merely determined by the name mapping, along with the long name.

The following screenshot shows the filenames of some of the built-in templates and stencils:

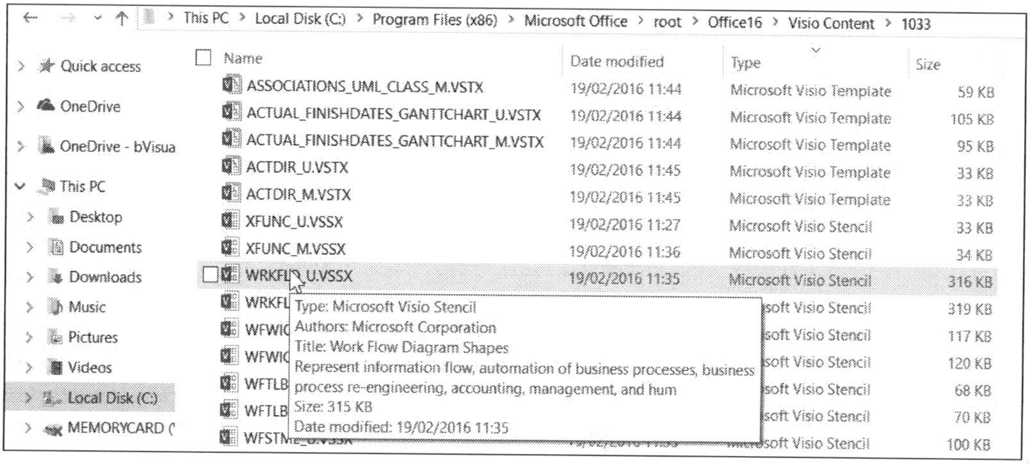


The `Visio.Application` object has useful properties and methods for finding the file path in code. The following screenshot shows the result of finding the `Path` and `Language` properties:

```
Immediate
?Visio.Application.Path
C:\Program Files (x86)\Microsoft Office\root\Office16\
?Visio.Application.Language
 1033
?Visio.Application.GetBuiltInStencilFile(visBuiltInStencilContainers,visMSMetric)
C:\Program Files (x86)\Microsoft Office\root\Office16\visio content\1033\sdcont_m.vssx
```

All the built-in Visio files are in a language sub-folder of the folder named `Visio Content` below `Application.Path`.

There is also a method, `GetBuiltInStencilFile()`, for getting backgrounds, borders, callouts, containers, and legends. These built-in stencils are used in the Visio UI. There is also a method, `GetCustomStencilFile()`, that provides access to any custom versions.

Remember that there are two possible extensions for stencils since Visio 2013, depending upon whether it can store macros (.vssm) or not (.vssx). Pre-Visio 2013 stencils can hold macros whether they are binary (.vss) or XML (.vsx). The following function, `StripExt()`, strips off the possible extensions, ignoring case:

```
Public Function StripExt(ByVal name As String)
Dim txt As String
    txt = Replace(name, ".vssx", "", 1, -1, vbTextCompare)
    txt = Replace(txt, ".vssm", "", 1, -1, vbTextCompare)
    txt = Replace(txt, ".vss", "", 1, -1, vbTextCompare)
    txt = Replace(txt, ".vsx", "", 1, -1, vbTextCompare)
End Function
```

All this means that searching for a stencil by full filename may require a little thought because there are so many permutations. This final function, `OpenGetMaster()`, is called if none of the loops find the required master. The `stencilName` parameter can be just the short filename of any built-in stencils, but should be the full path of any custom stencils. It opens and docks the required stencil into the active documents workspace.

```
Public Function OpenGetMaster(ByVal doc As Visio.Document, _
    ByVal name As String, ByVal stencilName As String) As Visio.Master

Dim stn As Visio.Document
On Error Resume Next
Set stn = doc.Application.Documents.OpenEx(stencilName, _
    Visio.visOpenRO + Visio.visOpenDocked)
If Not stn Is Nothing Then
    Set OpenGetMaster = GetDocMaster(stn, name, stencilName)
    Exit Function
End If

Set OpenGetMaster = Nothing
End Function
```

The preceding screenshot of the function contains the `On Error Resume Next` line because the following line may fail to open the specified stencil. In production code, it would be better to check for a file's existence first. The `Visio.Application` object has a `EnumDirectories()` method, which creates an array of folder and sub-folder names for a specified folder. There is a `MyShapesPath` and a `StencilPaths` property on `Visio.Application` which returns the file paths set using the **File** | **Options** | **Advanced** | **File Locations** dialog.

```
Public Function GetMaster(ByVal doc As Visio.Document, _
    ByVal name As String, ByVal stencilName As String) As Visio.Master
Dim mst As Visio.Master
    Set mst = GetDocMaster(doc, name, stencilName)
    If Not mst Is Nothing Then
        Set GetMaster = mst
        Exit Function
    End If
Dim win As Visio.Window
    For Each win In Visio.Application.Windows
        If win.Type = Visio.VisWinTypes.visDrawing Then
            'Window found
            If win.Document Is doc Then
                Exit For
            End If
        End If
    Next
Dim aryStencilNames() As String
    win.DockedStencils aryStencilNames
Dim stn As Visio.Document
Dim iStencil As Integer
    For iStencil = LBound(aryStencilNames) To UBound(aryStencilNames)
        If Len(aryStencilNames(iStencil)) > 0 Then
            Set stn = Application.Documents(aryStencilNames(iStencil))
            Set mst = GetDocMaster(stn, name, stencilName)
            If Not mst Is Nothing Then
                Set GetMaster = mst
                Exit Function
            End If
        End If
    Next iStencil
    For Each stn In doc.Application.Documents
        If stn.Type = visTypeStencil Then
            Set mst = GetDocMaster(stn, name, stencilName)
            If Not mst Is Nothing Then
                Set GetMaster = mst
                Exit Function
            End If
        End If
    Next
    Set GetMaster = OpenGetMaster(doc, name, stencilName)
End Function
```

All of the above functions to use in the following sub-function `DropAMaster()`. This looks for the specified Master name, in the optionally specified `stencilName`, and if found, drops a copy in the center of the active page.

```
Public Sub DropAMaster()
Dim doc As Visio.Document
Dim pag As Visio.Page
Dim shp As Visio.Shape
Dim mst As Master
Dim stencilName As String
Dim name As String
    Set pag = Visio.ActivePage
    Set doc = pag.Document
    name = "Person"
    stencilName = ""
    Set mst = GetMaster(doc, name, stencilName)

If Not mst Is Nothing Then
    Set shp = pag.Drop(mst, _
        pag.PageSheet.Cells("PageWidth").ResultIU * 0.5, _
        pag.PageSheet.Cells("PageHeight").ResultIU * 0.5)
End If

End Sub
```

The preceding `name` and `stencilName` values drop **Person** Master from the **Mastering Data** stencil in the following screenshot. This is because this stencil was searched before the open **ITIL Shapes** stencil, which also contains a Master named **Person**.

However, if the `stencilName` value was changed to **ITIL Shapes**, then the code would find and drop the **Person** shape from the correct stencil.

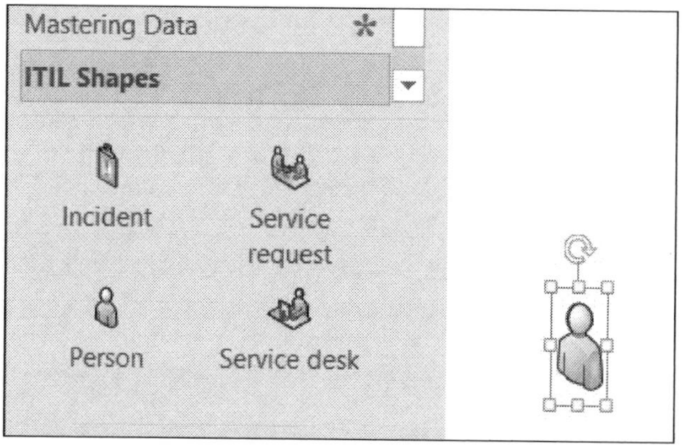


Lastly, if the `stencilName` value was changed to **WFOBME_M.VSSX**, then the code would open the **Work Flow Objects** built-in stencil and drop the **Person** shape from it, as shown in the following screenshot:

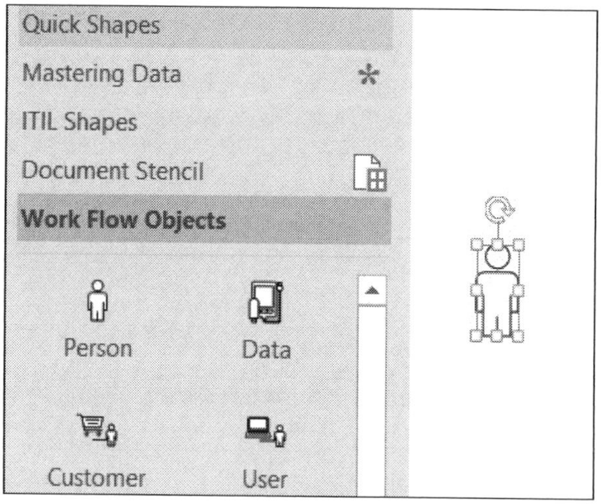


Note that the `Visio.Page` object also contains the `DropMany()` and `DropManyU()` methods, which are more efficient at dropping multiple shapes.

# Dropping and linking shapes to data

It is often necessary to drop multiple shapes and link each one of them to a different row in `DataRecordset`. For example, the following screenshot shows a document with an **External Data** window that contains `Personnel DataRecordset`. The diagram requires the Sales team to be added to the page.

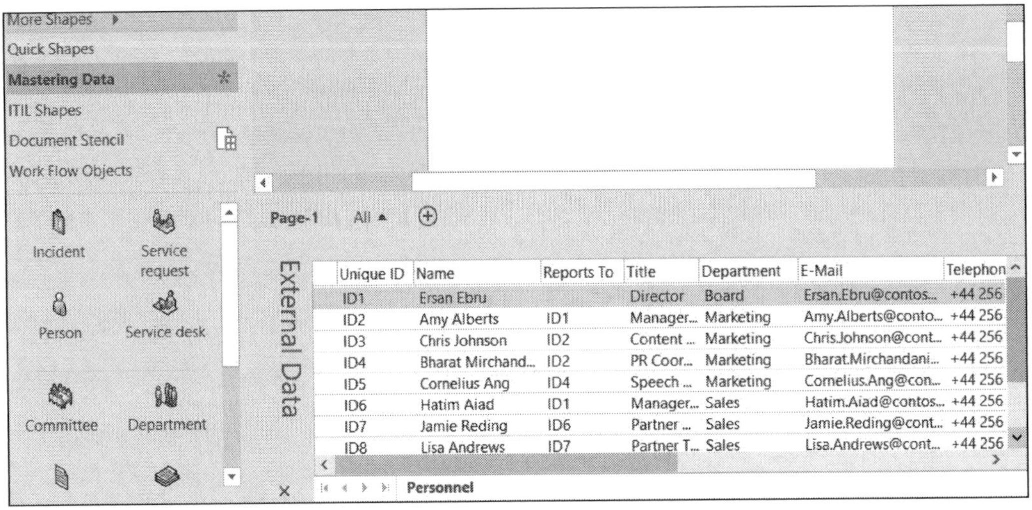


The following function, `GetDataRecordset()`, looks for `DataRecordset` with the given name in the specified document and returns it:

```
Public Function GetDataRecordset( _
    ByVal doc As Visio.Document, _
    ByVal name As String) As DataRecordset
Dim drs As DataRecordset
    For Each drs In doc.DataRecordsets
        If drs.name = name Then
            Set GetDataRecordset = drs
            Exit Function
        End If
    Next
    Set GetDataRecordset = Nothing
End Function
```

This function is used by the following sub-function, `DropManyLinked()`, filters the `Personnel DataRecordset`, gets the **Person** Master from the open **Work Flow Objects** stencil, and drops data-linked copies in a line along the bottom of the page.

```
Public Sub DropManyLinked()
Dim pag As Visio.Page
    Set pag = Visio.ActivePage
Dim doc As Visio.Document
    Set doc = pag.Document
Dim drs As DataRecordset
    Set drs = GetDataRecordset(doc, "Personnel")
    If drs Is Nothing Then Exit Sub

Dim aryRowIDs() As Long
    aryRowIDs = drs.GetDataRowIDs("[Department] = 'Sales'")
Dim mst As Visio.Master
    Set mst = GetMaster(doc, "Person", "Work Flow Objects")
Dim shpWidth As Double
Dim shpHeight As Double
    shpWidth = mst.Shapes(1).Cells("Width").ResultIU
    shpHeight = mst.Shapes(1).Cells("Height").ResultIU
Dim pinX As Double
Dim pinY As Double
    pinX = shpWidth * 2
    pinY = shpHeight * 2
Dim aryMsts() As Variant
Dim aryXYs() As Double
ReDim aryMsts(LBound(aryRowIDs) To UBound(aryRowIDs))
ReDim aryXYs(LBound(aryRowIDs) To ((2 * UBound(aryRowIDs)) + 1))
Dim iRow As Integer
    For iRow = LBound(aryRowIDs) To UBound(aryRowIDs)
        Set aryMsts(iRow) = mst
        aryXYs(((iRow + 1) * 2) - 2) = pinX
        aryXYs(((iRow + 1) * 2) - 1) = pinY
        pinX = pinX + (shpWidth * 2)
    Next iRow

Dim aryShapeIDs() As Long
    pag.DropManyLinkedU aryMsts, aryXYs, drs.id, aryRowIDs, _
        False, aryShapeIDs
    ApplyDataGraphics pag, aryShapeIDs, "Data Graphic"

End Sub
```

The last line calls the sub-function, `ApplyDataGraphics()`, shown in the following screenshot. This is a workaround for an issue that currently exists in Visio 2016. Specifically, there is a reserved User-defined Cell, named `User.msvLastAppliedDataGraphic`, in `DocumentSheet` that contains the name of the Data Graphic Master that was most recently used in the UI. Previously, it was possible to set this cell to the Data Graphic `Master` to use when the `DropManyLinkedU()` method was used.

```
Public Sub ApplyDataGraphics(ByVal pag As Visio.Page, _
    ByVal aryIDs As Variant, ByVal dgName As String)
Dim doc As Visio.Document
    Set doc = pag.Document
Dim dgMaster As Visio.Master
    Set dgMaster = GetMaster(doc, dgName, "")

Dim iShape As Integer
    For iShape = LBound(aryIDs) To UBound(aryIDs)
        pag.Shapes.ItemFromID(aryIDs(iShape)).DataGraphic = dgMaster
    Next iShape
End Sub
```

The result of running the preceding `DropManyLinked()` sub-function is shown in the following screenshot:

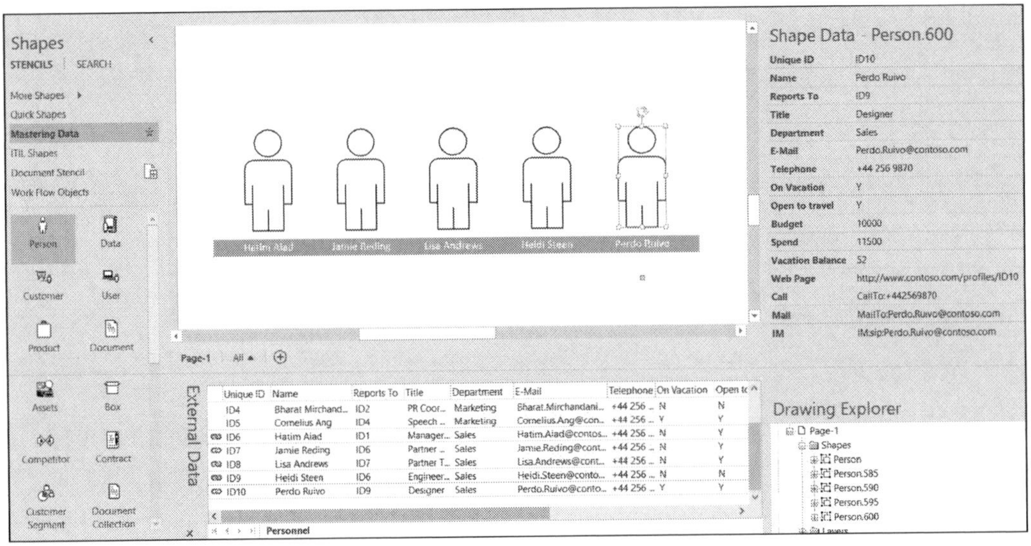

# Connecting shapes from data

The example `Personnel DataRecordset` has a `Reports To` column that is used by Organization Chart Wizard to create a hierarchy by connecting the shapes together. The data that connects two shapes together does not need to be in the same `DataRecordset`, especially if there are *many-to-many* relationships.

A lot of the VBA code in this chapter make increasing use of arrays. However, the VBA `IsArray()` and `IsEmpty()` functions do not really report an empty array. Therefore, the following function, `IsEmptyArray()`, will return `True` or `False` by forcing an error if necessary:

```
Public Function IsEmptyArray( _
    ByVal ary As Variant) As Boolean
    If Not IsArray(ary) Then
        IsEmptyArray = True
        Exit Function
    End If
On Error Resume Next
    Debug.Print LBound(ary)
    If Err.Number = 0 Then
        IsEmptyArray = False
    Else
        IsEmptyArray = True
    End If
End Function
```

Also, much of the code herein needs to get the index of `DataColumn`. However, the `DataColumn` object does not have an `index` property. Therefore, the following function, `GetColumnIndex()`, returns the `index` or `-1` if the specified column name does not exist in `DataRecordset`:

```
Public Function GetColumnIndex( _
    ByVal dCol As Visio.DataColumn) As Integer
Dim i As Integer
Dim dCols As Visio.DataColumns
    Set dCols = dCol.DataRecordset.DataColumns
    For i = 1 To dCols.Count
        If dCol Is dCols.Item(i) Then
            GetColumnIndex = i - 1
            Exit Function
        End If
    Next
    GetColumnIndex = -1
End Function
```

Now that the helper functions are defined, they can be used in the sub-function `LinkShapes()` to iterate through the shapes on the active page that are linked to `Personnel DataRecordset`. It checks to see if the **Reports To** shape is also present on the page.

```
Public Sub LinkShapes()
Dim pag As Visio.Page
    Set pag = Visio.ActivePage
Dim doc As Visio.Document
    Set doc = pag.Document
Dim drs As DataRecordset
    Set drs = GetDataRecordset(doc, "Personnel")
    If drs Is Nothing Then Exit Sub

Dim aryFromIDs() As Long
    pag.GetShapesLinkedToData drs.id, aryFromIDs

Dim iFromShape As Integer
Dim iToShape As Integer
Dim shpFrom As Visio.Shape
Dim shpTo As Visio.Shape
Dim aryRowIDs() As Long
Dim rowFrom As Long
Dim rowTo As Long
Dim data As Variant
Dim idTo As Variant
Dim aryToIDs() As Long
Dim scopeID As Long
    scopeID = Application.BeginUndoScope("Linking Shapes")
    For iFromShape = LBound(aryFromIDs) To UBound(aryFromIDs)
        Set shpFrom = pag.Shapes.ItemFromID(aryFromIDs(iFromShape))
        rowFrom = shpFrom.GetLinkedDataRow(drs.id)
        data = drs.GetRowData(rowFrom)
        idTo = data(GetColumnIndex(drs.DataColumns.Item("Reports To")))
        aryRowIDs = drs.GetDataRowIDs("[Unique ID] = '" & idTo & "'")
        For rowTo = LBound(aryRowIDs) To UBound(aryRowIDs)
            pag.GetShapesLinkedToDataRow drs.id, aryRowIDs(rowTo), aryToIDs
            If Not IsEmptyArray(aryToIDs) Then
                For iToShape = LBound(aryToIDs) To UBound(aryToIDs)
                    Set shpTo = pag.Shapes.ItemFromID(aryToIDs(iToShape))
                    shpFrom.AutoConnect shpTo, visAutoConnectDirNone
                Next iToShape
            End If
        Next rowTo
    Next iFromShape
    Application.EndUndoScope scopeID, True
End Sub
```

The preceding code then connects the **Person** shapes, using the default dynamic connector Master to connect the shapes together. The result is shown in the following screenshot:

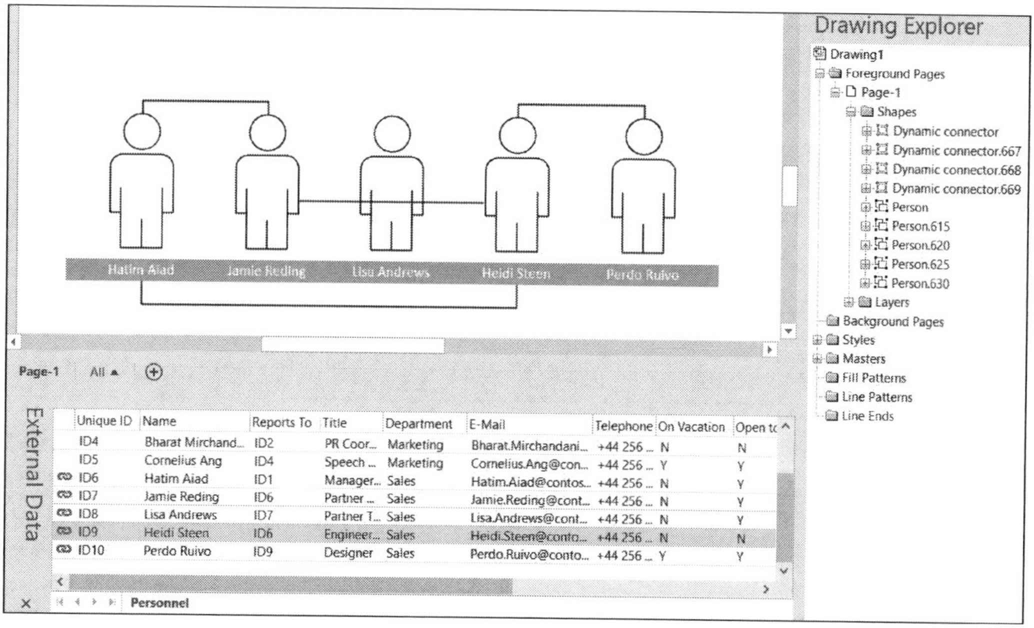


It may not look too clear at the moment, but the page layout can be quickly applied to choose an appropriate arrangement, as in the following screenshot:

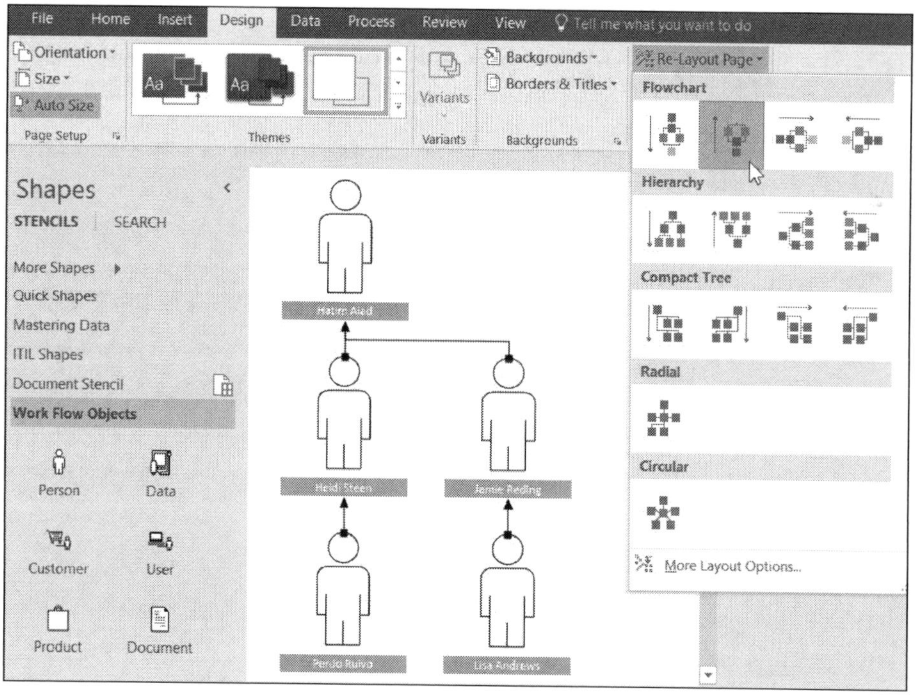

The second argument of the shape, the `AutoConnect` method, allows the direction of the connected shape to be specified. There is also an optional third argument that allows a 1D connector shape Master to be specified.

Sometimes, the `AutoConnect` method does not provide the required control because it only uses *dynamic glue*. This means that a connection point, or other, cannot be specified. There are the `Cell.GlueTo()` and `Cell.GlueToPos()` methods available for this purpose.

The dynamic connector shape is the only Master that you do not need to specify with the `AutoConnect()` method. In fact, this special Master does not even need to exist in Document Stencil because Visio automatically creates Master for you.

Once a dynamic connector exists as a Master in Document Stencil, then it can be customized. Indeed, some of the built-in templates already contain a modified version of a Dynamic connector. The **Connector** tool in the UI also uses dynamic connector Master.

> For more examples of *Dropping and Linked Data Shapes in Visio,* see `http://blog.bvisual.net/2015/06/14/dropping-and-connecting-linked-data-shapes-in-visio/`.

# Adding data-linked shapes to containers

Containers group shapes together visually. The normal user adds a container to the existing shapes using the **Insert** | **Diagram Parts** | **Container** button. The same action can be repeated in code using the `Page.DropContainer()` method. The container shape is added to the page and encloses the target shapes.

An alternative is to use the `Shape.ContainerProperties.AddMember()` method, where `Shape` is a container shape. The container can then expand to enclose the target shapes, which remain in their current positions.

The final alternative action is to move the target shapes into an existing container shape. In the following screenshot, the **Person** shapes are on the outside of the **Sales** container:

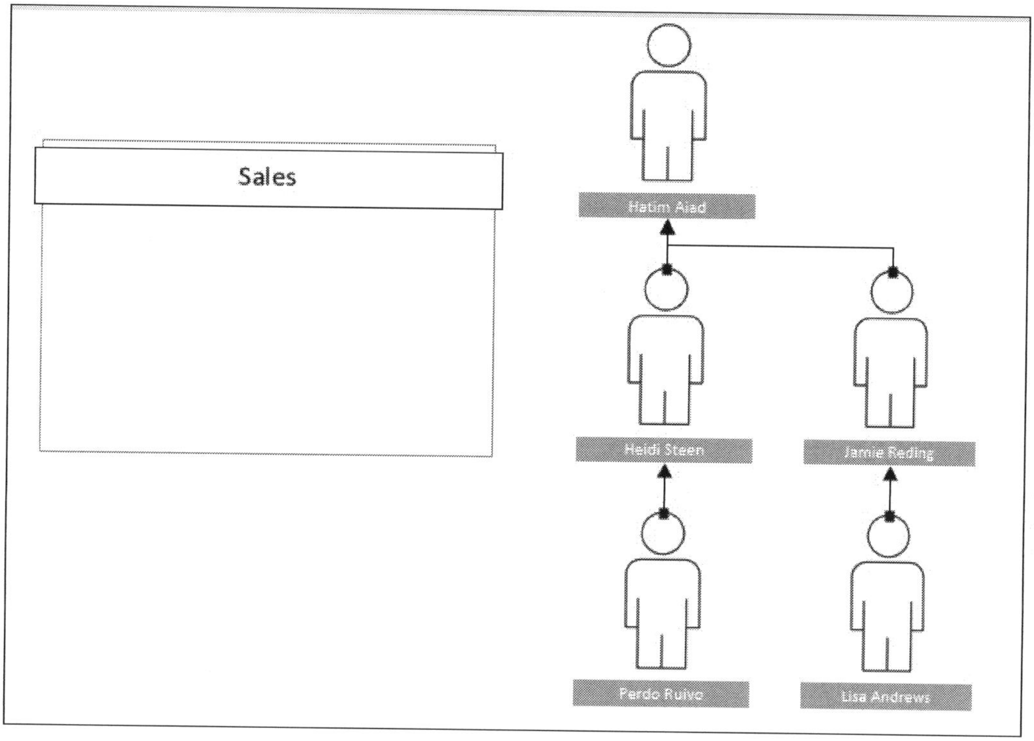

The following sub-function, `DropShapesInContainer()`, finds all the relevant containers by creating a selection of all the shape instances of the `Belt` Master. It gets the text of each container because this is the name of a department. It then finds all the rows from `Personnel DataRecordset` that belong to **Department**. It gets all the shapes that are linked to the **Personnel** row of the active page. Finally, it moves the shapes to the center of the container and adds it to the underlying container.

```
Public Sub DropShapesInContainer()
Dim pag As Visio.Page
    Set pag = Visio.ActivePage
Dim doc As Visio.Document
    Set doc = pag.Document
Dim mstCntnr As Visio.Master
    Set mstCntnr = GetMaster(doc, "Belt", "")
Dim sel As Visio.Selection
    Set sel = pag.CreateSelection(visSelTypeByMaster, 0, mstCntnr)
Dim drs As DataRecordset
    Set drs = GetDataRecordset(doc, "Personnel")
    If drs Is Nothing Then Exit Sub
Dim shpCntnr As Visio.Shape
Dim dept As String
Dim aryRowIDs() As Long
Dim iRow As Integer
Dim iShape As Integer
Dim aryShapeIDs() As Long
Dim shpPerson As Visio.Shape
Dim scopeID As Long
    scopeID = Application.BeginUndoScope("Move Shapes into Container")
    For Each shpCntnr In sel
        dept = shpCntnr.Text
        aryRowIDs = drs.GetDataRowIDs("[Department] = '" & dept & "'")
        If Not IsEmptyArray(aryRowIDs) Then
            For iRow = LBound(aryRowIDs) To UBound(aryRowIDs)
                pag.GetShapesLinkedToDataRow drs.id, aryRowIDs(iRow), aryShapeIDs
                If Not IsEmptyArray(aryShapeIDs) Then
                    For iShape = LBound(aryShapeIDs) To UBound(aryShapeIDs)
                        Set shpPerson = pag.Shapes.ItemFromID(aryShapeIDs(iShape))
                        shpPerson.Cells("PinX").FormulaU = shpCntnr.Cells("PinX").ResultIU
                        shpPerson.Cells("PinY").FormulaU = shpCntnr.Cells("PinY").ResultIU
                        shpPerson.AddToContainers
                    Next iShape
                End If
            Next iRow
        End If
        Debug.Print dept
    Next shpCntnr
    Application.EndUndoScope scopeID, True
End Sub
```

The resultant diagram will look like the following screenshot:

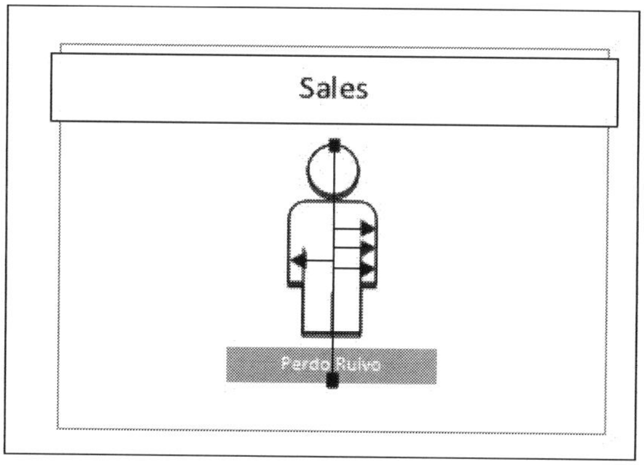


However, applying a layout to the **Person** shapes, either manually, perhaps using the **Design | Layout | Re-Layout Page** button, or in code, can change the appearance to something more useful, as in the following screenshot:

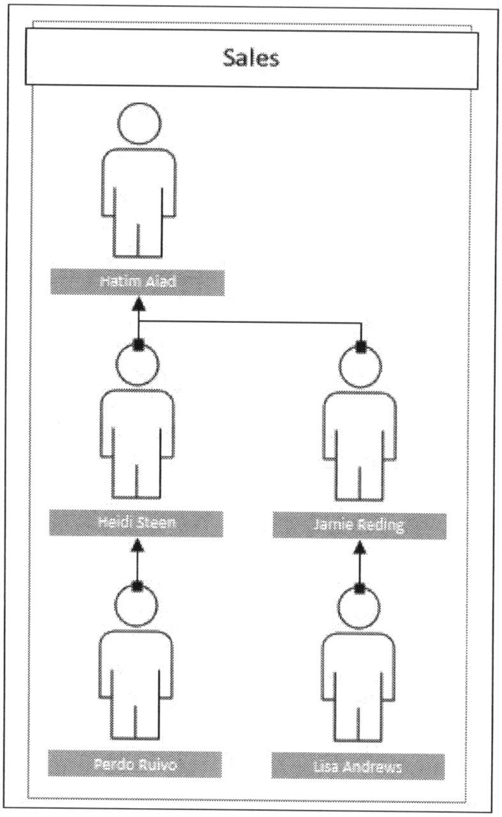

# Adding data-linked shapes to lists

Lists are a special type of container. Each item in a list is ordered from left to right, right to left, top to bottom, or bottom to top. These are the settings that can be applied to the list. In the following screenshot, the **Sales** container has been changed to a list ordering from left to right:

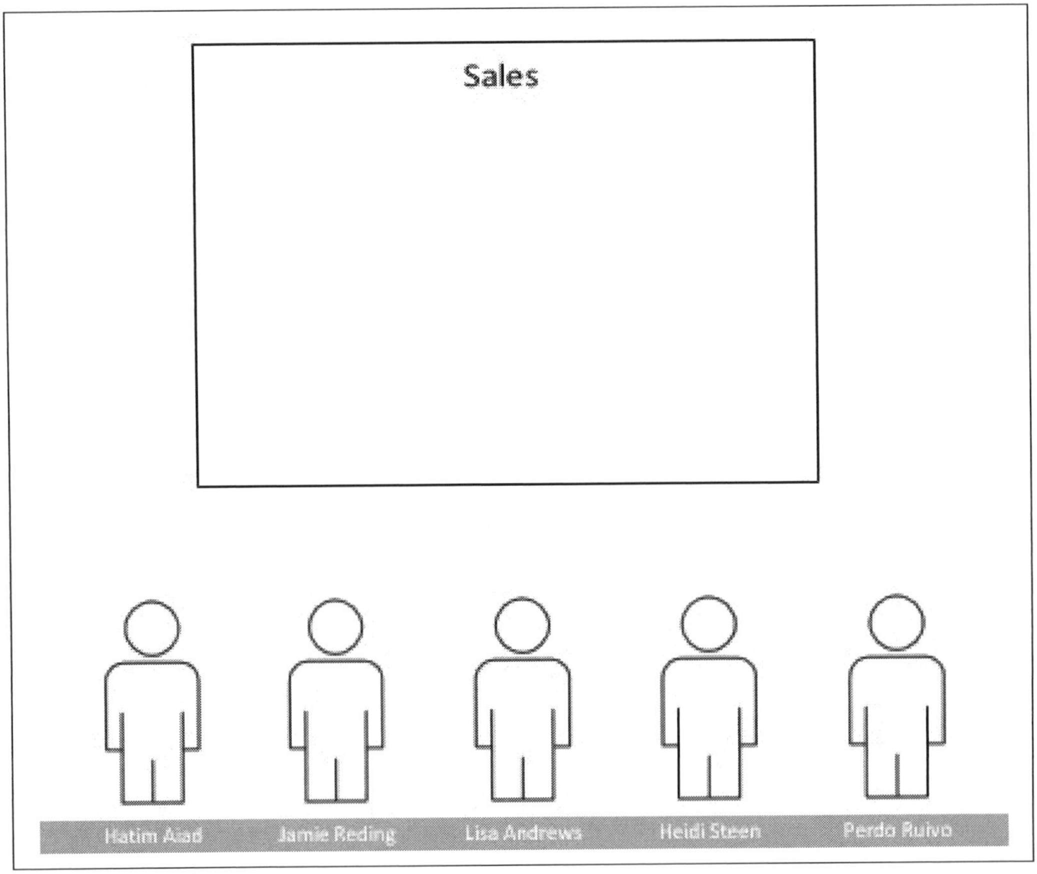

The code is almost identical for `DropShapesInContainer()`, except that the rows that move the **Person** shapes into the center of the container are replaced with the action to insert them into a list.

```
    For iShape = LBound(aryShapeIDs) To UBound(aryShapeIDs)
        Set shpPerson = pag.Shapes.ItemFromID(aryShapeIDs(iShape))
        shpList.ContainerProperties.InsertListMember shpPerson, iShape
    Next iShape
```

This results in the **Person** shapes being neatly aligned within the list container, as shown in the following screenshot. There is no need to lay out the shapes, of course.

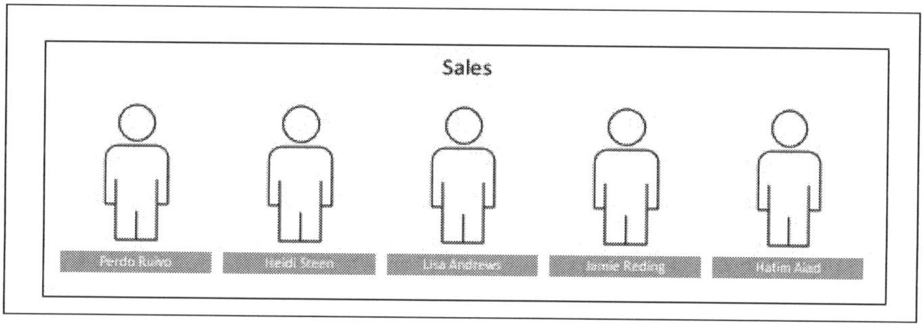


In reality, the **Person** shapes will be ordered according to some rule, rather than just looping through `DataRecordset`.

[ For more uses of lists in Visio diagrams, see `http://blog.bvisual.net/2014/12/31/get-scrabbled-with-visio/`. ]

# Adding Callouts to shapes

There is a built-in stencil called **Callouts** in the **Visio Extras** category, but the Callouts introduced as part of Structured Diagram API are something different. These are a special type of Shape that have some programmatic control. Any shape can have many Callouts associated with it. The names of Callout Masters in the built-in stencil can be read by moving the mouse over them in the **Insert | Diagram Parts | Callout** drop-down gallery, as in the following screenshot:

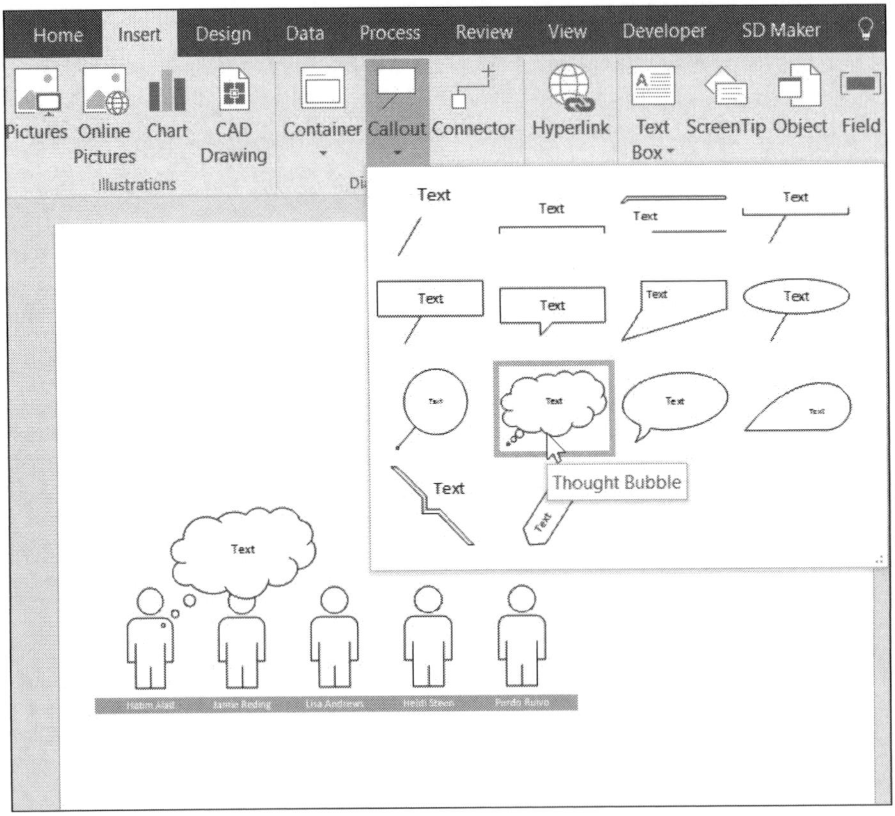

The following code, `AddCallouts()`, gets a reference to the **Thought Bubble** callout from the built-in stencil. It then loops through all the shapes in the active page that are linked to `Personnel DataRecordset`. It drops a new shape instance of the **Callout** Master and associates it with the **Person** shape, and inserts the name of **Person** Shape as text.

```
Public Sub AddCallouts()
Dim pag As Visio.Page
    Set pag = Visio.ActivePage
Dim doc As Visio.Document
    Set doc = pag.Document
Dim drs As DataRecordset
    Set drs = GetDataRecordset(doc, "Personnel")
    If drs Is Nothing Then Exit Sub
Dim dsEnabled As Long
    dsEnabled = doc.DiagramServicesEnabled
    doc.DiagramServicesEnabled = VisDiagramServices.visServiceAll
Dim scopeID As Long
    scopeID = Application.BeginUndoScope("Add Callouts")
Dim stn As Visio.Document
    Set stn = Application.Documents.OpenEx( _
        Application.GetBuiltInStencilFile( _
            visBuiltInStencilCallouts, visMSUS), _
            visOpenHidden)
Dim mstCallout As Visio.Master
    Set mstCallout = stn.Masters.ItemU("Thought Bubble")
Dim iShape As Integer
Dim aryShapeIDs() As Long
Dim shpPerson As Visio.Shape
Dim shpCallout As Visio.Shape

    pag.GetShapesLinkedToData drs.id, aryShapeIDs
    If Not IsEmptyArray(aryShapeIDs) Then
        For iShape = LBound(aryShapeIDs) To UBound(aryShapeIDs)
            Set shpPerson = pag.Shapes.ItemFromID(aryShapeIDs(iShape))
            Set shpCallout = pag.DropCallout(mstCallout, shpPerson)
            Set shpPerson = shpCallout.CalloutTarget
            shpCallout.Text = shpPerson.name
        Next iShape
    End If
    stn.Close

    Application.EndUndoScope scopeID, True
    doc.DiagramServicesEnabled = dsEnabled
End Sub
```

The resultant diagram is shown in the following screenshot:

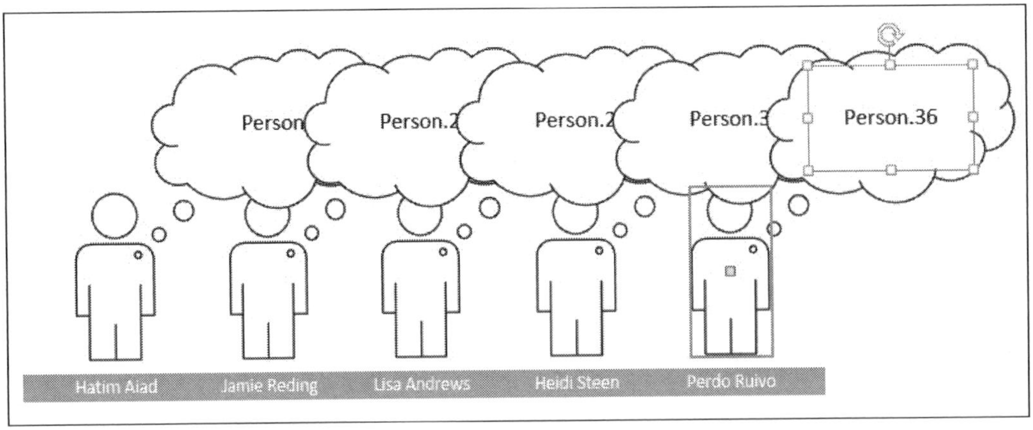


Callouts can be used for comments or notes, or even as additional placeholders for information held in the Shape Data rows in the target Shape.

> See `http://blog.bvisual.net/2014/04/08/adding-configure-callout-functionality-to-visio-callouts/` for tips on how to add the Configure Callout feature to Structured Diagram Callouts.

# Summary

In this chapter, we learnt how to create structured diagrams with data values found within `DataRecordsets`. We learnt how to connect shapes, add shapes to containers and lists, and how to associate Callouts.

In the next chapter, we will learn how to make these data-driven diagrams available to others to view and interact with.

# 10
# Sharing Data Diagrams

In previous chapters, you learned how to create data diagrams with Visio. Unfortunately, not everybody has the Visio application installed on their Windows PC.

This chapter discusses the various ways that a Visio data diagram can be shared with others, and it explains how Visio diagrams can become an interactive visual dashboard either within Visio (in SharePoint or Office365 web pages), in the Microsoft Visio Viewer (published as web pages), or as another file format.

This chapter includes some VBA macros that contain the principles for actions in any other coding language. There is some sample JavaScript for interacting with an embedded Visio document.

In this chapter, we will learn the following topics:

- Viewing with the Visio Viewer
- Embedding within SharePoint web pages
- Printing to paper, PDF, and XPS
- Publishing as web pages

# Thinking about sharing

This book is all about Visio as visual information. Shapes in Visio are obviously graphical, but they contain data and hyperlinks. There is no doubt that the richest experience of a Visio document is with the Visio application. However, this is not always possible, so an alternative experience is often necessary. Some of these methods can provide access to the data and hyperlinks, either fully or partly, but some methods reduce Visio to providing purely graphical output. Perhaps this is when Data Graphics are at their most important because they visualize the information without the viewer needing to select a shape.

There are also times when the data in shapes is sensitive, and providing access is not desirable.

# Viewing Visio documents without Visio

The simplest way to provide viewing of Visio documents without Visio is to use the Microsoft Outlook desktop application or Windows File Explorer. Microsoft Outlook uses a Visio previewer that can display Visio files either included as e-mail attachments or within SharePoint document libraries, as shown in the following screenshot:

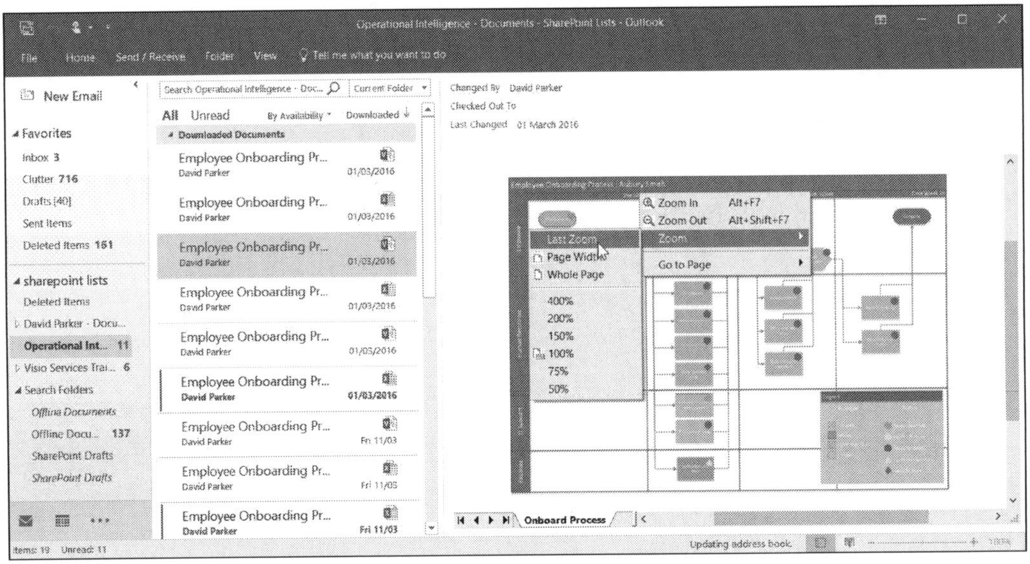


The Visio previewer is the Microsoft Visio Viewer control, but a lot of its functionality has been hidden to reduce it to viewing graphics only.

# Embedding the Viewer in a Windows desktop application

The control uses ActiveX technology and has an API that provides developers access to each shape and their data labels and values, as well as hyperlinks. It also has the ability to switch layers off and on. It is a shame that these functions are hidden inside Microsoft Outlook.

However, the Microsoft Visio Viewer control can be inserted into a Windows application, such as Microsoft Excel. It is listed as **Microsoft Visio Document** when the **Developer | Insert | ActiveX controls | More Controls** button is pressed, as shown in the following screenshot:

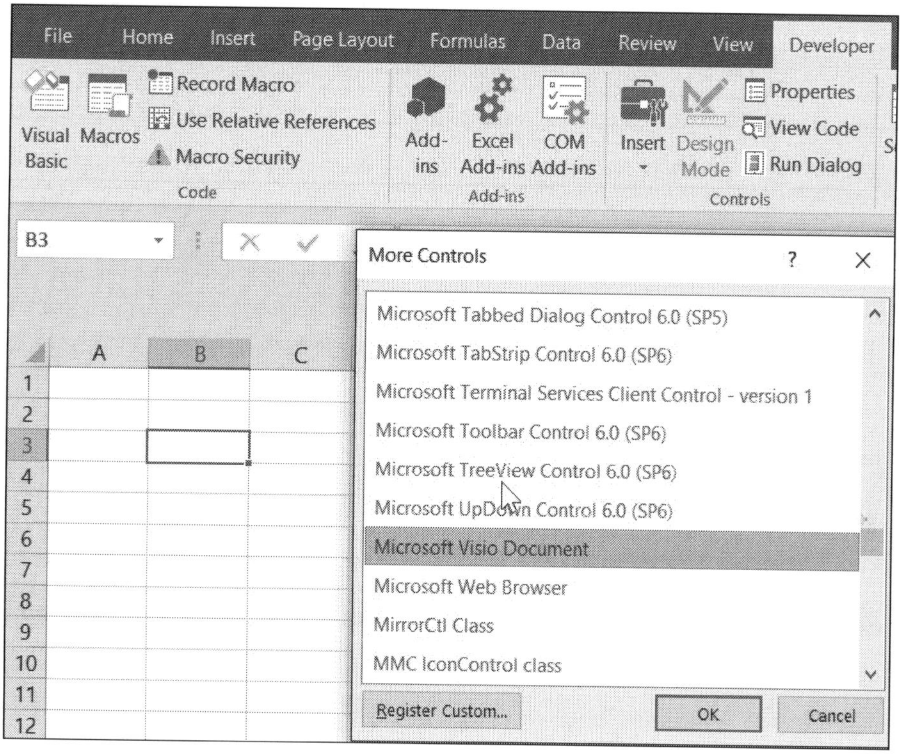

A Command Button can also be inserted into the worksheet, and the following VBA code, `CommandButton1_Click()`, will load a selected Visio document into the Microsoft Visio Viewer control:

```
Private Sub CommandButton1_Click()
Dim strFileToOpen As String

strFileToOpen = Application.GetOpenFilename _
    (Title:="Please choose a Visio Document to View", _
    FileFilter:="Visio Documents (*.vsdx;*.vsdm;*.vsd;*.vdx)," & _
        "*.vsdx;*.vsdm;*.vsd;*.vdx")
If strFileToOpen = "" Then
    MsgBox "No file selected.", vbExclamation, "Sorry!"
    Exit Sub
Else
    Viewer1.Load strFileToOpen
    If Viewer1.LastErrorCode <> 0 Then
        Debug.Print Viewer1.GetErrorMessage(Viewer1.LastErrorCode)
    End If
End If

End Sub
```

Notice that Windows File Explorer also uses the Visio Viewer to preview Visio files, as shown in the following screenshot, which shows a Visio file viewed within an Excel worksheet:

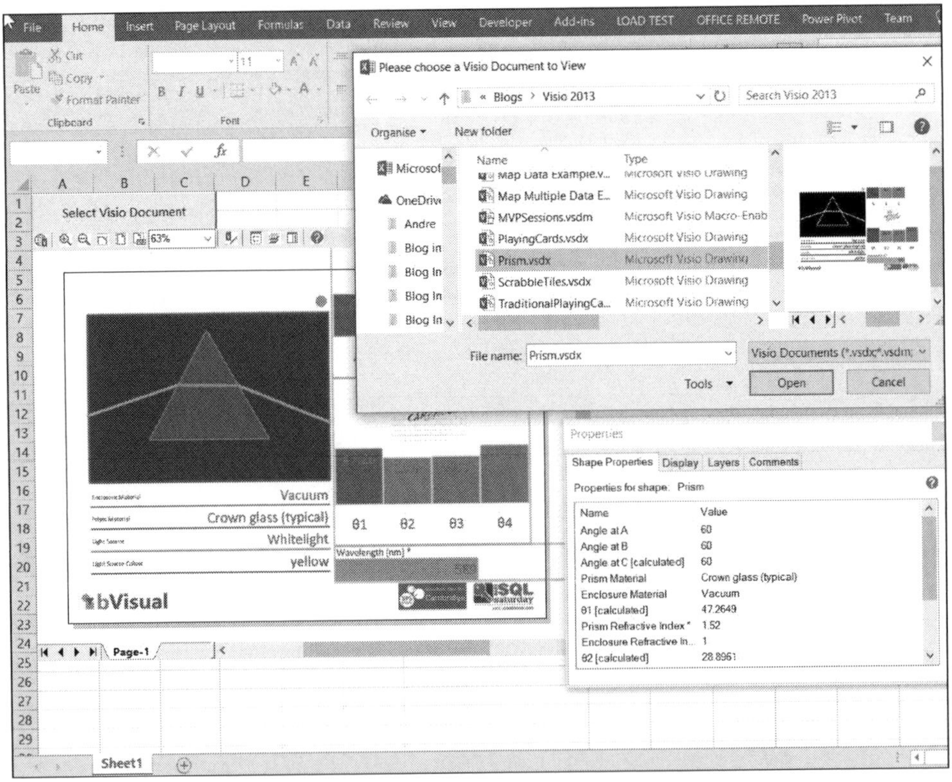

The Visio Viewer, used in this way, can display a toolbar that has buttons for zooming in and out and viewing the **Shape Properties** of a selected shape. It also has some **Display Settings**, which enable **Layers** to be switched on and off. The **Comments** tab is for pre-Visio 2013 documents only, as a new method for commenting was introduced after that version.

> For more details on the Microsoft Visio Viewer API, take a look at `https://msdn.microsoft.com/en-us/library/office/jj684248.aspx`.

The Microsoft Visio Viewer is free for all Microsoft Office license holders, and it can be downloaded separately from the Microsoft website.

> Take a look at `http://bvisual.net/Products/visViewer.aspx` for an example of an application that utilizes the Microsoft Visio Viewer.

# Embedding the Viewer in a web page

The control can be embedded within a web page, but it needs to be viewed using a browser that supports ActiveX. For example, the following screenshot is of Microsoft Internet Explorer (Microsoft Edge does not support ActiveX):

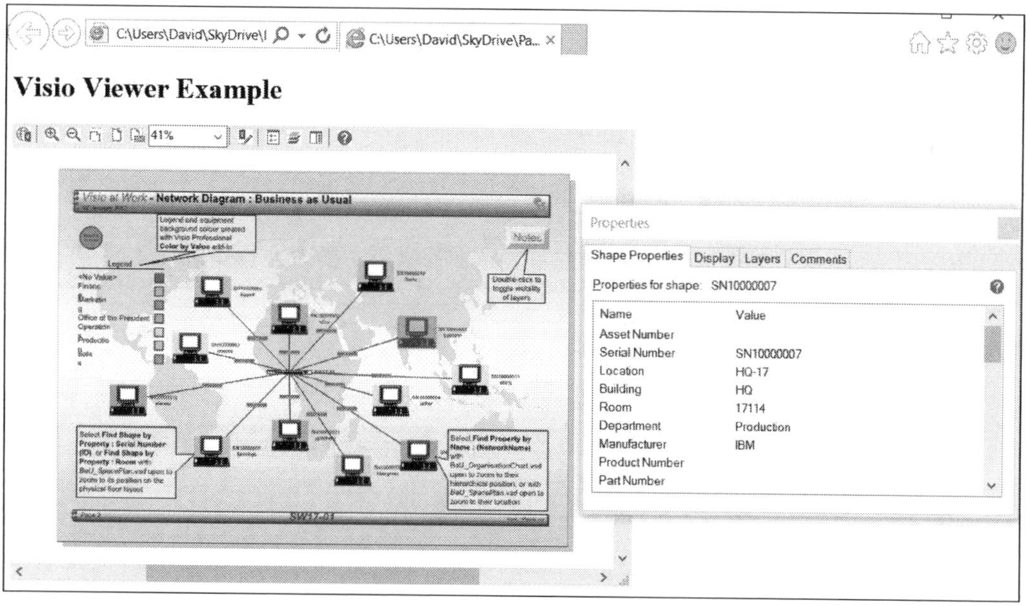

The following code is for the previously displayed web page. It merely embeds the Microsoft Visio Viewer control, which must be registered in the Windows system that runs it:

```
<!DOCTYPE html>
<html>
  <head>
    <h1>Visio Viewer Example</h1>
  </head>
  <body>
      <object id="DrawingControl1" height="500" width="700"
        classid="clsid:F8CF7A98-2C45-4c8d-9151-2D716989DDAB" >
           <param name="ToolbarVisible" value="1">
           <param name="Src" value="http://www.bvisual.net
           //examples/BaUNetworkDiagram.vsd">
        </object>
  </body>
</html>
```

## Viewing in SharePoint/Office365 web pages

Visio 2013+ documents that are stored in SharePoint 2013+ can be viewed directly by users with an Enterprise Client Access License. Pre-Visio 2013 documents need to be saved as VDW files to enable them to be viewed. Visio documents are viewed in the Visio Web Access control.

This control has a JavaScript Object Model that is quite similar to the API for the Microsoft Visio Viewer. The control also has an optional **Shape Info** panel that displays the **Hyperlinks** and **Shape Data** of a selected shape, as shown in the following screenshot:

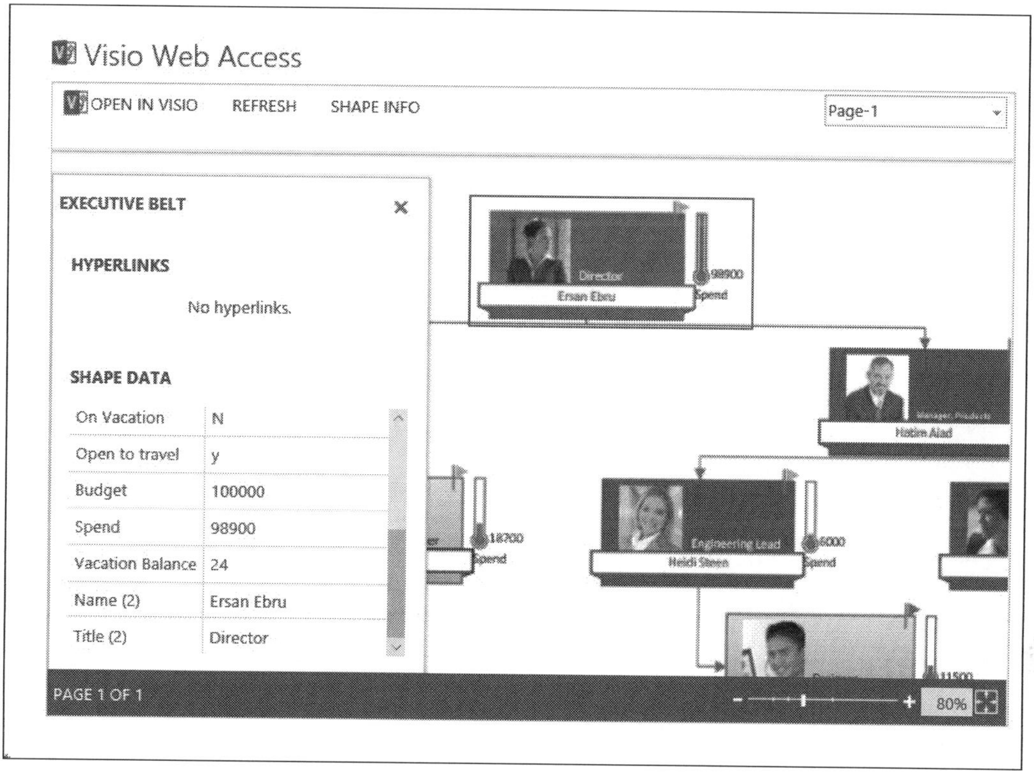


Like the Microsoft Visio Viewer control, the API only provides the labels and values of Shape Data rows. The Visio Web Access control also has inter-web-part linking features, but the JavaScript API usually provides greater and smoother interaction.

# Protecting data

If access is provided to a Visio document, then it may be necessary to prevent the unauthorized viewing of all or some of the data.

If the Visio file is stored in SharePoint, and a Rights Management Server is available, then it can be protected using the **Protect Diagram** button on the **File | Info** backstage, as shown in the following screenshot:

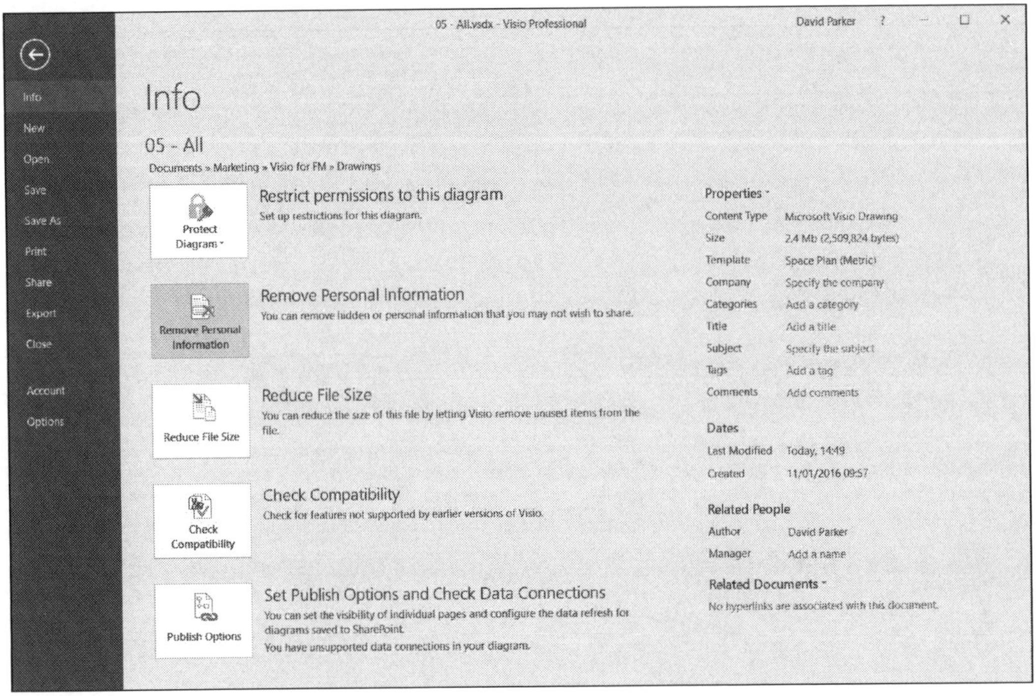


There may be more data cached in the external `DataRecordsets` than is stored in each shape. Therefore, the **Remove Personal Information** button opens the **Remove Hidden Information** dialog where these `DataRecordsets` can be erased with the **Remove data from external sources stored in the document** option, as shown in the following screenshot:

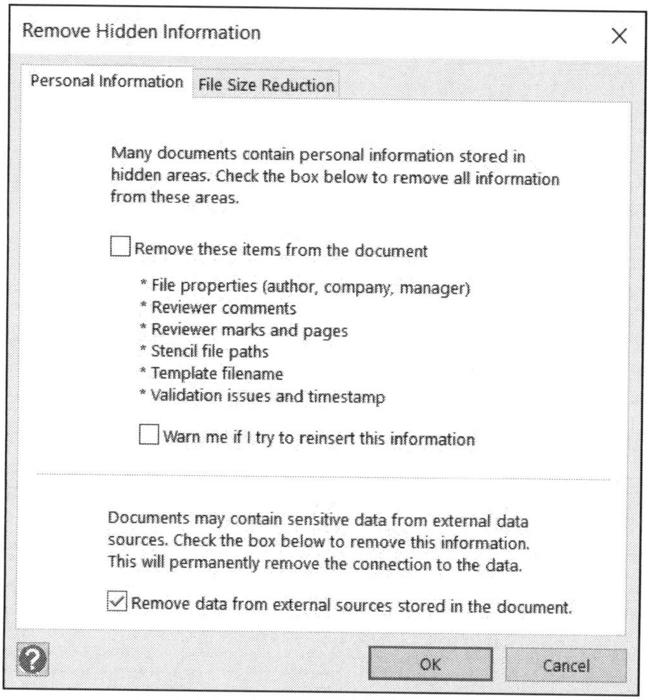


If the Visio document is stored in SharePoint, then the **Publish Options** button enables pages and data to be made invisible in documents viewed in the **Visio Web Access** control, as shown in the following screenshot:

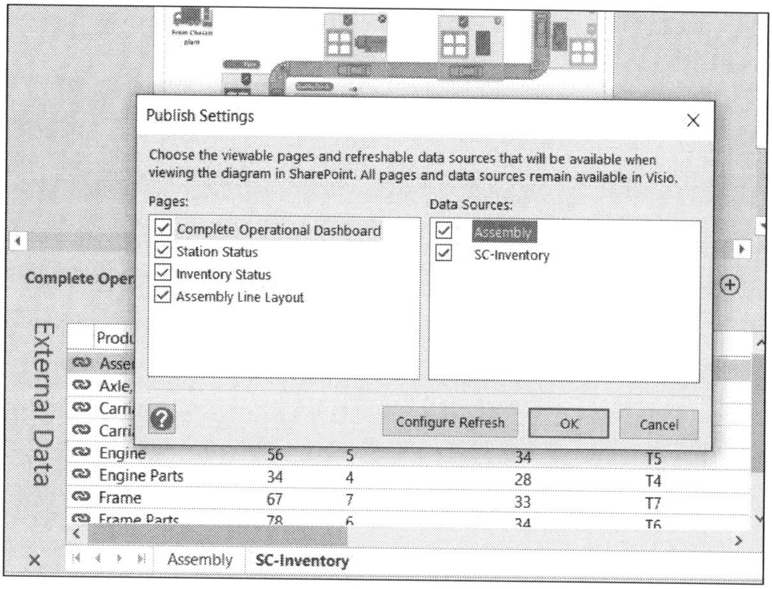

# Coming soon

Microsoft has committed to providing a Visio viewer application that does not use ActiveX in the near future. This will greatly improve the breadth of capabilities and possibilities. It should enable Visio documents to be viewed on any modern device, regardless of the operating system. It should include layer control, and it will hopefully include Shape Data and Hyperlinks.

# Sharing a Visio document

If a Visio document is stored in OneDrive, then a link to the file can be shared via an e-mail. The intended user can be provided with edit or view permissions, and the user can be forced to sign in with a Microsoft identity first, as shown in the following screenshot:

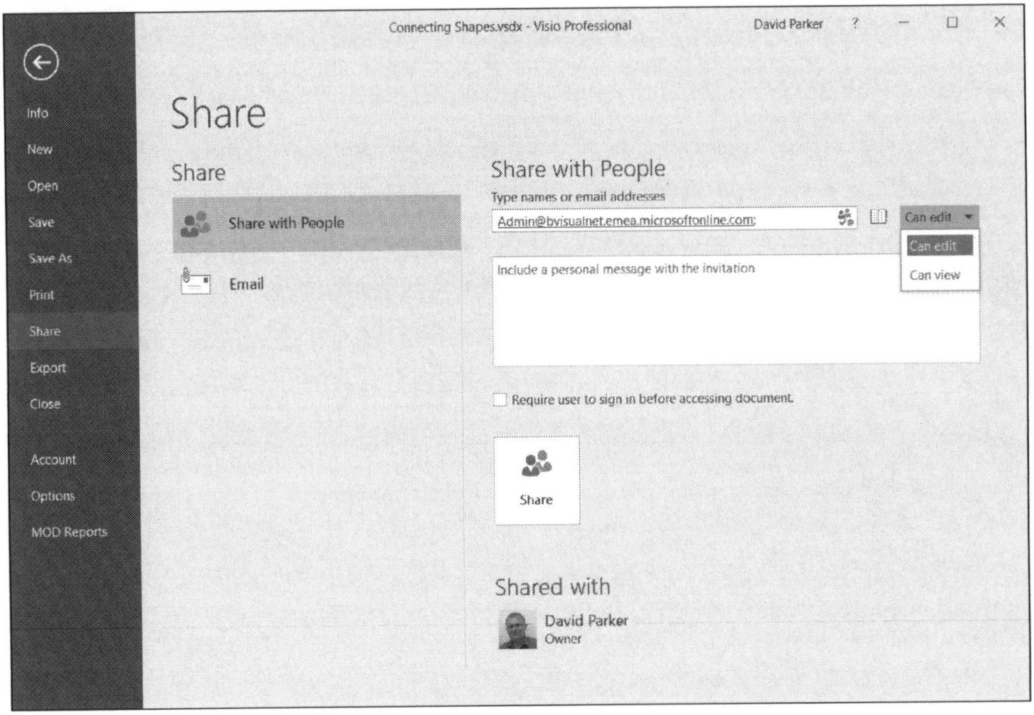


The preceding e-mail is sent automatically, but the **Email** option will create a proposed e-mail using the installed e-mail client.

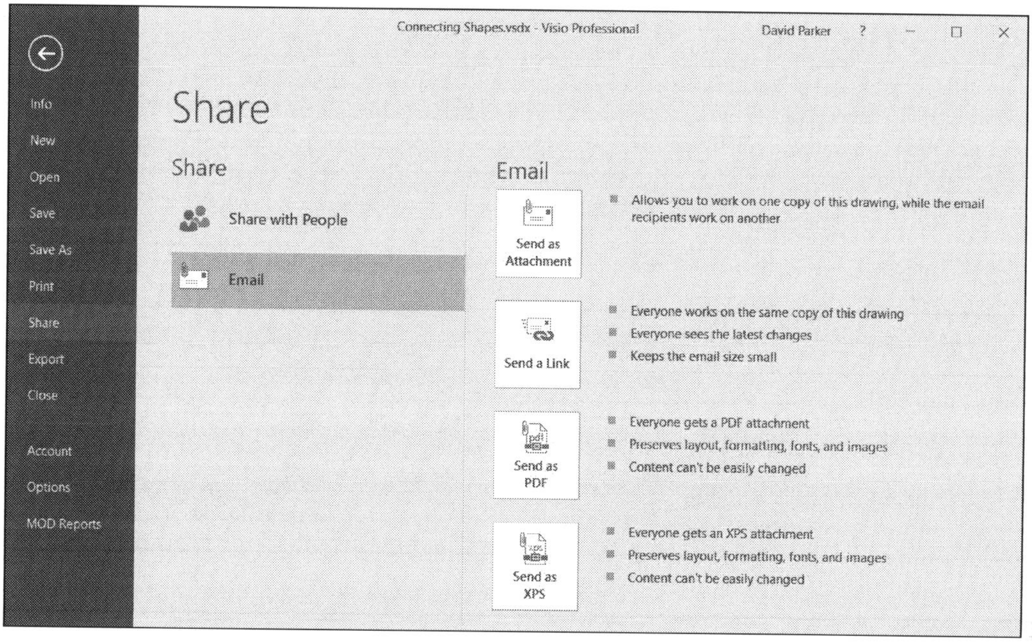


The PDF and XPS options are discussed in the next section.

# Exporting a Visio document

The following screenshot shows the **File** | **Export** options that are available:

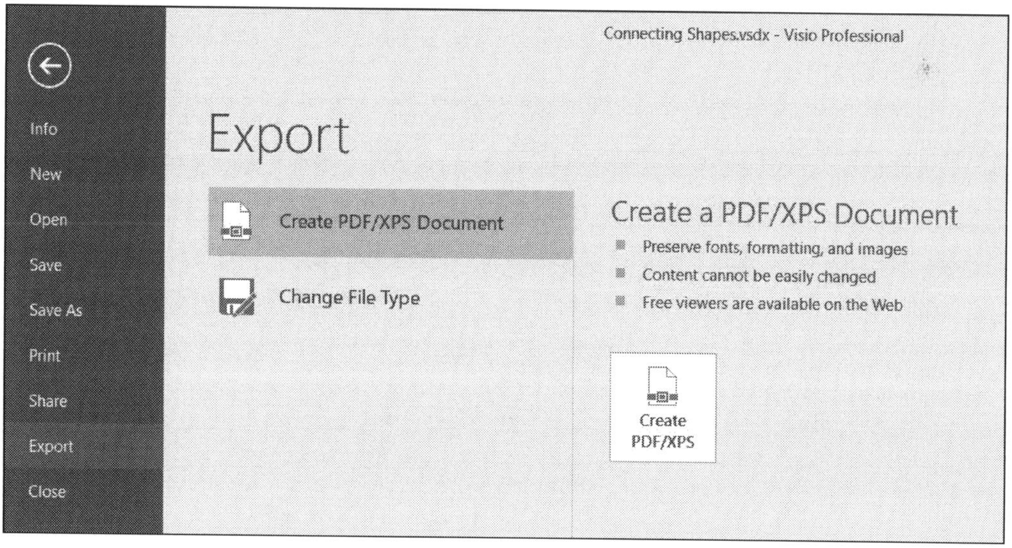

# Creating a PDF or XPS document

Microsoft has included the ability to create PDF and XPS documents from a Visio document. These have the ability to set the specific pages and some graphical properties. However, neither method provides the option to include Shape Data, and they only enable the first hyperlink on each shape. This is disappointing since both PDF and XPS are capable of much more.

These outputs can be created in code using the `Document.ExportAsFixedFormat()` method; take a look at `https://msdn.microsoft.com/en-us/library/office/ff766893.aspx` for more information.

The following screenshot is of the **Options** dialog for PDF, but XPS is the same except for the **PDF options, ISO 19005-1 compliant (PDF/A)**:

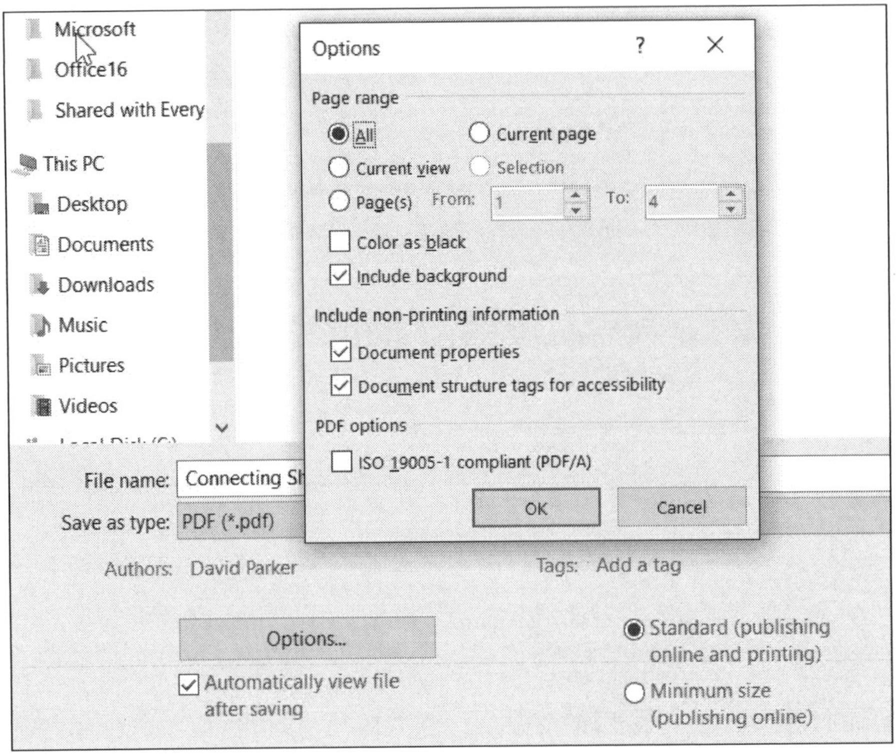


I have always felt that **XPS (Extensible Paper Specification)** is a good idea that has not been exploited by Microsoft. XPS has an API (take a look at `https://msdn.microsoft.com/en-us/library/system.windows.xps(v=vs.100).aspx`). Therefore, it is possible to enhance the XPS document with custom code to include data and hyperlinks. However, the current viewers will not reveal the extra information, and thus a custom viewer would also need to be coded.

# Changing the file type

The **Export** options include one that enables saving to different Visio file extensions. However, the pre-Visio 2013 XML format is not included, as shown in the following screenshot of **File** | **Export**:

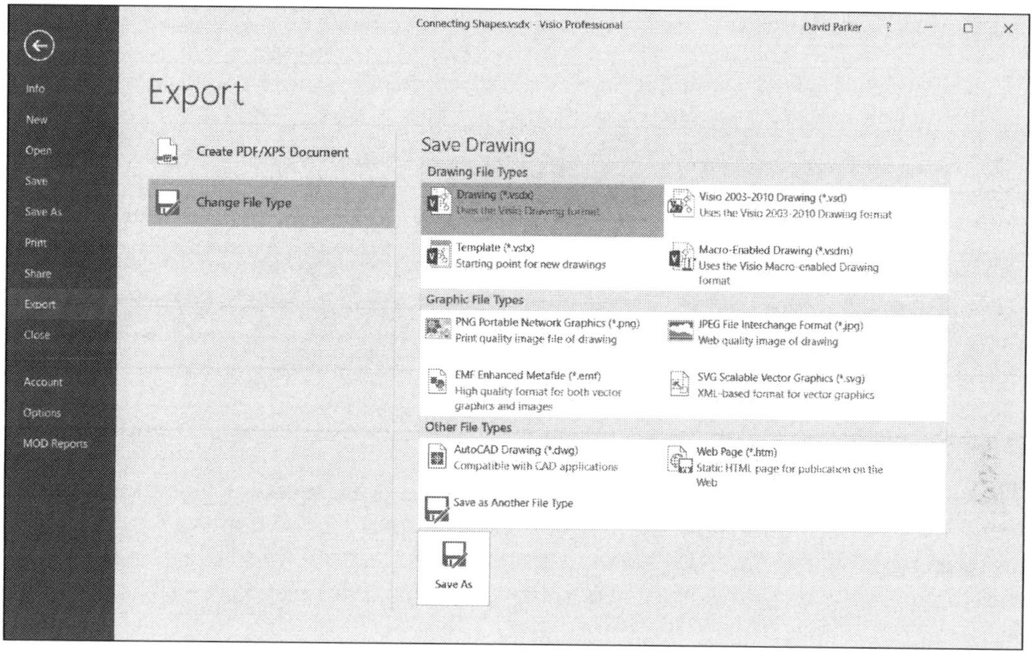


# Saving as SVG

The only graphical format that includes data with the graphics is SVG. Each of these graphical export options are for the selected shapes, or for the whole page. This option is available at the bottom of the **Save As** window, as shown in the following screenshot:

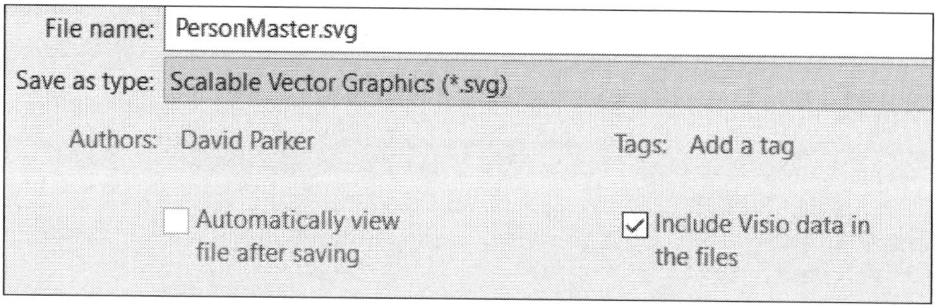

The SVG format is supported by most modern browsers and so the graphics are rendered acceptably, as shown in the following screenshot of Microsoft Edge:

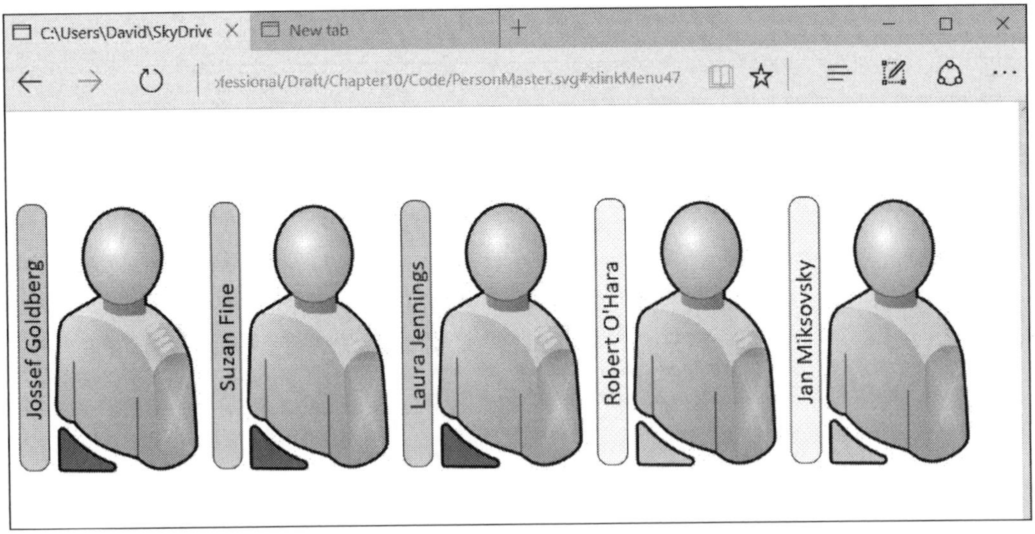


However, the graphics are not contained within any other element that allows them to be panned and zoomed easily. Also, the hyperlinks do not work. An examination of the SVG code that is created shows that both the Shape Data (`<v:custProps>`) and User-Defined Cells (`<v:userDefs>`) are exported, as shown in the following screenshot:

```
<?xml version="1.0" encoding="UTF-8" standalone="no"?>
<!DOCTYPE svg PUBLIC "-//W3C//DTD SVG 1.1//EN" "http://www.w3.org/Graphics/SVG/1.1/DTD/svg11.dtd">
<!-- Generated by Microsoft Visio, SVG Export PersonMaster.svg Page-1 -->
<svg xmlns="http://www.w3.org/2000/svg" xmlns:xlink="http://www.w3.org/1999/xlink" xmlns:ev="http://www.w3.org/2001/xml-events"
        xmlns:v="http://schemas.microsoft.com/visio/2003/SVGExtensions/" width="8.26772in" height="11.6929in"
        viewBox="0 0 595.276 841.89" xml:space="preserve" color-interpolation-filters="sRGB" onzoom="resetCoords()"
        onscroll="resetCoords()" onload="initCoords(evt)" class="st24">
    <v:documentProperties v:langID="2057" v:metric="true" v:viewMarkup="false">
        <v:userDefs>
            <v:ud v:nameU="msvNoAutoConnect" v:val="VT0(1):26"/>
            <v:ud v:nameU="msvLastAppliedDataGraphic" v:val="VT4(Data Graphic)"/>
            <v:ud v:nameU="msvNoApplyDataGraphicAfterLink" v:val="VT0(1):5"/>
        </v:userDefs>
    </v:documentProperties>

    <style type="text/css">
    <![CDATA[
    </style>

    <defs id="Patterns_And_Gradients">
    <defs id="Filters">
    <g v:mID="0" v:index="1" v:groupContext="foregroundPage">
        <v:userDefs>
        <title>Page-1</title>
        <v:pageProperties v:drawingScale="0.0393701" v:pageScale="0.0393701" v:drawingUnits="24" v:shadowOffsetX="8.50394"
                v:shadowOffsetY="-8.50394"/>
        <v:layer v:name="Data Graphic" v:index="0"/>
        <v:layer v:name="Flowchart" v:index="1"/>
        <a xlink:href="#xlinkMenu1" onclick="showHyperlinks(evt, 'xlinkMenu1')" onmousemove="promptHyperlinks(evt)"
                v:hyperlinks="url(#xlinkMenu1)">
            <g id="group1-2" transform="translate(45.3543,-342.992)" v:mID="1" v:groupContext="group">
                <v:custProps>
                    <v:cp v:nameU="ID" v:lbl="ID" v:prompt="ID (Prop.ID)" v:type="2" v:langID="2057" v:val="VT0(1):26"/>
                    <v:cp v:nameU="Name" v:lbl="Name" v:prompt="Name (Prop.Name)" v:type="0" v:langID="2057"
                            v:val="VT4(Jossef Goldberg)"/>
                    <v:cp v:nameU="Title" v:lbl="Title" v:prompt="Title (Prop.Title)" v:type="0" v:langID="2057"
                            v:val="VT4(President &#38; CEO)"/>
                    <v:cp v:nameU="Reports_To" v:lbl="Reports_To" v:prompt="Reports_To (Prop.Reports_To)" v:type="0"
                            v:langID="2057" v:val="VT4()"/>
                    <v:cp v:nameU="Department" v:lbl="Department" v:prompt="Department (Prop.Department)" v:type="0"
                            v:langID="2057" v:val="VT4(Office of the President)"/>
                    <v:cp v:nameU="Telephone" v:lbl="Telephone" v:prompt="Telephone (Prop.Telephone)" v:type="0" v:langID="2057"
                            v:val="VT4(425-707-9790)"/>
```

The code also reveals that the reason for the failure of the hyperlinks to work is because the `onclick` event is set to a non-existent JavaScript function called `showHyperlinks()`. Also, the `onmousemove` event is set to a non-existent JavaScript function called `promptHyperlinks()`. The reason for this becomes clear when a Visio document is saved as a web page, as we will see in the next section.

The SVG export can also be achieved in code, but `Application.ApplicationSettings.SVGExportFormat` should be set to include or exclude the data before using the `Page.Export()` method. Take a look at `https://msdn.microsoft.com/en-us/library/office/jj229319.aspx` for more information.

# Publishing as a web page

Visio has a method of exporting one or more pages of a Visio document as web pages. The following screenshot of the **Save as Web Page | General** dialog shows that a number of **Publishing options** can be set (dependent on the output format):

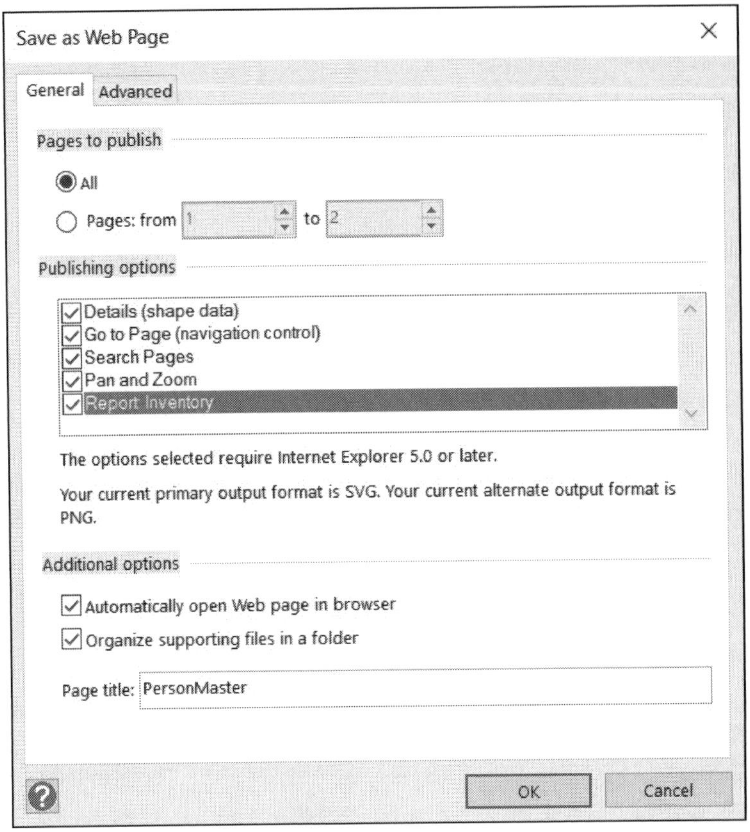


The output creates a main HTML file and a large number of supporting files that are best organized in a supporting folder. Also, note that reports can be included as extra pages within the output.

Visio documents used to be very presentable in Microsoft Internet Explorer using the **Vector Markup Language (VML)**, ActiveX widgets, and JavaScript. The following screenshot is from Visio 2016, running the Microsoft Internet Explorer 5 emulation:

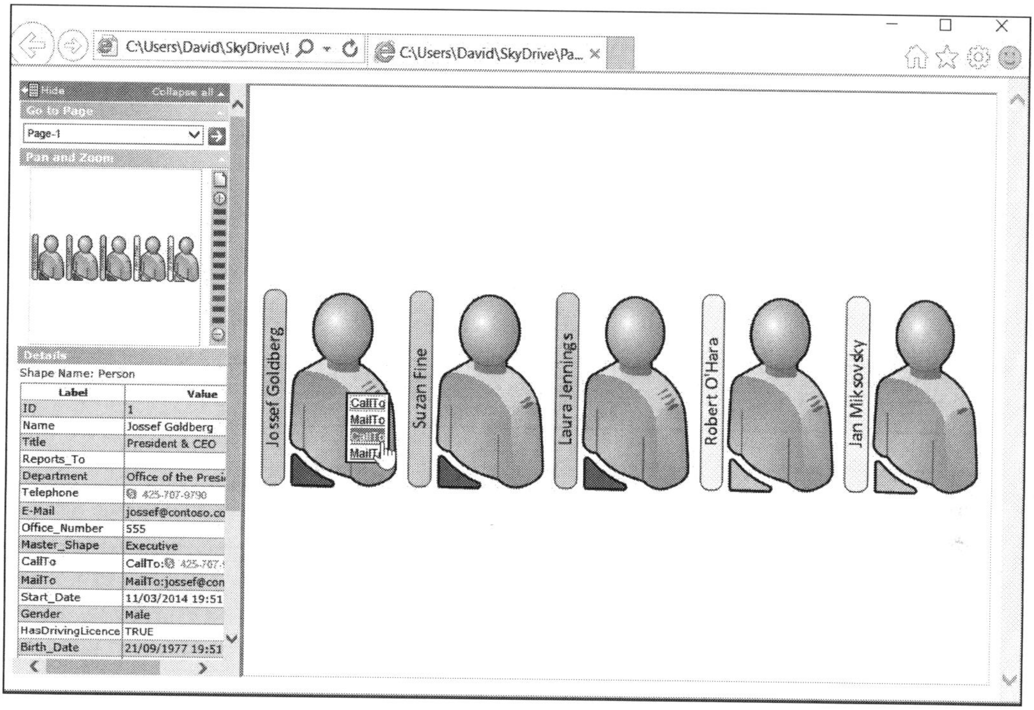


Multiple hyperlinks are available per shape. Shape Data is available for each selected shape or via the use of the search function. The selected shape from the search results is even zoomed to and indicated with an arrow, as shown in the following screenshot:

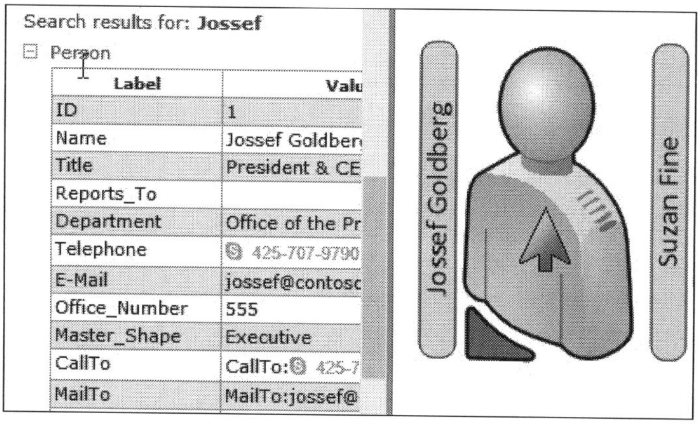

The browser world has moved on, and modern browsers are following the HTML5 protocol. VML is not supported in other browsers—not even in Microsoft Edge. However, SVG is supported, and the web pages can be set to use SVG, as shown in the following screenshot of the **Save As Web Page** publishing options dialog:

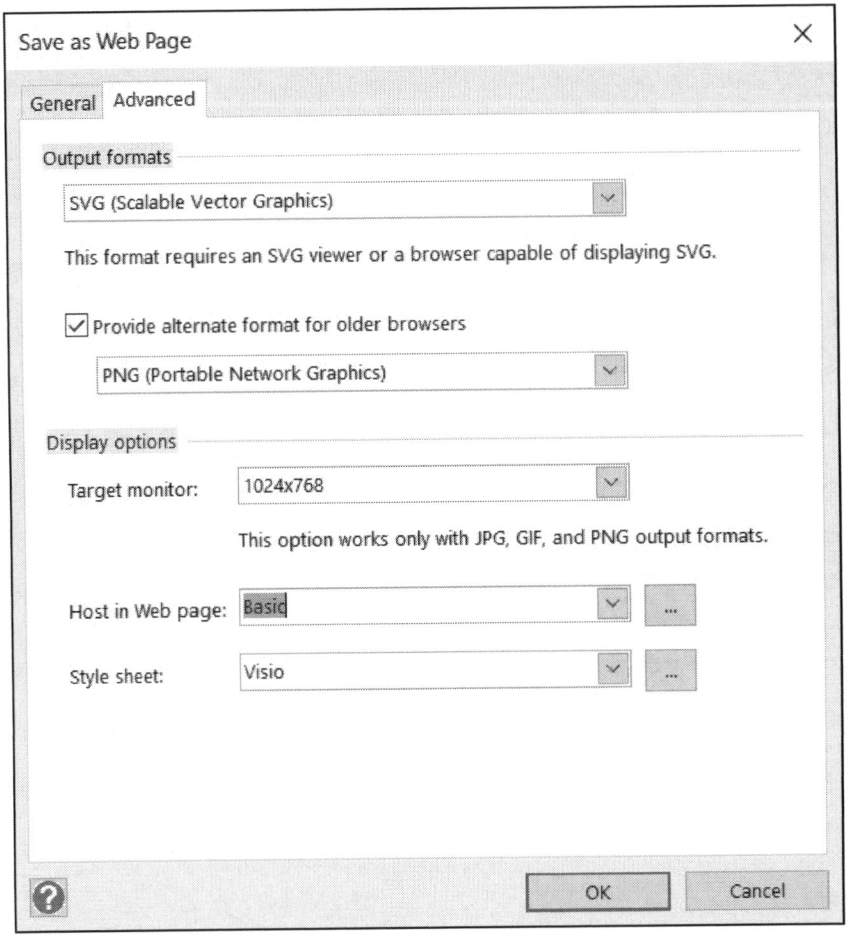

However, it is regrettable that Microsoft has let this functionality fall behind modern standards. The following screenshot is a typical output of a two-page long Visio document with a report page using SVG:

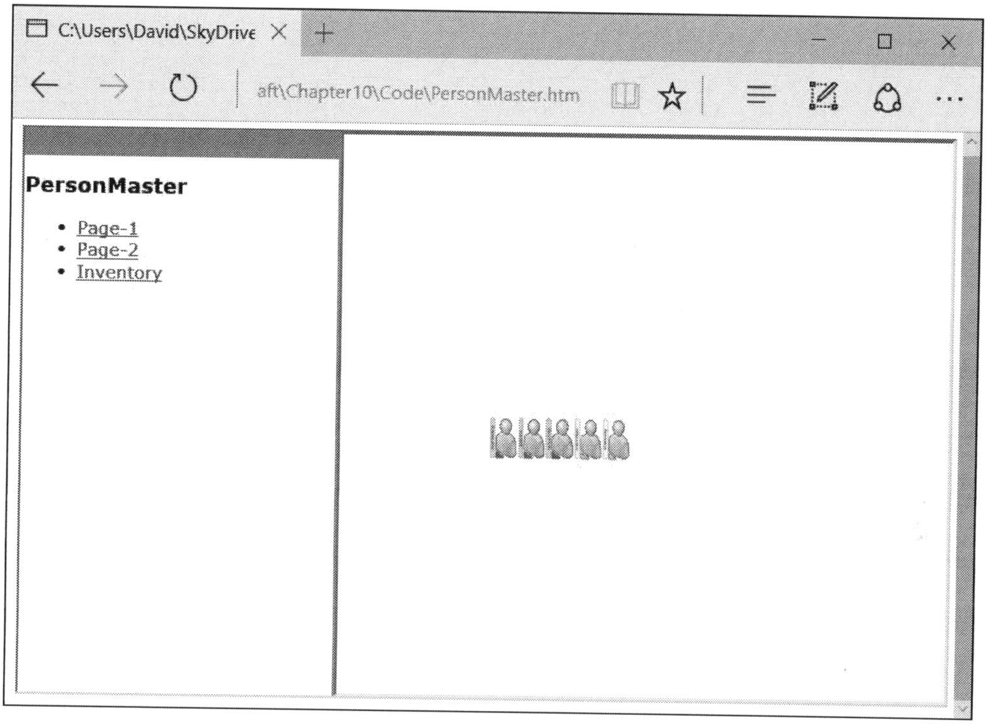

This is clearly not usable in practice. However, the supporting files are all present and include a file called `data.xml` that contains all of the data for each shape, as shown in the following screenshot:

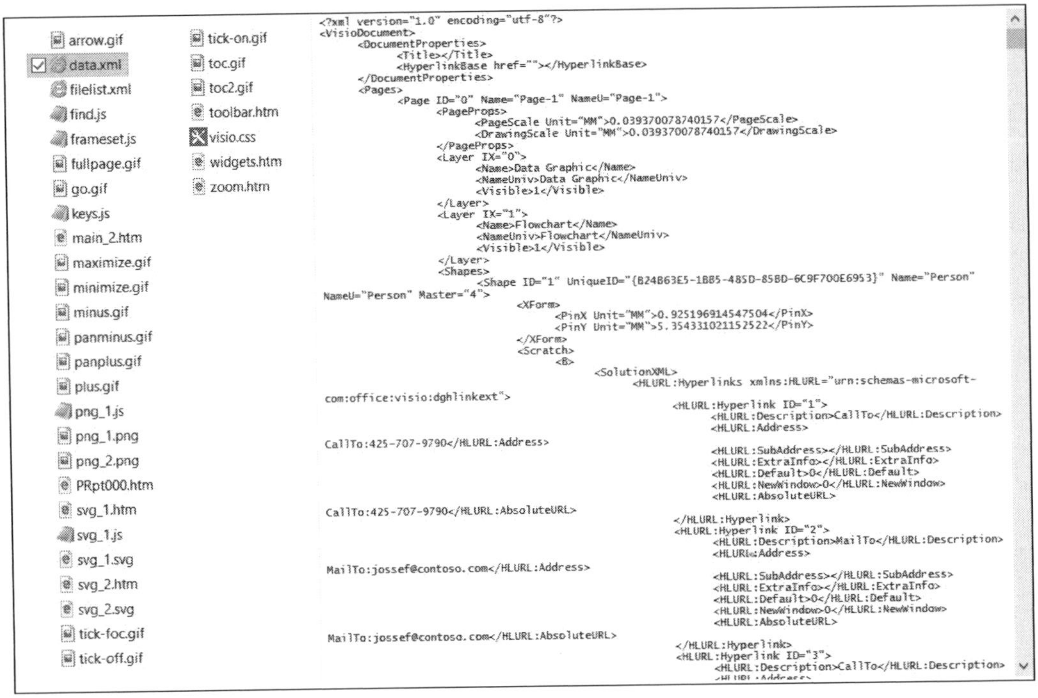


The supporting files also include the JavaScript files with the code that could have been referenced by the `onclick` and `onmouseenter` events found in the SVG output in the last section.

Therefore, these files could be adaptively reused by web developers to make presentable data diagram web pages. Hopefully, Microsoft will refresh their code soon.

> Take a look at `https://msdn.microsoft.com/en-us/library/office/ff768358.aspx` for more information on the `Application.SaveAsWebObject`.

# Summary

In this chapter, we learned about the different ways of sharing Visio documents, especially those that contain data and hyperlinks. This has included viewing Visio documents directly or by converting them into other formats.

In the next and final chapter, we will discuss the options for deploying solutions.

# 11
# Choosing a Deployment Methodology

In previous chapters, we learned about creating, viewing, and reading Visio documents. We started to learn some aspects of sharing Visio documents in *Chapter 6, Creating Custom Master Shapes*, and in this chapter, we will learn more ways of sharing professional looking Masters, Templates, and code.

In this chapter, we will learn the following topics:

- Sharing custom stencils
- Sharing custom templates
- Sharing custom code

## Sharing custom stencils

A **stencil** is a Visio document with a VSSX or VSSM extension and contains a number of Masters. The easiest method of sharing custom Masters is to add them to a custom stencil and simply distribute the file. The file can then be added to the `My Shapes` folder that is created by the Visio installation.

The location of the `My Shapes` folder can be viewed, and changed, by opening the **File Locations** dialog from **File** | **Options Advanced**, as shown in the following screenshot:

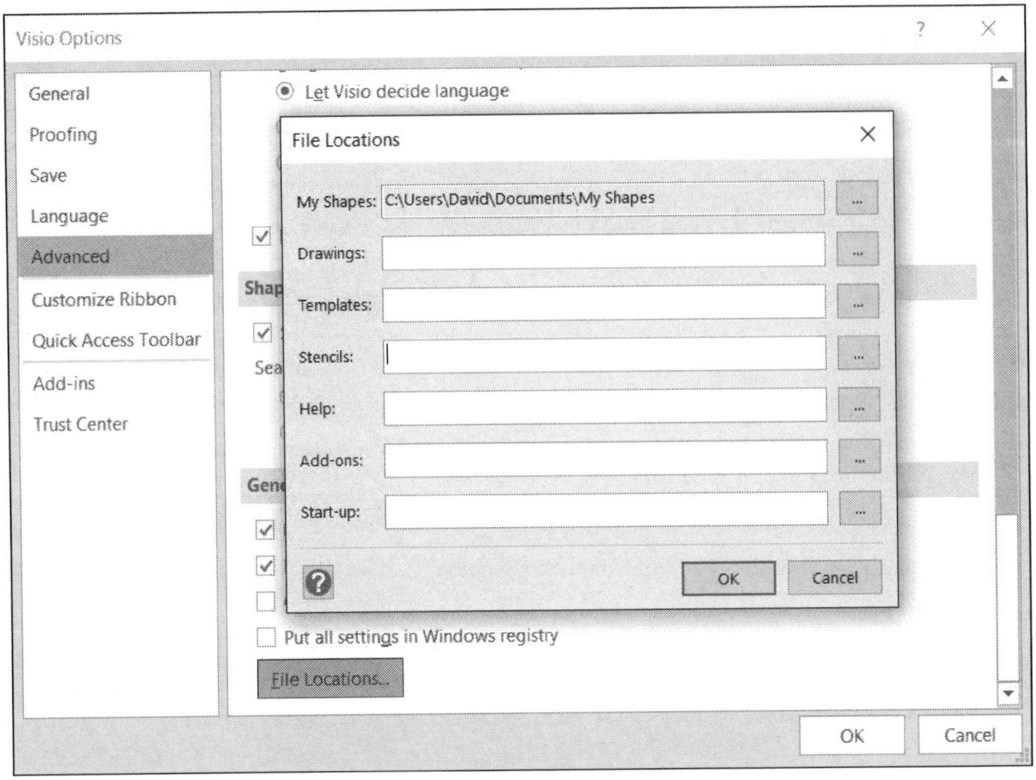


There can be only one `My Shapes` folder, but all of the other file locations can have multiple folders if the paths are separated by semicolons.

Visio will enumerate all subfolders within a specified folder, so a category and subcategory can be created with folder names. For example, the following screenshot of File Explorer shows that there are many stencils within a folder named `Metro Icons` inside the `My Shapes` folder:

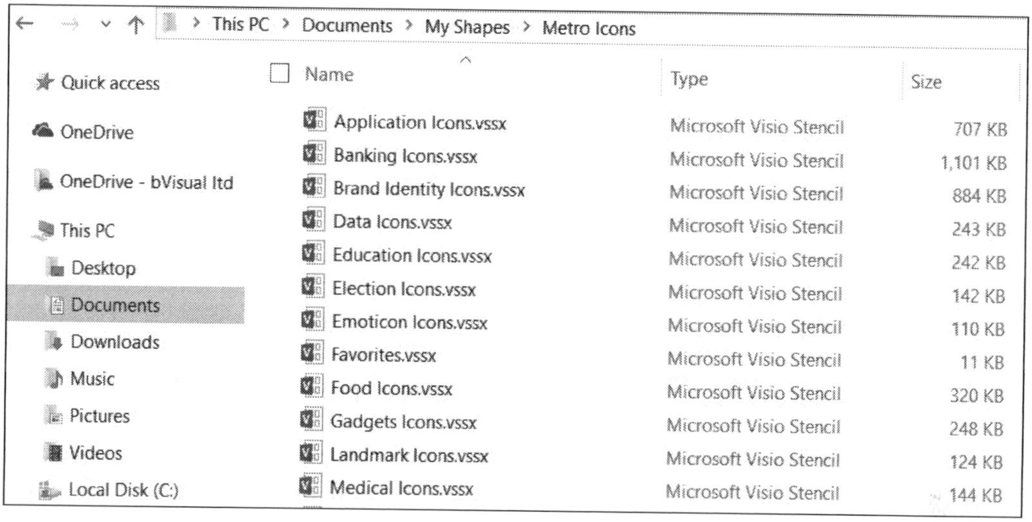


When viewed with Visio, the stencils appear under the **Metro Icons** category of **Shapes** | **Stencils** | **More Shapes** | **My Shapes**, as seen in the following screenshot:

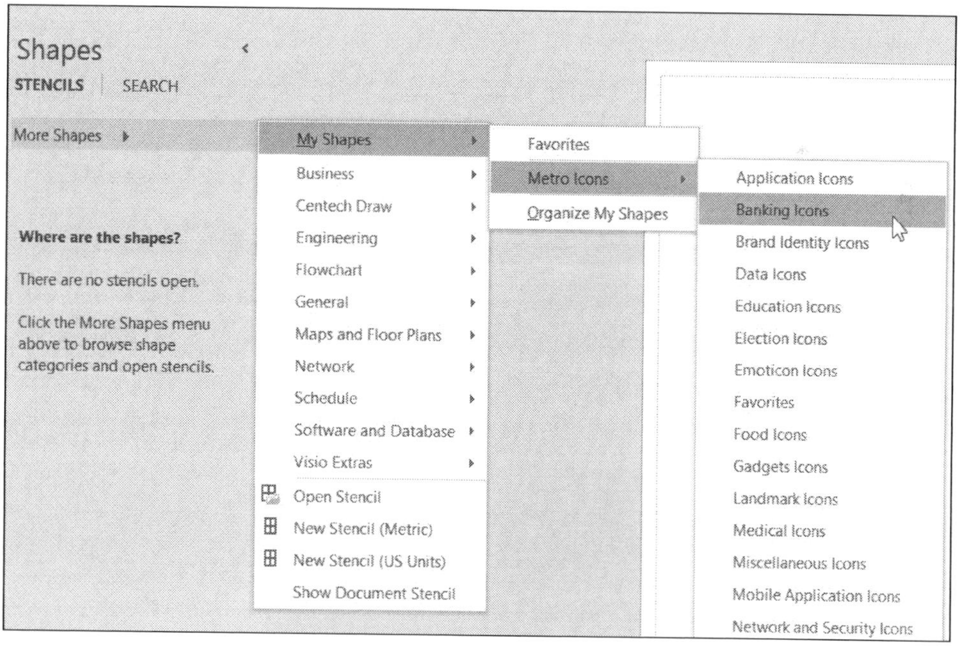

Notice that there is a stencil called **Favorites** inside the `My Shapes` folder already. This can be used for personal favorite Masters, but these are not intended for distribution to others.

A new stencil can be created with either the **Shapes | Stencils | More Shapes | New Stencil (Metric)** or **New Stencil (US Units)** command. Masters can be dragged and dropped onto the new stencil from a Document Stencil or from other stencils. If the Master has a Data Graphic defined, then it will also be copied to the **Masters** collection of the new stencil, as shown in the following screenshot:

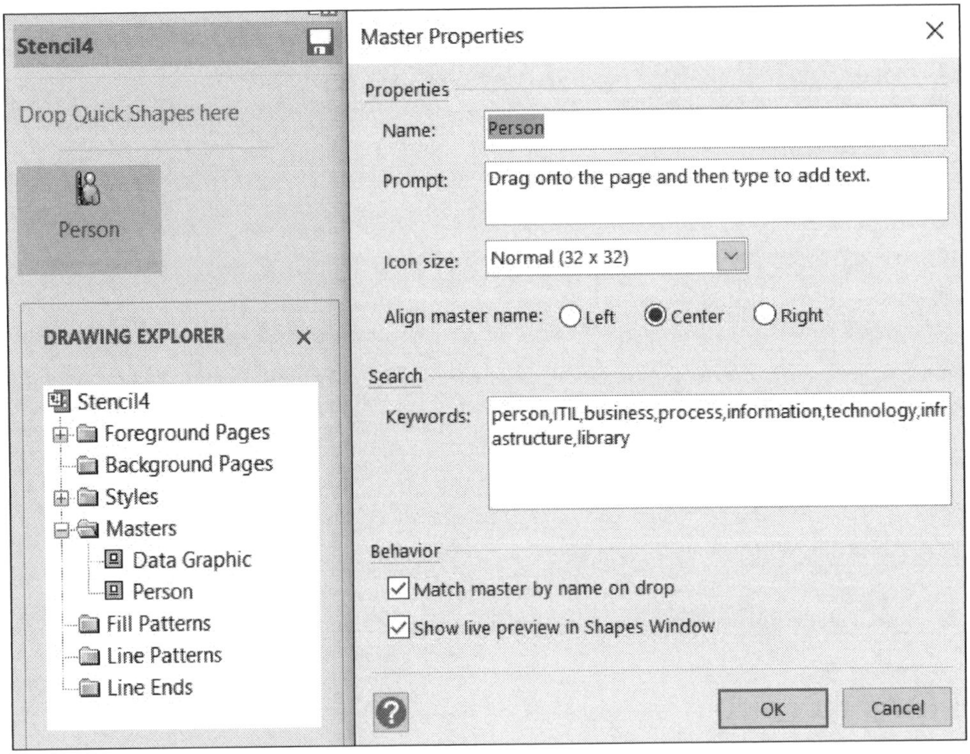


The **Master Properties** dialog can be used to set **Name, Prompt**, and **Keywords** to describe each Master. The **Icon size, Align master name**, and **Show live preview in Shapes Windows** fields control its appearance in the stencil.

The **Drawing Explorer** window of a stencil is available from the right-click menu of the header bar. The default caption in the header is the name of the stencil without the file extension. The **Properties** dialog provides for various details of the stencil, as shown in the following screenshot:

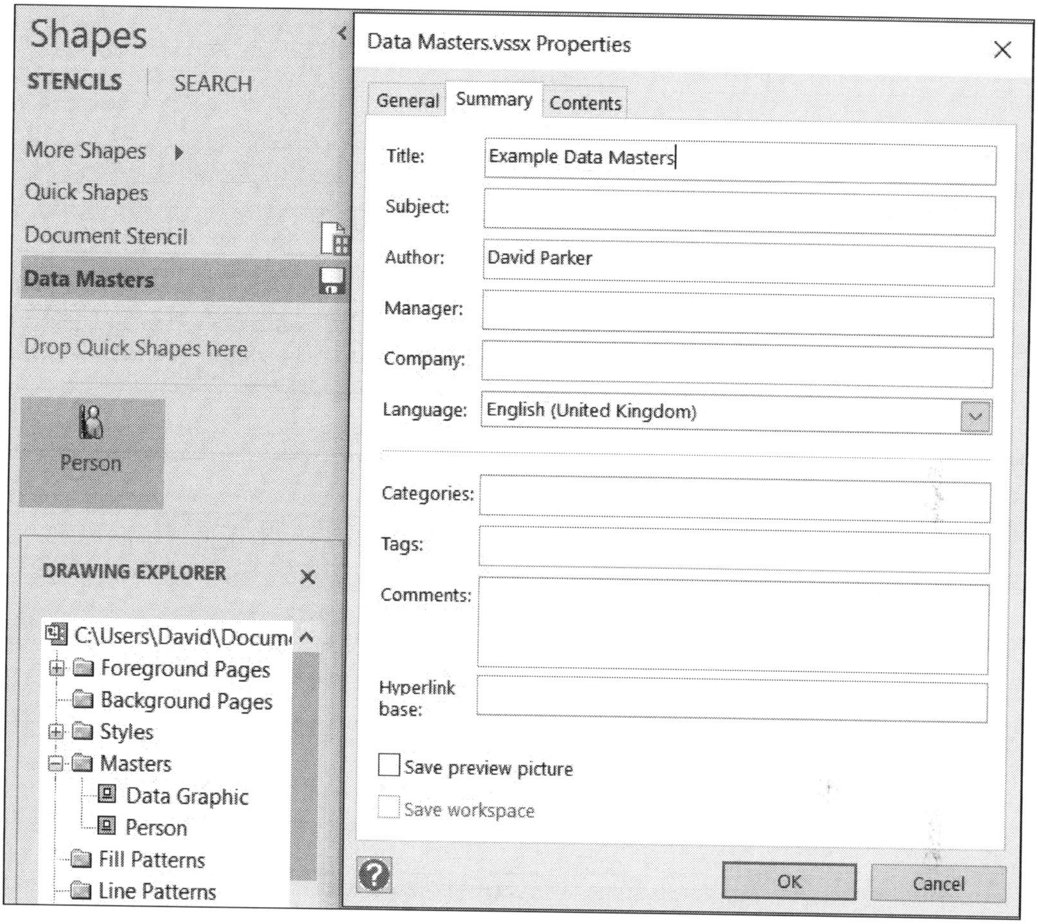

Any text in the **Title** property will be preferred over the stencil name as the caption in the header bar, as shown in the following screenshot:

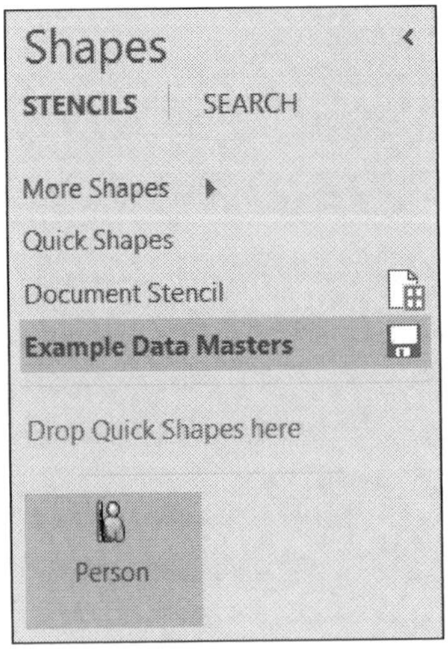


The displayed icon can be automatically generated every time the Master shape is updated by ticking the **Show live preview in Shapes Window** checkbox. Alternatively, the icon can be edited with the basic **Icon Editor**, as shown in the following screenshot:

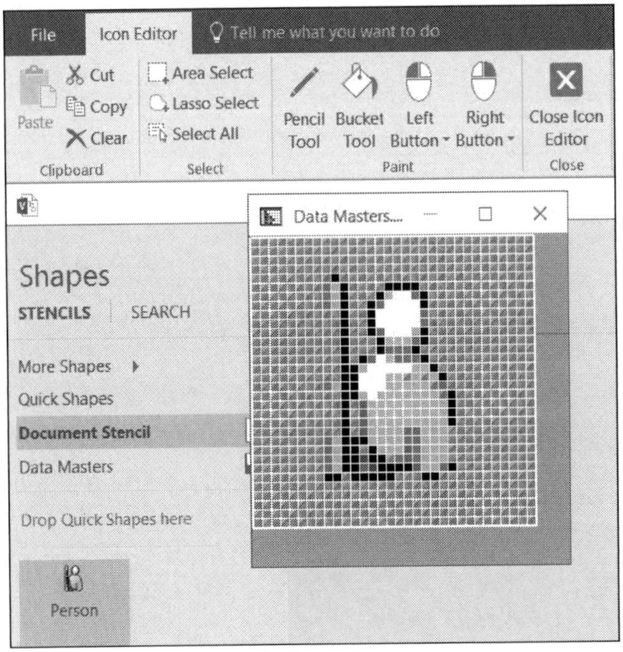

The `Master` object has an `ExportIcon()` method that can save the icon to a file, in one of two formats. The `Master` object also has an `ImportIcon()` method that can import from one of these formats. Take a look at `https://msdn.microsoft.com/en-us/library/office/ff767253.aspx` for more information.

# Sharing custom templates

*Chapter 6, Creating Custom Master Shapes*, includes some information about custom templates and should be read in addition to this section.

Templates are just Visio documents with a VSTX, or VSTM, extension that tells Visio that the default action is to create a new document based on it. The template document may contain no Masters in its Document Stencil, or it could contain any number of custom Masters. For example, a custom version of the dynamic connector Master is found in several of the Microsoft Visio-installed templates.

Templates do not need to include docked stencils, but they often do. The docked stencils can be ones that are part of the Visio installation, or they can be custom stencils.

The preview image of a Visio document is created from the shapes that are on the first page. Therefore, a preview image of a template can be created by adding some shapes to the first page.

However, the default image created is not very sharp, but this can be improved. First, tick the **Put all settings in the Windows registry** option in the **File** | **Options** | **Advanced** | **General** panel, as shown in the following screenshot:

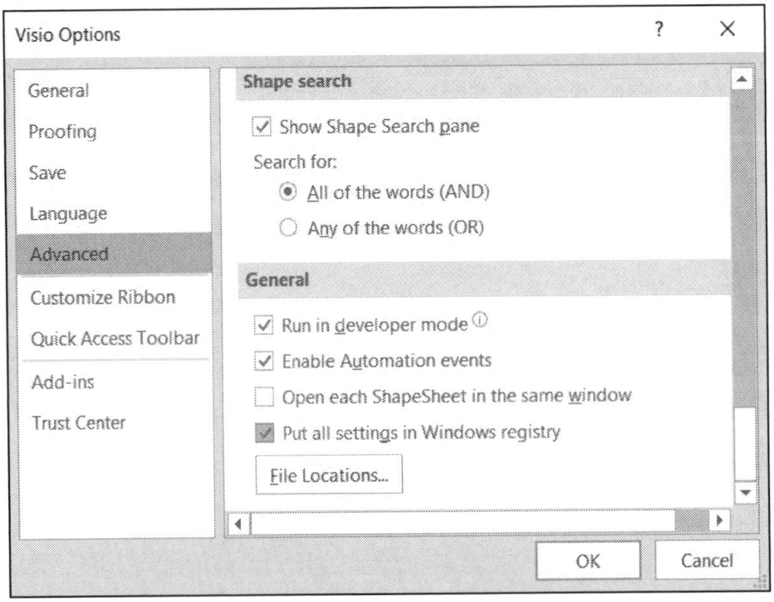


Then, close Visio to save extra settings into the Windows registry.

Next, run the `regedit.exe` command from the Windows Start button. This will open the **Registry Editor** window, so edit the value of the `ThumbnailDetailMaxSize` data in the `HKCU\Software\Microsoft\Office\16.0\Visio\Application` hive to, for example, **6000000**, as shown in the following screenshot:

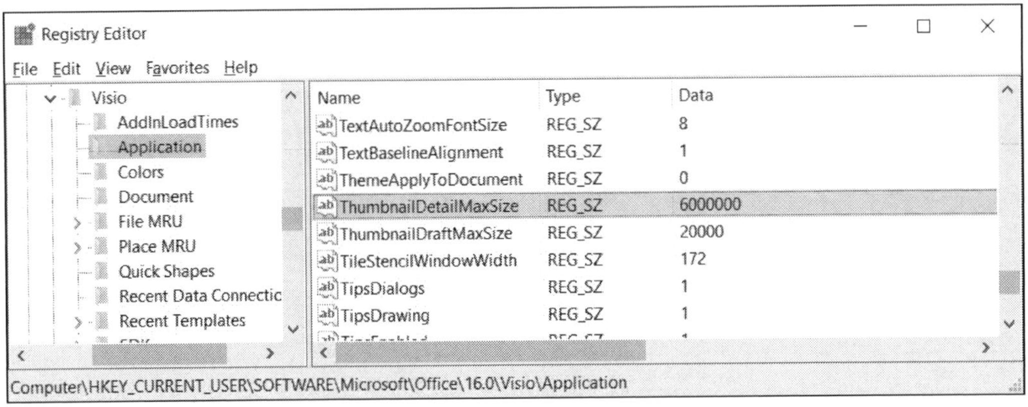

The description of the template can be entered in the **Comments** field of the **Properties** dialog, as shown in the following screenshot:

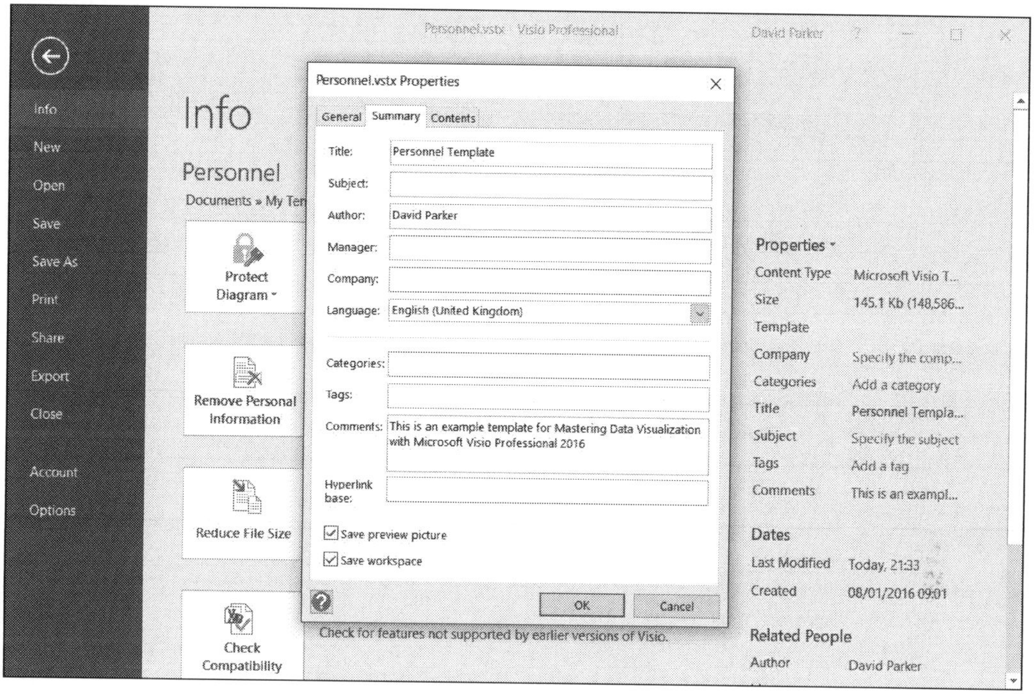


Notice that the **Save preview picture** option is ticked in the screenshot.

The ShapeSheet of the document can be opened from the **Developer** | **Shape Design** | **Show ShapeSheet** ribbon command. There is a cell in the **Document Properties** section called **PreviewQuality**. The default value is **0** (**visDocPreviewQualityDraft**), but setting it to **1** (**visDocPreviewQualityDetailed**) provides the opportunity to improve the quality of the preview image.

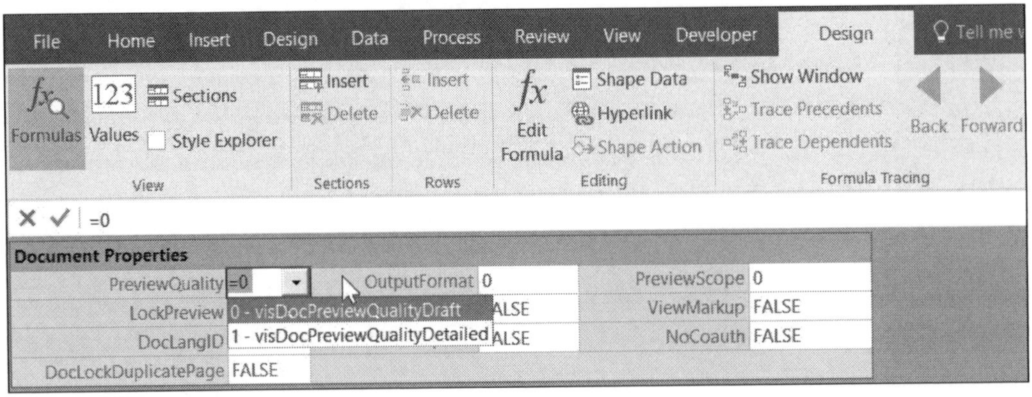


Once Visio is restarted, the enhanced preview image of the template and the description adds to the professional appearance, as shown in the following screenshot:

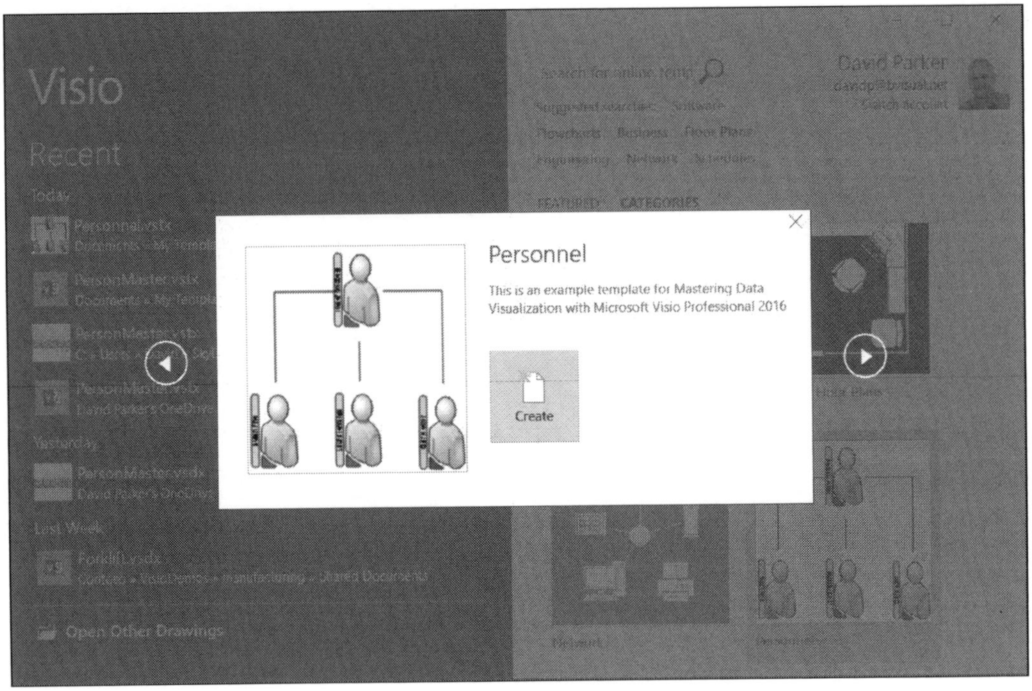

Once the template has been saved with the enhanced image, then the **LockPreview** cell in the **Document Properties** section of the **Document ShapeSheet** option can be set to **True** from the **False** default setting. The shapes on the first page can be deleted, and the preview image will stay as it was intended.

The `ThumbnailDetailMaxSize` data in the registry can also be reset back to its value.

An alternative to this process is to use the `Document.CopyPreviewPicture()` method from one document in another.

# Sharing custom code

All Visio documents can contain VBA code, but they must be saved with one of the macro-enabled extensions. Often, the best location for custom VBA code is in a stencil, saved with a VSSM extension. This is because it can be easily opened for read-only purposes by multiple documents and users.

This book has companion VBA code in a Visio stencil called `Mastering Data.vssm`. The project name, `Mastering_Data`, and other values can be set in the **Project Properties** dialog opened from the **Tools** menu.

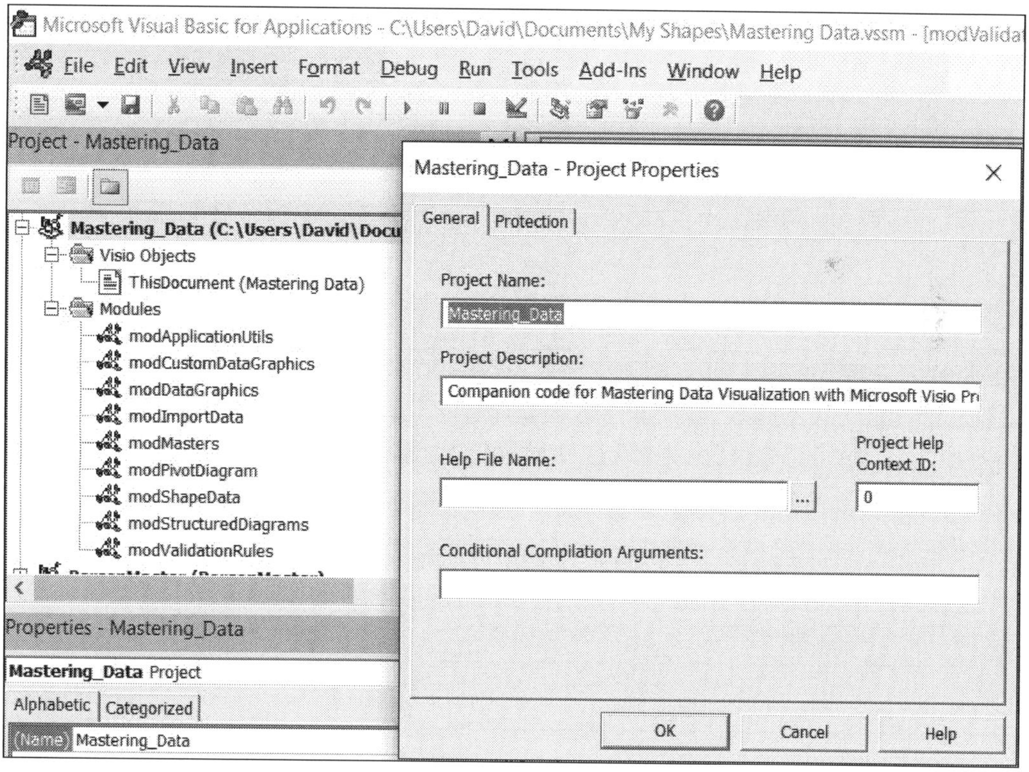

VBA projects can also be locked with a password on the **Protection** tab of the **Project Properties** dialog, as shown in the next screenshot:

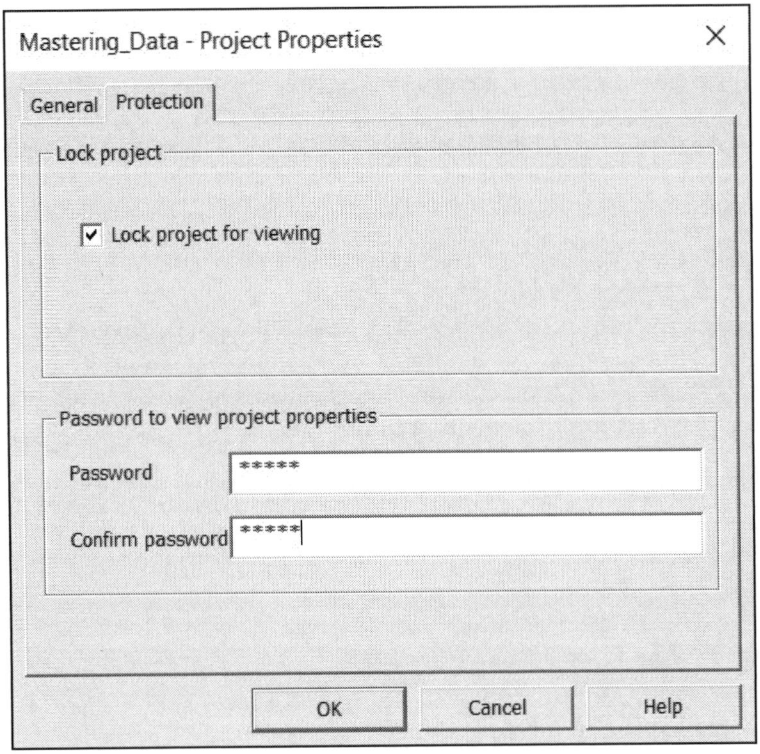


Locking code prevents idle tampering, but there are VBA password hacks available online.

The VBA project in a Visio document can also be signed with a digital signature, as shown in the following screenshot of the dialog opened by **Tools | Digital Signature**:

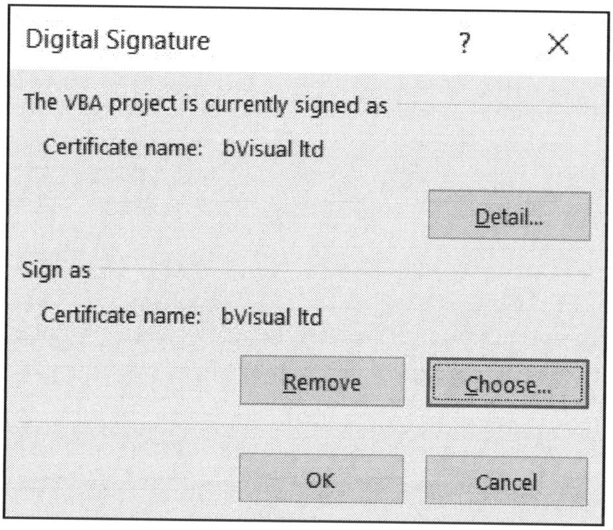


If a VBA project has a digital certificate applied to it, then it will automatically be removed if the project is edited by anyone else.

Code can also be written easily using VB.NET or C# as a VSTO add-in. Take a look at *Chapter 6, Creating Custom Master Shapes*, for more information on publishing a Visio VSTO solution.

# Summary

So, this was the last chapter. You learned about creating, reading, viewing, and sharing Visio data diagrams. Visio is more than graphics, and it is more than data. It is visual information that can be refreshable, and therefore, stay relevant and useful for assisting with business decisions. Correctly used, it provides the backbone of an operational intelligence system that can add real clarity to many parts of a business.

Visio will continue developing for many years to come, and Microsoft will add more ways to interact with Visio documents on the web. The skills outlined in this book will remain relevant and reusable. So, be smart, be clear, and be visual!

# Index

## Symbols



## A



## C

## D

# T



# U



# V

## W



## X

36163257R00186

Made in the USA
San Bernardino, CA
18 May 2019